CW01207552

Medieval Welsh Literature and its European Contexts

Medieval Welsh Literature and its European Contexts

Essays in Honour of Professor Helen Fulton

Edited by
Victoria Flood

D. S. BREWER

© Contributors 2024

All rights reserved. Except as permitted under current legislation nart of this work may be photocopied, stored in a retrieval system, published, performed in public, adapted, broadcast, transmitted, recorded or reproduced in any form or by any means, without the prior permission of the copyright owner

First published 2024
D. S. Brewer, Cambridge

ISBN 978 1 84384 721 2

D. S. Brewer is an imprint of Boydell & Brewer Ltd
PO Box 9, Woodbridge, Suffolk IP12 3DF, UK
and of Boydell & Brewer Inc.
668 Mt Hope Avenue, Rochester, NY 14620–2731, USA
website: www.boydellandbrewer.com

A catalogue record for this book is available
from the British Library

The publisher has no responsibility for the continued existence or accuracy of URLs for external or third-party internet websites referred to in this book, and does not guarantee that any content on such websites is, or will remain, accurate or appropriate

Contents

Illustrations

Full credit details are provided in the captions to the images in the text. The editor, contributors and publisher are grateful to all the institutions and persons for permission to reproduce the materials in which they hold copyright. Every effort has been made to trace the copyright holders; apologies are offered for any omission, and the publisher will be pleased to add any necessary acknowledgement in subsequent editions.

Contributors

Claudio Cataldi, Kore University of Enna

Catherine A. M. Clarke, Institute of Historical Research, University of London

Geraint Evans, Swansea University

Joseph Falaky Nagy, Harvard University

Victoria Flood, University of Birmingham

Marged Haycock, Aberystwyth University

Stephen Knight, University of Melbourne

Liz Herbert McAvoy, Swansea University/University of Bristol

Catherine McKenna, Harvard University

Daniel F. Melia, University of California Berkeley

Ad Putter, University of Bristol

Jan Shaw, University of Sydney

Elaine Treharne, Stanford University

Jonathan M. Wooding, University of Sydney

Introduction
Medieval Welsh Literature and its European Contexts

Victoria Flood

Medieval Welsh Literature and its European Contexts honours the influential research of Professor Helen Fulton. Its title takes its inspiration from Helen's 1989 monograph on the European influences and analogues of the fourteenth-century Welsh poet Dafydd ap Gwilym, and her subsequent field-defining research into the relationship between British, Irish, and European literary traditions.[1] The volume incorporates Irish alongside Welsh, and orients both in relation to the languages and literatures of continental Europe, the framework into which Helen has influentially integrated the study of literature in the Celtic languages. The linguistic and thematic range of the following pages responds to the diversity of Helen's work, including (to name but a few subjects) the multifaceted Welsh and Irish developments of the legend of Troy, the multilingual histories of Arthurian literature, the relationship between British literature and the Italian renaissance, and the wider history of writing in Welsh, both medieval and modern. Helen's expertise spans an inimitable range of historical periods, languages, and geographical contexts, and indeed stretches beyond what a single Festschrift might comfortably contain (for example, the present volume necessarily omits contributions relating to Helen's work on media and discourse analysis). She is a scholar whose influence spreads beyond a single discipline or field; whose scholarship combines the local and the international, and historicisation with theorisation; and who balances detailed linguistic and textual analysis with a deep awareness of the implications of such work for our understanding of lines of cultural contact, influence, and the flow of power in the medieval world.

This collection of essays brings together colleagues and former students of Helen from a geographical range as international as her research interests. From collaborators and friends in Celtic Studies from Europe, Australia, and North America, to those who have worked and studied with Helen in English Literature departments at the Universities of Swansea, York, and Bristol, this book is a labour

1 Helen Fulton, *Dafydd ap Gwilym and the European Context* (Cardiff: University of Wales Press, 1989).

of love from the scholars whose careers have been inspired by, and dialogically engaged with, Helen's research. It offers a window into a multidiscursive, multilingual field: a combining of disciplinary knowledges in response to a decidedly singular interdisciplinary researcher and teacher.

Responding to Helen's work on Welsh poetry, in the first chapter of this volume Catherine McKenna explores the early appearances of the animal *llatai* (love-messenger), a common trope in the work of the *cywyddwyr* (poets of the Welsh gentry working after the Edwardian conquest of Wales), detecting pre-conquest affinities. An enquiry both complementary and responsive to Helen's work on the love poetry of Dafydd ap Gwilym, McKenna discusses the twelfth-century poem *Rhieingerdd Efa*, a lover's eulogy by Cynddelw, in which the poet-narrator has been understood to address his desires regarding his beloved Efa to his horse. Offering a new reading of this poem, McKenna explores the text's rich complexities, revealing a playful work in which the poet is at once a figure marginalised from, and central to, the glories of the court, while his poetry itself wields a knowing cultural capital. This reading, alert to the cultural positionality of Welsh verse, is very much in the spirit of the shared interests of the author and the honourand. Continuing the volume's discussions of Welsh poetry, in Chapter 2 Marged Haycock explores the figure of the ale-wife in works of the late fifteenth and early sixteenth centuries. Responding to Helen's research into the urban contexts of medieval Welsh literature, this chapter details a vibrant, mostly unedited, collection of poetry from late-medieval and early Tudor Wales.[2] Haycock makes available significant new material for Welsh literary-historical study, as well as offering an important chapter in the history, and representation, of female industry – a fitting tribute to Helen's own scholarly innovations, editorial activities, and study of medieval urban life.

Chapter 3 is Stephen Knight's comparative study of Chrétien de Troyes's *Yvain* and the Middle English and Welsh versions of the same narrative. Exploring the meanings and uses of the natural world across this variegated international tradition, Knight traces a common concern with 'socialised nature' and 'naturalised society' felt in varying degrees across the texts. This critical position is in many respects complementary to Helen's work on the relationship between the natural world and magic in native Welsh prose, a formulation that represents a significant departure from nineteenth-century critical assumptions regarding 'Celtic magic', and which is alert both to the specificity of Welsh representations and those elements in common with pan-European medieval literary traditions, not least the Arthurian.[3] Helen's work on Welsh prose similarly provides the inspiration for the

2 See, for example, Helen Fulton, ed., *Urban Culture in Medieval Wales* (Cardiff: University of Wales Press, 2012); 'Trading Places: Representations of Urban Culture in Medieval Welsh Poetry', *Studia Celtica* 31 (1997): 219–30; 'The Outside Within: Medieval Chester and North Wales as a Social Space', in *Mapping the Medieval City: Space, Place and Identity in Chester c. 1200–1600*, ed. Catherine A. M. Clarke (Cardiff: University of Wales Press, 2011), pp. 149–68.

3 See, for example, Helen Fulton, 'Magic and the Supernatural in Early Welsh

next item in the volume, by Daniel F. Melia. Responding to Helen's 'broadening [of] the geographical and historical lens' through which scholars have approached medieval Wales, Melia situates the branches of the *Mabinogi* in the context of wider European legendary medieval narratives, which integrate genealogical and onomastic material and frame a claim to territorial ownership. A study that is at once expansive and geographically and linguistically specific, Melia's particular focus is on the territorial claims of the kingdom of Deheubarth in south Wales, which are raised as a counterpart to longstanding formulations of the familiar dynastic claims of the northern kingdom of Gwynedd. While presenting a new reading of the text, Melia is here comfortable with the polyvalence of the medieval past – an awareness he, like other contributors to this collection, associates with the nuanced and considered critical approaches of our honourand.

In Chapter 5 Joseph Falaky Nagy takes his inspiration from Helen's work on the Irish translation of Dares Phrygius's account of the Trojan war. A study of the story of the legendary Irish account of the Battle of Mag Tuired, the *Cath Maige Tuired*, Nagy suggests that the text exalts both the 'warrior excellence' and 'peace-making' of its Irish subjects that Helen first detected in the double Trojan and Greek contexts of Dares's heroes in Irish translation.[4] Equally in line with the volume's, and its honourand's, interest in Irish literature, located in its broader European as well as its more specifically geographically localised and determined contexts, Jonathan Wooding's chapter explores the relationship between Welsh and Irish hagiography, approached in the context of the pan-European cult of St Brendan of Clonfert. Wooding discusses the frequently overlooked references to Brendan that we find in Welsh hagiography, revealing a context that is at once local and international. Continuing the focus on the international contexts of medieval Celtic literatures and languages, in the next chapter Claudio Cataldi explores the early relationship between Irish, English, and European literatures and languages visible in the *Lorica of Laidcenn*, a Hiberno-Latin text with a strikingly rich, and in places rare, vocabulary, which attracted a vibrant tradition of insular glossing. Tracing linguistic and literary developments in the early Middle Ages with a place in manuscript traditions down to the sixteenth century, Cataldi's work speaks to the chronological range of Helen's own linguistic interests, at home both at the beginning and the end of the Middle Ages – and indeed, beyond.

Taking her cue from Helen's scholarship on the place of 'romantic Wales' in medieval English literary imaginings, Victoria Flood's chapter details the representation of England and Wales in the late fourteenth-century north-west Midlands

---

Arthurian Narrative: *Culhwch ac Olwen* and *Breuddwyd Rhonabwy*', *Arthurian Literature* 30 (2013): 1–26.

4 Helen Fulton, 'Historiography and the Invention of British Identity: Troy as an Origin Legend in Medieval Britain and Ireland', in *Origin Legends in Early Medieval Western Europe*, ed. Lindy Brady and Pamela Wadden (Leiden: Brill 2022), pp. 338–62.

poem *Sir Gawain and the Green Knight*.[5] Flood suggests that the Welsh affinities of the poem's geography are not (as has elsewhere been argued) suggestive of a direct Welsh source influence on the poem, but rather are indicative of the mediation of Welsh historical material within the English tradition through Geoffrey of Monmouth's twelfth-century *Historia regum Britanniae* – the insular reception of which has formed an important component of Helen's own research.[6] Liz Herbert McAvoy continues the volume's interest in the March, reappraising some of her own earlier arguments regarding the literary-religious culture of this region. Taking new inspiration from the European connectedness of Wales and the border region, as explored by Helen, McAvoy discusses the ways in which male-authored Middle English religious and devotional texts from the March and the west Midlands are suggestive of a distinctive interest in wider European female or 'female-coded' spiritual movements, as a point of resistance to, or escape from, the martial culture of the region.[7] Reading, alongside other significant sources, the works of the *Gawain*-poet – positioned in relation to the Middle English translation of the thirteenth-century German visionary, Mechthild of Hackeborn, McAvoy makes a case for the close relationship between continental constructions of female piety and literary culture in western Britain. In the next chapter of the collection, Catherine A. M. Clarke further discusses textual and cultural production in the border regions between England and Wales, a significant topic, and location, in Clarke's previous collaborations with the honourand.[8] Clarke addresses an emplaced, potentially auto-epitaphic, remembrance of a significant Marcher literary figure: a brass plaque bearing the verse epitaph of the chronicler Adam Usk, preserved at St Mary's church, in Usk. A curiously composed Welsh *cywydd*, the difficulties we face in reading this text's imperfect Welsh might, Clarke suggests, be approached as emblematic of Adam's 'complex, ambivalent relationship with his Welshness', and the multivocality of the March of Wales more broadly. This is a complexity to which Helen's own research into poetic voice and identity in postcolonial Wales has been similarly alert.[9]

5 Helen Fulton, 'Romantic Wales: Imagining Wales in Medieval Insular Romance', in *Cultural Translations in Medieval Romance*, ed. Victoria Flood and Megan Leitch (Cambridge: D. S. Brewer, 2022), pp. 21–44.

6 See, for example, Helen Fulton, 'Troy Story: The Medieval Welsh *Ystorya Dared* and the *Brut* Tradition of British History', *Medieval Chronicle* 7 (2011): 137–50.

7 Helen Fulton, 'Outside Within', pp. 149–68. For Helen's work on literary production in the Welsh March, see, for example, 'The Red Book and the White: Gentry Libraries in Medieval Wales', in *Crossing Borders in the Insular Middle Ages*, ed. Aisling Byrne and Victoria Flood (Turnhout: Brepols, 2019), pp. 23–39.

8 I refer here specifically to Clarke's project, *Mapping Medieval Chester* (2008) <https://medievalchester.ac.uk/> [last accessed 10th November 2023], which includes significant new editions and analyses by Helen of medieval Welsh poems to Chester. See also, Clarke, ed., *Mapping the Medieval City*.

9 See, for example, Helen Fulton, 'Class and Nation: Defining the English in Late-Medieval Welsh Poetry', in *Authority and Subjugation in Writing of Medieval*

In Chapter 11 Jan Shaw offers a theoretical perspective engaged with Helen's current research with the Borders and Borderlands research network, exploring the implications of conceptual engagements with borders for our understanding of pre-modern constructions of nation and empire. Shaw considers the Middle English translation of the French prose *Mélusine* in relation to its source, tracing the multiple configurations of place and power at work in the text – including the possibility of an audacious imagining entertained in the French, and foreclosed in the English: of the house of Lusignan as the rebuilders of Jerusalem. This chapter, engaged with both the spatial and temporal limits that constitute medieval conceptions of empire, is a fitting tribute to an honourand who, throughout her career, has been consistently engaged with such ideas. Similarly presenting intellectual and theoretical intersections with Helen's most recent work, Ad Putter's chapter responds to Helen's forthcoming study on the Welsh speakers of medieval Calais, with a focus on the role of Dutch in the life of the town during its status as an English settlement between 1347 and 1558.[10] Putter explores a rich multilingual situation in many respects comparable to that of late medieval Wales, but this is a history that is not simply analogous but connected. Putter suggests that Dutch remained a dominant language throughout the English occupation, as part of a wider multilingual context that also included the mother tongue of the town's Welsh immigrants. What is more, just as scholars increasingly recognise the importance of Welsh as a significant language in late medieval Britain, so, Putter suggests, was Dutch a familiar competency during this period, not least among English merchants.[11] A study with implications for our understanding of both continental and insular linguistic perceptions, this chapter enriches our appreciation of medieval multilingualism as a new chapter in a history in which Helen's work has been so influential.

Modelling connective research between the literature of Wales and English literary production into the eighteenth and nineteenth centuries, in the final essay of this collection Geraint Evans, Helen's co-editor of the monumental *Cambridge History of Welsh Literature*, extends the principles of both his and the honourand's scholarship to a post-medieval archival context, exploring Percy Bysshe Shelley's ownership of a Welsh Bible and illuminating a significant context in Shelley's biography.[12] A striking example of the multilingual encounters that necessarily

---

Wales, ed. Ruth Kennedy and Simon Meecham-Jones (New York: Palgrave Macmillan, 2008), pp. 191–212.

10 Helen Fulton, 'Mobility and Migration: Calais and the Welsh Imagination in the Late Middle Ages', in *The Hundred Years War and European Literary History*, ed. Daniel Davies and R. D. Perry (Manchester: Manchester University Press, 2024), pp. 145–67.

11 See, in particular, Helen Fulton, 'Negotiating Welshness: Multilingualism in Wales Before and After 1066', in *Conceptualizing Multilingualism in England, c. 800– c. 1250*, ed. Elizabeth M. Tyler (Turnhout: Brepols 2012), pp. 145–70.

12 Helen Fulton and Geraint Evans, eds, *The Cambridge History of Welsh Literature* (Cambridge: Cambridge University Press, 2019).

disrupt, and enrich, understandings of national literary canons, this is a reminder, Evans concludes, of all that can be uncovered when we think beyond university department specialisms – just as Helen has done. Articulating further admiration for Helen's interdisciplinarity, the volume concludes with Elaine Treharne's tribute to Helen – from one Welsh medievalist to another – which provides an overview of Helen's scholarly work and achievements. This precedes a select bibliography of Helen's publications between 1978 and 2023, a deeply influential body of work with which contributors are engaged throughout the volume.

Many of the essays in this collection pay tribute to Helen's writings on the powerful role of space and place in the formation of medieval political and national identities – not least in the literature of the Welsh March. Helen is a scholar who is at once aware of the very constructed nature of the nation, and its emotional valences and political importance, not least in the contexts of medieval and modern Wales. It is to her that the discipline of English Studies, to which Helen has influentially brought to bear the findings and practices of Celtic Studies, in large part owes an awareness that was previously all too often forgotten: that Welsh is the fourth language of medieval Britain. Further, it is impossible to overstate the importance of Helen's role in mediating the literature of medieval Wales to a wider academic readership, from her edition of the apocrypha of Dafydd ap Gwilym, to her current Leverhulme Trust-funded work on a new edition and translation of the Welsh political poetry from the Wars of the Roses.[13] In many respects, Helen is a decidedly difficult scholar to present with a Festschrift – for her work is ongoing, and her contributions ever-growing. Indeed, we write this just as Helen has been awarded a major European Research Council grant for her project 'The Medieval March of Wales c. 1282–1550' (MOWLIT), a course of research that brings together literature, history, codicology, and cartography to explore the production and circulation of manuscripts containing Welsh, English, Latin, and French, and to map the territories and shifting boundaries of the Marcher lordships for the first time. This volume is intended to honour her career so far, which continues to yield new discoveries and develop new paradigms for reading medieval Welsh with, and as, European literature.

13 Helen Fulton, ed., *Selections from the Dafydd ap Gwilym Apocrypha* (Llandysul: Gwasg Gomer, 1996). For Helen's previous work on Welsh poetry from the Wars of the Roses, see 'Guto'r Glyn and the Wars of the Roses', in *Gwalch Cywyddau Gwŷr: Essays on Guto'r Glyn and Fifteenth-Century Wales*, ed. Dylan Foster Evans, Barry J. Lewis, and Ann Parry Owen (Aberystwyth: University of Wales Centre for Advanced Welsh and Celtic Studies, 2013), pp. 53–68.

1

Horseplay: Another Look at *Rhieingerdd Efa*

Catherine McKenna

Helen Fulton's work in medieval Welsh poetry focuses on the *cywyddwyr* of the fourteenth and fifteenth centuries, whereas mine deals with the poets of the princes – the *beirdd y tywysogion* – of the twelfth and thirteenth. Studies of these two bodies of Welsh poetry often have an intertextual dimension. Discussions of twelfth- and thirteenth-century poetry point backward to its reverence for *hengerdd*, the 'old poetry' associated with the sixth through ninth centuries, and forward to aspects of the poetry of the *cywyddwyr* that it foreshadows. Studies of fourteenth- and fifteenth-century poetry, similarly, juxtapose consideration of its formal and thematic innovations with attention to its embeddedness in the tradition of the *beirdd y tywysogion*. In this essay, I propose a slight adjustment to the standard reading of a poem by the great twelfth-century poet Cynddelw, a poem that has been regarded as making the earliest known use of the device of the *llatai*, or love messenger, which features regularly in the poetry of the even greater fourteenth-century poet Dafydd ap Gwilym. It has been read as a forward-pointing poem, in other words. Helen Fulton has written about the *llatai*, and indeed about its appearance in this poem by Cynddelw, and so it seems appropriate to offer this reflection on *Rhieingerdd Efa* as a token of my deep respect for her work and in celebration of a long and treasured friendship.

The poem in question is titled in both of its earliest manuscript sources *Rhieingerdd Efa ferch Madog ap Maredudd*. *Rhieingerdd* (maiden song) is a term used for a poem in praise of a woman.[1] In this case, that young woman is Efa, the daughter of the Powys prince Madog ap Maredudd, who died in 1160. The poem

1 These sources are the Hendregadredd Manuscript, Aberystwyth, National Library of Wales, MS 6680B, fols 48v–50v, and the Red Book of Hergest, Oxford, Jesus College MS 111, col. 1425–28. I have rendered the title in Modern Welsh orthography. The standard edition of the poem is Nerys Ann Jones and Ann Parry Owen, eds, *Gwaith Cynddelw Mawr I* (Cardiff: University of Wales Press, 1991), pp. 55–75. All quotations from the modernised orthography text of the poem in this edition, pp. 64–66. Hereafter *Gwaith Cynddelw Mawr*.

itself is undated, but it may reasonably be assumed to have been composed between 1150–60. It is a 134-line poem in syllabic *awdl* measures, with six monorhyming sections, or *caniadau*, each of which begins with the phrase 'gorfynnawg drythyll' (ll. 1, 21, 39, 71, 91, 113). *Gorfynnawg* (*gorfynnog* in Modern Welsh) has to do with desire and has both positive and negative connotations. It can mean 'high-spirited, ardent, eager', but it can also mean 'envious, jealous, malicious'.[2] Similarly, *trythyll* can describe someone who is 'lively, high-spirited', but also one who is 'voluptuous, wanton, lascivious, lustful, licentious, lecherous'.[3] Both words are adjectives, but slippage between adjective and noun is very common in medieval Welsh poetry, so that the rendering of this phrase as adjective + noun, 'spirited prancer' in the translation of Joseph Clancy, does no great violence to its sense.[4] What that translation does, however, is to introduce a horse into a poem in which, I would argue, the poet has been very careful to do no more than *suggest* the presence of a horse. My first question about the way in which this poem has been read is basically: is there actually a horse in *Rhieingerdd Efa*?

It has been taken for granted that Cynddelw is addressing his horse as *gorfynnawg drythyll* in the opening line of each *caniad* (and again in the third line of the fifth *caniad*; l. 93). As suggested in the opening paragraph, a number of scholars have described this device as the first appearance in Welsh poetry of the *llatai*, or love messenger, and, more specifically, of the horse as *llatai*. In the introduction to their edition of the poem, Nerys Ann Jones and Ann Parry Owen write that:

> Y mae i'r gerdd fframwaith sy'n dod yn amlwg iawn ym marddoniaeth Dafydd ap Gwilym ddwy ganrif yn ddiweddarach: y bardd … yn cyfarch ei negesydd (march yn yr achos hwn) … ac yn ei yrru ati i geisio adfer y sefyllfa. Y mae'n ddiddorol sylwi bod hon yn un o'r enghreifftiau cynharaf yn ein barddoniaeth o farch yn cael ei yrru fel llatai at ferch.[5]
>
> (The poem has a framework which will become very prominent in the poetry of Dafydd ap Gwilym two centuries later: the poet … greeting his messenger [a horse in this case] … and sending him to her [the beloved] to try to remedy the situation. It is interesting to note that this is one of the earliest examples in our poetry of a horse being sent as a *llatai* to a girl.)

The Modern Welsh paraphrase of *Rhieingerdd Efa* in Jones and Parry Owen's edition points up the ambiguity nicely: the horse has to be inserted into the text,

2 *Geiriadur Prifysgol Cymru Online* (*GPC*) (Aberystwyth: Centre for Advanced Welsh and Celtic Studies, 2016) <http:www.geiriadur.ac.uk> [last accessed 14th November 2022], s.v. *gorfynnog*.

3 *GPC*, s.v. *trythyll*.

4 Joseph P. Clancy, trans., 'A Love Poem for Efa', in *Medieval Welsh Poems* (Dublin: Four Courts, 2003), pp. 141–44. I quote Clancy's translation at several points in this article because of its elegance.

5 *Gwaith Cynddelw Mawr*, p. 56. Helen Fulton refers in passing to the role of the horse as *llatai* in this poem in her invaluable study *Dafydd ap Gwilym and the European Context* (Cardiff: University of Wales Press, 1989), p. 167.

which opens '[Farch] awchus bywiog' (eager, lively [horse]). For the editors, as for translators like Clancy, there is very definitely a horse in the poem. But would that have been true for a twelfth-century audience at the court of Madog ap Maredudd or, conceivably, at the court of Efa's husband, Cadwallon ap Madog ap Idnerth of Maelienydd (although the poem is likely to have been composed before her marriage)?[6] What might have been the cues for that first audience? We might imagine the speaker enacting his relationship, as rider, to his horse. This conjures a Monty Python-esque image that might strike some as too frivolous for a courtly poem that is, in part at least, a eulogy of Efa and, by implication, of her aristocratic family and princely father. I would argue, however, that there is a light, tongue-in-cheek aspect to the tone of this poem; that it owes as much to popular traditions as to the influence of twelfth-century European *fin'amors* or *amour courtois*. Nevertheless, it is fair to assume that the audience of a contemporary performance would have had to rely for their interpretation on the language of the poem as it unfolded in time. And the phrase 'gorfynnawg drythyll' would not necessarily have immediately evoked a horse.

There are horses aplenty in the poetry of the *beirdd y tywysogion*. Nerys Ann Jones's study of 'Horses in Medieval Welsh Court Poetry' includes an appended list of 'vocabulary used for describing horses in early and medieval Welsh poetry', which claims not to be exhaustive, but which includes terms from 20 of these poets, including Cynddelw.[7] Neither *gorfannawg* nor *trythyll* appears in this list. Indeed, there are just eight instances of *trythyll*, or its lenited form *drythyll*, in the poetry of the princes, seven of them in the *Rhieingerdd Efa* and the eighth in a poem on the signs portending Judgment Day, in which those who rise include 'mud a drud a drythyll' (the mute and the arrogant and the *drythyll*), which would seem to imply a sense of *drythyll* whose connotations are negative – closer to 'wanton, lascivious' than to 'lively' or 'prancing'.[8] *Gorfynnawg* appears nowhere in the poetry of the princes outside this poem.

The twelfth-century audience would have had to puzzle over the unusual opening phrase of *Rhieingerdd Efa*. This would probably not have surprised them,

6 On the date of the poem in relation to Efa's marriage to Cadwallon, see *Gwaith Cynddelw Mawr*, p. 55. On the likelihood that it was intended for courtly performance, see Ann Parry Owen, 'Rhieingerdd Efa ferch Madog ap Maredudd. Cynndelw a'i Cant', *Ysgrifau Beirniadol* 14 (1988): 56–86 (p. 66); and Fulton, *Dafydd ap Gwilym and the European Context*, pp. 80–81.

7 Nerys Ann Jones, 'Horses in Medieval Welsh Court Poetry', in *The Horse in Celtic Culture: Medieval Welsh Perspectives*, ed. Sioned Davies and Nerys Ann Jones (Cardiff: University of Wales Press, 1997), pp. 82–101 (pp. 91–97).

8 It is possible, however, that *drythyll* in this instance refers to persons who are alive at the time of the Last Judgment, as opposed to those rising from the dead. See Catherine McKenna, ed., 'Arwyddion cyn Dydd Brawd', in *Gwaith Llywelyn Fardd I ac Eraill o Feirdd y Ddeuddegfed Ganrif*, ed. Kathleen Anne Bramley *et al.* (Cardiff: University of Wales Press, 1994), II, pp. 71–83, l. 63; Catherine McKenna, 'Welsh Versions of the Fifteen Signs before Doomsday Reconsidered', in *Celtic Folklore and Christianity*, ed. P. K. Ford (Santa Barbara, CA: McNally and Loftin, 1983), pp. 91–101.

as a store of esoteric vocabulary is one of the tools of the trade that a distinguished poet like Cynddelw, a *pencerdd*, would have been expected to have at the ready. The repetition of the phrase would not only have marked the beginning of each *caniad*, as did a change in the end rhyme, but would have drawn attention to its ambiguity and invited an interpretation that developed along with the progression of the poem. We must not forget that twelfth-century court poetry was published through performance. What Eric Falci has written of poetry in general, as a form of art, is especially true of poetry consumed in performance:

> A poem unfolds in time, both as a compositional arrangement and also as something like a score for a performance by voice [even if that voice is the subvocal one of a silent reader] [...] A poem is both artifact and happening, and central to our understanding of poems is some kind of account of how they move or proceed.[9]

At first, it would not have been clear that the phrase 'gorfynnawg drythyll' was addressed to anyone. Given the fact that both words are fundamentally adjectival, and given the absence of any clear mark of a vocative, a listener or even a reader might have taken the opening 'gorfynnawg drythyll' as descriptive of the speaker's mood and manner, as 'gorfynt a dygaf / wrth ar a folaf, a folais-i gynt' (I bear desire / for the one whom I praise, whom I praised once before). It might be understood that he endures and presents his *gorfynt*, which carries connotations of envious desire as well as of passion, in a way that is eager (but also perhaps somewhat envious) and lively (but also perhaps lustfully so). Certainly, the pairing of 'gorfynnawg' and 'gorfynt' does more than provide the line with an echo of the consonant sequence g-rf-n; it draws attention to the centrality of this pair of related multivalent terms.

Nothing changes immediately with the second *caniad*. In line 21, 'Gorfynnawg drythyll, gorwyth iolwyf' (I passionately implore), the opening phrase might once again describe the speaker's manner. It is only at the opening of the third *caniad* that an imperative verb tells the audience that someone is being addressed, inviting the listener to identify the *gorfynnawg drythyll*, the one who is both *gorfynnawg* and *drythyll*, as that addressee. The speaker instructs that implied presence in line 39, 'Gorddyfn-di fyned' (accustom yourself to going) to the court of the prince of Powys, or 'prepare to go', as the editors' paraphrase has it. One might well hear or read this as the speaker's injunction to himself, but another idea has been introduced in line 23, in the second *caniad*: 'Gorfelyn, called, colledig wyf' (golden, so wise, I am lost). The term 'gorfelyn', a compound of the intensifying prefix *gor-* and *melyn* (yellow), typically refers to hair colour. *Geiriadur Prifysgol Cymru* assigns to it a range from 'bright yellow, golden' to 'auburn'. It is unlikely that the poet is identifying himself as blond for no particular reason. He might be describing the girl, whose golden mantle he mentions in the previous line, and who is elsewhere in the poem described as having hair that is *gwinau* (auburn), but *gwinau* would

9 Eric Falci, *The Value of Poetry* (Cambridge: Cambridge University Press, 2020), p. 7.

seem to denote a darker shade than *gorfelyn*.[10] It is perhaps the most plausible reading to understand *gorfelyn* as a nominalised adjective and a term for a horse, perhaps a chestnut of some sort, even a palomino, and to take it as vocative.[11] The editors of *Rhieingerdd Efa* certainly take Gorfelyn to be the name of the horse, a name descriptive of his colour analogous to horse names to be found elsewhere in medieval Welsh texts, such as *Gwineu Gwddf Hir* (Long-necked Bay), *Melynlas* (Greyish-Yellow), and *Melyngan* (Whitish-Yellow, or perhaps Yellowish-White).[12] Thus, there is at this point a hint of a horse in the poem that may have cast a new light for the audience on the phrase 'gorfynnawg drythyll' when they heard it at the beginning of the third *caniad*, and they may have thought of that horse when the phrase recurred four more times (ll. 71, 91, 93, 113).

The phrase itself remains, nevertheless, formally a pair of adjectives. This fact of grammar links speaker and implicit horse through the two shared and ambivalent qualities. In other words, even as the audience comes to accept the presence of a horse in the poem, it is possible to understand *gorfynnawg drythyll* as describing the horse's manner as he visits the court in the speaker's stead, rather than as a strictly nominal epithet. The gradual disclosure of the horse's presence enables identification of speaker and messenger, even as it increasingly distinguishes the speaker's distance from the court – 'Nid af-i ar hirdwf ni dâl hirdaith' (I will not go to the long-bodied one, it's not worth the long journey) (l. 77) – from the messenger's imagined access thereto. As Nerys Ann Jones has written of the function of horses in *rhieingerddi*, 'When it is described at all, the lover's horse more often than not reflects its owner's emotions, eager and passionate'.[13] And in relation to this poem specifically, Ann Parry Owen points to the identity of speaker and horse-messenger: 'y march yn fywiog ac yn eiddgar ei symudiadau, a'r bardd yn fywiog ac yn eiddgar ei feddwl oherwydd ei draserch tuag at Efa'[14] (the horse lively and ardent in his movements and the poet lively and ardent in his mind because of his passion for Efa). 'Lively and ardent' though the horse, and the poet's emotions, may be, the fact that it is a horse rather than another animal with whom the speaker identifies, and whom he will address in the imperative, is significant. It was a common trope in medieval art and literature and, indeed, going as far back as Plato's *Phaedrus*, to represent a horse as the passionate, emotional aspect of the human spirit and the rider as the faculty of reason, keeping the horse under control. Although the poet is *gorfynnawg, drythyll*, just like the horse, it is *his* horse that embodies those passionate qualities, and he has it under control.

10 Although *GPC* s.v. *gorfelyn* offers *gwinau* as one definition.

11 I am very grateful to Jessica Hemming for sharing with me her forthcoming work on horse colour terms in medieval Welsh literature.

12 *Gwaith Cynddelw Mawr*, p. 71, n. to l. 23. On the names of horses, see Rachel Bromwich, 'The Triads of the Horses', in *The Horse in Celtic Culture*, pp. 102–20 (pp. 104–05); Jones, 'Horses in Medieval Welsh Court Poetry', pp. 92–93.

13 Jones, 'Horses in Medieval Welsh Court Poetry', p. 83.

14 Parry Owen, 'Rhieingerdd Efa ferch Madog ap Maredudd. Cynndelw a'i Cant', p. 81.

The projection of the speaker's own qualities onto a faintly glimpsed horse, what might even be described as a reification of the speaker's emotions *as* a horse, develops and intensifies quite rapidly in the third and subsequent *caniadau* with additional imperative verbs: 'gorthrych' (look upon) (l. 40), 'dywed' (tell) (l. 51), 'dywan' (return) (l. 52), 'na chêl' (don't conceal) (l. 53), 'gorddyfn' (accustom yourself) (l. 71), 'na chymedd' (don't reconcile) (l. 75), 'na chymer' (don't accept) (l. 76), 'gorddyfn' (l. 91), 'syll' (watch that) (l. 93), 'gorddyfn' (l. 113). A gap is opened between the message of unfulfilled aspiration and the subject – the poet – who is experiencing it. The device is one of several in *Rhieingerdd Efa* that allows to be deployed the trope of love of an unattainable lady at a distance, within what Helen Fulton has described, in a discussion of the poem, as 'a conservative native tradition of aristocratic praise-poetry'.[15] While the *gorfelyn* is instructed to carry the emotional content, the poet stands aside, as it were. He does not risk offending Efa or angering her father with the temerity of his desire, but rather dissociates his passion and to some extent himself, as court poet, from emotions that might be deemed socially unseemly.

The playful ambiguity with which Cynddelw simultaneously admits to being *gorfynnawg, drythyll,* and distances himself from those qualities, is apparent as well in a certain equivocality about the object of his desire. It is, of course, nominally Efa, his patron's daughter. It is she who is:

Cymrawd ewyn dwfr a'i dyfriw gwynt,
Cymraëg laesdeg o lys dyffrynt;
Cyfleuer gwawr ddydd pan ddwyre hynt,
Cylfiw eiry gorwyn gorwydd Epynt

(Twin of foam on wind-ruffled water,
Soft-voiced her Welsh, of the valley's court;
Bright as daybreak when it takes its way,
Hue of snow glowing on Epynt's slope) (ll. 3–6)[16]

Such seemly praise constitutes a substantial part of the poem – just under 20% of its 134 lines, by my count, although it is impossible to be precise because it is difficult to distinguish in every case a line of praise from an expression of unsatisfied longing. More time and space – about 30% of the poem – are devoted to that longing, to lament on the part of the speaker that the one whom he desires rejects him, causing him to suffer. This is typical of courtly love literature, of course, but there are aspects of Cynddelw's deployment of the trope that are noteworthy in light of his role as a Welsh court poet. Some of the plaintive passages are conventional enough within the tradition of *fin'amors*, such as:

15 Fulton, *Dafydd ap Gwilym and the European Context*, p. 81.

16 Here I quote the translation of Joseph P. Clancy, see above, n. 4. Elsewhere, except as noted, translations are my own.

Ym mhwyllad newid, neud ydwyf – am fun
Yn anhun anhedd, ced rhys porthwyf.
Gorthewis-hi wrthyf-i gwerth fy hirglwyf,
Nid gorthaw a wnaf wrth a garwyf

(Mind in a whirl, for a girl I am now
Unsettled, sleepless, though I endure it.
She stayed silent, pay for my lasting pain:
I will not stay silent to the one I love) (ll. 25–28)[17]

In other passages, however, it is or seems to be in his role as a poet, rather than a would-be lover, that Cynddelw feels himself to have been repudiated. He complains that:

Gwarfardd wyf iddi o ddylyed,
Gwâr air i'm cyfair ni'm cyfaered:
A chen ni'm caro, na'm cerydded – fyth:
O'm ceryddawdd, nawdd na'm diddoled.

(I am by right her courteous poet,
No courteous word comes my way;
And though she may not love me, let her never find fault with me:
If she found fault, let her not deprive me of patronage.) (ll. 59–62)[18]

Here, romantic love seems to serve as a coded reference to the relationship of poet and patron in the pre-conquest courts of the Welsh princes. One might even read this quatrain as saying 'of course Efa doesn't love me in a romantic way, I just want her to admire and reward me as a poet'. The poem supports such a reading more convincingly, I would argue, than the slightly different interpretation 'even though she rejects the romantic overtures I've made to her, don't let her fire me!' It is understood, in other words, that the claim of romantic love is merely a trope, and that the real issue at stake is Cynddelw's status at the court of Powys. As Helen has put it, 'The poet's attitude to Efa, expressing devotion, torment, and the hope of reward, is a displacement of his position in relation to his lord and patron: his duty is to praise in return for material gifts. His apparent humility masks the reality of special privileges and status conferred on court-poets'.[19]

The centrality to the poem of the court, and the poet's position in it, is apparent from the opening of the third *caniad*. The very first of the imperative verbs that signal the presence of a second Other, not the would-be love object Efa, but an equine messenger, is *gorthrych*:

17 Clancy's translation.

18 My translation. I defer to the editors' reading of MS *kerytad* as a preterite tense form, but it is more consistent with the orthography of the manuscript to read it a third person present/future indicative, which makes equally good sense.

19 Fulton, *Dafydd ap Gwilym and the European Context*, p. 81.

Gorthrych lys Leisiawn ei hystlyned,
Llys y daw deon i'w darymred:
Llys Efa i feirdd y'i digoned,
Llysaidd ei hirdwf o'i heurdudded.

(Look upon the court of the Lleisiawn,[20] her kin,
A court where noblemen come to attend her:
Efa's court was made for poets,
Courtly her tall form with its golden mantle.) (ll. 40–43)

This passage effectively identifies Efa with the court; to praise her and to desire her favour is essentially to praise and to desire the favourable response of the court.

In his role as poet, as contrasted with his adopted role as rejected lover, Cynddelw unabashedly vaunts his own poetic prowess. He is rather haughty about what seems to him inadequate appreciation thereof, by Efa and perhaps by the entire court:

Ni thewais ermoed o'i moli mal drud,
Ni phair gosymud i'm gosymdaith,
Ac ni'm rhif rhiain (rhyfedd a waith!)
Ac im oedd ei llaw, fy llawenrhaith;
Ac nid oes fardd dwfn, dinus gyfiaith,
A garwy yn hwy o hir obaith.

(Like an idiot, I never ceased praising her,
She makes no move toward my support,
And the maiden doesn't esteem me (amazing turn of events!)
And her hand used to be for me my happy recompense;
And there is no poet in the world, skilled in language,
Who can love any longer out of endless hope.) (ll. 79–84)

This passage is reminiscent of the poems called *bygwth* (threatening poems), in which a court poet threatens to leave, or even to disgrace, his patron if he is not properly appreciated and rewarded.[21] In another reference to his status and skill, even as he urges the (probable) horse to assist him, Cynddelw asserts that 'gorddawn ced cyrddfawr, cerddawr cyfraith' (a great favour is the gift of one splendid in song, a poet by law) (l. 72).

In the final *caniad* of *Rhieingerdd Efa*, Cynddelw the affronted poet emerges fully from his guise as wounded lover. It opens, of course, with the phrase *gorfynnawg drythyll*, and the first couplet is something of a conundrum: 'Gorfynnawg drythyll, gorddyfn-di gywir / Ail Gwyn Gorfynnawg, gorpwy enwir' (ll. 113–14). The editors

20 The Lleisiawn are the descendants of Lles, founder of the dynasty of Powys.

21 See Rhian M. Andrews, 'Cerddi Bygwth a Dadolwch Beirdd y Tywysogion', *Studia Celtica* 41 (2007): 117–36; Catherine McKenna, 'Bygwth a Dychan mewn Barddoniaeth Llys Gymraeg', in *Beirdd a Thywysogion: Barddoniaeth Llys yng Nghymru, Iwerddon a'r Alban*, ed. Morfydd E. Owen and Brynley F. Roberts (Cardiff: University of Wales Press, 1996), pp. 108–21.

take *Gwyn Gorfynnawg* (Spirited White) to be the name of a horse known to a now-lost tradition, a horse that the speaker's own imagined horse resembles. Their paraphrase (in my translation) renders the couplet as 'Eager lively horse, become familiar with a faithful one, / one like Gwyn Gorfynnawg, may he overcome injustice', referencing himself, Cynddelw, as the faithful one who hopes to overcome the injustice of Efa, with *Ail Gwyn Gorfynnawg* functioning as a vocative phrase parallel to *gorfynnawg drythyll*.[22]

In the following 20 lines, the speaker's preoccupation with his status as court poet, rather than lover, becomes increasingly clear. 'Mal ydd arddunaf, y'm harddunir' (as I honour, so shall I be honoured) (l. 116), he declares, making explicit the objective of his praise. And Efa's approval would stand him in good stead: 'A ddywaid rhiain ni rhygeblir' (what the maiden says won't be rejected) (l. 120). Unfortunately, she has withheld that approval: 'Nid amgen y'm rhydd, ni'm rhybuchir' (she rewards me no more, I'm not wanted) (l. 122). When he is away from his homeland, he is well-known as the poet of Llywelyn, understood by the editors to be Llywelyn ap Madog, Efa's brother. And Llywelyn is 'enwawg' (renowned) (l. 127), everywhere that Cynddelw goes in his life. Thus, it behooves the royal family to show him proper respect: 'Anwar fy lluchfar oni'm llochir' (savage my anger if I am not appeased) (l. 128). The threat is no longer veiled.

As he brings the poem to a close, Cynddelw suggests that he is on his way to seek more appreciative patrons, and perhaps to disseminate an unflattering portrait of the prince of Powys and his court: 'Pellynnig fy nghof yng Nghaerwys dir, / Pell ydd wyf i'm nwyf, oni thelir' (My mind is far off in the land of Caerwys, / I am away in all my intensity unless there is recompense) (ll. 131–32). Now, it has of course been the fiction of the poem that Cynddelw is already somewhere other than at court, that he has been driven away by Efa's disdain; that is why he needs a messenger to bring the burden of his emotion to her attention: 'Ni af-i ar hirdwf ni dâl hirdaith / I ar draed awel y drydedwaith' (I won't go to the tall one, the long trip isn't worth it, / On the wind's feet for a third time) (ll. 77–78). Yet, to exist as a heard poem, *Rhieingerdd Efa* must be performed for her, in the court. There is no evidence of poems being sent to patrons in writing in the pre-conquest period, and little evidence of their being performed by a *datganiad*, a reciter, in lieu of the court poet himself. As Ann Parry Owen writes in her fine study of the poem, 'cerdd i'w datgan o flaen y llys ydyw, ac nid datganiad cyhoeddus o'i serch' (it is a poem to be recited before the court, and not a public declaration of his love).[23] Indeed, the text of the poem calls attention to its own public performance in the court – as opposed to its pretended conversation with a horse – when the speaker asks 'A glywch chi, ddeon, a ddywedir' (Do you hear, good people, what is being said?) (l. 119).

Cynddelw's distance from the court is metaphorical, an aspect of his sense of alienation as underappreciated court poet, as the horse is metaphorically a rep-

22 *Gwaith Cynddelw Mawr*, p. 74, n. to l. 114.

23 Parry Owen, 'Rhieingerdd Efa ferch Madog ap Maredudd. Cynndelw a'i Cant', p. 66.

resentation of his emotion in relation to the situation. To quote once again from Ann Parry Owen's analysis, 'defnyddio'i ddychymyg a wna'r bardd i ddiriaethu sefyllfa neu syniad sy'n hanfodol "haniaethol": mae'n trawsnewid pellter meddyliol ... i dermau diriaethol, sef pellter daearyddol' (the poet uses his imagination to concretise a situation or an idea that is essentially 'abstract': he transforms mental distance ... into concrete terms, i.e., geographical distance).[24] He is at court, both actually, as the poet performing his poem, and figuratively, within that poem, as the horse that embodies his emotions, which are *gorfynnawg* and *drythyll.* At the same time, the physically present performing poet is absent from court by virtue of his alienation, as he is absent from it within the drama of the poem.

This analysis of the implicitly threatening message of *Rhieingerdd Efa* might seem to suggest that it is a more serious poem than I actually believe it to be. So much about it is playful, from the presence in the poem of an imaginary horse that would not have been physically present at the performance, to the adoption of some of the conventions of *fin'amors* in the poet's praise of Efa – although neither his adulatory descriptions of Efa nor his declarations of suffering ever violate standards of seemliness. And, as a kind of footnote to this rereading of the poem, I would suggest that Cynddelw takes a further step away from the possibility of offending Efa and her male kin by suggesting that it may be one of her handmaidens who is the actual object of his sexual desire.

This theme is introduced in the first *caniad*, with the opposition of a third person plural verb, *rhifynt* (they esteemed) to the third person singular 'ni'm rhifai' (did not esteem) (l. 8). The subject of the plural verb appears in the next line and contrasts the plural 'rhianedd' (maidens) (l. 9) with the singular 'rhiain' (maiden) that is the subject of 'ni'm rhifai', all the while sustaining the alliteration on *rh-*. Unlike Efa herself, these girls liked *Rhieingerdd Efa.*[25] Cynddelw recounts visits to these maidens, describing how they would watch him from the window like seagulls and send him a *traul ateb* (a response causing weakness or anguish, according to the editors; Joseph Clancy translates 'unmanning, the answer they'd send me', l. 16). He would love to love them, he says, but they do not love him. Still, they thought about

24 Parry Owen, 'Rhieingerdd Efa ferch Madog ap Maredudd. Cynndelw a'i Cant', p. 66.

25 J. E. Caerwyn Williams found this reference sufficiently disconcerting to suggest that *Rhieingerdd Efa* was actually a different poem, the title of which had attached itself to this one at some point in the course of transmission. See 'Cerddi'r Gogynfeirdd i Wragedd a Merched, a'i Cefndir yng Nghymru a'r Cyfandir', *Llên Cymru* 13 (1970): 3–112 (86). This is possible, of course, but the fact is that the poem under discussion here was preserved with that title in the medieval manuscript tradition. I would suggest, rather, that the allusion to the poem in its opening lines as a poem that has already been performed is part of the playfully self-conscious fiction of the poem itself. It is both in process of becoming in the course of its performance for Efa, and already in existence before that performance as a complete and complex composition, just as the poet himself is both present, in order to perform the poem, and absent, exiled from court by Efa's disapprobation.

him: 'Am Gynddelw Brydydd yd bryderynt' (they cared about Cynddelw the poet) (l. 20). And so concludes the first *caniad*.

In the second, the speaker seems to introduce the theme of his unreciprocated love for the unattainable princess, Efa. It opens, of course, with the phrase *gorfynnawg drythyll*, and then:

> ... gorwyth iolwyf
> Gorddawg pall eurawg pell nas gwelwyf.
> Gorfelyn, called, colledig wyf,
> Collais gall ateb y neb a'm nwyf.
>
> (... with passion I plead,
> Sprightly gold-mantled maid, far from my sight.
> Golden steed so discreet, I am lost:
> I've lost discreet words from her who stirs me.) (ll. 21–24)[26]

There are a couple of words here – 'gorwyth' and 'gorddawg' – that are somewhat difficult to decode,[27] and this quatrain introduces what may or may not be the name of the implicit horse, as discussed above. The gist of the passage is clear enough, however: there is a golden-mantled one who is far away, and the speaker is no longer receiving from a person who excites his passions the sort of response – a response that was in some way wise or rational – that he used to. Given the pall 'eurawg' (golden mantle), it is reasonable to assume that this person is Efa, but it should be borne in mind that she has not yet been named within the text of the poem. It is only the *llawforynion* (handmaidens) who have been present to the poem up to this point, and Cynddelw has lamented that 'llawen y'u carwn-i ceni ni'm cerynt' (gladly I loved them, although they loved me not) (l. 17).

Thus, when he launches into the 14-line complaint that follows in lines 25–38, it is not immediately clear that Cynddelw is not referring to one of these maidens. The one who has rejected him is a 'bun' (l. 25), a term used frequently in *cywyddwyr* poetry to refer to a female love object; it carries no connotation of exalted social status or the absence thereof. He addresses her as '[m]einwen', a noun compounded of two adjectives meaning 'slender' and 'fair' that also occurs with some frequency in poems addressed to women. It is only in the final couplet of the *caniad* that the other shoe drops when the speaker addresses the woman whose silence and rejection he has been bemoaning as '[m]erch peniaeth' (lord's daughter) (l. 37). And it is in the fourth line of the following *caniad* that he will refer to the court of Powys as 'llys Efa' (l. 42, discussed above).[28] As a result of Efa's relatively late entrance onto the stage of the poem, I would suggest that there hovers over the entire poem the possibility that the poet has an actual love interest at court, but that it is someone

26 Clancy's translation.

27 See *Gwaith Cynddelw Mawr*, p. 71, nn. to ll. 21 and 22; s.v. *gorddog, gorwyth* in *GPC*.

28 This is the only instance of her name in the poem other than the reflexive reference to *Rhieingerdd Efa* in l. 10.

more appropriate to his own social standing than the prince's daughter.[29] This possibility runs as a kind of subtle leitmotif through the poem, reinforcing the decorum of the praise itself as a way for Cynddelw to maintain an appropriate social distance from Efa corresponding to the physical distance that he claims she has imposed. As I have argued, it is appropriate recognition as a poet that Cynddelw really wants from Efa and her family, not romantic love. Even though it is metaphorical, that representation of sexual desire is softened and ambiguated by these hints at the presence of a theoretically more attainable sweetheart among Efa's attendants.

In light of the ways in which, as I hope to have shown, the poem concerns itself more with Efa as patroness, emblem of the court of Powys, than with Efa as love object, it is noteworthy that, with the mention of the *merch peniaeth*, Cynddelw's tone shifts from that of pining lover to that of the poet keeping track of his accounts payable: 'Ni'm dawr, ferch peniaeth, pryd na'th welwyf / Nid er ceisiaw tâl tros a ganwyf' (I don't mind, lord's daughter, that I may not see you, / It isn't in order to seek payment for what I sing) (ll. 37–38). Although he has already referred to the favourable reception of *Rhieingerdd Efa* by the handmaidens, and although he will in the final *caniad* make explicit his sense of the value of his poetry and its importance to the prestige of Madog and his family, here Cynddelw suggests that his intention is merely to establish or re-establish a good relationship with Efa, not to demand payment on the spot for his poems. He will get to that later.

There was of course a disparity of status between Cynddelw as court poet and Efa as daughter of the prince, a disparity that precluded an actual romantic attachment between them. A young woman of royal blood was, in twelfth-century Wales, as elsewhere throughout medieval Europe, a valuable capital asset, to be invested by means of marriage into another princely family, with the expectation of political rewards. Nevertheless, the court of a twelfth-century Welsh prince would not have been enormous, and the *bardd teulu*, the household poet, held a position within it that is recognised in all redactions of the Laws of Court. He was entitled to certain perquisites and gifts, including a horse. Thus, despite their social inequality, the poet is likely to have been on relatively familiar terms with the prince himself and members of his family. The occasional joke would not have been out of the question. It has been suggested that *Rhieingerdd Efa* might have been composed for the occasion of Efa's wedding to Cadwallon ap Madog ap

29 There is evidence that Cynddelw composed, on at least one occasion, the kind of love poem to a woman to whose romantic affections he actually aspired, complete with a complaint about the jealous husband, such as we associate with Dafydd ap Gwilym – as indeed with love poets in other medieval linguistic traditions. The Hendregadredd manuscript contains a brief *awdl* of eight lines in *cyhydedd naw ban* under the title *Kynddelw a gant yr awddl hon*, Cynddelw sang this *awdl*. See *Gwaith Cynddelw Mawr*, pp. 51–54. Helen Fulton takes note of this poem's 'lowered register' in *Dafydd ap Gwilym and the European Context*, pp. 59–60, 63–66, where she also discusses the theme of the jealous husband as it occurs in medieval French popular love lyrics. Fulton discusses the Cynddelw *awdl* at p. 93.

Idnerth, and we know that humour and even hilarity were not unheard of at weddings.[30] I believe, however, that we need not establish a connection between the poem and Efa's wedding in order to understand it. This poem lies squarely within the tradition of formal praise that was the *bardd teulu*'s primary social function, and of assertion of the poet's rights and privileges that routinely accompanies such praise. Yet in its playfulness, it participates in and avails of the intimacy of courtly circles everywhere and at every period.

A horse that is and is not there, that is and is not the poet himself; an aristocratic young woman of whom the poet pretends to be enamoured, while at the same time there are other girls in the poem with whom he flirts; a princess who is both herself and the court that she inhabits; a poet who maintains a seemly distance from his patroness, while at the same time demanding proper respect for the cultural capital he controls. Cynddelw weaves all these paradoxes into a piece of dazzlingly rich ambiguity, a poem that reinforces and reproduces the values of the aristocratic milieu within which he lived and worked. The lady, and the court she represents, are glorious, much to be desired; the poet enacts the praise that sustains that glory in the world outside the court; hence, while in one sense abject, the poet is essential, an integral part of the social structure here emblematised as an unattainable lady and her would-be love.

30 Parry Owen, 'Rhieingerdd Efa ferch Madog ap Maredudd. Cynndelw a'i Cant', pp. 62–64. Simon Rodway discusses the role of the poet at weddings, albeit for the most part in a later period, in 'What Did Medieval Welsh Poets Do at Weddings: A Re-examination of the *Cyfarws neithior*', in *Cyfarwydd mewn Cyfraith: Studies in Honour of Morfydd E. Owen*, ed. Sara Elin Roberts *et al.* (Bangor: Cymdeithas Hanes Cyfraith Cymru, 2022), pp. 124–41.

2

Ale-wives in Welsh Poetry c. 1450–c. 1650

Marged Haycock

One of John Skelton's most famous satires is 'The Tunnyng of Elynour Rummynge', written c. 1517. It describes a tavern in Leatherhead, Surrey, and its ageing proprietor, Elynour, 'her skynne lose and slacke', 'brystled with here', portly and malign. 'She is a tonnysh gyb; / The devyll and she be syb', brewing 'noppy ale' and presiding over a rough lot of travellers, tinkers, and unruly women including drunken Alice, 'full of tales, / Of tydynges in Wales'. Skelton is clearly drawing on casual racial and class prejudice and routine misogyny, as well as literary models such as the popular carol, 'The Gossips' Meeting', and the tavern scene in *Piers Plowman*. Despite the tropes Skelton has recourse to, we know that Elynour was a real woman, capable of running her own business, and that is surely part of what made her such a ready target.[1] Analogous caricatures regularly cited include the misericord in St Laurence's Church, Ludlow, showing a cheating ale-wife being dispatched to Hell by devils; she is identified by her measuring jug, and her escoffion suggestive of presumption and vanity.[2] Similar iconography can be seen in a few Doom wall-paintings in England, such as those in St Thomas's Church, Salisbury, and Holy Trinity, Coventry.[3] The confessions of the dishonest taverner and brewster in the Chester

1 John Skelton, *Poems*, ed. Robert S. Kinsman (Oxford: Clarendon Press, 1969), pp. 53–70. See p. xii, n. 1 and p. 154 on the document showing that she was living in Leatherhead in 1525 when she was accused of selling her beer 'at excessive price by small measures'.

2 Peter Klein, *The Misericords and Choir Stalls of Ludlow Parish Church* (Ludlow: Ludlow Parochial Church Council, 1986), accessible online at <https://www.misericords.co.uk/ludlow.html> [last accessed 30th April 2022].

3 For relevant details of St Thomas's, Salisbury, see Sarah Nash, 'The Doom Paintings of St Thomas's Church, Salisbury' <https://archaeology-travel.com/england/doom-painting-st-thomas-church-salisbury/> [last accessed 30th April 2022]; for Coventry see 'Holy Trinity Church, Coventry, Warwickshire', in *Medieval Wall Painting in the English Parish Church*, ed. Anne Marshall (2018) <https://reeddesign.co.uk/paintedchurch/coventry-doom.htm> [last accessed 30th April 2022].

play of the Harrowing of Hell[4] – adulterating her brew with ashes and herbs – also form part of the dossier taken to support Thomas Wright's assertion back in 1875, and reiterated *con forza* by Judith M. Bennett, that 'the ale-wife was an especial subject of jest and satire'.[5] Various reasons have been advanced for this demonisation: rank misogyny, propaganda as the ale trade became increasingly professionalised and controlled by men, the ambiguous territory and social space such women inhabited,[6] or, as Ralph Hanna adds, a more general and perennial distrust of people trading in food and drink. Hanna also notes the relative thinness of the literary dossier: 'Given both the paucity of overt references to ale-wives in the literature and women's prominence in the medieval brewing trade, the most misogynistic aspect [...] may be the general elision of the feminine'.[7]

This chapter is an attempt to bring some 'tydynges from Wales' to bear on the matter, as our honorand has done with distinction over many decades. I hope it speaks to her interests in late medieval commerce, women's work, the connections between lived life and literary depictions, and the textual study of poetry in Welsh. The focus here is a handful of poems – some unedited, most overlooked – about ale-wives from late medieval and Tudor Wales. All, like Elynour Rummyng, were flesh and blood women undoubtedly known in their communities and to the audiences who would have heard the poems being performed. The poems offer a more rounded view than is often assumed, bringing into question Judith Bennett's assertion that ale-wives were universally hated, and that they 'are never praised for the essential product they provide; they are never honoured for their good trade and nappy ale; they are never held up as epitomes of goodwives and good neighbours'.[8] On the contrary, the Welsh poems – albeit with some calculated and deliberate ambivalence in their characterisation – acknowledge the skill and craft of these women and their key role in oiling companionship and good cheer.

Before turning to those literary texts, a word about the advances made by economic and social historians in the field that was first opened up for England by Eileen Power, and subsequently in seminal works by Peter Clark and Judith Bennett.[9]

4 Robert M. Lumiansky and David Mills, eds, *The Chester Mystery Cycle Vol. I*, Early English Text Society Supplementary Series 3 (Oxford: Oxford University Press, 1974), pp. 337–39.

5 Thomas Wright, *History of Caricature and Grotesque in Literature and Art* (London: Chatto and Windus, 1875), pp. 139–40 (Wright was born and brought up in Ludlow); Judith M. Bennett, 'Misogyny, Popular Culture, and Women's Work', *History Workshop Journal* 31.1 (1991): 166–88.

6 Well-discussed by Barbara A. Hanawalt, *'Of Good and Ill Repute': Gender and Social Control in Medieval England* (Oxford: Oxford University Press, 1998), pp. 104–23.

7 Ralph Hanna III, 'Brewing Trouble: on Literature and History – and Alewives', in *Bodies and Disciplines: Intersections of Literature and History in Fifteenth-Century England*, ed. Barbara Hanawalt and David Wallace (Minneapolis, MI: University of Minnesota Press, 1996), pp. 1–17 (p. 6).

8 Bennett, 'Misogyny', p. 174.

9 Eileen Power's outline was published in Elaine Power, *Medieval Women*, ed. M. M.

In Wales, as elsewhere, there had been millennia of home production of ale, and in royal courts and the gentry and larger houses, surplus was regularly consumed in feasts and hospitality. The lavish provision of ale and mead, as well as a good range of wines, continued as an emblem of nobility and social cohesion and a very marked component of the gentlewoman-ideal in praise poetry, especially from the late fourteenth century onwards.[10] As for retailing ale, the picture is complicated by the fact that women were undoubtedly selling occasional surplus on a sporadic *ad hoc* basis from the back door, and that evidence of more commercialised activity in Wales comes mainly from the towns, such as Caernarfon and Ruthin, and over the border from Chester and Shrewsbury, which were much frequented by the Welsh traders, pilgrims and poets.[11] Assize of Ale and other prime sources are often lacking, but Matthew Stevens has worked the rich seam of court records from the small borough of Ruthin in the Vale of Clwyd, Denbighshire, for the period 1312–21.[12] He shows that brewing there was almost exclusively the preserve of women, most of them married, and moreover that Ruthin's brewsters were 'both the best documented and often the wealthiest of the borough's women'.[13] He argues that such wives, not just widows in dower, had more agency than historians such as Judith Bennett had found to be the case in England – being able to conduct themselves independently of their spouse in a legal setting, possessing property, and transacting business.

Postan (Cambridge: Cambridge University Press, 1975); Peter Clark, *The English Alehouse: A Social History, 1200–1830* (London: Longman, 1983); Judith M. Bennett, *Ale, Beer and Brewsters in England: Women's Work in a Changing World 1300–1600* (Oxford: Oxford University Press, 1996). For Wales, see sections in Llinos B. Smith's illuminating overviews: 'Towards a History of Women in Late Medieval Wales', in *Women and Gender in Early Modern Wales*, ed. Simone Clark and Michael Roberts (Cardiff: University of Wales Press, 2000), pp. 14–49; and 'In Search of an Urban Identity: Aspects of Urban Society in Late Medieval Wales', in *Urban Culture in Medieval Wales*, ed. Helen Fulton (Cardiff: University of Wales Press, 2012), pp. 19–49.

10 For examples and discussion, see Marged Haycock, *'Where Cider Ends: There Ale Begins to Reign': Drink in Medieval Welsh Poetry*, H. M. Chadwick Memorial Lecture 10 (Cambridge: Department of Anglo-Saxon, Norse, and Celtic, 1999).

11 Jane Laughton, 'The Alewives of Later Medieval Chester', in *Crown, Government and People in the Fifteenth Century*, ed. Rowena E. Archer (Stroud: St Martin's Press 1995); Helen Fulton, 'The Outside Within: Medieval Chester and North Wales as a Social Space', in *Mapping the Medieval City: Space, Place and Identity in Chester c. 1200–1600*, ed. Catherine A. M. Clarke (Cardiff: University of Wales Press, 2011), pp. 149–68; Helen Fulton, 'Trading Places: Representations of Urban Culture in Medieval Welsh Poetry', *Studia Celtica* 31 (1997): 219–30; Diane Hutton, 'Women in Fourteenth-century Shrewsbury', in *Women and Work in Pre-Industrial England*, ed. Lindsey Charles and Lorna Duffin (London: Routledge, 1985), pp. 82–99.

12 Matthew Frank Stevens, 'Women Brewers in Fourteenth-century Ruthin', *Transactions of the Denbighshire Historical Society* 54 (2005/6): 15–31; Stevens, *Urban Assimilation in Post-Conquest Wales: Ethnicity, Gender and Economy in Ruthin 1282–1348* (Cardiff: University of Wales Press, 2010), pp. 117–53.

13 Stevens, *Urban Assimilation*, p. 139.

Moving on to the fifteenth and sixteenth centuries, when permanent ale-houses and longer-life hopped beer were becoming more common, it is thought that the industry became increasingly controlled by men, although the evidence from Wales is patchy and, as Llinos Smith warns, we may be misled by 'changes in recording procedures whereby husbands were held liable for fines which were, in practice, incurred by their wives'.[14] She suspects – and consideration of the poems discussed below seems to confirm it – that brewing remained a predominantly female activity. Our poems indicate furthermore that there were Welsh women, seemingly *femmes soles*, in rural Ardudwy (near Harlech), Corwen, and Conwy, who were, like Elynour Rummynge, brewing and running their own ale-houses or *tafarnau*.[15]

The Dishonest Ale-wife

Richard Hughes of Cefnllanfair (c. 1565–1619) was a poet known to be fond of stock characters and situations.[16] His *englyn* to 'The Dishonest Ale-wife' (*I Dafarnwraig Anonest*) strikes a very similar note to Skelton, though much compressed: we see the same connection with the devil, the false accounting, and the way she is likened to one of her own brewing containers, just as Elynour is a *tonnysh gyb*.[17]

Rhyw siad anynad, un ynni – â diawl
Yn dilyn camgyfri';
Rhyw gwr[r]og yn rhagori,
Rhyw ddiawles yw'n hostes ni!

(An ill-tempered jade, of the same nature as the devil
practising false reckoning;
like a vessel,[18] lording it,
our hostess is a she-devil!)

The English loan-words – 'siad' (jade), 'hostes' (hostess; the first attestation), 'cwrrog' (vessel) – may be especially fitting if this maligned woman, if a real person at all, was operating in London, where Richard Hughes spent a good deal of his

14 Smith, 'Towards a History of Women', p. 33.

15 The word most commonly used for an ale-house in the Welsh sources is *tafarn*, an old loan word from Latin *taberna*, but first attested in the thirteenth century. *Tafarn* was also used occasionally for a place with lodging, an inn. Attested earlier, but seldom used, is *cyfrdy* (< *cwrw(f)* 'beer, ale' + *tŷ* 'house'), later, *tŷ cwrw*; also *dioty* 'drinking house'. A tavern in the early English sense, a place selling wine, usually in a town, is marked as a *tafarn win* or *gwindafarn*; similarly, *medd-dŷ* (mead-house).

16 Nesta Lloyd, ed., *Ffwtman Hoff: Cerddi Richard Hughes, Cefnllanfair* (Swansea: Cyhoeddiadau Barddas, 1998), p. liii.

17 Lloyd, *Ffwtman Hoff*, pp. 41 and 112.

18 The editor takes *gwrog* in line 3 to be a variant of *gwriog* 'married (woman)', rather than the lenited form of *cwrrog* 'vessel', a loan-word from English *currock*. For the use of *cwrrog* in satire, see Huw Meirion Edwards, *Gwaith Prydydd Breuan a Cherddi Dychan Eraill o Lyfr Coch Hergest* (Aberystwyth: Centre for Advanced Welsh and Celtic Studies, 2000), p. 115.

career, in the retinue of the Earl of Essex, and as a footman in the court of Elizabeth, and then James I. But it is possible that the establishment was in the town of Pwllheli, just east of Hughes' ancestral home at Cefnllanfair. That borough was developing rapidly as a centre of commerce and trade, and Hughes's family were burgesses with business interests there – just one example of the permeability of town and country in the period.[19] Another member of Elizabeth's Guard, the prolific poet Siôn Tudur (d. 1602), has left vivid pictures of companionship at taverns, with roaring gorse fires, toasted rye bread, double backgammon tables and games of dice, but sadly with no details of ale-wives.[20]

Gweurul and Annes of Ardudwy and Merioneth, by Dafydd Llwyd ap Huw

While Richard Hughes's *englyn* is disappointingly predictable, the next pair of poems, both in the strict *cywydd* metre, offer more novelty. They are grounded in the tradition of request poems, whereby a poet might ask his patron for a substantial gift for himself, such as a buckler, a horse, a harp, a fine bed coverlet and hangings, a pair of spectacles, a beehive, or a team of oxen.[21] In exchange, he offered the poem itself, a well-wrought *cywydd*, praising the patron and publicly recited in his hall; corresponding poems of thanks would further advertise the patron's largesse and standing. Towards the end of the medieval period, poets often asked for a gift on behalf of another patron, on occasion requesting a person, often to carry out a certain task. So Wiliam Cynwal asks his fellow poet, Siôn Tudur, for the *crwth* player, Rhys Grythor, lingering in jest on that musician's drunkenness in the genre's obligatory section of description. Huw Pennant requests a biddable old servant, Elin Rolant,[22] second to none for her cleanliness, and eager to be 'brushing [the floor] three or four times a day'.

The first of the pair we are concerned with here, by a little-known poet, Dafydd Llwyd ap Huw, is extant only in a defective manuscript eaten by rodents,[23] and in

19 T. Jones Pierce, *Medieval Welsh Society: Selected Essays*, ed. J. Beverley Smith (Cardiff: University of Wales Press, 1972), pp. 127–93. He notes, p. 188, that the *Penlan* (later Penlan Fawr Inn, partly dating from the sixteenth century) and the *Cock* are the only taverns of the period whose names have survived.

20 E.g. *Gwaith Siôn Tudur*, ed. Enid Roberts, 2 vols (Cardiff: University of Wales Press, 1980), I, pp. 593–95.

21 The classic study is Bleddyn Owen Huws, *Y Canu Gofyn a Diolch c. 1350 – c. 1650* (Cardiff: University of Wales Press, 1998), with an accompanying genre anthology, *Detholiad o Gywyddau Gofyn a Diolch* (Swansea: Cyhoeddiadau Barddas, 1998).

22 Huws, *Y Canu Gofyn*, pp. 73–74, 233.

23 Aberystwyth, National Library of Wales, MS Peniarth 97, p. 50. See further, Daniel Huws, *Repertory of Welsh Manuscripts and Scribes c. 800–c. 1800*, 3 vols (Aberystwyth: National Library of Wales, 2022), I, pp. 376–77. The defective Peniarth 97 text was included in W. Leslie Richards, 'Gwaith Dafydd Llwyd o Fathafarn', Unpublished MA dissertation (University of Wales, Aberystwyth, 1947), pp. 290–92. The

a later, poor text from the Tan-y-bwlch manuscript.[24] It has been suggested that Dafydd may be identified with Dafydd Llwyd ap Hywel, a gentleman-poet from Cynfal near Maentwrog in Ardudwy, but that remains uncertain.[25] In a *cywydd* of 86 lines, the poet addresses one Siôn ab Wmffre on behalf of another Siôn, the son of Gruffudd ap Harri of Tonfannau, on the west coast between Tywyn and Llangelynnin, Merioneth.[26] These two Siôns are second cousins, both scions of the fine stock of Derwas,[27] and, as is usual in this genre, the opening is devoted to reminding the addressee of his nobility and landedness ('yn wr da, aer o dir'), his wisdom ('yn ddoeth odiaeth'), his bravery and his readiness with his wine ('gwrol winffraeth').[28]

Then he turns to the cousin, always sincere where love is in the question ('carwr sy cywir o serch'). What does Siôn want? None other than Gweurul,[29] a dark impetuous woman ('gwraig ddu[30] chwidr') whom he desires not on account of any physical attraction, but for profit, in order to procure 'good beer, undefiled, loved by men' for Llangelynnin, 3 miles (5 km) from his seat at Tonfannau. Cheekily invoking the patron saint of lovers, the poet continues,

Myn Dwynwen, mae amdani
Yma ryw sôn mawr a si,
A bod y ferch a ercha'
Yn cael clod am ddiod dda.

---

cywydd's first line is 'Y llew doniog llydanwyn' (The bountiful lion, broad and fair), and the attribution at the end is to Dafydd Llwyd.

24 Aberystwyth, National Library of Wales, MS Minor Deposit 1206, p. 249, dated c. 1700–68; Huws, *Repertory*, I, pp. 105–06; the attribution in the Tan-y-bwlch manuscript is to 'Dd Lloyd ap Huw'.

25 A. Cynfael Lake, 'Gwaith Huw Llwyd o Gynfal', *Journal of the Merioneth Historical and Record Society* 9 (1981): 67–88 (67), notes that the names Hywel and Huw often alternate. This Dafydd Llwyd of Cynfal was the father of poet and soldier, Huw Cynfal, and grandfather of Morgan Llwyd, the noted divine. Evidence of Dafydd Llwyd's poetic ability, as well as his other accomplishments can be seen in Huw Machno's elegy for him (Dafydd died, aged 90, in 1623), preserved in Oxford, Bodleian Library, MS Welsh e.10, and printed in *Gweithiau Morgan Llwyd o Wynedd, Vol. II*, ed. John H. Davies (Bangor: Jarvis and Foster, 1908), pp. 305–08.

26 That the poem was regarded as a request poem is signalled by the rubric '[...] gowydd i ofyn Gweyryl [ferc]h Thomas dros Siôn ap [Gruffudd] ap Hari o'r Ton fane' (a *cywydd* to request Gweurul daughter of Thomas on behalf of Siôn ap Gruffudd ap Harri of Tonfannau), as noted by Glenys Davies, *Noddwyr Beirdd ym Meirion* (Dolgellau: Merioneth Record Office, 1974), pp. 206–07, adding that Siôn ap Gruffudd was alive in 1570.

27 Gruffudd Derwas (1374–1455), son of Meurig Llwyd of Nannau, near Dolgellau.

28 Texts are given here in modern orthography.

29 The form of this personal name varies: Gweurul (as here), Gweurful, Gweurfyl, Gwerfyl, Gwerful, Gweirful, and Gweryl.

30 This is ambiguous since *du* can cover 'gloomy, angry', even 'villainous'.

(By Dwynwen, there's a lot of talk and rumour here about her, that
the girl he loves is praised for good drink).

The text is very defective in places, but Gweurul is clearly a force to be reckoned with – still hale though desiccated and squinting, quick with her stinging tongue, and ready to 'fill us up gladly so long as the money lasts'. Not so if payment is not forthcoming; she claims her vat has run dry and shuts up shop. The later text, though garbled, accuses her – as so many of her kind – with false reckoning and avarice.[31] For all this, if she were to come south across the foaming sea via Barmouth, she would find the companionship in Merioneth finer than anything in her native Ardudwy, with 'fine men making cheer and praising the black drink', and virtuous wives and fair maidens and young men paying on the dot. So please, Siôn ab Wmffre, give thin-faced Gweurul to deserving Merioneth.

The second part of the *cywydd* seems to propose a straight exchange for a year with another ale-wife, one Annes daughter of 'Sir' Gruffudd. Like Gweurul, she is mistress of her brewing craft, doing good with her hand ('a wna lles â'i llaw'), but she is physically and temperamentally her opposite: Annes is a lovable woman, fat and well-grown ('un dewferch gain dyfiad'), possessed of steadfastness ('sadnes'), easily roused to a quarrel but quick to make it up ('hawdd y cymyd'). Stout of belly ('tordew'), she is a forceful and remarkable woman ('taer od fenyw').

Who are these women and what is going on here? The rubric of the poem discussed below states that Gweurul ferch Thomas was from Pen-y-sarn Hir, and this is undoubtedly the place now called Pen-sarn, due south of Harlech, almost half way between Llanbedr and Llanfair-juxta-Harlech in the commote of Ardudwy.[32] This would indeed be a good spot for an ale-house: although very rural, it lies on the River Artro, navigable beyond here, and on the Sarn Hir, the old Bronze Age way leading travellers and drovers up towards Harlech and thence north-east in the direction of Trawsfynydd.[33] Annes is not firmly located, but her father, parish priest Syr Gruffudd ap Siôn Daeliwr, may perhaps be identified with the Griffith ap John Tailor who was holding the benefice of Llanfair-juxta-Harlech in October 1554.[34] Of course, Annes may well have been living some distance from Llanfair, and certainly the talk of exchange would more naturally lead us to suppose that she was living in Merioneth, perhaps near Llangelynnin. And indeed, there is a record of a burial of

31 'Cam gyfri pot dan drotian / A mynnu er hyn mwynai rhan' (Counting wrongly a potful as she scurries about, and yet demanding the full sum of money).

32 For older forms such as *Tythyn Pen y sarn hir* (1636), *Penysarnhir* (1795), see Melville Richards, 'Welsh *sarn* "Road, Causeway" in Place-names', *Études celtiques* 11 (1966): 383–408 (388, 395).

33 See Rhian Parry, *Cerdded y Caeau* (Talybont: Y Lolfa, 2022), pp. 20–21.

34 Arthur Ivor Pryce, *The Diocese of Bangor in the Sixteenth Century* (Bangor: Jarvis and Foster, 1923), p. 14. I am most grateful to Professor G. Aled Williams for directing me to this source. He notes (personal communication) that Gruffudd's predecessor, Dafydd ap Gruffydd, was deprived of his living, marked as 'married', and surmises that Gruffudd was a recusant, and unmarried in 1554.

one Agnetta Griffith, on 7th November 1623 in Llangelynnin, and another on 25th July 1635.[35] But any identification is very rash with such common names.

Clearly the main purpose of the poem, apart from praising the two cousins, is to amuse them and their audience – whether in a noble house or perhaps in the very ale-houses mentioned – with a contrast between the thin crone Gweurul and stolid Annes. Neither is presented as physically alluring and thus a threat to respectability,[36] but both clearly have the authority and wit to control their establishments and lay down the law if need be.

Gweurul and Annes of Ardudwy and Merioneth, by Rhisiart Phylip

Dafydd Llwyd's poem was answered by Rhisart Phylip of Ardudwy (c. 1565–1641), a prolific member of a family of professional poets from Mochras, on the coast some 3 or 4 miles (6 km) from Pen-y-sarn Hir.[37] The interpretation of this unedited 109-line *cywydd*, too, is not easy. Seemingly, it is extant only in the late Tan-y-bwlch manuscript.[38] As this is a collection from Ardudwy, however, this manuscript's rubric has value, stating explicitly that this is a reply to Dafydd Llwyd's poem, and, as noted above, giving us a location for Gweurul. The poem confirms a connection with 'bro Decwyn' ([St] Tecwyn's region), the parish of Llandecwyn being only 7 or 8 miles (11 or 12 km) north of Pen-y-sarn. The *cywydd* begins conventionally, addressing Siôn ap Gruffudd of Tonfannau (Merioneth), whose request was tendered by Dafydd Llwyd – he is a vine of the island ('gwinwydd ynys'), a gentle stag who deserves praise ('yn hydd mwyn yn haeddu mawl'), but above all a generous fellow in company ('camp iawn rodd, cwmpnïwr wyt'), lord of the old drinking companions ('pen rhaith y cwmpniwyr hen'). As for his request for the wry-mouthed Gweurul ('Gweryl ferch gyriawg'), with her flavourful pure ale ('cwrw perflas pur'), that is not something to which his cousin would agree. Although she is unappealing – thin, unwholesome ('un afiach gul yw'), foul-mouthed ('diful fant'), dark and rough ('du a garw'), an old crone ('drygen hen') – there's nothing to beat her ale ('nid oes bwrw ar gwrw Gwerful'), and cousin Siôn will not let her leave Ardudwy.

He then is lavishly praised, a lusty young blade, ready with bow and arrow, horse and hound, a byword for generosity, his payment equal to the wealth of Cheapside. A trusty companion ('cwmpnïwr glân'), he relishes the best drink of ale from the

35 The will of Agnes Griffith, widow, in 1661 would seem too late: Rhisiart Phylip died in 1641. Agnes's will is available online through the National Library of Wales website <http://hdl.handle.net/10107/815194> [last accessed 11th November 2023].

36 See Lumiansky and Mills, *Chester Mystery Cycle, Vol. 2*, p. 275, for the 1533 regulations in Chester that prohibited women between the ages of 14 and 40 from running ale-houses.

37 J. Gwynfor Jones, 'Phylipiaid Ardudwy: Aspects of their Bardic Contribution in Late-sixteenth and Seventeenth-century Wales', *Journal of the Merioneth Historical and Record Society* 13 (2001): 313–47.

38 National Library of Wales, MS Minor Deposit 1206, p. 251.

thin old squinting woman ('y ddiod orau / o gwrw gan goeg wreigan gul') and there are many others too who love her. The poet suggests that the proposed object of exchange, Annes, 'fat, day and night in Merioneth', whose countenance inhibits well-being ('bryd ludd les'), is the better-known of two evils, and just the ticket for Siôn Tonfannau in his dotage. Of course, if Gweurul *were* to go south, and be treated well, she would produce abundant drink, vatfuls like aqua vitae ('fitied fal acyfeiti'). If her barrels were drunk dry late at night, she would happily provide a jugful to last until morning and – countering any slur implied by Dafydd Llwyd – the poet adds that she would give customers five pots of ale for the price of three ('a chyfri [...] / am driffot bumpot y bydd'). We must conclude that Rhisiart Phylip is advertising Gweurul and her establishment – his 'local', perhaps, superior to anything in Merioneth – as well as praising the two gentlemen and playing to a gallery who relished casual banter about older women while admiring their produce.

Gwerful ferch Gutun at the Conway Ferry Tavern

Unlike the unedited items above, this short request poem of 36 lines for a harp strung with horsehair (*Cywydd i Ofyn Telyn Rawn*) has had a certain amount of attention. This is partly because scholars in the past – its first editor, Leslie Harries, and others – have assumed it to be by the renowned fifteenth-century woman-poet, Gwerful Mechain of Powys.[39] This was a temptation since it opens with the lines 'Gwerful wyf o gwr y lan, / O'r Fferi, orhoff arian' (I am Gwerful from the water's edge, from the Ferry, very partial to silver). But in none of the four extant copies is it attributed to Gwerful Mechain (daughter of Hywel Fychan), but rather to an unidentified Gwerful daughter of Gutun,[40] an ale-wife connected with a place

39 Leslie Harries, 'Barddoniaeth Huw Cae Llwyd, Ieuan ap Huw Cae Llwyd, Ieuan Dyfi a Gwerful Mechain', Unpublished MA dissertation (University of Wales, Swansea, 1933), p. 124; Ceridwen Lloyd-Morgan, '"Gwerful, ferch ragorol fain": golwg newydd ar Gwerful Mechain', *Ysgrifau Beirniadol* 16 (1990): 84–96 (88–89); and Lloyd-Morgan, 'Women and their Poetry in Medieval Wales', in *Women and Literature in Britain, 1150–1500*, ed. Carole Meale (Cambridge: Cambridge University Press, 1996), pp. 185–201 (p. 191). The text is most easily consulted in Cathryn A. Charnell-White, ed., *Beirdd Ceridwen: Blodeugerdd Barddas o Ganu Menywod hyd tua 1800* (Swansea: Cyhoeddiadau Barddas, 2005), pp. 108–09. English translations include Joseph P. Clancy, *Medieval Welsh Poems* (Dublin: Four Courts Press, 2003), pp. 337–38; Katie Gramich, *The Works of Gwerful Mechain* (Peterborough, ON: Broadview Press, 2018), pp. 140–45.

40 The earliest witness is London, British Library, MS Additional 14875, fols 5v–6r, in a portion of the manuscript dated 1570–71 by Huws, *Repertory*, I, pp. 606–07. The rubric states that this is a request poem for a harp ('Kowydd i ovyn telyn'), and that the woman was an ale-wife from Tal-y-sarn ('y dyvarnwraig o dal y sarn'). At the end, the name is given as 'Gwerfyl ach Ryttyn' (Gwerful daughter of [the] Gutun; the definite article was often used before shortened personal names and names used affectionately, cf. German *der Peter*). Another copy, Cardiff, Central Library, MS 4.156, p. 192, was written in 1736–37 by Margaret Davies of Coetgae-du, Trawsfynydd. A knowledgeable anthologist and literary historian, Davies would

called Tal-y-sarn. Unfortunately, Enid P. Roberts, while rightly rejecting Gwerful Mechain's authorship, muddied the waters by implying some connection with the later Gweurul we have met above – the dark, thin ale-wife of Pen-y-sarn Hir in Ardudwy, daughter of Thomas ap Rhys.[41] Even allowing for some confusion between Pen-y-sarn and Tal-y-sarn, these two individuals are *not* the same: the one here at 'the Ferry' is Gwerful daughter of Gutun.

Where is that? A place called Y Fferi is mentioned by the poet Iocyn Ddu ab Ithel Grach as he traces an itinerary of debauchery across north-east and mid-Wales and over Offa's Dyke. 'Yn y Fferi offerennais' (In the Ferry I celebrated Mass), he records, possibly with obscene sense.[42] One clear candidate here is Tywyn y Fferi, named for the ferry across the River Conwy, on the east bank south of Degannwy in the parish of Eglwys Rhos.[43] In our present poem, the fact that the request for the harp is made to one Ifan ap Dafydd, who belongs to the best ones in [the cantref of] Rhos ('i'r rhai gorau'n Rhos'), favours the Conwy identification, clinched by the presence of nearby Tal-y-sarn, in the same parish.[44] If the triangulation offered here is correct, Gwerful ferch Gutun's establishment was in a prime spot, on a route heavily traversed across the centuries, close to the site of the bridges built by Telford and Stephenson.

---

have signalled had Gwerful Mechain been the author; instead she notes the attribution to Gwerful, 'yr hon oedd dafarnwraig' (who was a tavern-wife). Other later copies include Aberystwyth, National Library of Wales, MS Cwrtmawr 169, p. 79, and Aberystwyth, National Library of Wales, MS 112B, p. 4.

41 Enid Roberts, *Dafydd Llwyd o Fathafarn* (Caernarfon: Eisteddfod Genedlaethol Cymru, 1981), p. 12, where she calls the Ardudwy woman 'Gwerful Fychan or Fechan'. William Owen Pughe had also placed the poem later, 'the production of a jolly Landlady of the sixteenth century', see Nerys A. Howells, *Gwaith Gwerful Mechain ac Eraill* (Aberystwyth: Centre for Advanced Welsh and Celtic Studies, 2001), p. 29.

42 Barry J. Lewis, ed., *Gwaith Madog Benfras ac Eraill o Feirdd y Bedwaredd Ganrif ar Ddeg* (Aberystwyth: Centre for Advanced Welsh and Celtic Studies, 2007), poem 18, pp. 295–307, discussed by Huw Meirion Edwards, '"Rhodiwr fydd clerwr": sylwadau ar gerdd ymffrost o'r bedwaredd ganrif ar ddeg', *Y Traethodydd* 149 (January 1994): 50–55.

43 As noted by Lewis, *Gwaith Madog Benfras*, p. 303.

44 For Tal-y-sarn, see Richards, 'Welsh *sarn*', p. 392. The village of Tal-y-sarn, Dyffryn Nantlle, can be discounted since there is no ferry known there. For details on the Conwy ferry and the one further up-river at Tal-y-cafn, both with taverns or alehouses nearby, see H. R. Davies, *A Review of the Records of the Conway and the Menai Ferries* (Cardiff: University of Wales Press, 1942). For a different identification with a place in eastern Montgomeryshire (a propos Gwerful Mechain), see Lloyd-Morgan 'Gwerful', 89, n. 17, citing D. Machreth Ellis, 'Enwau Lleoedd Sir Drefaldwyn', Unpublished MA dissertation (University of Wales, 1935), p. 806, who gives a map reference to a dwelling by a ferry on the River Severn near Llandrinio. For the name Ferry in Llandysilio and in Guilsfield see Peter Barton, ed., *Montgomeryshire Placename Database* (2004): <https://doi.org/10.5284/1000245]> [last accessed 30th April 2022].

After naming and locating herself, the speaker presents herself as wholesome, white-smocked ('cryswen lwys'),[45] ready to give an excellent welcome to men with money – the second mention of the word 'arian' in the first six lines. This is no mean ale-house, neither is there mention of brewing. To ensure good cheer ('cydfod gwŷr'), Gwerful provides plentiful food for her guests ('byd diwall i'm lletywyr') and entertaining song ('a chanu'n lân gyfannedd') while serving mead, the noblest of native drinks. But what is missing is a harp, a *sine qua non* for the performance of poetry.[46] So she has sent to her kinsman, one Ifan ap Dafydd, described – with bathos perhaps – as 'a baron giving bread'. She traces his line to the finest in the cantref of Rhos, confident that he will not let her down. The harp she requests is described according to the requirements of the genre, albeit briefly, noting the 'warp' of its strings ('ysto' o rawn'), the set of pegs running from end to end, with tuning-horn and sounding board, and a neck like one of the geese ('fal un o'r gwyddau').[47] As for Ifan, his reward will be the poem itself, plus a roast and mead, a good welcome when the cuckoo sings, and his dinner – for tuppence ('er dwy geiniog'). The comic sting in the tail, that he will have to pay for his drink and victuals at their Spring tryst, is consonant with the fronting of money early on in the poem and raises the question whether this is indeed the tavern-keeper, Gwerful ferch Gutun, singing, or another poet ventriloquising,[48] using her persona to make a request on her behalf, while advertising the delights of the Ferry tavern. This was a strategy employed occasionally in request poems of the later medieval period, which sometimes also saw suppliants, especially those of less noble status, being satirised.[49] The humour here derives from the mismatch between the traditional mores expressed by the genre – one good thing exchanged for another ('da dros dda'), and gifts possessing a worth no money can buy[50] – and the explicitly mercenary concerns of the speaker.

45 But conceivably a metaphor for the whitewashed tavern.

46 The poet Gruffudd Fychan in asking for a harp says how ashamed he felt when forced to perform a *cywydd sengl*, that is a poem unaccompanied by the harp: *Gwaith Sefnyn, Rhisierdyn ac Eraill*, ed. Nerys A. Jones and Erwain Haf Rheinallt (Aberystwyth: Centre for Advanced Welsh and Celtic Studies, 1995), p. 145, poem 11, ll. 15–18.

47 For other poems requesting a harp, see Huws, *Canu Gofyn*, p. 270; Sally Harper, *Music in Welsh Culture before 1650: A Study of the Principal Sources* (London: Routledge, 2007), pp. 18–20, 43, who notes the 'over-riding bardic preference for the horsehair-strung *telyn rawn*' as opposed to the harsher bray harp.

48 Lloyd-Morgan, 'Gwerful', pp. 88–89, wondered whether Gwerful Mechain might not have assumed the persona of a tavern-keeper, noting the playful irony of the poem, discussed further, Lloyd-Morgan, 'Women and their Poetry', p. 191.

49 Huws, *Canu Gofyn*, p. 116: 'Datblygodd ail fath lle'r oedd y bardd yn ganolwr ac yn erchi ar ran trydydd person, weithau drwy dadogi'r cywydd ar yr eirchiad a llefaru drwy ei enau ef' (There developed a second class [of request poems] where the poet was an intermediary, asking on behalf of a third party, sometimes attributing the cywydd to the suppliant and assuming their voice). See further, pp. 143–59, on the way suppliants were presented.

50 Huws, *Canu Gofyn*, p. 134, notes that, in over 650 poems, there are only very rare mentions of money.

Lleucu's Tavern at Corwen, by Hywel Gethin

The final poem in the dossier is by Hywel Gethin of Clynnog Fawr in Arfon, on the north coast of the Llŷn peninsula. Only three poems by him have survived, but he can be approximately dated by an allusion by a fellow-poet, Tudur Penllyn (1420–85/90). Tudur's informal series of *englynion* shows Hywel taking part in one of the pretend wedding feasts (*coeg neithiorau*) where poets would come together and take pot shots at one other.[51] Alongside bandy-legged Gutun Owain ('bongam'), wily Lewys Môn ('dyrys'), Lewys Daron and many others, there is the lob, Hywel Gethin ('drel'), listening to Tudur playing the buffoon ('yn canu hoywan dail').

In a more sober vein is Hywel's own *cywydd* praising the four sons of Rhys ap Hywel ap Madog of Abercain (Bercin), Llanystumdwy (who was living in 1469), and comforting their mother Mawd after Rhys's death. Madog Fychan, the oldest son, was living in 1485.[52] This was a prosperous region, with some of the best land in Eifionydd sustaining several noble seats, some of them belonging to the descendants of Einion ap Gruffudd ap Hywel, brother of Syr Hywel y Fwyall 'Sir Hywel the Axe', the constable of Cricieth Castle, who had been praised – like Einion's son, Ieuan – by Iolo Goch in the fourteenth century.[53]

The 52-line *cywydd* with which we are concerned, describing the tavern of Lleucu ferch Bleddyn, was edited in exemplary fashion by Édouard Bachellery, who was struck by the fact that 'il présente une certaine originalité'.[54] Lleucu was operating in Corwen, on the River Dee, in the commote of Edeirnion, 13 miles (21 km) south of Ruthin and 14 miles (23 km) west of Llangollen. There is no evidence that Corwen was a market town in the fifteenth century;[55] it was more a staging post at a point where many of the northern droving routes converged before heading east to Llangollen and Wrexham and on to England. Beasts from Ardudwy, Harlech, Anglesey, and Llŷn would all come this way with thirsty drovers – and entertainers

51 Thomas Roberts, ed., *Gwaith Tudur Penllyn ac Ieuan ap Tudur Penllyn* (Cardiff: University of Wales Press, 1958), pp. 61–62.

52 Hywel Gethin was wrongly assigned to the period 1570–1600 by Ebenezer Thomas (Eben Fardd) who was misled by his source, Aberystwyth, National Library of Wales, MS Minor Deposit 55 (Swansea 1), 'Y Piser Hir', c. 1788, p. 74, in the hand of David Ellis (d. 1795). This wrong date was perpetuated by several authors into the twentieth century, until corrected by É. Bachellery in 1950 (see below, n. 54). Eben Fardd, anxious to bring into prominence the work of a fellow Clynnog inhabitant, printed the *cywydd* in *Y Brython*, June 1860, p. 233. This and other poems to the nobility of the area are discussed in detail by Iwan Llwyd, 'Noddwyr Beirdd Sir Gaernarfon', Unpublished MA dissertation (University of Wales, Aberystwyth, 1986).

53 D. R. Johnston, ed., *Gwaith Iolo Goch* (Cardiff: University of Wales Press, 1988), pp. 6–15. For details of the Abercain estate, see Colin Gresham, *Eifionydd: A Study in Landownership from the Medieval Period to the Present Day* (Cardiff: University of Wales Press, 1973), pp. 185–92.

54 É. Bachellery, 'Le poète Hywel Gethin et le MS. British Museum Additional 14967', *Études celtiques* 5 (1949–51): 248–59 (p. 251).

55 Pace Bachellery, 'Le poète Hywel Gethin', p. 255.

and poets undoubtedly following. The poet Guto'r Glyn drove sheep to England for Sir Bened ap Hywel (d. 1464), parson of Corwen, and enjoyed there 'medd, cwrw ... mêl cwyraidd' (mead, beer ... honey like wax), from a man famed more than anyone for spending in wine houses ('Mawr yw d'air am roi d'arian / Mewn gwindai mwy nog undyn').[56]

The *cywydd* to Lleucu ferch Bleddyn conforms in several respects to the conventions used to praise gentlewomen. First there is her flawless pedigree: although not identifiable in the genealogies, she is 'Eigr enwog o ryw Ynyr' (an Ygraine of the line of Ynyr Fychan), that is, the house of Nannau near Dolgellau – and is therefore distantly related to Hywel Gethin's patrons in Llanystumdwy, who may well have been dispatching their cattle along the road to Corwen. Lleucu's father's family could claim descent from Rhirid Flaidd, the twelfth-century magnate praised by the Powys poet, Cynddelw Brydydd Mawr. Furthermore, this fair woman of noble lineage was begotten from the bloodline of Engelfield (Flintshire), right back to dukes ('Rhywiog wen, ei rhyw a gaid / O waed Tegeingl at dugiaid'). Well-networked, then. Indeed, 'Mae'r glod am y wraig lwydwen[57] / O gaer Gaint i Geiriog wen' (the praise of the grey-haired woman is heard from Canterbury to fair Ceiriog). As befits what Bachellery calls 'un personnage assez cossu', she dispenses largesse in the house where the string resounds to her praise. Nothing is ever whispered about *buying* a drink. Like others of her class, she is a by-word for gold and silver, and 'Ni phalla [...] o roi i gerddwyr' (doesn't fail [...] to give support to poets) perhaps by paying them directly, or in kind. Here, they are paid 'gold and mead', substantial reward for the itinerant poet, presumably to perform in her tavern. In this case, she is very likely calling the tune.

We are a full 19 lines into the *cywydd* before her brew is mentioned. The poet would not even take 'sugar and wine instead of the ale of her manufacture' ('Ni ddewiswn seugr a gwin dros cwrw o'i gwaith'). Indeed, there's such great call for 'Osai o'r ŷd' (the champagne of grain)[58] that even the men of Chester are clamouring for Corwen beer. She brews a veritable treacle or medicinal salve ('Triagl o ddŵr trwy glawdd iach') from a pure water source, producing the finest of drinks served

56 Guto'r Glyn, 'Awdl foliant i Syr Bened, person Corwen (Poem 43)', ed. R. Iestyn Daniel <www.gutorglyn.net> [last accessed 11th November 2023].

57 *Llwydwen* is ambiguous, being a compound of *llwyd* (grey-haired, old, but also blessed, pious) + *gwen* (fair, blessed), hence Bachellery's translation 'cette femme sage et belle'.

58 *Osai* (E. *Osey, Osaye*), a sweet strong wine, is often referred to by the Welsh poets, both in lists of wines and in love poetry. See Ifor Williams, 'Osai', *Bulletin of the Board of Celtic Studies* 10 (1939–41): 305, for its connection with Portugal rather than Alsace, quoting Salzman, *English Trade in the Middle Ages* (Oxford: Clarendon Press, 1931), pp. 401 and 407, in favour of Sierra de Ossa east of Lisbon, or the valley of the River Odese. Azoia near Lisbon is suggested by Michael Freeman, '*Pots of Osey*: Portuguese Wine in Late Medieval England and its Place of Origin', in *De Mot en Mot: Aspects of Medieval Linguistics*, ed. Stewart Gregory and D. A. Trotter (Cardiff: University of Wales Press, 1997), pp. 17–36.

in the finest tavern. The terms used here bring to mind the metaphors used in the love poetry of the period. Then follows a picture of the happy establishment ('tŷ dedwydd') over which she presides, a wholesome contrast to Elynour Rummynge's place in Leatherhead:

> Cywain a wna, canwn [n]i
> gerdd addwyn, bob gradd, iddi,
> cwrw i fardd fal Caer Fyrddin
> i'w roi i lawr ar ei lin.
> Odid fyth, a daed yw 'vo,
> os yf dyn, y saif dano:
> Un yn floesg yn ei nef wledd,
> un arall yn ei orwedd,
> un a ymladd yn amlwg,
> un heb ryw gas yn bwrw gwg,
> un a gwsg fegis oen gwan,
> ail â'n grupl yno i gropian!
> Cadarn fal gwin Ffrainc ydyw,
> cryf iawn, iarll y kyrvav yw!

> (She garners – we sing –
> pleasing song of every [poetic] order,
> ale for a poet as [in] Carmarthen[59]
> to set down on his lap.
> It's a rare thing – and what a good[brew]! –
> if a man drinks, that he can stand upright.
> There's one there, his speech slurred in his heavenly feast,
> another one flat out,
> one fighting in full view,
> one without any provocation scowling,
> one sleeping like a weak lamb,
> another like a cripple going on hands and knees.
> It's potent like the wine of France,
> it's very strong, the earl of ales!)

The poem ends as it began, wishing Lleucu every success, health, and grace, having provided us with the earliest full picture in Welsh poetry of an ale- or tavern-wife in situ, one which most gives the lie to claims that such women were universally hated and never praised for their produce.

This chapter has discussed poetry in strict metre from the long sixteenth century, and has tried to show the variety of attitudes manifest within the small group dealing in detail with ale-wives. No comparable material survives for male

59 Possibly a reference to the famous Eisteddfod of Carmarthen c. 1450/51 which tightened up the rules relating to grades of poets and metres. See John Morris-Jones, *Cerdd Dafod* (Oxford: Oxford University Press, 1925), pp. 349–50.

brewers and mine hosts. By the end of the period, however, popular free-metre poems and ballads begin to proliferate, taking in the delights and dangers of drink, dialogues between drunkards and tavern-wives, reflections on public houses as a liberating space for men seeking escape from domestic and marital cares, the 'Jolly Welsh-Woman' on the razzle at the Sign of the Crown in London,[60] and many other related matters that must await further investigation.

60 'English Broadside Ballad Archive 34969 (Anon, c. 1688–92)', in *English Broadside Ballad Archive* (University of California at Santa Barbara, 2014) <http://ebba.ds.lib.ucdavis.edu/ballad/34969/xml> [last accessed 12th May 2022].

3

A Forest, a Spring, and a Lion: Nature in Three Romances

Stephen Knight

This study will look at three parallel medieval romances in French, Welsh, and English: Chrétien de Troyes's *Le Chevalier au Lion* or *Yvain*, the Welsh *Iarlles y Ffynnawn* (The Lady of the Fountain), and the English *Ywain and Gawain*. Such a cross-cultural comparison resembles in several ways the wide-ranging European research of Helen Fulton, who I had the great pleasure of meeting as a leading undergraduate at the University of Sydney, and who, throughout her subsequent career, has produced significant works on both Welsh romance and constructions of the natural world in literature in the Celtic languages.[1] The recurring concern of my essay will be how my three texts handle details of the natural contexts that characters, especially knights, experience on their varied adventures. While nature is not dealt with in the romances in terms of producing wealth for major landowners nor, in all but a few cases, supporting the life of the land-dwelling poor, the natural context of both life and travel is realised variously as an evaluative setting for the knightly adventurers, negative or positive – and at times both.

Chrétien's poem *Yvain* can be dated with some confidence between 1170 and 1180. The Welsh prose text, *Iarlles y Ffynnawn*, is less certain in date, although it is usually located by modern scholars in the mid- or late twelfth century. In his discussion of the text, R. L. Thomson cautiously dates its composition to 'the end of the twelfth century'.[2] The English poem *Ywain and Gawain* is usually dated in the early to mid-fourteenth century. Its author evidently knew the story of *Yvain* well. Jessie

1 Helen Fulton, 'Individual and Society in *Owein/Yvain* and *Gereint/Erec*', in *The Individual in Celtic Literatures*, ed. J. F. Nagy (Dublin: Four Courts Press, 2001), pp. 15–50; 'Magic Naturalism in the *Táin Bó Cúailnge*', in *Narrative in Celtic Tradition: Essays in Honor of Edgar M. Slotkin*, ed. Joseph F. Eska, CSANA Yearbook 8–9 (Hamilton, NY: Colgate University Press, 2011), pp. 84–99.

2 R. L. Thomson, 'Owain: Chwedl Iarlles y Ffynnon', in *The Arthur of the Welsh: The Arthurian Legend in Medieval Welsh Literature*, ed. Rachel Bromwich, A. O. H. Jarman, and Brynley F. Roberts (Cardiff: University of Wales Press, 1991), pp. 159–69 (p. 159).

L. Weston accepted the French as a source for the English poem, but also argued that, in several instances, *Iarlles y Ffynnawn* may have been known to the English adaptor.[3] She argued that three main instances show this (I will detail these during my analysis of the Welsh text, below), potentially remembered from an encounter with an oral version of the Welsh text, presumably translated into English. In the pages that follow, the three texts will be discussed in their likely order of production: French, Welsh, English. This is also, I suggest, the order of their complexity, which is highest in French and simplest in English. My discussion will be divided into the four major sections of the action as laid out by Chrétien, and each section will deal with all three texts, before moving on to the next section of the narrative.

The First Knight at the Spring

At the beginning of *Yvain*, a minor knight at Arthur's court, Sir Calogrenant, tells his colleagues about a recent and wretched adventure of his. This name, R. S. Loomis argued, comes from a negative title given to Sir Kay as 'Cai Lo Grenant' (Kay the Grumbler). He will justify the title early in this story.[4] Calogrenant was riding, seeking adventure, when he found himself on a path, 'leading through a thick forest. The way was very treacherous, full of thorns and briars'.[5] This hostile-seeming natural context is normal for knights on journeys, which pose real threats. The forest is Brocéliande, an often-magical location in Arthurian story, first mentioned in Wace's mid-twelfth-century *Roman de Rou*. This familiar forest is not as forbidding as many will be, and Calogrenant soon leaves it, entering 'into open country'.[6] Here he encounters civilisation, firstly of the military kind: a fortress 'with a deep and wide moat all around'.[7] The 'vavasour' who owns the castle invites the knight to dismount and a maiden takes him to 'the most beautiful meadow in the world, enclosed roundabout with a small wall'.[8] A pleasant meadow after a difficult journey is a common feature in medieval romance, and it is usually positive, as here. Calogrenant rides on, and soon he sees a clearing with wild bulls fighting in it, and,

3 Jessie L. Weston, '"Ywain and Gawain" and "Le Chevalier au Lion"', *Modern Quarterly of Literature and Language* 1 (1898): 98–107 (103).

4 R. S. Loomis, 'Calogrenanz and Crestien's Originality', *Modern Language Notes* 43 (1928): 215–22 (216–21).

5 References to *Yvain* are from Chrétien de Troyes, 'The Knight with the Lion (Yvain)', in *Four Arthurian Romances*, trans. William W. Kibler and Carleton W. Carroll (London: Penguin, 2004), pp. 295–380 (p. 297). Hereafter *Yvain*.

6 *Yvain*, p. 297.

7 *Yvain*, p. 297.

8 *Yvain*, p. 298. The title 'vavasour' means 'a vassal of a vassal', not a lord who holds his feudal property directly from the king, but one holding land from a royal vassal. Yvain himself, though of noble blood, is himself not (or at least not yet) a great land-owning lord, and in a way is himself at the vavasour financial and social level, from which he will ascend grandly. The conflict inherent in this development is a part of the social context of the chivalric romances. See further Stephen Knight, *Arthurian Literature and Society* (London: Macmillan, 1983), pp. 74–77.

as if to match this natural violence, sitting on a stump is 'a rustic lout, as black as a mulberry, indescribably big and hideous' – a clearly racialised romance allusion, although here first and foremost connected with a distinctive natural scene.[9] When asked if he is 'a good creature or not?', the churl replies, 'I stand here and watch [...] I am lord over my beasts'.[10] Calogrenant asks for advice on where to find an adventure, and this apparently anti-heroic force of nature tells him to 'go to a spring near here [...] that boils and yet is colder than marble. It is shaded by the most beautiful tree that Nature ever formed. Its leaves stay on in all seasons; it doesn't lose them in even the harshest winter'.[11] The spring is a place of natural beauty that can accommodate natural violence. The churl says that, beside the spring, there will be a stone, and 'if you will take some of the water in the basin and cast it upon the stone', a storm will rise and all the animals will run away: 'stags, does, deer, boar, and even birds will fly before it'.[12] Calogrenant goes to the spring, sprinkles the hollow stone with water from the basin, and a terrible storm appears: 'all the clouds pell-mell dropped rain, snow and hail'.[13] When the storm stops, he sees 'gathered upon the pine tree so many birds – believe it if you will – that not a leaf or branch could be found that was not completely covered by birds'.[14] Then the knight of the spring arrives, descending on Calogrenant 'faster than an eagle, looking as fierce as a lion'.[15] The animal comparisons suggest the knight is hyper-natural, and he is certainly a far better warrior than Calogrenant: with one blow of his huge lance, he knocks Arthur's knight off his horse and immediately rides away, leaving Calogrenant 'shamed and defeated'.[16] He makes his way back to the world of Arthur, via the house of the hospitable vavasour, to tell his story at court. Yvain says at once that he will avenge his relative, Calogrenant. In response to this, Yvain is insulted by Sir Kay (and we might remember here Loomis's theory regarding 'Cai Lo Grenant'). The king hears of this discussion and declares that he wants to see the spring and will leave for that purpose within two weeks, but Yvain, concerned that otherwise either Kay or Gawain would receive the right of the first battle at the spring, heads off there himself, the very next day.

In the Welsh prose text, the hero is not Yvain but, evidently a related name, Owein, son of Urien, originally a legendary historical figure from sixth-century Northumbria. The opening account of the journey to the spring is narrated by Cynon ap Clydno, another legendary hero of the British Old North: his father was one of many named as dying at the Battle of Catraeth (c. 600 CE), in the early Welsh poem *Y Gododdin*. The Welsh text is only about a quarter of the length of the French

9 *Yvain*, p. 298.
10 *Yvain*, p. 299.
11 *Yvain*, pp. 299–300.
12 *Yvain*, p. 300.
13 *Yvain*, p. 300.
14 *Yvain*, p. 300.
15 *Yvain*, p. 301.
16 *Yvain*, p. 301.

Yvain. The earlier view that the two texts had a common source, a Celtic story that probably came to Chrétien through Brittany, is now questioned. As Regine Reck has recently reported, that opinion

> is no longer widely held, given that the differences between them [the French and Welsh texts] do not necessarily depend on their both being derived from such a (postulated) text, but can be satisfactorily explained by the process of adaptation of a foreign source into a new social, cultural, and literary context.[17]

It is uncertain which language had the prior version, but Reck and others evidently privilege the French source. However, the matter of how these texts handle the natural world rather differently does not, perhaps fortunately, depend on an opinion in the matter of precedence.

Cynon starts with a detailed account of his initial journey, which is both longer and contains more references to the natural world than that of Calogrenant in *Yvain*:

> I made me ready and travelled the bounds of the world and its wilderness. And at long last I came upon the fairest vale in the world, and trees of an equal height in it, and there was a river flowing through the vale, and a path alongside the river. And I travelled along the path till mid-day; and on the other side I travelled till the hour of nones. And then I came to a great plain, and at the far end of the plain I could see a great shining castle, and a sea close to the castle.[18]

This benign, positively natural, journey leads him to find 24 maidens sewing silk in the hall of the castle, by a window. This episode occurs a good deal later in the French: when Yvain is at the Castle of Pesme Avanture and sees as many as 300 oppressed maidens sewing. The Welsh text ascribes to the maidens' host a set of directions given to Cynon, which take him to a 'great clearing', where he meets the antagonist of *Yvain*: a black giant with an iron club. The giant hits a stag so it bellows, summoning more animals, including 'serpents and lions and vipers', who 'bowed down their heads and did him obeisance, even as humble subjects would do to their lord'.[19] As in *Yvain*, this figure gives Cynon directions on how to reach the spring, where he will see 'a great tree with the tips of its branches greener than the greenest fir trees'.[20] When he gets there, he pours water on the slab as instructed, and there is a great storm. Unlike the French and English accounts, after the storm there are no leaves on the tree, but (as in the French and English) there are very many birds, and their songs are extremely fine.

17 Regine Reck, '*Owain* or *Iarlles y Fynnawn*', in *Arthur in the Celtic Languages: The Arthurian Legend in Celtic Literatures and Traditions*, ed. Ceridwen Lloyd-Morgan and Erich Poppe (Cardiff: University of Wales Press, 2019), pp. 117–31 (p. 120).

18 References are to 'Lady of the Fountain' [*Iarlles y Ffynnawn*] in *The Mabinogion*, trans. Gwyn Jones and Thomas Jones (London: Dent, 1993), pp. 129–51 (p. 130). Hereafter *Lady of the Fountain*.

19 *Lady of the Fountain*, pp. 131–32.

20 *Lady of the Fountain*, p. 132.

In this part of the story, the English text basically follows *Yvain*, with some minor differences. The knights here talk of hunting at court, which does not occur in the other two versions, and the first visitor to the spring, Colgrevance, has vengeance on Kay's early grumbling by saying he is like 'A brok [badger] omang men forto stynk' (l. 98).[21] The English author does not insert a direction-giving vavasour with maidens, but he does make Colgrevance's journey more naturally alarming, with:

> ... many a wild lebard,
> Lions, beres, bath bul and bare,
> That rewfully gan rope [howl] and rare [roar] (ll. 240–42)

This list is the first of the items which Weston finds to be like the one in *Iarlles y Ffynnawn*, and both the Welsh and the English are here a good deal longer than the French.[22] When he heads off, the knight soon discovers seated before him, 'the fowlest wight / That euer yit man saw in sight' (ll. 245–46). When this ugly figure rises, 'als a beste than stode he still' (l. 274). Following his instructions, Colgrevance soon finds the tree, not a pine as in the French or just a tree as in the Welsh, but 'the fayrest thorne / That euer groued sen God was born' (ll. 533–54). It is permanently green and remains so after the storm, as in the French text. Colgrevance is soon beaten and back at court.

The Hero Goes to the Spring

When Yvain departs from the court, his journey is described more fully in terms of threatening nature than was Calogrenant's. He rides 'over mountains and across valleys, through forests deep and wide, through strange and wild places, crossing many treacherous passes, many dangers, and many straits, until he reached the narrow path, full of thorn bushes and dark shadows'.[23] This is the typical knightly natural journey into danger, but he crosses no meadow, and sees no river or lake and its attendant castle – features that often appear in such a journey after a difficult forest-crossing and suggest a journey that leads finally to socialisation of a positive kind, if also to chivalric conflict. Yvain meets the vavasour and his maiden, but this scene is much faster paced than in Calogrenant's account; and Yvain finds the pine tree more quickly than before and pours the whole basin of water over the stone. The storm is also more briefly described, but the triumphant fight with the knight of the spring is much fuller in detail than was Calogrenant's – and of course Yvain is successful.

The next sequence, where Yvain wins the love of his lady, Laudine, is full, but without natural detail, occurring as it does in the lady's city. There is a brief episode where his lady's handmaid, and Yvain's ally, Lunete, tells Yvain that the otherwise

21 References are to Albert B. Friedman and Norman T. Harrington, eds, *Ywain and Gawain*, Early English Text Society Original Series 254 (London: Oxford University Press, 1964). Hereafter *Ywain and Gawain*.

22 Weston, '"Ywain and Gawain" and "Le Chevalier au Lion"', p. 103.

23 *Yvain*, p. 304.

unmentioned figure of hostile nature, the 'Savage Damsel', usually sends warning of attacks on the spring, and asks if anyone has heard from her that Arthur is coming.[24] Yvain's answer is no, but Lunete urges him to plan for the event. Arthur's arrival at the spring is also quick and under-detailed in natural terms. When he and his people have settled at Laudine's castle, they find that 'the hunting and hawking by the river were excellent', but these activities are not described in any detail.[25] The story moves on swiftly as Yvain, with his wife's permission to be absent for a year, goes off jousting with Gawain. There is some discussion in the text about the tensions Yvain feels between his chivalric and amatory commitments, but the two knights ride to tournament adventure without any natural or travel details given, just as there is little detail of the tournaments themselves. It is Yvain's absence that is central, not the knightly activity. Both this self-proving knighthood, and the lack of natural and travel detail, are changed when the damsel arrives bearing Laudine's angry message, taking back the magic ring she has given to protect her tournament-enjoying husband. Suddenly Yvain desires 'to flee entirely alone to a land so wild that no one could follow or find him'.[26] When he immediately leaves, alone, 'such a great tempest arose in his head that he went mad; he ripped and tore at his clothing and fled across fields and plains'.[27] He meets a youth, takes his bow and arrows, and then stalks 'wild animals in the forest and killed them and ate their raw flesh'.[28] Now a wild man in wild nature, he meets a hermit to whom he seems a 'naked stranger'.[29] The hermit gives him bread and water and, in return, 'he plunged again into the woods and hunted stags and does', and brings them to the hermit.[30]

This sequence of action and reaction is a good deal shorter in the Welsh text, unlike its somewhat amplified first section. Owein's journey starts on the morning after Cynon's story, and this follows the 'journey into society' pattern, making, as did Cynon, the visit to the vavasour in an essentially benign environment:

> And when he saw day on the morrow he donned his armour and mounted his horse and he went his way to the bounds of the world and desolate mountains. And at last he hit upon the valley that Cynon had told him of, so that he knew for sure that it was the one. And he travelled along the valley by the side of the river; and the other side of the river he travelled until he came to the waterway. And he travelled the waterway till he could see the castle. And he came to the castle.[31]

24 *Yvain*, p. 315.
25 *Yvain*, p. 326.
26 *Yvain*, p. 330.
27 *Yvain*, p, 330.
28 *Yvain*, p. 330.
29 *Yvain*, p. 330.
30 *Yvain*, p. 331.
31 *Lady of the Fountain*, p. 135.

In the castle little happens. Owein dines with the lovely maiden and the 'yellow-haired' castle-owner, who is not a 'vavasour' as we find in the feudal allusion of the French. The host gives directions, and in the morning Owein departs to see the churl with the club.[32] In one short paragraph, Owein visits him, follows his advice, and arrives at the spring and activates it. In this version, as also happened with Cynon, the leaves on the tree do not survive the storm. Owein badly wounds the knight summoned with the storm, and follows him to the 'great shining city', which here seems rather grander than in the more urbanised context of the French and English texts.[33] Here Owein meets and marries his lady, named only as the titular Lady of the Fountain.[34] The Welsh text lets Owein and his lady's marital happiness last for three years before Arthur and his people arrive. Arthur's journey is slightly brisker than Owein's, and much more so than Cynon's. Thomson comments that the journeys of Cynon, Owein, and Arthur to the spring are in the 'proportion ... 33: 9: 7'.[35] In this version, Cei insists on being the first to face Owein, the new knight of the spring. Cei is quickly beaten, and the next day tells Arthur, 'unfairly was I overthrown yesterday'.[36] Cei seeks another battle, and this time he is badly hurt, as well as quickly unhorsed. Then Owein defeats them all, except for Arthur and Gwalchmei. Gwalchmei is the earlier Welsh name for Gauvain/Gawain: 'gwalch' means hawk, and 'mei' is almost certainly the month, so making him the 'Hawk of May', a natural allusion.

After these knightly events, developed at some length in the Welsh version, Arthur asks Owein to travel with him in knightly fashion. In this version, Owein is permitted by the Lady of the Fountain to leave for three months, despite her distress at the situation.[37] Yet it is only after three years that he receives her angry message, addressed 'to a false treacherous deceiver'.[38] The next day, much as in the French (although here he is even more intensely wretched), Owein travels away from human society in misery:

> It was not for Arthur's court that he made but the bounds of the world and desolate mountains. And he was wandering thus till his clothes perished, and till his body was nigh perished, and till long hair grew all over his body; and he would keep company with wild beasts and feed with them till they were used to him. And therewith he came down from the mountains into the vale, and made for a park, the fairest in the world, and a widowed countess owned the park.[39]

32 *Lady of the Fountain*, p. 135.
33 *Lady of the Fountain*, p. 136.
34 *Lady of the Fountain*, p. 136.
35 Thomson, 'Owain: Chwedl Iarlles y Ffynnon', p. 164.
36 *Lady of the Fountain*, p. 142.
37 *Lady of the Fountain*, p. 144.
38 *Lady of the Fountain*, p. 144.
39 *Lady of the Fountain*, p. 144.

The next section will see him venture back into social good health – only awaiting his amatorial recovery.

In the English version, much as in *Yvain,* the adventurous hero hurries off from the court and makes a knightly journey a good deal briefer than in the previous account of the journey made by Colgrevance. The text simply tells us:

> He passed many high mowntayne
> In wildernes, and mony a playne,
> Til he come to that lethir sty [ugly path]
> That him byhoved pass by [go along] (ll. 597–600)

While he finds 'curtaysi' and 'honowre' at the 'toure' where he stops (ll. 605–06), nothing is said of the people he meets there, nor of any advice they might have given. He leaves the next day, 'And with the cherel [churl] sone gan he mete' (l. 612). The English text dwells a little on this figure: Ywain 'had wonder that nature / Myght mak so fowl a creature' (ll. 617–18). But the 'creature' does not give advice on Ywain's journey, and the hero rides on:

> ... he lighted in that place
> And sone the bacyn has he tane
> And kest water on the stane (ll. 620–22)

As in French, after the storm:

> The fowles light opon the tre;
> Thai sang ful fayre opon that thorn,
> Ryght als thai had done byforn. (ll. 626–28)

Events in the castle are developed very much as in *Yvain,* although with some affinities with the Welsh version. This is the second of the three sequences that Weston sees as linking *Ywain and Gawain* with *Iarlles y Ffynnawn.*[40] The lady here is named 'Lady Alundine, / The Dukes daughter of Landuit' (ll. 1254–55). Alundine is a very rare name, presumably based on Chrétien's Laudine, daughter of the duke of Laudunet. The English author may well have been influenced by the name of the sizeable Glamorgan town, Llantwit Major. He indicates no sense of the lady's Lothian origins, and neither does the Welsh author, who simply, as we have seen, names this character 'the Lady of the Fountain'.

The English text celebrates the couple's developing romance at least as much as the French, but little is made of the royal arrival: the text simply tells that King Arthur 'come to the well, / With al his knyghtes euerilkane' (ll. 1268–69). He and his men are welcomed, and Arthur speaks in elevated natural terms to the lady:

> ... 'Lady white so flowre
> God gif the joy and mekil honowre,
> For thou ert fayre with body gent' (ll. 1421–23)

40 Weston, '"Ywain and Gawain" and "Le Chevalier au Lion"', p. 103.

The king and his huge party enjoy themselves in the beautiful natural world of which Ywain is now the master:

> And ilk day had thai solace sere [various entertainment]
> Of huntyng and als of reuere [hawking];
> For thare was a ful fayre cuntre,
> With wodes and parkes grete plente,
> And castels wroght with lyme and stane,
> That Ywayne with his wife had tane. (ll. 1443–48)

After this entertainment, the king will 'no langer lende [stay], / Bot til his cuntre wil he wende' (ll. 1449–50). Gawain prays Ywain: 'Forto wende with tham infere' (l. 1454). He urges him not to abandon his chivalry for his lady. Ywain agrees, and his lady 'was loth him to greve' (l. 1499). She asks that he return 'this day twelmonth' (l. 1507) and gives him her ring to ensure that 'in nane anger sal ye be' (l. 1529). The word 'anger' might seem like a scribal error for 'danger', but Friedman and Harrington's gloss for the word in this line is 'trouble, affliction', which is certainly apt.[41] The chivalric departure is very briefly recounted: 'The knightes thus thaire ways er went / To justing and to turnament' (ll. 1561–62). The knights' activities are similarly briefly noted and, after more than a year, when they return to the king, Ywain realises 'He had forgeten his leman' (l. 1584). He is upset and can hardly 'hald fra wepe' (l. 1589), and at once a damsel arrives and says to the king that she greets him, and Gawain, 'And al thi knyghtes bot Sir Ywayne'. Of Ywain, she observes:

> 'He es ateyned for trayture,
> A fals and lither losenjoure;
> He has bytrayed my lady' (ll. 1601–03)

After a lengthy and searching speech, she says directly to Ywain: 'Thou es / Traytur untrew and trowthles' (ll. 1625–26), and simply takes the ring and leaves, 'ne no man wist where sho bycome' (l. 1636). Ywain mourns, recognises 'al es for myne owen foly' (l. 1647), and then:

> For wa he wex al wilde and wode.
> Unto the wod the way he nome;
> No man wist whore he bycome. (ll. 1650–52)

His marital and chivalric joys are drawn into conflict, as in the other versions of the story, and now he runs wild, alone, wretched: desocialised in nature.

The Hero Alone

In his new miserable state, Yvain receives help. A maiden recognises him from a scar on his face, tells her mistress who he is, and he is given some very fine ointment associated with Morgan the Wise. Chrétien also mentions Morgan elsewhere in *Yvain*

41 Friedman and Harrington, *Ywain and Gawain*, p. 134.

(l. 2957) and, as there, here there is no sense of her malice, her dangerous power, or her personal connection to King Arthur – matters often raised elsewhere. Although the maiden's mistress told her to be very careful with the costly ointment, she uses it all on him. He is soon back in sanity and health, and she throws the empty ointment box away: she will pretend to have lost it and so hide her use of all. Her mistress is cross it has gone, but still wants Yvain to be helped. The very grateful Yvain wonders how he can help these generous ladies and sees an opportunity to do so when the vicious Count Alier attacks the lady's town. Yvain beats some of his knights, then chases and captures the count himself. The lady, like others in this story, would like Yvain to stay as her husband or lover, but he moves on, back into nature – to encounter the radically natural:

> Deep in thought, my lord Yvain rode through deep woods until he heard from the thick of the forest a very loud and anguished cry. He headed immediately towards the place where he had heard the cry, and when he arrived at a clearing, he saw a dragon holding a lion by the tail and burning its flanks with its flaming breath.[42]

Yvain finds that 'Pity summoned and urged him to aid and succour the noble and honourable beast'.[43] He cuts the dragon in half with one blow of his sword. As the dragon had the lion's tail in its mouth, Yvain cut a little off – but 'only as much as he had to, and he could not have taken off less'.[44] After doing that, Yvain feared the lion would attack him, but the lion behaved 'nobly and splendidly', standing up on his hind paws, bowing his head and extending his forepaws to Yvain 'in an act of total submission'.[45] Yvain and the lion set off together, the lion deferring to the knight in terms of direction and, when Yvain kills a deer to eat, the lion waits until he has finished before devouring the rest; later in the day, the lion kills another deer and carries it for their dinner. Very soon, they find themselves at the spring beside the basin, beneath the pine tree. Yvain faints when he realises this: he falls, his sword cuts his neck and, as he lies there bleeding, the lion thinks he is dead. The lion positions the sword on a fallen tree and starts to run towards the sword and his own death, but Yvain awakes and restores order.

Yvain's resocialisation with the noble side of nature, in his relationship with this finely courteous lion, seems to begin the knight's movement towards recovery as a person, although he does not recognise this. Yvain laments his errors and says that he deserves his misery. Yet things move onwards. He is overheard by a person who is being held prisoner in the chapel by the spring, and she calls to him. It is Lunete: three of her lady's men have taken against her because of her support of Yvain. She is to be executed for treason the following day, unless a knight fights the three men: only Gawain or Yvain could do that, and Gawain is away looking for the queen

42 *Yvain*, p. 337.
43 *Yvain*, p. 337.
44 *Yvain*, p. 337.
45 *Yvain*, p. 337.

(evidently an allusion to the abduction of Guinevere in Chrétien's *Le Chevalier de la Charrette*). The hero replies that he is Yvain and will rescue her tomorrow. He nearly fails to do that. After leaving the spring, he finds a place to stay, a 'baron's stronghold', whose owner has his own problems – the bestial giant Harpin of the Mountain has taken the owner's sons prisoner, and now wants the daughter for his pleasure.[46] The mother is Sir Gawain's sister, and, of course, Yvain agrees to help. In the morning he worries he will miss saving Lunete, but the lord and his daughter beg him to stay. Harpin arrives and, after a brutal battle, Yvain kills him. When the daughter asks who they shall say saved them, he calls himself 'the Knight with the Lion' and hurries off.

Yvain and his lion reach the spring with no travel difficulty, 'for the road was straight and clear and he knew it well'.[47] He sees Lunete stripped to her shift, ready for execution, and moves against the three men. They insist that he send the lion to a distance. Yvain fights well but, before long, the three 'injured him and began to overpower him'.[48] The lion returns, tears the seneschal apart, and attacks the others. They fight and, when Yvain 'saw his lion wounded, the heart in his breast overflowed with wrath, and rightly so. He struggled to avenge his lion'.[49] Yvain does so well that the two men soon submit, and he has them burnt on their own fire. The text assures readers that this 'is right and just', because 'those who wrongfully condemn another should die by the same death to which they have condemned the other'.[50] Aside from Lunete nobody recognises him, including his own lady. When she asks his name he says he is 'the Knight with the Lion', and then departs 'in great sorrow'.[51] Lunete goes with him a long way, and agrees when he asks her 'never to reveal who had been her champion'.[52] The lion is badly hurt and Yvain, remarkably, 'carried it along, stretched out on the inside of his shield'.[53] They find lodging with 'the lord of Blackthorn', and here begins a lengthy narrative that will lead to the end of the story.[54] The lord has two daughters and no sons, so – reflecting the new rules of primogeniture in twelfth-century France – the older sister will inherit all their father owns, and the younger one will have effectively nothing. Georges Duby has written about this rule being quite new, and it is clear that the noble but property-less knights who appear so often in French romance, including Yvain himself, are essentially generated by this new law, meant to keep properties large and strong.[55]

46 *Yvain*, p. 342.
47 *Yvain*, p. 348.
48 *Yvain*, p. 351.
49 *Yvain*, p. 351.
50 *Yvain*, p. 352.
51 *Yvain*, p. 353.
52 *Yvain*, p. 353.
53 *Yvain*, p. 353.
54 *Yvain*, p. 353.
55 Knight, *Arthurian Literature and Society*, pp. 76–77. See further, Georges Duby, *The Chivalrous Society* (London: Arnold, 1977), ch. 7: 'Youth in Aristocratic Society'.

The romance hero usually wins a lady and a land, a situation that could indeed happen in reality, although a more common recourse for younger property-less nobles was to go on Crusade and win land there, or gather enough gold to buy one back at home.

The younger Blackthorn sister wants a knight to fight for her, but Gawain is, as we know, unavailable, off seeking Guinevere. The sister finds her natural surroundings as bleak as her financial position, as she 'galloped through the mire just as over the smooth and level road', chasing 'the Knight with the Lion' so he can be her knight.[56] Yvain comes to a place named in French 'Pesme Avanture' (translated by Kibler as 'Dire Adventure'), and a new episode is inserted into the narrative.[57] The town is under constant threat from the two sons of a demon. The King of the Island of Maidens, the town's owner, has sent maidens each year – now as many as 300 – to stop the demons taking the town, and they work as seamstresses in 'a meadow enclosed with huge, round, pointed staves', a sort of industrial prison.[58] The maidens have a supervisor, are seriously underpaid, but make much money for the king. This sequence seems to be, like the disinherited sister story that frames it, a contemporary social reference, here to the growing number of towns, including Troyes itself, which were delivering wealth through new forms of trade and, as here, manufacture.[59] The trade activities themselves are apparently seen as anti-natural, as with the stake-surrounded meadow where they occur. Whatever Chrétien's wider meaning for this sequence, for Yvain these threats are manageable. The demon's sons attack the town, and he fights them, with his lion's help. After this, Yvain rejoins the younger sister, and is reunited with Arthur's court and, especially, with Gawain, after which he will return, with some complications, to the spring and his lady.

Not only is the Welsh text much shorter than *Yvain*, the sequence from the hero's rejection by his lady to their happy ending is merely a seventh of the length of the same sequence in French. After his dismissal by his lady, the text simply says 'he made for the bounds of the world and desolate mountains'. There he wandered 'till his clothes perished, and till his body was nigh perished, and till long hair grew all over his body; and he would keep company with wild beasts and feed with them till they were used to him'.[60] The sequence *Yvain* offered with the hermit is omitted here. Owein immediately leaves wild nature and reconnects with society: when 'he came down from the mountains into the vale, and made for a park, the fairest in the world, and a widowed countess owned the park'.[61] The treatment with ointment (here said to be worth 'sevenscore pounds'), and the defeat of the young earl who harasses the countess, take just two pages in the Kibler and Carroll edition. After

56 *Yvain*, p. 358.
57 See above, n. 5.
58 *Yvain*, p. 360.
59 Knight, *Arthurian Literature and Society*, pp. 91–92.
60 *Lady of the Fountain*, p. 144.
61 *Lady of the Fountain*, p. 144.

this, Owein 'desired nothing save to travel the bounds of the world and its wilderness' – and, as in the French, wild nature has a benign possibility in the form of the lion.[62] As Owein travelled:

> he heard a loud roaring within a forest, and a second, and a third. And he came thither, and when he had come he could see a huge craggy hill in the middle of the forest, and a grey rock in the side of the hill; and there was a cleft in the rock and in the cleft was a serpent, and beside the serpent was a pure white lion.[63]

It is likely that the Welsh author uses a serpent because, to the Welsh, a dragon is a fine beast and was already in medieval times seen as a national image (it is held that the lords of Aberffraw took it as their symbol after the Romans withdrew in the fifth century). The serpent is dealt with very quickly, without the precise detail of the French – here Owein simply 'cut at it with the sword until it was in two halves on the ground'.[64] The lion's tail is not cut and the lion is pure white, like the grand white stags that recur in Welsh romance, and are elsewhere associated with the theme of sovereignty, itself transmitted (as we find, for example, in the first branch of the *Mabinogi*) through a woman.[65] The story of Yvain/ Owein/ Ywain clearly has the hero gaining sovereignty through a woman, and perhaps this is why the Welsh author made the lion white.

The Welsh text does not offer the human/natural scene where the hero swoons, his sword cuts him, and the lion almost commits suicide, but this is far from the only abbreviation in *Iarlles y Ffynnawn*. When he is at the spring with the lion, Owein hears Luned in her prison, not she him, as in the French and the English. Here she has only two male harassers, and Owein does not tell her who he is. He simply asks her if she is sure that 'if that young man knew of this, he would come to defend thee?' Her answer is: 'Sure, between me and God'.[66] She then directs him to a place to lodge that night, in civilised country, on 'the road alongside the river, and after a while thou wilt see a great castle with many towers thereon'.[67] He is not guided in this way in the French or in the English texts, where he merely finds the castle. Here Luned controls his nature-wandering. The local earl says that the castle and its people are being attacked by 'a savage monster', although he is not here named Harpin.[68] In the following battle, as in the French, the lion breaks out to help his master fight – very dramatically jumping from the castle rampart. The monster is killed and Owein hurries to save Luned. When Owein is evidently struggling in the fight, the lion breaks out of what had been Luned's prison and kills

62 *Lady of the Fountian,* pp. 145, 147.
63 *Lady of the Fountain,* p. 147.
64 *Lady of the Fountain,* p. 147.
65 Rachel Bromwich, 'First Transmission to England and France', in *Arthur of the Welsh*, pp. 273–98 (p. 284).
66 *Lady of the Fountain,* p. 148.
67 *Lady of the Fountain,* p. 148.
68 *Lady of the Fountain,* p. 148.

both his opponents. From this point the Welsh version is nearly over. It omits the two sisters' narrative and the complicated Pesme Avanture episode, as well as the climactic fight with Gawain, and the final difficult encounter between the hero and his lady. But it does have an unusual short final episode, and this will be dealt with in the section below, 'The Hero Back in Society'.

Events in the English text again come very close to those in *Yvain*, but it is notable that from about line 1500 the travel details become consistently sparse, presumably for purposes of abbreviation. Here, simply, we read: 'On a day als Ywayne ran / In the wod, he met a man' (ll. 1657–58). Ywain takes the man's bow and arrows, finds the hermit, shares his bread, and then catches wild animals for him. Soon he sleeps under a tree and is found there, naked, by a lady and her 'twa bourewemen' (l. 1711). One of the maidens recognises him, and speaks of his quality at greater length than her one-line praise of him in *Yvain*. Then the ointment sequence follows, although, as Friedman and Harrington observe, the discussion of the ointment by the women is cut back and can at times become obscure.[69] This episode is the third in *Ywain and Gawain* where Weston argues that the English author is using a brief sequence from the Welsh text (probably via memory of an English oral translation) rather than his French main source, which does not have this discussion about the excellent use of the costly ointment.[70]

Here too the travel details are brief, and little physical context is noted. When Ywain is better, the maiden simply 'helped him up on his hors ryg, / And sone thai come until a bryg' (ll. 1834–35). They reach the lady's castle where they encounter the troublesome Sir Alers (an English version of the French Count Alier), and Ywain 'and his feres' (l. 1913) kill Alers's men and force him to agree to a full restoration of the lady's property. Naturally, the lady invites Ywain to stay, saying invitingly 'Mekyl mirth war us omell [would be between us]' (l. 1970), but Ywain again declines and rides 'With hevy herte and dreri chere / Thurgh a forest by a sty [path]' (l. 1976–77). (Almost exactly the same phrase is used at line 599, where 'lether', meaning 'narrow' is added to 'sty'. The English text can be repetitive and limited in vocabulary at times.) Very soon Ywain hears the dragon and lion fighting and, after freeing the lion the hero, still in despair, swoons, his sword cuts him, and the lion attempts to kill himself, but Ywain comes round in time. This is all the same as in the French, but with rather less detail and setting. Then, as in Chrétien, from her chapel cell Lunet hears Ywain and tells him about her trouble with her lady's very hostile steward and his two brothers. She has been unable to find Gawain to defend her against execution because he is busy rescuing the queen. As in the French, Ywain tells her who he is, and that he will fight for her tomorrow, but asks her not to reveal his name. The text then simply notes his departure: 'Than rade he forth into frith [forest], / And hys lyoun went hym with' (ll. 2207–08). Ywain and the lion come straight to the castle threatened by 'Harpyns of the Mowntain'. In the

69 Friedman and Harrington, *Ywain and Gawain*, p. xxx.

70 Weston, '"Ywain and Gawain" and "Le Chevalier au Lion"', p. 103.

morning, Ywain goes to Mass and then says he must leave, 'Til other place byhoves me fare' (l. 2359), but he is asked to stay, so, for the sake of the lady's brother, Sir Gawain, he waits until the monstrous giant arrives, and rides out with his lion. The lion watches as they fight but, when he sees Ywain hit heavily, he joins in, and they defeat the giant together. Naturally, Ywain is begged to stay, but refuses 'for me bus go [it behoves me to go]' (l. 2504), and he hurries off, again on a journey very briefly told – 'The neghest way than gan he wele, / Until he come to the chapele' (ll. 2507–08). By the chapel he sees a fire, and Lunet in her smock, about to be executed. He states that with God and righteousness on their side, he and the lion will be four against three. The French Yvain does similarly mention God, righteousness, and the lion, but as his own three true supports rather than as part of a fighting foursome.[71] The steward insists the lion be sent away, but not put in a cell as in the French and the Welsh. The fight is hard, the lion is worried, so 'hasted him ful hard' (l. 2611) and returns to tear the steward to pieces. Although Ywain tries to make him stop, the lion fights on and is wounded. Soon they are victors, and the folk there offer 'to wirship him [Ywain] ever on al wise' (l. 2648). The lady, who has not recognised him, asks him to return with them 'Forto sojorn thare a stownd' (l. 2653) until he is healed of his wounds. But he refuses – and says to himself about her: 'Thou ert the lok and kay also / Of al my wele and al my wo' (ll. 2681–82). So yet again in this lonely hero section Ywain leaves. Lunet goes with him for a while, and he calls her 'Gude leman' (l. 2688), which seems to be a sign of their closeness rather than any rival attraction. He asks for secrecy and for her to try to reconcile his lady with him. She says she will, that she is ever grateful to him, and they separate.

Ywain is worried about the lion's wounds and, as in the French, he carries the lion on his apparently very large shield. When he rides off again, the details are sparse: 'Forth he rides by frith and fell, / Til he come to a fayre castell' (ll. 2711–12). At the castle he meets with generous people, notably two of the lord's daughters: 'Twa maydens with him thai left / That wele were lered of lechecraft' (ll. 2735–36). They soon heal both Ywain and his lion, and 'When he was helyd he went his way' (l. 2742). So ends Ywain's lengthy period of misery and conflict, with only the lion for company – heroic nature with him in his lonely natural environment. The next section will describe the social encounters he will have that introduce him to people central to the lengthy build-up to his climactic fight with Gawain, that will bring his rapprochement with his chivalric world, and will be followed by re-entry to his amatory world.

The Hero Back in Society

Free again from the distractions of battle, Yvain hurries off, still with the lion, meets the younger sister, and they go to King Arthur's court so he can fight for her. In a pointed natural image, when the older sister sees Yvain with her sibling, she 'turned

71 *Yvain*, p. 349.

blacker than the earth'.[72] But she has reason to hope for victory, for she has managed to engage the newly returned Gawain as her warrior. The two heroes do not recognise each other as they fight long and hard, but finally agree to stop, each stating that the other has fought better than himself. This indicates knightly camaraderie – perhaps the scene also shows some dissent from primogeniture, as King Arthur, faced with a draw, imposes an arrangement where the young sister does receive some property. Yvain and his lion, after their historically intriguing sub-plot narratives at Pesme Aventure and in the sisters' dispute, both receive medical care (the lion for his old wounds: he did not fight against Gawain). Then they hurry to the spring, Yvain believing that 'There he would cause so much thunder and wind and rain that she [his wife, Laudine] would be compelled to make her peace with him'.[73] The hero-stimulated storm is very terrible, and Lunete argues to her lady that, if she could find the man who killed the giant Harpin and slew the three knights who were going to burn her, then Laudine should accept this 'Knight with the Lion'. After making her lady swear to this on 'a very precious reliquary', Lunete rides off to seek Yvain and, to her surprise, finds him at the spring.[74] When they return, Laudine is angry when she is told the identity of the knight with whom she has sworn to be, and says she would rather 'put up with the storms and high winds all my life' than be made to 'love a man who doesn't love or respect me'.[75] Yvain immediately admits to her his 'foolishness' and says 'I acknowledge my guilt and wrong'.[76] So they are reconciled, and the poem ends with Lunete very happy 'now that she had established an unending peace between the noble Sir Yvain and his dear and noble lady'.[77]

The Welsh version quite lacks the complexity of the final sequence of *Yvain*. Immediately after Owein and the lion have rescued Luned from the two young men who planned to burn her, the text says: 'And then Owein, and Luned with him, went to the dominions of the Lady of the Fountain. And when he came away thence, he brought the lady with him to Arthur's court, and she was his wife so long as she lived'.[78] This version of the story adds one curious final sequence. Apparently, after he and his lady had settled at Arthur's court, Owein comes to 'the court of the Black Oppressor' and fights with him.[79] He beats the Oppressor; and then the lion, the text simply says, leaves him. But Owein goes to the Black Oppressor's court, where he finds 'four-and-twenty of the fairest ladies that any one had ever

72 *Yvain*, p. 369.
73 *Yvain*, p. 376.
74 *Yvain*, p. 378.
75 *Yvain*, p. 379.
76 *Yvain*, p. 380.
77 *Yvain*, p. 380.
78 *Lady of the Fountain*, p. 150.
79 *Lady of the Fountain*, p. 150.

seen.'[80] But 'they were sad as death', their clothes were poor, and they said they had all come with their lords to this house, its master had killed their men, stolen their horses, clothes and wealth, and imprisoned them. This seems to be another version of *Yvain*'s Pesme Avanture episode, as Thomson has commented, with many fewer maidens and without any link to modern urban manufacturing, and with an unusually benign outcome for the villain.[81] After hearing what the ladies have said, Owein walks outside and sees the Black Oppressor approaching him 'with joy and affection, as though he were his brother'.[82] Owein ties him up, and the man says 'there was a prophecy that thou shouldst come hither to subdue me'.[83] He admits he has been a 'despoiler', but if Owein will grant him his life he will become a 'hospitaller, and I will maintain this house as a hospice for weak and for strong so long as I live, for thy soul's sake'.[84] Owein agrees, but he also takes the twenty-four ladies, with their horses, wealth and clothes restored to them, to Arthur's court, where they either stay or leave, according to their wishes. Owein himself remains with Arthur 'as captain of the war-band, and beloved of him'.[85] This final sequence seems to critique, and somewhat optimistically reverse, evil practices among the strong – so it is a moral addition to, and partial reworking of, the abbreviated, especially finally, Welsh version of this story.

This apparent addition may well be meant to emphasise the Welshness of this story. Thomson has noted in his edition of the text: 'The general impression that comes from reading the various versions of the *Yvain* story carefully and in parallel is that all are very close to the French except for the Welsh one'.[86] This dissimilarity has been linked by Helen Fulton to the way in which the French texts 'endorse the social and economic outcomes of certain kinds of behaviour by certain kinds of individual', but 'the Welsh romances privilege collectivism and the strength of the group above the behaviours or desires of its individual members'.[87] So while in the conclusion of *Yvain* the hero rights his personal wrongs, then rules alone with his countess and her land, in *Iarlles y Ffynnawn* Owein acts for the oppressed public, and then returns to court as a leader in the royal world. The Black Oppressor episode with which the Welsh text finishes notably resembles Peredur's fight in his own romance against another Black Oppressor, who lost an eye fighting the Worm of 'The Dolorous Mound': Peredur kills him, takes his treasure, and continues his

80 *Lady of the Fountain*, p. 150.
81 Thomson, 'Owain: Chwedl Iarlles y Ffynnon', pp. 165–66.
82 *Lady of the Fountain*, p. 150.
83 *Lady of the Fountain*, p. 151.
84 *Lady of the Fountain*, p. 151.
85 *Lady of the Fountain*, p. 151.
86 R. L. Thomson, ed., *Owein or Chwedyl Iarlles y Ffynnawn* (Dublin: Institute for Advanced Studies, 1968), p. xxvii.
87 Fulton, 'Individual and Society', p. 24.

own adventures. The names are slightly different: in *Peredur* he is 'Y Du Trahawc'; in *Iarlles y Ffynnawn*, 'Y Du Traws'.[88] The names mean the same but, under Owein's influence, he is redeemed, in a final moment of positivity.

In the English version, the elder sister needs to acquire a knight to fight for her land – primogeniture is not assumed as it was in the French. Whereas Chrétien developed a complicated process until Gawain was her knight, here she simply engages Gawain at the start of things. Gawain is also the choice of the younger sister, but he declines. She hears of 'the Knight with the Lion', so goes to hunt for him, and with great fortune – and speedy travel, as is common now in the poem – comes to the castle where he has been. For no clear reason, her need of 'lecheing' (l. 2823), medical treatment, is mentioned, and another maiden pursues Ywain on her behalf. She quickly meets Lunet, who takes her to the place where she parted with him. The maiden rides on to the castle where he stayed and then chases him down. This all happens quickly and easily:

> Than toke sho leve and went hir way,
> With sporrs sho sparid noght hir palfray;
> Fast sho hyed with al hyr myght,
> Until sho of him had a syght
> And of hys lyoun that by him ran. (ll. 2891–95)

The maiden asks him to help the younger sister. Ywain replies, 'Glady with the wil I gane [go]' (l. 2926). The pair ride on, again with no travel details, and come to 'The Castle of Hevy Sorowe', the English equivalent of Pesme Avanture. Here they find 'many maidens' who are working on 'silk and gold-wire', all poorly dressed and afflicted 'of hunger, of threst and of calde' (ll. 2966, 2967, 2974). They say they are all from 'Maydenlande' and they have been sent by their king (it is not clear why there is a king of the land of women), to calm down the 'twa champions' who threaten him – they are also 'the devil sons / Geten of a woman with a ram' (ll. 3017–19). As in *Yvain*, the maidens work for cash and get little themselves, but the English author lacks the French sense of modern urban business and its vulgar owners: the castle authorities here are just a normal knight and lady who take their ease 'under a tre / Opon a clath of gold' (ll. 3084–85). Chrétien's element of contemporary politics is one of the cuts made in the English version, which, as Friedman and Harrington comment, leave inconsistencies in the sisters' narrative.[89]

As we expect, Ywain is ready to fight the dubious 'champions'. They insist on the lion being locked 'in a chamber' (l. 3185), then attack Ywain with their huge clubs and an enormous shield called a 'talvace' (l. 3158 – a French word of uncertain origin). But the lion, with 'Ful grete sorow' (l. 3211), sees Ywain's difficulty, digs his way out, and the demonic pair are soon destroyed. As usual Ywain is offered the daughter's hand. He rejects it but does ask for the female workers/prisoners to be

88 Jones and Jones, *Mabinogian*, pp. 173–74.
89 Friedman and Harrington, *Ywain and Gawain*, p. xxxi.

freed, and takes them with him, 'with ful faire processione' (l. 3348), to the nearby town. He and the maiden hurry away, and their travel is again thinly described:

Al the sevenight traveld thai.
The maiden knew the way ful wele
Hame until that ilk castele
Whare sho left the seke may (ll. 3360–63)

The younger sister is still not well, but at least is cheerful and optimistic and, in the morning, she and her knight ride off in the same brisk manner:

... forth thai went.
Until that town fast gan thai ride
Whare the ky; sojourned that tide (ll. 3386–68)

The next day is the last one possible for her challenge. There is much discussion between the sisters and the king. Ywain leaves the lion in his own bedroom, and then the two knights meet. In heavy armour their faces are concealed, and they do not recognise each other. As they begin to fight the onlookers realise: 'Thai saw never under the hevyn / Twa knightes that war copled so evyn' (ll. 3595–96). It is a very long fight, over a hundred lines of poetry, as it was in French (the episode, and the whole sisters' sequence, does not occur in the Welsh text). The warriors finally agree to stop fighting, exchange names, and then show each other great affection. They explain to Arthur that the conflict is effectively a draw, and he imposes some inheritance-sharing on the older sister. The knights disarm, and the lion 'out of the chamber brak' (l. 3778) to celebrate his master's victory. As a result, the townspeople flee in fear, but then realise this is the famous 'Knight with the Lion'. They all settle down, but not Ywain. He immediately 'hies him fast to found [travel]' (l. 3830), 'Bot he get grace of his lady, / He most go wode or for luf dy' (ll. 3833–84). Simple travel details follow: 'He rides right unto the well' (l. 3837), and there causes an enormous storm. The lady is very troubled, and Lunet takes this opportunity, at considerable length, to say she needs 'the Knight with the Lion', and makes her lady swear on 'the chalis and the mes-boke' (l. 3908) that she will do that. Lunet rides off on her quest for Ywain – unlike in French (this episode is also not in the Welsh text), she shows no surprise to see him at the spring. When the lady is told this new knight-protector is in fact Ywain she is taken aback but admits she has sworn to accept him and says: 'What man so wil mercy crave, / By Goddes law he sal it have' (l. 4003–4). She accepts him and, of course, 'Was he never are so blith' (l. 4008). After this, the end is rapid, simply recording their joy, and the honour and pleasure of Lunet, who 'has maystri / Next the lord and the lady' (ll. 4017–18):

And so Sir Ywain and his wive
In joy and blis thai lad thaire live.
So did Lunet and the liown
Until that ded haves dreven tham down. (ll. 4023–26)

Only the English text records the happy presence of the lion at the end, and this poet simply ends with a prayer to Christ for, if it be his will, all of us to find a place 'In heveyn-blis' (l. 4030).

To sum up the narratives and their relationship with nature, we might look to the texts' conclusions. In *Yvain*, the hero rejoins the community with the sisters, and then with Gawain. Little is linked to nature in his renewed social world, though Yvain does make the storm at the spring rage very seriously, wanting to make his lady really feel she needs him – and, somewhat ironically, she at first says she would prefer to 'put up with the storms and high winds all my life' than be with a man who 'doesn't love or respect me'.[90] The Welsh text does not use the ending of the French story, suggesting clearly it has a different basis from *Yvain*. As Reck comments, it ends with what is, in Welsh tradition, 'the more conventional channel of military success'.[91] This, while the oddest social triumph the hero has in the whole Welsh text, also is a reversal of anti-natural behaviour. In the English version, Ywain's travels with the sisters and fight with Gawain are briefer and less nature-linked than the distinctly limited natural references in French, but at least the lion appears to remain with the hero to the end. This presents a satisfying final element of the socialised nature, and naturalised society, that has been a recurrent feature of the story, variously treated in its three major languages, whether in context, travel, dialogue, or symbolism, and even the lion and the fountain in the titles of the French and Welsh versions of this intriguing romance.

90 *Yvain*, p. 379.

91 Reck, '*Owain* or *Iarlles y Fynnawn*', p. 121.

4

Territorial Narrative in the *Mabinogi*[1]

Daniel F. Melia

Professor Helen Fulton has long been concerned both with broadening the geographical and historical lens through which we see medieval Wales, and also with applying all the scholarly tools available in looking at native Celtic material. In particular, she has often been concerned with the uses of the past in Wales and medieval Europe, as in her studies on the Arthurian tradition at Caerleon, and in her interpretation of the fourteenth-century itinerary poem by Iolo Goch, the locations in which Helen used to illustrate the origins of monastic manuscript production in medieval Wales.[2] I mean here to continue in this same spirit to examine some of the ways in which the elements of legend, genealogy, and onomastics seem to be functioning as a territorial and dynastic claim in the *Mabinogi*, particularly in the First Branch, but also, by connection or contrast, in the Third and Fourth Branches.[3]

Polyvalence is also a subject with which Helen is comfortable, and I hasten to point out that my reading here is not a claim about the ultimate meaning of any part of the *Mabinogi*. I wish to illustrate, however, some features that work together in

1 This paper includes material from 'Legendary Politics in the *Mabinogi*', a paper presented at the 3rd Poznán Conference of Celtic Studies, 9th July 2018, and from 'Sticky Figures: The Afterlife of Pre-Christian Supernatural Beings in Medieval Celtic Texts', delivered 24th October 2015 at the Symposium, *Thinking About Celtic Mythology in the 21st Century*, University of Edinburgh. See further, Daniel F. Melia, 'Sticky Figures: The Afterlife of Pre-Christian Supernatural Beings in Medieval Celtic Texts', *Cosmos* 32 (2016): 21–38.

2 Helen Fulton, 'Caerleon and Cultural Memory in the Modern Literature of Wales', in *Germano-Celtica: A Festschrift for Brian Taylor*, ed. A. Ahlqvist and P. O'Neill (Sydney: Sydney University Press, 2017), pp. 101–19; Helen Fulton, 'Ceredigion: Strata Florida and Llanbadarn Fawr', in *Europe: A Literary History, 1348–1418*, 2 vols, ed. David Wallace (Oxford: Oxford University Press, 2016), I, pp. 438–54.

3 All references to the *Mabinogi* are from Ifor Williams, ed., *Pedeir Keinc y Mabinogi* (Cardiff: University of Wales Press, 1964), hereafter *Pedeir Keinc y Mabinogi*; translated by Patrick Ford, *The Mabinogi and Other Medieval Welsh Tales* (Berkeley, CA: University of California Press, 1977), hereafter *Mabinogi*.

the text to present a kind of foundational history for the native lordships of South Wales, in a setting in which much of the horizon in the medieval legendary history of Wales, then as now, has been taken up by Gwynedd and the progeny, real or alleged, of the Sons of Cunedda. There are several ways in which *Pwyll*, the First Branch of the *Mabinogi*, differs from the other branches: it is unusually focused on a single family and its claim to rule; it involves dynastic marriage with an actual otherworld being; unlike the other branches it lacks any references in the Welsh Triads; and its geographical references are concentrated on cantred names, rather than on individual placenames (unlike the Fourth Branch).[4] Each of these elements is overdetermined in the text, being repeatedly emphasised.

Medieval (and presumably earlier) Celtic narratives that we would now call pseudo-history, legend, or saga, keep track of significant chronology by pedigree, and significant territory by onomastics.[5] Cross-indexing is provided by collections of Triads in Wales and Ireland. The discussion of the placenames 'Slechta' in the *Cattle Raid of Cooley*, and 'Talebolion' in the *Mabinogi*, are prominent examples of self-conscious uses of onomastics to identify territory and its ownership in the context of the audience contemporary with the version of the tales.[6] The inclusion of the birth tales of prominent characters in both Irish and Welsh traditions (Cuchulainn, Conchobor, Pryderi) points as well to the crucial role that individuals can play in claims of genealogical authenticity and relative dating. Genealogical tracts, pedigrees, and onomastic tales (*dindshenchus*, 'the lore of places' in Irish) interact in virtually all our surviving sources, as can be seen in *Pwyll*.

This nexus, the conjunction of genealogy, onomastics, and individual histories in historical narratives, is not, of course, exclusive to Celtic-speaking peoples, either in the Middle Ages or earlier. The story of the foundation of the Kievan Rus' in the *Russian Primary Chronicle*, explaining how the Viking, Rurik, and his three sons were invited to found the kingdom by the local Slavic tribes, or the account of the demise of the court of Attila the Hun in Germanic narratives such as *Volsungasaga* and the *Nibelungenlied*, are quite reminiscent of the foundation stories of the Scottish Kingdom of Dalriada by the three sons of Erc, and the legend of the Sons of Mil in Ireland, which serve as explanations of political relations at a later period.[7]

4 Rachel Bromwich, ed. *Trioedd Ynys Prydein* (Cardiff: University of Wales Press, 2006).

5 Kuno Meyer, ed., *The Triads of Ireland* (Dublin: Hodges, Figgis, & Co, 1906). Available online in *Corpus of Electronic Texts* (University College Cork, 2011) <http://www.ucc.ie/celt> [last accessed 16th November 2022].

6 Cecile O'Rahilly, ed. and trans., *Táin Bó Cúalnge from the Book of Leinster* (Dublin: Dublin Institute for Advanced Studies, 1967), from l. 513; *Mabinogi*, p. 34 n. 28.

7 Horace G. Lunt, 'What the Rus' Primary Chronicle Tells Us about the Origin of the Slavs and of Slavic Writing', *Harvard Ukrainian Studies* 19 (1995): 335–57; 'Volsunga Saga' from the collection of *Fornaldarsögur* (Tales of Olden Times), for which see

John Kelleher used to say in his classroom lectures at Harvard that the medieval Irish genealogical tracts and *Banshenchus* (genealogies of women from important families) were constitutional documents.

I argue in this chapter that the attention to similar matters of genealogy, onomastics, and personal history, particularly in the First and Third Branches of the *Mabinogi*, indicates a deep concern with establishing a counter-narrative for Deheubarth (mainly Dyfed plus Seisellwg) to the hegemonic history of Gwynedd that foregrounds the Men of the North, the descendants of the Sons of Cunedda.

The *Bildungsroman*

In the beginning, the story of Pwyll, 'Pendefig Dyfed', appears to be mainly a princely *Bildungsroman*. Pwyll begins by making the mistake of claiming another hunting nobleman's slain boar but learns to behave nobly by taking the place of the offended otherworld king, defeating his enemy, enlarging his kingdom, and protecting the chastity of his wife for a year. In doing so, he earns the additional title of 'Pen Annwn' (Chief of the Otherworld), which establishes him as having sovereignty over both Dyfed and its otherworld counterpart, a realm that he has increased in size as he will do for Dyfed. He next seeks a wife, which further engages him with the otherworld with respect to sovereignty. He then learns not to act without having taken advice, when he needs Rhiannon to rescue him after having offered her previous betrothed, Gwawl ap Clud, the opportunity to reclaim her. Last, he naively accepts the accusation that Rhiannon has killed their infant son, who has actually been supernaturally abducted, and forces her, as a punishment, to behave in the manner of a horse until their son is returned to them and given the name Pryderi by his mother. Pwyll has thus learned noble behaviour, courtesy, prudence, and justice, which are necessary attributes of a good ruler. Each of these learning opportunities also brings him into contact with otherworld figures and foreshadows his future career in this world. As Helen Fulton has remarked of the Arthurian tradition in Wales, this material is engaged with a 'discourse of historical naturalism that claimed authority from earlier, often unnamed, sources and elided the boundaries between what we now think of as fiction and history'.[8]

Margaret Clunies Ross, 'The Icelandic *fornaldarsaga*', in *Poetry in fornaldarsögur*, ed. Margaret Clunies Ross (Turnhout: Brepols, 2017); Hermann Reichert, ed., *Das Nibelungenlied: Vol. VII* (Berlin: De Gruyter, 2005); Marjorie O. Anderson, *Kings and Kingship in Early Scotland* (Edinburgh: Birlinn Ltd, 1980), pp. 229–30; John Carey, *The Irish National Origin-Legend: Synthetic Pseudohistory*, E. C. Quiggin Memorial Lecture 1 (Cambridge: Department of Anglo-Saxon, Norse and Celtic, 1996), p. 151.

8 Helen Fulton, 'Historiography: Fictionality vs Factionality', in *Handbook of Arthurian Romance: King Arthur's Court in Medieval European Literature*, ed. Leah Tether and Johnny McFadyen (Berlin: De Gruyter, 2017), pp. 151–66 (p. 15).

Genealogical Signals

The characters in the Four Branches, including Pwyll, Rhiannon, Pryderi, Bran, Manawydan, and Llew Llaw Gyffes, do not include any historical persons, and some of them – indeed, most – appear to be of legendary or mythological origin. The name Rhiannon, for instance, can be seen as being derived from **rigan-tona* (great queen), with a similar semantic charge as appears in the name of the Irish battle-goddess, Morrigan < **mor-rigain*. Rhiannon is strongly connected with horses, as was the Gaulish goddess Epona, being able to outrun any horses that Pwyll sends after her and being wrongly punished by being made to wear horse trappings and to carry guests to Pwyll's court on her back.[9] These mythic and legendary motifs seem particularly appropriate in the setting of the first branch, in which Pwyll learns the virtues of a ruler by his interactions with the otherworld.

I have elsewhere discussed possible reasons for the persistence of certain mythological and legendary characters and features in medieval Irish and Welsh narrative, for which the real historical audience consisted of Christians who were fully aware of the pre-Christian nature of much of this material:

> Myth and legend do not survive unless they continue somehow to serve some audience, and, on the level of what we might call 'authorizing metaphor', the tale of Pwyll and Rhiannon can be seen to have relevance in twelfth and thirteenth-century Wales. The Norman incursions of the eleventh century and the Edwardian *reconquista* of the thirteenth century had disrupted the native Welsh nobility, and narratives emphasizing native conceptions of sovereignty and legitimacy would have had a certain appeal to a Welsh speaking audience.[10]

In this case, and cases like it, the metaphoric aptness presents what I term an element of 'stickiness'.[11] Historically illustrative and/or metaphoric stories and story patterns connected to pre-Christian deities and otherworld figures find continuing use because they provide orderliness to the imagining of the relationship of the past to the present. Ancient Greek city-states had legends of founding deities: for example, Athena in Athens, or Poseidon in Troy, or Romulus and Remus in Rome. The ultimate appeal in ancient Roman argumentation, after all, was to the *mos maiorum* (the custom of our ancestors). Political authority derives in major part from a shared sense of history, from knowing the deeds of your ancestors and the part they played in shaping your own present polity. In the third book of his *Politics*, Aristotle said that the Polis was not merely the physical fabric of the city-state, nor its geo-

9 *Mabinogi*, pp. 4–5; Sioned Davies, ed., *The Mabinogion* (Oxford: Oxford University Press, 2007), p. 230. For a contrary view, disputing Rhiannon's connection to Epona, see Ronald Hutton, *Pagan Britain* (New Haven, CT: Yale University Press, 2014), p. 366.

10 Melia, 'Sticky Figures', p. 33. See also Marc Morris, *A Great and Terrible King: Edward I and the Forging of Britain* (London: Hutchinson, 2008).

11 Melia, 'Sticky Figures'.

graphical boundaries, but rather the citizens' shared understanding of its history and purpose.[12] Virgil provided the Julian rulers of Rome with an origin story in the *Aeneid*, and, closer to home, Geoffrey of Monmouth provided a similar origin story for the sovereignty of Britain, for the recently implanted Plantagenet kings.[13]

Rhiannon identifies herself to Pwyll as the daughter of Hyffaid Hên, Hyffaid the Old, or the lineage-founding ancestor, as Patrick Ford has argued.[14] We might compare the use of *Hên* to *Mór* (the Great) in Irish genealogical tradition. There was a historical Hyffaid, son of Bleddri, who ruled Dyfed in the ninth century. According to Triad 68, he was one of the three kings sprung from peasant stock (*meibion eillion*). Rachel Bromwich has argued that, as in the case of the famous Merfyn Vrych (825–44), the first Welsh King of Gwynedd not claiming descent from Cunedda, Hyfaidd claimed kingship through his mother, which seems metaphorically congruent here.[15] I would not argue that Rhiannon's father is necessarily meant to be *that* Hyfaidd, but the association of the name with the kingdom of Dyfed is, I think, the point here. Her father's name links her to the land of Dyfed, underlining her role as a local representative of sovereignty.

Her otherworldly suitor, Gwawl ap Clud, 'Wall (?) son of the River Clyde', is presumably from further north. He might represent a long-lasting literary trace of the British Kingdom of Strathclyde, or an atavistic name among the *Gwyr y Gogledd* (Men of the North) (Cunedda and his descendants), who dominated the rule of Gwynedd, and thus much of medieval Wales, after migrating from Strathclyde and Rheged during the Middle Ages.[16] My own guess is that the name is a learned joke ('Hadrian's/Antonine Wall, son of the River Clyde').

Also congruent is the claim of Hywel Dda (ruled 942–50), a scion of the House of Dinefwr, to rule over territories in Deheubarth. Hywel's father, Cadell ap Rhodri Mawr, was the second son of the union of Rhodri Mawr, King of Gwynedd (844–78) and his wife, Angharad of Seisyllwg. Upon Rhodri's death, his eldest son, Anarawd, became sovereign of Gwynedd, and Cadell succeeded his maternal uncle in Seisyllwg. It is thus through his mother, Angharad, that Anarawd, King of Gwynedd, belongs to a dynasty named after a place in Llandeilo in South Wales. In this way, the legendary metaphor of the king marrying the local goddess of sovereignty is echoed in some of the key dynastic history of Deheubarth in the ninth and tenth century.

12 Aristotle, *Politics*, trans. H. Rackham. Loeb Classical Library 264 (Cambridge, MA: Harvard University Press, 1932), pp. 70–71, pp. 184–85.

13 Neil Wright, ed., *The Historia regum Britannie of Geoffrey of Monmouth. 1, Bern, Burgerbibliothek, MS. 568* (Cambridge: D. S. Brewer, 1984).

14 Patrick K. Ford, 'Llywarch, Ancestor of Welsh Princes', *Speculum* 45.3 (1970): 442–50.

15 Bromwich, *Trioedd Ynys Prydein*, pp. 256–57.

16 Wendy Davies, *Wales in the Early Middle Ages* (Leicester: Leicester University Press, 1989).

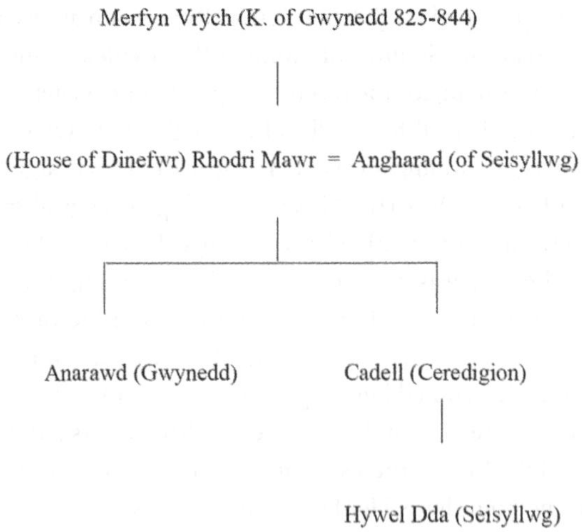

Figure 1 Genealogy of Hywel Dda.

Geography

As Proinsias MacCana observes:

> As a compositional element in narrative, [place names] are often loaded with the kind of multiple reference and resonance that is characteristic of myth. Placenames and their lore were more than an attribute or a simple constituent of cultural consciousness, they were in a sense its living index, its semiotic system.[17]

The Stanzas of the Graves (*Englynion y Beddau*), some of which may date to the ninth century, are a good example of the evocative use of place intertwined with legendary narrative and genealogy in Welsh tradition.[18] As John K. Bollard notes in his *Landscapes of the Mabinogi*, most of the individual placenames found in the Four Branches are clustered in Gwynedd, though a few crucial ones from Pwyll are in Deheubarth (for the *cantrefi* of Wales, see Map 1).[19] Geography has been much discussed in the context of the *Mabinogi*, and has been the basis of several arguments put forward in aid of identifying authorship or thematic unity in the Four

17 Proinsias MacCana, 'Placenames and Mythology in Irish Tradition: Places, Pilgrimages and Things', in *Proceedings of the First North American Congress of Celtic Studies held at Ottawa from 26th–30th March 1986*, ed. G. W. Mac Lennan (Ottawa: University of Ottawa, 1988), pp. 319–41.

18 Thomas Jones, 'The Black Book of Carmarthen "Stanzas of the Graves"', *Proceedings of the British Academy* 53 (1967): 97–137.

19 John K. Bollard, 'Landscapes of *The Mabinogi*', *Landscapes* 10.2 (2009): 37–60.

Map 1: Royal Commission Map of the Welsh *cantrefi*. Royal Commission Map giving an approximate indication of the boundaries of the larger cantrefs of Wales, based on the list given by Gruffudd Hiraethog (d. 1564) in Aberystwyth, National Library of Wales, MS Peniarth 147. Reprinted with the permission of the Royal Commission on Ancient and Historical Monuments of Wales.

Branches. A globalising view is offered by Alfred Siewers, who is of the opinion that 'the composer envisioned a type of Welsh Old Testament, anchored in a union of topography and traditions, but as a "map" of cultural identity resisting amalgamation into the conquering Norman culture'.[20]

In 1975, Brinley Rees argued that the First and Third Branches (*Pwyll* and *Manawydan*) were concerned with Dyfed, the Second Branch (*Branwen*) with Powys, and the Fourth Branch (*Math*) with Gwynedd. He further argued that the kingdoms represented different Dumezilian functions: Knowledge/Sovereignty (Gwynedd), War (Powys), and Fertility/Productivity (Dyfed).[21] Christina Chance, in a 2009 paper given at the Harvard Celtic Colloquium, discussed the use of terms such as *Prydein, Ynys y Kedeirn* (the Island of the Mighty), and *Lloegr* (?south-east England), chiefly in the Second Branch, arguing that that branch indicates a desire to elucidate ethnic and political identity for Wales (*Cymru*) proper.[22] Brynley F. Roberts sees the emphasis and specificity of placenames as evidence that the author was from North Wales, while Glenys Goetinck, Proinsias MacCana, and Ifor Williams favour a southern perspective.[23] It is obvious enough, though, that the First Branch is geographically and dynastically concerned with Deheubarth, with Dyfed in particular, and that *Math* is largely geographically confined to Gwynedd.

Individual placenames are very scarce in the First Branch: Arberth and Glyn Cuch, which are locatable, and Pen Llwyn Diarwya, where Pwyll spent the night on his way to Glyn Cuch and his confrontation with Arawn, which is not. On the other hand, names of cantrefs are highly prominent, which they are not in the other branches. To begin with, Pwyll is Lord over the seven cantrefs of Dyfed ('Pwyll, Pendefig Dyfed a oed yn arglwyd ar seith cantref Dyfed')[24] – namely, Emlyn, Cemais, Gwarthaf, Penfro, Deugleddyf, Pebidiog, and Rhos. The closing paragraph of the First Branch relates that, after Pwyll's death, his son Pryderi 'gained the three cantrefs of Ystrad Tywi and the four cantrefs of Ceredigion': Cantref Mawr, Cantref Bychan, and Cedweli, plus Is Aeron, Uch Aeron, Buellt, and Penweddig (the four cantrefs of Ceredigion), constituting together the Kingdom of Seisyllwg.[25] One might also count by alliance Teyrnyon in Gwent Is Coed. We see here the record of the assembling of a sizable kingdom, comprising the bulk of Deheubarth.

20 A. K. Siewers, 'Writing an Icon of the Land: *The Mabinogi* as a Mystagogy of Landscape', *Peritia* 19 (2005): 193–228.

21 Brinley Rees, *Ceinciau'r Mabinogi* (Llandysul: Gomer Press, 1975).

22 Christina Chance, 'Ethnicity, Geography, and the Passage of Dominion in the "Mabinogi" and "Brut y Brenhinedd"', *Proceedings of the Harvard Celtic Colloquium* 29 (2009): 45–56.

23 Brynley F. Roberts, 'Where Were the Four Branches of the *Mabinogi* Written?', in *The Individual in Celtic Literatures*, ed. Joseph Falaky Nagy, (Dublin: Fourt Courts Press, 2000), pp. 61–73; Glenys Goetinck, '*Pedair Cainc y Mabinogi*: yr Awdur a'i Bwrpas', *Llên Cymru* 15 (2001): 249–69; Proinsias MacCana, *The Mabinogi* (Cardiff: University of Wales Press, 1977); *Pedeir Keinc y Mabinogi*, p. xli.

24 *Pedeir Keinc y Mabinogi*, p. 1; trans. *Mabinogi*, p. 37.

25 *Pedeir Keinc y Mabinogi* p. 27; trans. *Mabinogi*, p. 56.

This collection of territories is underlined in the Third Branch, in which Pryderi betroths his widowed mother, Rhiannon, to Manawydan, the eponym of that branch (just as Angharad of Seisyllwg was betrothed to Rhodri Mawr) along with the rule of the seven cantrefs of Dyfed, thus underlining both Rhiannon's role as representative of sovereignty and the unity of Dyfed and Seisyllwg. The early popular and legal existence of these area names is indicated by the medieval charters archived at Llandaf Cathedral in Cardiff, which involve the places mapped by Wendy Davies: in Deheubarth (from west to east): Mathri, Castelldwyran, Penally, Tanby, Conarth, Llandowror, Dinefwr, Llandeilo, Builth, Llan-gors, Talgarth, Llanfihangel, Cwm Du. Only three are in Gwynedd: Llangadwalader, Deganwy, and Aberffraw, and three in Powys: Llangollen, Bangor, and Chester.[26]

The Triads and Giraldus Cambrensis

The intertextuality among the Four Branches and other medieval Welsh narrative traditions is illustrated by the appearance of names from the *Mabinogi* in the Welsh Triads. There are ten references to the *Mabinogi* in the Triads, though none are in the First Branch, and the only one that refers to characters from that branch is number 26. Number 26 is interesting, however. It is the longest of all the Triads, save for number 51 ('Three Men of Shame') which appears only in the Red Book of Hergest and which is highly dependent on the *Historia Regum Britanniae* of Geoffrey of Monmouth. Number 26 also reports two varying traditions of the story that appears early in the Fourth Branch:

> Ac ar hynny at Uath uab Mathonwy yd aethant wy. 'Arglwyd', heb y Guydyon, 'mi a gigleu dynot y'r Deheu y ryw bryuet ni doeth y'r inis honn eirot'.
>
> (They [the sons of Dôn] went to Math son of Mathonwy. 'Lord,' said Gwydion, I have heard that some kind of animals that have never been in this island have come to the South'.)[27]

The sons of Dôn are here fomenting a war so as to provide an occasion for Gilfaethwy to rape Math's foot-holder, Goewin. They report that the new animals, swine, belong to Pryderi and that they can get some from him. Pryderi refuses them on the grounds that he has promised his people that he will not give any away until the pig population has doubled, but Gwydion trades him phantom horses, dogs, and shields for the pigs. War is provoked when the magical animals return to their state as mushrooms the following day. Triad 26 from Aberystwyth, National Library of Wales, MS Peniarth 16, records the 'The Three Powerful Swineherds of the Island of Britain', Drystan, Pryderi, and Coll – listing Pryderi second: 'A Phyderi mab Pwyll Pen Annwuyn, a getwis moch Pendaran Dyfed ac Glyn C6ch yn Emlyn' (And Pryderi son of Pwyll, Lord of Annwfn, who guarded the swine of Pendaran Dyfed in Glyn Cuch in Emlyn). By contrast, the versions of this triad in the Red

26 Davies, *Wales in the Early Middle Ages*, p. 98.

27 *Pedeir Keinc y Mabinogi*, p. 68; trans. *Mabinogi*, p. 92.

Book of Hergest and the White Book of Rhydderch place Pryderi first of the three swineherds and report that the swine belonged to Pwyll, presumably brought from Annwfn, and were given to Pendaran Dyfed:

> Pryderi vab P6yll Pen Annwn, 6th voch Pendaran Dyuet y tatmeth. Ac y sef moch oedynt: y seithlydyn a duc P6yll Pen Annwn ac a'e rodes y Pendaran Dyuet y datmaeth, Ac y sef y lle y katwei, y Glyn Kuch yn Emlyn. A sef acha6s y gelwit h6nn6 yn wrueichiat: kany allei neb na th6yll na threis arna6.
>
> (Pryderi son of Pwyll, Lord of Annwfn, with the swine of Pendaran Dyfed, his foster-father. These swine were the seven animals which Pwyll Lord of Annwfn brought, and gave them to Pendaran Dyfed his foster-father. And the place where he used to keep them was in Glyn Cuch in Emlyn. And this is why he was called the Powerful Swineherd: because no one was able either to deceive or to force him.)[28]

I agree with Rachel Bromwich (*contra* Ifor Williams) that these entries are not incorporated glosses, but indicate that multiple versions of elements of the narrative of the Four Branches were known at the time.[29] The medieval Irish and Welsh Triads were indexes of traditional story material, like the tenth-century Irish 'Seventy-Two Tales known by a *Filid in Scelaib*', and, like that document and many genealogical and onomastic sources, recorded story material that, like folktales and other oral material, existed in multiform by their nature.[30] The theft of the swine is important to the overall structure of the Four Branches because it is the ultimate cause of Pryderi's death in the climactic battle between the forces of Gwynedd and Deheubarth. Thus, among many other themes, *Math* completes the heroic biography of Pryderi, running from his *enfance* in the First Branch, to his battlefield death and burial in the Fourth. There is so much other foregrounded narrative material in *Math*, however, that I would argue that the conclusion of the tale of Pryderi is as much aimed at chronological coherence as it is about Pryderi as a central character.

The Triads and the Llandaf Charters are evidence for the circulation of names and narratives connected with the traditional stories and lore (genealogical, legendary/mythological, and onomastic) found in the Four Branches. An indication of real-world interest in the rule and extent of Deheubarth in the period between, say, 1000 CE and 1400 CE, is found in an anecdote from the works of Giraldus Cambrensis:

> After their midday nap, the bishop [of Hereford] and noblemen went into a certain orchard as the day was already drawing to a close, bringing Rhys with them, and sat down there together. As Gerald the archdeacon was coming in with the others and sitting down, Rhys started to jest and joke, taking Gerald as his target and […] said

28 Bromwich, *Trioedd*, pp. 50–52.

29 Bromwich, *Trioedd*, pp. 50–52.

30 Proinsias MacCana, *The Learned Tales of Medieval Ireland* (Dublin: Dublin Institute for Advanced Studies, 1980), pp. 41–49.

> 'That archdeacon over there and the men of his family, who are called "Geraldines" have descended from my aunt Nest, the sister of my father, Gruffed, and they are certainly noble and able men, but only in a particular corner of Wales, the cantref of Pembroke'.
>
> To which the archdeacon answered: 'No, the sons of Nest held the seven cantrefi of Dyfed in Wales [...] Two daughters of Nest, my mother Angharad and Gwladus, were married to two barons, those of Rhos and Pembroke. Besides these six, or seven barons, she also had a son, David, bishop of St Davids, who exercised the rights of bishop over nearly all of South Wales.[31]

That is to say, the ruling families of South Wales in the late twelfth century had differing views on the balance of genealogical power in the south. It seems to me that, in this exchange, both Rhys and Gerald are nervous about the status of their personal lineages. Nest, of course, was the progenitrix of the Geraldines, who figure so prominently in Irish and Norman as well as Welsh history. It is notable that Rhys already identifies that lineage by its name, and that he is interested, at least jokingly, in cutting them down to size. Gerald de Barry reports himself as reminding Rhys, his first cousin once removed, of the cantrefs of Dyfed controlled by their mutual close relatives, and of the family's reach into the Church as well.

The reader will have noted that there is an opportunity here to attempt to identify some moment in the history of Wales when the particular constellation of political arrangements seen in the Four Branches was current. My argument here, however, is that, though there may have been such a moment in the passage of time, referring to it is not the purpose of the story. The upper-class folk in Gerald's anecdote think of their family power in the same terms, linking history, genealogy and named places, as the author and characters in the Four Branches. The interweaving of history, genealogy, legend, and even myth (or its narrative afterglow) is in aid of making a claim of *ethos*, in the ancient Greek sense, the culture of a particular area or polity, rooted in its agreed-upon legendary and real history. To begin with, Pwyll adds Morgannwg and Gwent to Deheubarth, so we are not seeing a literal picture of rule of Rhys ap Gruffydd (c. 1170). Rhiannon is not a depiction of Giraldus's mother, Angharad de Windsor, and neither Gerald de Barry nor his brothers seem to be likely models for Pryderi. The Four Branches is not a *roman à clef* but it is true, I think, that its original audience was expected to feel an echo in their own experience of the world of the legendary past depicted in such concrete political terms in that work.

My contention here is that the legendary history related in the Four Branches, and particularly in Branches One and Three, mainly concerning itself with

31 Translation by Paul Russell in lecture, 'Gerald on Himselves: The Multiple Lives of Gerald of Wales', Department of English, Virginia Polytechnic and State University, 16th February 2022, based on the Latin version of text in Giraldus Cambrensis, *Opera*, 8 vols, ed. J. S. Brewer, James F. Dimock, and George F. Warner (London: Longman, Green, Longman, and Roberts, 1868), I, pp. 58–59.

Deheubarth in general and Dyfed and Seisyllwg in particular, is aimed at providing a counter-narrative to the legendary history of Gwynedd, which, outside the Four Branches, constitutes a large part of surviving medieval Welsh legendary and historical material. The poems attributed to Aneirin, Taliesin, and Llywarch Hen, glorifying the ancient northern kingdoms of Rheged and Gododdin along with the histories attributed to Nennius (*Historia Brittonum*), and in the *Annales Cambriae* and the *Brut y Tywysogion*, plus the early, and thus dubious, genealogies, mainly concern themselves with events in Gododdin and Rheged and the establishment of the over-kingdom of Gwynedd under the sons of Cunedda, himself an early fifth-century immigrant from Gododdin.[32]

According to the *Historia Brittonum*, which dates from the ninth century, Cunedda (< *Cuno-dagos, 'good/protective, hound') was the son and grandson of men with Roman names, Edeyrn < Eternus, and Padarn Beisrudd < Paternus (red cloak), an epithet implying service in a Roman legion. By some means, perhaps connected with the collapse of Gododdin, along with the other northern British kingdoms in post-Roman Britain, Cunedda ends up in Wales. Legendarily, he had nine sons, with the most notable lineage stemming from Einion Yrth, whose son, Cadwallon Lawhir (Longhand), was the father of Maelgwn Gwynedd (d. 547), the consolidator of the power of Gwynedd and the target of Gildas's scorn in his *De Excidio et Conquestu Britanniae*.[33] Looking only at what happens to have been preserved in writing, it is clear that the rulers of Gwynedd dominated the pseudo-history of Wales in the Middle Ages. From a southern perspective, it is easy to imagine that a counter-narrative composed of similarly powerful legendary material was desirable. It is not that there were not kingdoms in Deheubarth in the post-Roman period. We know that there was an Irish kingdom in the south in the fifth and sixth centuries, attested to by the large number of Ogham stones still extant. The history of these kingdoms did not, however, get recorded in the same way that the dynastic real and pseudo-history of the sons of Cunedda did.

The emphasis on the consolidation of Seisyllwg, enumerated cantref by cantref, and of the creation of Seisyllwg by Pryderi, would seem to be intended to parallel Maelgwn Gwynedd's reign in the North. As pointed as the geographic extent of Pryderi's rule is the long account of Rhiannon's humiliation of her otherworldly suitor, Gwawl ap Clud, who is presumably from the far north, the Kingdom of Strathclyde. But did anyone really care about such foundational stories? Llywelen ap Gruffud actually wrote a letter to Henry III, claiming that Wales was independent

32 David N. Dumville, ed., *The Historia Brittonum III: The 'Vatican' Recension* (Cambridge: D. S. Brewer, 1985), ch. 62; J. Williams (ab Ithel), ed., *Annales Cambriae* (London: Longman, Green, Longman, and Roberts, 1880); Thomas Jones, ed. and trans., *Brut y Tywysogion or, the Chronicle of the Princes: Peniarth MS. 20 Version* (Cardiff: University of Wales Press, 1952).

33 Gildas, *The Ruin of Britain, Fragments from Lost Letters, the Penitential, Together with the Lorica of Gildas*, ed. and trans., Hugh Williams (London: Alfred Nutt, 1899), chs 33–35.

because he, Llywelen, was directly descended from Kamber, the son of Geoffrey of Monmouth's Brutus of Troy, whose portion was Wales.[34] So in the thirteenth century, the political usefulness of a pseudo-historical genealogy is clear. And why might they, or we, care about such beliefs? As the twentieth-century cultural critic Marc Holthof observes of the constant reinvention, and thus continuity, of 'tradition':

> In his *Wahrheit und Methode* Hans-Georg Gadamer stresses the importance of tradition. He claims (following Heidegger) that a fundamental unity exists between thought, language, and the world. It is through language that the horizon of the 'now' comes into being. This language, however, is always marked by the past. Through language the past lives on in the present and thus represents tradition. According to Gadamer, the Enlightenment made an important mistake when it failed to take these 'prejudices' and traditions seriously: the burden of the past was too easily discarded. Gadamer claims that it is tradition which shapes our ways of understanding and interpreting the world through language. And this tradition, he is well aware, does not exist of itself. It must constantly be embraced, confirmed, and cultivated. It also requires (but Gadamer doesn't tell us this) reinterpretation and pure make-belief.[35]

In William Faulkner's words, 'the past is never dead. It's not even past'.[36]

34 J. Goronwy Edwards, ed., *Calendar of Ancient Correspondence Concerning Wales* (Cardiff: University of Wales Press 1935).

35 Marc Holthof, 'The Prince Consort's New Clothes, on the Kilt and the Internet', *Andere sinema: Tweemaandelijks filmtijdschrift* 123 (Sept 1994), trans. Tom Paulus <https://www.nettime.org/nettime/DOCS/1/prince.html> [last accessed 26th July 2023].

36 William Faulkner, *Requiem for a Nun* (London: Vintage, 2015), p. 85.

5

Making War, Love, and Porridge in the *Cath Maige Tuired*

Joseph Falaky Nagy

In her characteristically insightful article comparing the vernacular Irish and Welsh retellings of the story of the downfall of Troy as derived from Dares's *De excidio Troiae historia*, Helen Fulton says, concerning the medieval Irish author's aspirational identification with both the besiegers and the besieged: 'This, then, is the Irish heritage, combining the warrior excellence of the Greeks and the peace-making of the Asians [that is, the Trojans and their allies]'.[1] In this, my modest tribute to Helen, I explore the contrast laid out in her observation operating in another paradigmatic story of divinely-tinged peoples of a bygone heroic age in conflict – in what is perhaps the major example of what could be called mythological epic to have survived from pre-Norman Ireland. This is the *Cath Maige Tuired*, 'Battle of Mag Tuired', a text, dating from the late first millennium CE, that has come down to us in a single manuscript.[2] As we shall see, the *Cath Maige Tuired* evinces an awareness of the story

1 Helen Fulton, 'History and *Historia*: Uses of the Troy Story in Medieval Ireland and Wales', in *Classical Literature and Learning in Medieval Irish Narrative*, ed. Ralph O'Connor (Cambridge: D. S. Brewer, 2014), pp. 40–57 (p. 52).

2 Elizabeth A. Gray, ed. and trans., *Cath Maige Tuired: The Second Battle of Mag Tuired*, Irish Texts Society 52 (Naas, Co. Kildare: Irish Texts Society, 1982). Gray's edition/translation is cited here throughout, with reference to the individual sections (§). Her series of articles interpreting the text, '*Cath Maige Tuired*: Myth and Structure', has provided readers (including the author of this piece) with indispensable guidance. Gray's latest contribution to our understanding of the text takes into account scholarship about the *Cath Maige Tuired* that has appeared since the publication of her landmark edition: 'Tuatha Dé and Fomoiri in *Cath Maige Tuired*', in *Myth and History in Celtic and Scandinavian Traditions*, ed. Emily Lyle (Amsterdam: Amsterdam University Press, 2021), pp. 49–70. On the history and other contents of the manuscript containing the *Cath Maige Tuired* (London, British Library, MS Harley 5280), see John Carey, *A London Library, an Irish Manuscript, a British Myth? The Wanderings of 'The Battle of Moytirra'* (London: Irish Texts Society, 2014). An Early Modern Irish telling of the story, substantially different from the *Cath Maige Tuired*, is to be found in Brian Ó Cuív, ed., *Cath Muighe Tuireadh* (Dublin: Dublin Institute for Advanced Studies, 1945).

of Troy and even makes the claim that the story it tells took place at the same time as the war between the Greeks and the Trojans. I will argue that the need for 'warrior excellence', similar to what is highlighted by Helen in relation to the *Togail Troí*, pointedly underlies the narrative dossiers that the *Cath Maige Tuired* compiles for two of its main characters. One is Núadu, the king of the Túatha Dé Danann (peoples of the goddess Danu), a people said to be of mysterious, magical, and supernatural origins, who in primeval times came to Ireland to take possession of it, wresting control away from another, distantly related people already occupying the island, the Fir Bolg. The other paradigmatic warrior is Lug, a figure who assumes leadership of the Túatha Dé Danann in their preparations to stave off yet another invasion of the island, this time launched by the equally mysterious and supernatural Fomoiri, a transmarine host eager to place their own candidate, the deposed king of Ireland Bres (who had succeeded Núadu) back on the throne. That balancing complement to 'warrior excellence' – namely, 'peace-making' and other pursuits that depend on strategies for success other than war and violence – also finds representation among the chief *dramatis personae* of the *Cath Maige Tuired*, pre-eminently in the figure of the Dagda, who receives this epithet (Good God) from the Túatha Dé Danann in acknowledgment of his versatility and ability to multi-task (§81).

Four Imports: The Lia Fáil

The most salient and telling details given at the beginning of the *Cath Maige Tuired* in regard to the arrival of the Túatha Dé Danann have to do with their four 'calling cards', talismanic objects they bring with them to Ireland (§3–6). One of them, the Lia Fáil (Stone of Ireland), unlike the other objects, is not introduced in association with any member of the Túatha Dé Danann, but with kings in general, whom the stone is able to identify by calling out when a rightful king sits or stands on top of it.[3] While it is not a weapon, the importation of this stone clearly expresses the intention of the Túatha Dé Danann not only to settle in Ireland but to dominate it, eliminating rivals and formulating kingship, as it had existed before their arrival, on their own terms.

The *Cath Maige Tuired* presents another detail that indicates the total commitment of the newcomers to this mission, which irreversibly takes them on the path to war:

> Roloisc[s]et a mbaraca fo cétóir iar torrachtain críce Corcu Belgatan [.i. Conmaicne mara andíu éat-sen], cona pedh a n-aire for teiched cucu. Gu rrolíon an déi 7 an céu tánic denaib loggaib an ferodn 7 an áer robo comfocus dóib. Conid as sin rogabad a tíchtain a nélaip cíach.

3 This is but one of the many rocks prominently on display in the story of the Battles of Mag Tuired (which means 'Field of Pillars'). Their ubiquity and significance (including their associations with memory, the past, and death) are insightfully explored by Rebecca Blustein, 'Poets and Pillars in *Cath Maige Tuired*', in *Myth in Celtic Literature*, ed. Joseph Falaky Nagy, CSANA Yearbook 6 (Dublin: Four Courts Press, 2007), pp. 22–38.

> (Upon reaching [Ireland], they at once burned their boats so that they would not think of fleeing to them. The smoke and the mist which came from the ships filled the land and the air which was near them. For that reason it has been thought that they arrived in clouds of mist) (§9).[4]

In other words, for the Túatha Dé Danann, who come from the mysterious north, there is no turning back on this momentous martial undertaking, where they will encounter and defeat the Fir Bolg settlers in the first of two battles that take place at Mag Tuired (Moytirra in modern-day County Sligo). Mist can dissipate, and magically induced mist can be reintroduced in order to cover a hasty retreat or reconsideration. But the burning of their boats commits the Túatha Dé Danann to their chosen new home and, 'do or die', makes unavoidable whatever the future holds for them.

Even though the more rational understanding of the mist as smoke emanating from burning ships is clearly the explanation favoured by the author for the obscurity associated with the coming of the Túatha Dé Danann, it is only one of the two explanations offered. As discounted as it may be, the magical variant account of their arrival, clearly presented as the older, is included and stands as an alternative. It expresses a very different view of the Túatha Dé Danann, their quest for the domination of Ireland as symbolized by the Lia Fáil, and their ability to reverse course, if circumstances were to demand.

In fact, the invasion proves successful, but at a cost. The Túatha Dé Danann inflict massive losses upon the settled inhabitants, the Fir Bolg, who are said to lose not only their king but also a vast number of their armed men. The Túatha Dé Danann, however, also suffer substantial losses as well as the trauma of the mutilation of their king, Núadu, who loses his hand or arm (*lám*) – a wound that renders him obsolete as a king (§10–12). And yet, even in the setting of this jarring introduction of casualties into the lives of the Túatha Dé Danann, who not only inflict death but now are suffering it themselves, there is still strong evidence of the renewability that is one of the features of the charmed life that the Túatha Dé Danann lead. This is after all, only the first battle fought at Mag Tuired (the one against the Fir Bolg), and not the one that the text is leading us to, the second battle, which will once again produce a victory of the Túatha Dé Danann, against an even

4 In a poem from a different source, the *Lebor Gabála Érenn* (Book of the Taking[s] of Ireland), a massive medieval compilation of lore concerning Ireland's legendary history, including the episode of the Túatha Dé Danann's invasion of Ireland, another reason is given for the Túatha Dé Danann's burning of their ships – to prevent the Fomoiri from using them to invade Ireland. See R. A. S. Macalister, ed. and trans., *Lebor Gabála Érenn: The Book of the Taking of Ireland*, 5 vols, Irish Texts Society 31 (Dublin: Irish Texts Society, 1941), IV, p. 244. Is the idea here that otherwise the vessels, like magical cable-cars, automatically would have gone back to the northern realms from which both the Túatha Dé Danann and the Fomoiri came, and would have brought another wave of invaders to Ireland?

vaster array of opponents (the Fomoiri, yet another set of invaders eager to impose their lordship over the island and its inhabitants).[5] That the latter conflict, fought in the same location, is in some ways a rematch is perhaps suggested by what the *Cath Maige Tuired* says about the defeated Fir Bolg – that those who survived the battle found refuge among the Fomoiri and on the islands between Ireland and Britain, from which many of the Fomoiri would later launch their attack on Ireland (§13). Of course, two battles fought in the same place involving at least some of the same protagonists does not constitute the full-blown 'Everlasting Fight' motif to be found elsewhere in medieval Irish literature and later oral tradition, but the iteration does stand out, as if the two battles were multiforms of a pattern that gestures toward the timeless.[6]

Núadu's loss of his *lám* (hand, or arm), a consequence of the first battle, not only affects his effectiveness as a warrior but also brings about a crisis of leadership: with a maimed Núadu disqualified from the kingship, whom would the Lia Fáil recognize as the correct king for the Túatha Dé Danann to choose in his place? In fact, the text does not tell us whether the king-detecting stone was consulted (perhaps it should have been), but the crisis leads to the selection of Bres, a candidate who, while physically perfect (his name, his father declares, will become a by-word for anything beautiful, *cruthach*, §21), turns out to be a disastrous ruler. Not only does he lack the judgment and generosity required of a king, but he also humiliatingly exploits the Túatha Dé Danann, his mother's side of the family, and colludes in their exploitation with his father's people, the Fomoiri. It is with these people that the Túatha Dé Danann had contracted *caratrad* (an alliance or friendship) even before coming to Ireland, on the basis of the siring of a son, Lug, by a man of the Túatha Dé Danann upon a woman of the Fomoiri (§8). In the aftermath of the demise of Núadu's kingship, it had been argued by the women of the Túatha Dé Danann that the selection of Bres as Núadu's successor would only strengthen this bond between the peoples. But after Bres, judged by the Túatha Dé Danann to have gone too far in his exploitation of them, is deposed by his subjects and goes in exile to the Fomoiri, the latter discard whatever *caratrad* still existed between them and the Túatha Dé Danann, and proceed with a plan to invade Ireland and show who its *real* overlords are – whatever the Lia Fáil might 'think'.

5 The first Battle of Mag Tuired is the subject of a later medieval text, ed. and trans. John Fraser, 'The First Battle of Moytura', *Ériu* 8 (1916): 1–63.

6 'Recurrent battle (everlasting fight)' is Motif 162.1.0.1.*, provided with citations, in Tom Peete Cross, *Motif-Index of Early Irish Literature* (Bloomington, IN: Indiana University Press, 1952). Mícheál Hoyne has argued that it was a third battle fought at Mag Tuired, in 'historical' time – 1398 CE – that inspired the aforementioned Early Modern Irish retelling of the story of the Second Battle. Mícheál Hoyne, 'The Political Context of *Cath Muighe Tuireadh*, the Early Modern Irish Version of the Second Battle of Magh Tuireadh', *Ériu* 63 (2013): 91–116.

Four Imports: Núadu's Sword

Clearly, what the Lia Fáil represents (kingship) thematically resonates throughout the *Cath Maige Tuired*, and so do the other three magical objects that the opening of the text tells us were brought to Ireland by the Túatha Dé Danann. In contrast to the collectively shared (or owner-less) stone for determining royal legitimacy, the other imports are associated with leading figures in the tribe. Two of them are weapons: the spear of Lug and the sword of Núadu, each of which, our text says, spells doom for anyone facing its owner in combat (§4–5). Lug's weapon is introduced by the text as already having been brought to Ireland at the same time as or shortly after Lug's parents were united, he was conceived (§8), and an alliance was thereby formed by the Túatha Dé Danann with the Fomoiri. And yet Lug did not participate in the battle with the Fir Bolg and only enters the story later in the *Cath Maige Tuired.* So we wonder: did Lug take possession of the spear at some later stage of his life and thereby define it as his, or did the spear's association with him predate and define the child Lug, whom the text calls 'a gen mbúadha' (the wondrous [or victorious] child) (§8). Neither the *Cath Maige Tuired* nor any other surviving source sheds light on this point.

Núadu with his sword, and Lug with his spear, are thus characterized as 'terminators' whom, or whose weapons, no enemy can resist. In contrast, the fourth object, associated with the third member of what might be called a triumvirate, the Dagda, is a cauldron – not an implement of violence, like those objects specifically associated with his two leading colleagues among the Túatha Dé Danann, but instead a means for hospitality and provision: 'Ní tégedh dám dimdach úadh' (No company ever went away from it unsatisfied [or ungratified]) (§6). The association of this object with the Dagda highlights the range of his power that extends beyond the battlefield, where the legitimacy of kingship as proclaimed by the Lia Fáil, often must be defended with weapons such as those possessed by Lug and Núadu. This is not to say that the Dagda is defenceless in battle. He possesses a deadly weapon, a *lorg* (cudgel, staff), which he promises to wield with devastating effect in the battle against the Fomoiri (§119).[7] Moreover, the validity of his later reign, in succession to those of Núadu and Lug, would doubtless be acknowledged by the Lia Fáil. But, significantly, what identifies him here in the list of the four imports, where the Dagda is first mentioned in the *Cath Maige Tuired*, sustains life, not death or some intangible sense of royal rectitude. The cauldron offers a supply of food that is inexhaustible or never-ending, no matter how many guests or subjects come to partake

7 Other texts depict the Dagda playfully using the same cudgel to heal or revive those he has battered to death: see Joseph Falaky Nagy, 'How Time Flies in the *Cath Maige Tuired*', in Lyle, *Myth and History*, pp. 95–115 (pp. 100–02). No such magical power to reverse the damage caused by the weapon is attributed anywhere to Núadu's sword or Lug's spear. Apart from the ambiguous case of Cridenbél (see below), the Dagda is not shown actually slaying anyone in the *Cath Maige Tuired* – although in the aftermath of the battle, the Dagda's harp, when he reclaims it from the Fomoiri, demonstrates that it has a murderous mind of its own (§163–64).

of it. Given the usual limitations of resources and those imposed by time (including the seasons), food and the nourishment it provides usually run out, but, thanks to the magical properties of the cauldron, such limitations do not apply. In other words, unlike the mastery over others via separation and death that Núadu's and Lug's weapons bring about, the Dagda's vessel brings people together, no matter who approaches it.

Ironically, Núadu, a dispenser of death with his sword, has his *lám* sliced off in the first battle (§ 11) by someone else's sword, and he will meet his end, perhaps by the edge of yet another sword, in the second battle (§133). His return to kingship, after the departure of Bres, becomes possible because the missing hand or arm is replaced with an artificial one that moves as well as its predecessor (§ 11). Later there is even full recovery and replacement of the replacement, when Núadu's original *lám* is innovatively reattached by Míach, the son of Dían Cécht, the physician who had supervised the original prosthesis (§33).

Unfortunately for the young genius, his father proves to be murderously resentful of the *enfant terrible*'s extraordinary accomplishment. There is no evidence in the text that Núadu was anything but satisfied with what Míach had accomplished; but is it just coincidence that Dían Cécht's deadly rage against his son manifests itself in an attack on his son with a sword – not specifically Núadu's sword, but his signature kind of weapon? In the initial assault, Dían Cécht does not strike his son with the sword but throws it at him, as if it were a spear (§34). The verb used here, *do-léici* (releases, launches), would be more appropriate for describing what might be done with Lug's weapon. Since Míach is able to heal the wound he receives from the sword-as-projectile, Dían Cécht attacks him with it two more times, but now the verbs used indicate that the weapon is being used to strike blows.[8] Remarkably, even the slashing wounds to his head that Míach sustains when he is thus attacked, he is able to heal.

It is, however, as a result of the damage caused in the fourth attack that Míach finally succumbs, when, in a grisly conclusion to the sequence of attacks, Dían Cécht lands a blow that cuts out his son's brain ('co nderba a n-inchind', §35). Ultimately, one excision (of Núadu's *lám*), in itself not lethal, ironically leads to an excision of the seat of the mind itself, a wound from which (we are told) there is no possible recovery. This *coup de grâce* severs the link between medical tradition, which in its collective memory could have preserved Míach's healing techniques for future generations, and his innovative knowledge, by which body parts – even Míach's head, as badly damaged as it was before that final blow – could be regenerated.

8 In §34: *atcomaic* (from *ad-cumaing* 'strikes, cuts', *Electronic Dictionary of the Irish Language* [*eDIL*], ed. E. Gordon Quin (print edition, Dublin: Royal Irish Academy, 1913–76), Gregory Toner, Máire Ní Mhaonaigh, Sharon Arbuthnot, Marie-Luise Theuerkauf, and Dagmar Wodtko [www.dil.ie]., s.v.) and *bissis* (from *benaid* 'beats, strikes', eDIL, s.v.). See Gray's notes on these 'striking, cutting' verbal forms (including *co nderba* – see below) in her edition, pp. 85–86.

Four Imports: Lug's Spear

The spear-wielding Lug, meanwhile, has at least two opportunities in the *Cath Maige Tuired* to demonstrate his marksmanship, though in ways more metaphorical than literal. In both these instances, he penetrates closed spaces and breaks through confinement. Emerging from his fosterage in a foreign land, he comes as a stranger to the court where the Túatha Dé Danann are assembled in Tara. To convince them of his worthiness to be accepted into their company, Lug is willingly hemmed in with game-boards, matches, and players, to test how well he can play. (The board game played here is *fidchell*, a game of strategy bearing a general resemblance to chess.) Lug triumphs in all the matches with a strategy the text calls 'an cró Logo' (?the eye of Lug's needle), by means of which he passes through like a well-aimed spear to multiple victories, despite all the attacks, defences, and obstacles he must encounter while playing (§69).[9] This *cró* also allows Lug (and this episode) to thread a way through the limitations of time and space as pointed out by a parenthetical textual comment that expresses doubt about the knowledge of *fidchell* in Ireland as early as the era of the Battles of Mag Tuired: 'Acht masa i n-uamas an catha Troíanna ro-hairged in fidceall ní torracht hÉrinn and sin í. Úair is a n-áonaimsir rogníadh cath Muigi Tuired 7 togail Traoí' (But if *fidchell* was invented at the time of the Trojan war, it had not reached Ireland yet, for the Battle of Mag Tuired and the destruction of Troy occurred at the same time) (§69).[10] Still, as in the case of the question of whether the Túatha Dé Danann arrived in mist or burnt their ships, even though this objection is raised, the author does not exclude from the tale he tells this detail of Lug's triumph via his invincible *cró* in multiple simultaneous *fidchell* matches at Tara.

9 *Cró* (eDIL, s.v. 1 *cró*), which has a wide range of other meanings (including 'enclosure, pen, container'), perhaps refers to a way of entrapping an opponent's pieces in this board-game, but I propose that, with the understanding of the word in connection with needlework, we have here a parallel to the demonstration of skill by Lleu, Lug's cognate counterpart in medieval Welsh tradition, when in the Fourth Branch of the *Mabinogi* he hits a bird while he is sewing – presumably, what he throws is a needle. See Ifor Williams, ed., *Pedeir Keinc y Mabinogi* (Cardiff: University of Wales Press, 1930), p. 80. For another interpretation of Lug's *cró*, see Valéry Raydon, 'Le *cró Logo* "enclos de Lug" (*Cath Maige Tuired*, § 69)', *Études Celtiques* 42 (2016): 123–33. A second challenge issued to Lug in the hall of the Túatha Dé Danann may also involve throwing and accuracy. The strongman of the Túatha Dé Danann, Ogma (said in §75 to be the Dagda's brother), picks up a *márlicc* 'flagstone' from the floor and throws it out through the wall. Lug not only returns the missing stone to its original position in or on the floor but also restores the part of the wall that had been removed by Ogma's cast (§72). It is, however, only the verb used in describing Ogma's action (*focairtt*, from *fo-ceird*, eDIL, s.v.) that unambiguously means 'throw'. The meaning of the verb used for Lug's putting back both the stone and the part of the wall, on the other hand, could still involve throwing but can mean just '(re-)places, puts (back)' (*du-* or *docorustar*, from *ad-cuirethar*, eDIL, s.v.).

10 On this passage, see Tomás Ó Cathasaigh, 'Three Notes on *Cath Maige Tuired*', *Ériu* 40 (1989): 61–68 (67–68).

Later in the story, Lug pierces through a blockade mounted by his nine well-intentioned foster fathers, who fear for Lug's life were he to engage in battle with the Fomoiri (§95, 129). Freed from restraint and embracing his leadership role with gusto, he heads straight towards the fray. When he arrives on the scene, Lug fights not with projectile weapons but with incantation, until he confronts his mother's father, one of the battle-leading kings of the Fomoiri, Balor, who has already dealt a grievous blow to the Túatha Dé Danann in the fierce struggle by slaying Núadu. To counter the uncovered poisonous eye of his grandfather, Lug resorts to a sling, shooting a stone, which, with deadly accuracy matching that of Lug's spear, strikes and propels the eye out through the back of Balor's head. The eye is thus turned into a projectile itself, still functioning as a kind of death-ray, to cast a lethal look upon the Fomoiri themselves, upon whom it falls. Even the rest of Balor's body is swept up in the momentum of Lug's cast, as it collapses, more destructive than any spear, upon those behind him with crushing effect (§133–35).

This slaying of a maternal kinsman by means of a well-aimed cast echoes a similar, though far less successful, attempt that takes place at an earlier stage of the battle. Rúadán, the son of Bres and Brigit (the daughter of the Dagda), is, together with his dethroned father, on the side of the Fomoiri in the conflict. As someone who can consort with his mother's kin as well as his father's, despite the ongoing conflict between them, he is sent by the Fomoiri to spy on the Túatha Dé Danann. What they want to ascertain is how the Túatha Dé Danann manage to revive their grievously wounded warriors so that, in no time, they return to the battle in their previous condition. Also, the Fomoiri need to find out how their enemy can so efficiently repair and sharpen their weapons, damaged or blunted in battle but made as good as new by the next day. After Rúadán returns with his spy's report, the Fomoiri send him back with the mission to slay Goibniu the smith, who is at the head of the spectacularly efficient assembly line churning out refurbished weaponry. The Túatha Dé Danann's well for healing their wounded, as managed by a team headed by Lug's paternal grandfather Dían Cécht, is presumably also accounted for in Rúadán's report (§123).

Back among the Túatha Dé Danann, and at the weapon repair shop with the intention of slaying Goibniu (to whom the text elsewhere refers as Lug's *bráthair* (brother or uncle) (§75), Rúadán is handed a freshly sharpened spear, as if he were going to engage in combat and cast it against his father's people.[11] Instead, in a

11 See Gray's note in her edition of the *Cath Maige Tuired*, p. 95, on *a bráthair* in §75. In §8 Lug's father Cían is said to be the son of Dían Cécht. In the passage previously mentioned, §75, Dían Cécht is the other of the two *bráthair.* Among the materials constituting the *Lebor Gabála,* we find the statement that all three of these members of the Túatha Dé Danann, Dían Cécht, Goibniu, and Lug, as well as even the Dagda and Núadu, are sons (presumably by different fathers) of Ethliu, a name that may be a variant of Eithne, the name given to Lug's mother in the *Cath Maige Tuired* (Macalister, *Lebor Gabála,* p. 244, *Cath Maige Tuired* §8; on these names, see Clare Dagger, 'Eithne: The Sources', *Zeitschrift für celtische Philologie* 43 (1989): 84–124 (93–96).

(failed) anticipation of Lug's casting a weapon (a stone) against his own maternal kinsmen, so as to make them collapse upon themselves, Rúadán throws the spear not forward at the charging Fomoiri but backward at his mother's people, specifically Goibniu. Wounded, but having enough presence of mind to pull out the spear and throw it at his attacker, Goibniu slays Rúadán. The smith then takes a dip in Dían Cécht's healing well and returns to work, as good as new.

Both difference (Rúadán fails; Lug succeeds) and similarity (the use of projectiles) emerge in a comparison of these two episodes of confrontation with maternal kinsmen. Proving more effective than the hapless Rúadán's spear-turned-boomerang, Lug's slingshot makes it possible for him triumphantly to pierce through the protective barriers afforded by normal relations among kinsfolk and to slay his mother's fearsome father.[12]

Four Imports: The Cauldron

We have seen that sword and spear keep reappearing in the events associated directly and indirectly with Núadu and Lug in the *Cath Maige Tuired*. Also, the essence of leadership that the Lia Fáil validates is a running theme throughout the story, even if the object itself receives no mention beyond the listing of the four artefacts introduced to Ireland by the Túatha Dé Danann. Similarly, while the cauldron of plenty owned by the Dagda receives no mention beyond the catalogue of imports, the themes it connotes – hospitality, the bringing together of guests, and the desirability of ample provision – recur in most of the *Cath Maige Tuired*'s Dagda episodes. While his own cauldron makes no appearance, stand-ins are to be found, even including bodies of consumers that can contain seemingly limitless amounts of food. While the stories featuring them ultimately demonstrate the Dagda's power, these cauldrons (both literal and metaphorical) nearly entrap him, as if the Dagda were expected to dispense food no matter how outrageous the demand, or as if he himself possessed a bottomless stomach, which even the Dagda's cauldron might be hard-pressed to fill.

As an example of the exploitation and injustice that the Túatha Dé Danann experience during Bres's reign, the *Cath Maige Tuired* tells the story of Cridenbél, a poet who, with the threat of satire, bullies the Dagda into supplying him with food. His displaced mouth – we are told that it grows out of his chest – and his name, 'Heart-Mouth', make even more conspicuous his parasitical behaviour and his insatiable appetite for food (§26–30). He demands the three best portions of whatever food the Dagda receives while working for the tyrannical Bres, a circumstance in which the Dagda is already being exploited. The sort of unwelcome guest that one might expect at a hypothetical feast where a cauldron of plenty is in operation,

12 On the detail of this spear's being compared to a weaver's beam and the implement's becoming known as a *gai máthri* 'spear of the maternal kin' on account of this incident, see Blustein, 'Poets and Pillars', pp. 35–36, n. 46, and Ó Cathasaigh, 'Three Notes', pp. 61–64.

Cridenbél views the Dagda himself as such a cauldron. In those three best portions that he demands and receives, there is in fact plenty of food for the satirist to enjoy: each is the size of a pig (§29). It is clear from what he shares that, not only is the Dagda honest and generous even with someone as undeserving as Cridenbél, but also as a consumer himself he normally eats a huge amount.

Without the sustenance provided by the food extorted from him, the Dagda starts to waste away. The Mac Óc (another member of the Túatha Dé Danann and the Dagda's son, as we know from other texts, but never so identified in the *Cath Maige Tuired*) notices the Dagda's condition and, taking pity, advises him on how to free himself from this parasitical relationship.[13] Taking three 'scildei óir' (shillings of gold) (§28) from his purse, the Mac Óc tells the Dagda to hide them in the next portions of food that he will surrender to Cridenbél. When swallowed, they will kill the pest, says the Mac Óc. As coached by the latter on his defence before the king, who will accuse him of poisoning Cridenbél, the Dagda is to say that, after all, he was giving Cridenbél the 'best' of what he had in his possession – the gold. Both the ruse and the defence work, and the Dagda is finally rid of his nemesis.

The details in this episode, including the fact that, even in a state of servitude, the Dagda is given a meal of gigantic dimensions (as much as three pigs plus), resonate with the larger-than-life capacity of his never-empty cauldron. And it is worth emphasizing that the Dagda's reputation for generosity, implicit in the owning of such an object, remains intact. That he *did* give the persistent Cridenbél what he had that was of greatest value (the three pieces of gold) is accepted by Bres, who had suspected foul play, after an autopsy is performed on the corpse. So the Dagda's cauldron may not be a weapon overtly, like Núadu's sword or Lug's spear, but this episode proves that food, such as that which fills the Dagda's cauldron – and the best of portions, however interpreted – can be weaponized in both their presence and absence, proving to be just as effective as instruments of either aggression or resistance.

We also see in this episode a notable association of the Dagda (or, really, of the Mac Óc) with something new that is being introduced to Ireland – in fact, with even more recent an import than the cauldron and the other three objects brought by the Túatha Dé Danann, or the game of *fidchell* that Lug plays with the Túatha Dé Danann. The gold given to the Dagda to be used against the victimizing satirist is specifically money – shillings, introduced to the Irish of the late first millennium CE via trade contact with the Anglo-Saxons across the Irish Sea, or with the Vikings who had established and settled in the port-cities of Ireland.[14] The hiding of money

13 On the complex relationship between the Mac Óc (also known as Óengus) and the Dagda, see Gray's edition of the *Cath Maige Tuired*, pp. 127–28, and Nagy, 'How Time Flies', pp. 102–05.

14 The seeming anachronism of shillings in the world of the Túatha Dé Danann was highlighted by John Carey, 'Myth and Mythography in *Cath Maige Tuired*', *Studia Celtica* 24–25 (1989–90): 53–69 (60–61). Cf. Gray's note on §28 in her edition of the *Cath Maige Tuired*, pp. 81–82.

in food may be part of a plot to overturn more than the extortionist poet. The judgment resulting from the Dagda's trial, that the three golden shillings are indeed more valuable than the food they replaced or were hidden in, undermines the basis of the barter economy that obtained in Ireland well into the second millennium. Payment with the precious coins proves literally indigestible for the satirist, an undesirable but expected member of the cast of traditional characters operating in early medieval Ireland. The value and use of money proves to be a new idea for Bres as well, an unfashionable ruler who had suspected before he was proven embarrassingly wrong that the Dagda had resorted to a 'luib éccinéol' (poisonous herb) (§29), as if he were a sinister counterpart to the leech and herbalist Dían Cécht. With the discreet introduction of minted coinage into the picture, the satirist is undone, the king's reign draws ever closer to an end after his initial judgment proves to be flawed, and the Dagda can now eat to his heart's content.

Even more indulgence of this larger-than-life variety, darkened by the spectre of death hovering over it, appears in another episode of the *Cath Maige Tuired* that once again features the Dagda (§88–93). It is set after the banishment of Bres and the appointment of Lug as the *pro tempore* leader of the Túatha Dé Danann. He dispatches the Dagda to the camp of the Fomoiri, who, after landing in Ireland, are preparing for the upcoming battle. The Dagda's mission, laid out by Lug, is to find out more about the size of the forces of the Fomoiri and to arrange for a truce with them, so as to allow the Túatha Dé Danann more time to collect their forces. This proves to be an especially dangerous mission, comparable to the Dagda's experience with the satirist. In that previous episode, the Dagda was threatened with satire unless he shared so much of his food that he could not sustain himself on what was left. The Fomoiri, accepting the Dagda as a guest, claim to be fearful that he will satirize them if he does not receive enough food to satisfy his notorious appetite. This concern turns out to be a sarcastic pretence, when his Fomorian host tells the Dagda that he will be killed unless he can consume more food than the Fomoiri think even a figure possessed of such a notoriously large appetite (and cauldron) could possibly eat. The meal prepared for the guest is intimidating indeed: a gigantic amount of porridge, containing grain, milk, and whole animals, all cooked together in a Fomorian king's cauldron (§89). Surely this vessel is a mocking parody of the Dagda's own cauldron, which can contain enough food to satisfy any guest, except that now it is the Dagda himself who is the guest. The contents, however, do not stay put in the cauldron for collective sharing but are poured out, as the Dagda's own special serving, into an anti-cauldron, a dug-out pit, eating out of which serves to subject the Dagda to further indignity and embarrassment. Affirming the ironic treatment of a guest whom the hosts view as an enemy, Indech, the king and host in whose cauldron the porridge now cooling in the ground was prepared, delivers to the Dagda the ultimatum that he will be slain if he cannot eat all of it. Hence, he should eat his fill, lest the hospitality be deemed inadequate and the unsatisfied guest resort to public reproach. The Fomoiri, in other words, are making a Cridenbél out of the Dagda in their malevolent merriment – not, however, that it is an outlandish comparison to make, given the frequent association of the threat of satire with voracious visitors in medieval Irish storytelling tradition.[15]

Showing that he can 'get' as well as he can 'give', the Dagda does manage to consume the entire meal prepared in mockery. He uses what are probably utensils suitable for use with his own cauldron: a huge *líach* (spoon) with which he scoops up the hunks of meat in the stew, and a *gabol gicca* (fork) that he is said to cart away afterwards. The Dagda even uses his fingers when he scrapes out some of the food left at the bottom of the pit along with the gravel (§90–93). But this triumphant demonstration of appetite and capacity in the face of what seemed an overwhelming challenge produces in the eater considerable impairment. With a belly described by the *Cath Maige Tuired* as now as big as a cauldron, he falls asleep and is the object of Fomorian laughter (§92). No wonder that they find him funny: the cauldron-belly hanging down from the Dagda's body now makes it as grotesque a representation of eating excess as Cridenbél's body was, with the mouth protruding from its middle. Beneficial though the Dagda's cauldron may be, he cannot escape from the image of it, which burdens him with the obligations and consequences that ownership of such a cornucopia entails.

In the aftermath of his perilous diplomatic visit, the Dagda has the last laugh on the Fomoiri. Hampered by his belly, he leaves their camp after his nap, albeit slowly, and encounters on the way an attractive woman. She is strong enough to throw him to the ground, or he is too weak to resist the manhandling. In their coy dialogue she continues the mockery to which the Dagda was subjected before among the Fomoiri, but now the element of mutual sexual attraction is added to the mix. In contrast to the Cridenbél episode, the Dagda is expected to 'give' (and actually wants to), but in this situation it is not his food that is to be shared. To make him capable of satisfying the woman, who, it turns out, is the daughter of Indech, the king of the Fomoiri in whose cauldron the Dagda's enormous meal was prepared, she beats him until he defecates enough so as to make it possible for him to carry her – all that she claims she is asking for, but which leads, one suspects by mutual consent, to their passionate embrace. Cridenbél was undone, and the Dagda restored to health, by the introduction of the dangerously inedible additive (coinage) into the food provided to the satirist by the Dagda when he was challenged to live up to the reputation symbolized by his cauldron. Here, the tables are turned, and the person making demands on the Dagda needs to rid him of the internalized cauldron that prevents him from performing the services that might be expected from someone of notorious appetite.

15 The classic example of this intersection is the Middle Irish account of the picaresque adventures of the aspiring poet Mac Conglinne, who so easily resorts to satire when he is inhospitably treated, and whose appetite, at least in his visionary account of travel to a land of food, rivals the ravenousness of the demonically possessed king whom he is trying to exorcise: Kenneth Jackson, ed., *Aislinge Meic Conglinne* (Dublin: Institute for Advanced Studies, 1990).

After the sex, the woman at first attempts to dissuade the Dagda from joining in the battle, but then she finally relents, even offering to work against her father and her people in the conflict to come. Hence the Dagda returns to the Túatha Dé Danann with his mission accomplished and even more achieved: a temporary peace has been gained, which will allow the Túatha Dé Danann to prepare better for the coming encounter; he has won a massive food challenge and survived, seemingly unscathed, the combined satire of the Fomoiri and Indech's daughter; and he has acquired a new ally for the Túatha Dé Danann.

And yet, in an odd way, perhaps the Dagda does *not* return from this exploit completely intact, at least according to an alternate telling of the story to which the *Cath Maige Tuired* alludes, but that it does not necessarily accept. In the midst of his earthy adventure following the overwhelming meal, and after the Dagda has risen from the ground, now piled high with his faeces, and taken the girl on his back, 'dobert téorae clochau ina cris. Ocus dofuit cech cloch ar úair aire – ocus atberud batar íat a ferdai derocratar úad' (he put three stones in his belt. Each stone fell from it in turn – and it has been said that they were his testicles which fell from it) (§93). Still echoing the Cridenbél incident and the weighing of losses and gains that informed it, this episode presents its own version of the three shillings. Whether they are stones picked up by the Dagda and put in his belt (to steady himself as he carries the woman?) or his actual testicles (of which he has at least and maybe more than three?), they fall off and are lost, just as the three shillings that come out of the Mac Óc's bag are 'invested' in Cridenbél and never return to either the Dagda or the Mac Óc's purse.[16] It is as if the loss of the stones were a necessary precondition to the love-making and the resulting alliance formed between the Dagda and Indech's daughter. This hint of castration, however, adds an element of diminution to the proceedings. Will the Dagda emerge from the encounter with less or no ability to regenerate? – there is no mention anywhere of progeny resulting from this union with this unnamed princess. And is the loss of the 'stones' a sexual foreshadowing of the debilitating wound that, according to sources other than the *Cath Maige Tuired*, the Dagda will receive in the forthcoming battle at the hands of another royal woman of the Fomoiri (the wife of the slain king, Balor)?[17] Is even the Dagda, though relatively peaceable compared to Lug or Núadu, ultimately subject to the process whereby warriors live and die through violence – ironically, suffering from a grievous blow delivered to him by an opponent with whom under other narrative circumstances he might have been making love instead of war?

16 Patrick K. Ford notes: 'As he carries the girl along, his masculinity falls from him and, in the form of testicles as stones, becomes part of the earth'. 'The Which on the Wall: Obscenity Exposed in Early Ireland', in *Obscenity: Social Control and Artistic Creation in the European Middle Ages*, ed. Jan M. Ziolkowski (Leiden: Brill, 1998), pp. 176–90 (p. 185).

17 Macalister, *Lebor Gabála*, p. 236; Ó Cuív, *Cath Muighe Tuireadh*, pp. 7, 48.

6

Locating St Brendan in Medieval Wales

Jonathan M. Wooding

The Irish saint Brendan of Clonfert was widely known in medieval Europe through the pan-European popularity of the *Navigatio Sancti Brendani abbatis* (Voyage of St Brendan the Abbot), which describes his journey to a promised land in the ocean.[1] Alongside the sometimes overwhelming literary celebrity inspired by this tale (which could be described as a 'hagiographical romance'),[2] St Brendan had a medieval cult of more conventional type, traceable through dedications and hagiography.[3] This cult also had an international reach, if not on the scale of the reception of the *Navigatio*, with churches dedicated to Brendan in Brittany, England, the Isle of Man, and Scotland – but not in Wales, where no medieval dedications to Brendan are recorded. Brendan features in a handful of Cambro-Latin and Welsh sources. None of these explicitly try to place him in Wales, but some hagiographical traditions linked to Saint-Malo in Brittany do so. Given the proximity of Ireland to Wales, as well as the extent of commemoration of other Irish saints in Wales, a more

1 For the wide reception of the *Navigatio*, see *Navigatio sancti Brendani*, ed. Giovanni Orlandi and Rossanna Guglielmetti (Florence: Edizioni del Galluzzo, 2014), pp. cxxxii–ccli. A comprehensive bibliography is provided by Glyn S. Burgess and Clara Strijbosch, *The Legend of St Brendan: A Critical Bibliography* (Dublin: Royal Irish Academy, 2000), pp. 49–78. Translations of the *Navigatio* and its many adaptations are published in Ray Barron and Glyn S. Burgess, ed. and trans., *The Voyage of St Brendan: Representative Versions of the Legend in English Translation* (Exeter: Liverpool University Press, 2002). On the wider literary 'cult' of Brendan, see Clara Strijbosch, *The Seafaring Saint: Sources and Analogues of the Twelfth Century Voyage of Saint Brendan* (Dublin: Four Courts Press, 2000).

2 Hippolyte Delehaye, *The Legends of the Saints*, trans. Donald Attwater (New York: Fordham University Press, 1962), p. 5; Richard Sharpe, *Medieval Irish Saints' Lives* (Oxford: Oxford University Press, 1991), p. 17.

3 Jonathan M. Wooding, 'The Medieval and Early Modern Cult of St Brendan', in *Saints' Cults in Celtic Britain and Ireland*, ed. Steve Boardman, John Reuben Davies, and Eila Williamson (Woodbridge: Boydell Press, 2009), pp. 180–204.

visible cult of Brendan might be expected.[4] Brendan thus could be seen as another example of what Karen Jankulak has termed the phenomenon of the 'absent saint' – prominent British and Irish saints who feature significantly in Welsh sources but are not obviously culted there.[5] My study of this question is offered as a tribute to our honorand's own inspiring studies of the international context of medieval Welsh literature, as well as on the nexus between settlement history and literary narrative.

Co-ordinates of St Brendan

Brendan moccu Altai, also known as 'Brendan of Clonfert' and 'Brendan the Navigator', was an early Irish monk and abbot. The Irish annals, in a possibly contemporary entry, record that he died at his principal monastery of Clonfert (County Galway) in 575 CE.[6] Early sources consistently trace his ancestry to the Alltraige, a people who lived in the region around Tralee (County Kerry), as we find in Adomnán of Iona's (d. 704) *Vita Sancti Columbae*, where Brendan is 'Brendenus mocu Alti', and the *Navigatio*, where he is 'Sanctus Brendanus ... nepotis Althi'.[7] The *Life* of St Brendan, a separate work to the *Navigatio*,[8] describes his early life and edu-

4 For references to Irish saints in Welsh Lives and calendars, see Pádraig Ó Riain, 'The Irish Element in Welsh Hagiographical Tradition', in *Irish Antiquity*, ed. Donnchadh Ó Corráin (Cork: Tower Press, 1981), pp. 291–303. At least 21 pre-1800 churches arguably evince dedications to Irish saints: Brigit (15), Patrick (2), Colman (2), Aidan (1), and Barrwg (1), in Elizabeth Evans *et al.*, 'Medieval Churches in Wales: The Welsh Historic Churches Project and its Results', *Church Archaeology* 4 (2000): 5–26 (21–26).

5 Karen Jankulak, 'Present yet Absent: The Cult of St Samson of Dol in Wales', in *St Samson of Dol and the Earliest History of Brittany, Cornwall and Wales*, ed. Lynette Olson (Woodbridge: Boydell Press, 2017), pp. 163–80 (pp. 179–80); Karen Jankulak and Jonathan M. Wooding, 'The British Cult of St Gildas', in *Actes du Colloque Saint Gildas*, ed. Bernard Merdrignac and Georges Provost (Gourin: Éditions des Montagnes Noires, 2011), pp. 25–42 (pp. 29–40).

6 The date is calibrated from annals of various dates using the concordance of Dr Daniel P. McCarthy; see Wooding, 'The Medieval and Early Modern Cult', p. 184.

7 *Vita Sancti Columbae* I.26, in Alan Orr Anderon and Marjorie Ogilvie Anderson, ed. and trans., *Adomnán's Life of Columba* (London: Methuen, 1961), p. 52; Wooding, 'The Medieval and Modern Cult', pp. 187–88. Later sources affiliate him to the Cíarrage Luachra, but on the basis that the latter had by then absorbed the Alltraige.

8 The *Life* of St Brendan survives in a number of Latin (*Vita Sancti Brendani*) and Middle Irish (*Betha Brénnain*) versions of shared origin, which I generalise here as the '*Life* of St Brendan'. The *Navigatio* is itself titled '*Vita*' in many manuscripts, but modern scholarship uses *Navigatio* exclusively for the more famous voyage tale and reserves *Vita* for the Latin version of the *Life*. For useful discussions of the *Life* see Séamus Mac Mathúna, 'The Irish Life of St Brendan: Textual History, Structure and Date', in *The Brendan Legend: Texts and Versions*, ed. Glyn S. Burgess and Clara Strijbosch (Leiden: Brill, 2006), pp. 117–58; Orlandi and Guglielmetti, *Navigatio*, pp. lxxviii–cii; Séamus Mac Mathúna, 'The Structure and Transmission of Early Irish Voyage Literature', in *Text und Zeittiefe*, ed. Hildegard L. C. Tristram (Tübingen: Gunter Narr, 1994), pp. 313–57.

cation under St Erc at Ardfert (County Kerry), but Brendan's main career is seen to centre on Connacht, where he is reported to have founded several monasteries, including Clonfert. Stories of Brendan's travels in hagiography, of course, take him much further afield, most famously deep into the Atlantic, but also on visits to Britain. Adomnán describes a visit of Brendan to visit St Columba in the Hebrides. Serial visits in the *Life* of St Brendan take Brendan to visit Gildas – another 'absent saint' in Wales – and to found two monasteries one of which has, among other candidates, been claimed for a site in Wales (see below). We have no particular reason to regard these as historical travels, but such references in hagiography can also be a guide to where a saints' cult was established, or where hagiographers visited in search of one.

Whatever his notoriety in his own lifetime, Brendan became best known through the writing of the *Navigatio*, probably early in the ninth century.[9] It is most likely that this engaging work developed an already strong association in hagiography between Brendan and the historical Irish enterprise of monastic pilgrimage (*peregrinatio*) in the ocean. The core of the *Life* of St Brendan, a more conventional hagiographical narrative of the saint's life, seems to have existed prior to the *Navigatio*. Its own voyage episodes, as we will see, influenced hagiography in Wales and Brittany.[10]

St Brendan and St Malo

The earliest source that connects Brendan to Wales – and the only one that unequivocally locates him in Wales – is *Vita Sancti Machutis*, the Breton-Latin *Life* of St Malo, a Welsh-born bishop of Alet in Brittany. The *Vita Sancti Machutis* survives in a number of versions of uncertain priority. Space prevents our wading into the unresolved debates here. Two versions are likely to best reflect the contents of the original *Vita*, the one by a deacon of Alet named Bili, the other (surviving in longer and shorter forms) anonymous.[11] Bili's version can be reliably dated through its

9 See Jonathan M. Wooding, 'The Date of *Nauigatio S. Brendani abbatis*', *Studia Hibernica* 37 (2011): 9–27; Guglielmetti and Orlandi, *Navigatio*, pp. cii–cxix, propose a slightly earlier date in their recent edition; also see David Dumville, 'Two Approaches to the Dating of *Nauigatio Sancti Brendani*', *Studi Medievali* 29 (1988): 87–102.

10 For detailed study, see also Mac Mathúna, 'The Structure', pp. 318–34. Episodes from the *Life* quoted in other sources, as well as indications that the *Navigatio* itself used the *Life* as a source, suggest that it is older than the *Navigatio*, though surviving versions are all later in date. A contrary assessment is made by Pádraig Ó Riain, 'Hagiography Without Frontiers: Borrowing of Saints across the Irish Sea', in *Scripturus Vitam: Festgabe für Walter Berschin zum 65. Geburtstag*, ed. Dorothea Walz (Heidelberg: Mattes Verlag, 2002), pp. 41–48 (p. 42).

11 Séamus Mac Mathúna, 'Contributions to a Study of the Voyages of Saint Brendan and Saint Malo', in *Irlande et Bretagne, vingt siècles d'histoire*, ed. Catherine Laurent and Helen Davis (Rennes: Terre de Brume, 1994), pp. 40–55 (pp. 43–45). See also David Yerkes, ed. and trans., *The Old English Life of Machutus* (Toronto: University of

dedication to Bishop Ratwili of Alet (865–72 CE) and will form the basis of the following discussion, though reference will be made to the anonymous version on some points.[12] Both Bili's and the anonymous version provide similar details concerning Malo's early life, such as his birth in Gwent and his early years in Nantcarvan, where he received his formation at a monastery under the leadership of Brendan.[13] This is clearly the important monastery later known as Llancarfan (in Glamorgan), and this Brendan is also clearly to be understood as Brendan the Navigator.

Of particular interest for our enquiry is why Brendan is claimed to have lived and worked in South Wales. He is not given a backstory in the *Vita Sancti Machutis*, but the voyage he makes, as we will see, corresponds in detail with a voyage sequence in the *Life* of St Brendan. The latter contains two voyages in search of a promised land (*terra promissa* or *terra secreta*), the first ending unsuccessfully after five years, and the second, of two years duration, ending in success. In the *Navigatio* there is only a single voyage of seven years to the Promised Land of the Saints (*Terra Repromissionis Sanctorum*), mostly different in detail to the voyages in the *Life*. In Bili's *Vita Sancti Machutis*, Malo and Brendan make a single voyage, of seven years (Bili ch. XV), corresponding to the first (five-year) voyage in the *Life* of St Brendan. In the anonymous *Vita Sancti Machutis* a further voyage precedes the main voyage, but its detail is unrelated to any in the extant Brendan tradition. The destination of the Malo-Brendan voyage is an ocean island named *Yma* or *Ima*. In the anonymous version (ch. VII) it is presented as a 'more remote place' (*remotior locus*), of a type desirable for Malo to seek in his pursuit of the eremitic vocation; it is later (Anon. ch. IX) said to be inhabited by angels.[14] In Bili's version (ch. XV) it is a place to which Brendan was minded to travel as Malo advanced in his monastic formation.[15] This suggests that *Yma* is a desirable destination for a monk who wanted to find a place of higher retreat (*potioris peregrinationis locus*), and ultimately burial (*locus resurrectionis*), but that it was also an interim paradise, a place set aside for immortal beings to live until the final judgement.[16]

Toronto Press, 1984), pp. xxxiii–xxxvi for a succinct account of the editorial issues.

12 The text of Bili is cited from Gwenäel Le Duc, ed., *Vie de Saint-Malo, évêque d'Alet: Version écrite par le diacre Bili* (Rennes: CirDoMoc, 1979); the anonymous *Vita* is cited from *Mélanges d'histoire Bretonne (VIe–XIe siècle)*, ed. Ferdinand Lot (Paris: H. Champion, 1907).

13 Bili II (ed. Le Duc, p. 31) named *Nantcarvan* (and later *Vallis Carvan*, IV, ed. Le Duc, p. 39), it is *Vallis Carvana* in the anonymous *Life* (III ed. Lot, p. 297). Cf. *Vita Sancti Finniani*, ed. W. W. Heist (Brussels: Société des Bollandistes, 1965), p. 98; Gwynedd O. Pierce, *The Place-Names of Dinas Powys Hundred* (Cardiff: University of Wales Press, 1968), pp. 67–70.

14 Anonymous, *Life*, ch. VII (ed. Lot, p. 304) and IX (ed. Lot, p. 305).

15 Bili, ch. XV (ed. Le Duc, p. 63).

16 Thomas Charles-Edwards, 'The Social Background to Irish *Peregrinatio*', *Celtica* 11 (1976): 43–59 (43); Ananya Jahanara Kabir, *Paradise, Death and Doomsday in Anglo-Latin Literature* (Cambridge: Cambridge University Press, 2001). For the promised land as both interim paradise and place of monastic vigil, see Jonathan

In their main voyage Malo and Brendan encounter a dead giant named Milldu, whom they resurrect and baptise (Bili chs XVI–XVII). They ask him if he knows *Yma* and he describes to them an island he has seen at a distance across the sea, which seemed inaccessible behind a shining golden wall. He tries to tow them to this island but fails in the attempt and accepts death again (Bili ch. XVIII). The travellers then land elsewhere and find a jewelled fountain, which Brendan blesses (Bili ch. XIX–XX). They land on the back of a whale at Easter, where they celebrate Mass (Bili ch. XXIII). These incidents in their voyage resemble ones in the *Life* of St Brendan, albeit with somewhat different takes upon the same motifs; such adaptation of motifs from tale to tale is characteristic of the genre of Irish voyage-tales (*immrama*). In his own *Life* Brendan resurrects a dead giant (ch. 68), but in this case it is a young girl. The voyagers arrive at the high-walled island (ch. 69) where the incumbents lower down a tablet to tell them it is not the promised land. They then encounter a beautiful stream (ch. 71), but Brendan's blessing of it reveals it to have issued from the Devil.[17] The main motifs of the episodes and their ordering thus suggest that the author of the *Vita Sancti Machutis* had access to a copy of the *Life* of St Brendan, earlier than now survives and perhaps with episodes closer to those in *Vita Sancti Machutis* than are now found in the extant versions.[18] The fact that the giant is male, for example, is significant for its convergence with theories of the origins of the motif in the *Life* of St Brendan.[19]

If the version of the *Life* of Brendan available at Saint-Malo included the second voyage, however, the author did not draw upon it. A narrative in which Malo failed in an ocean quest before choosing to seek a different *locus* of *peregrinatio* in Brittany was sufficient to his purpose. The *Vita Sancti Machutis* transfers to Malo some of the special monastic leadership that Brendan evinces in his *Life*. It is Malo, for example, who reassures the brethren in the encounter with the whale, whereas it is Brendan in his *Life* and the *Navigatio*. Malo, however, does not need to usurp Brendan's

M. Wooding, 'The Location of the Promised Land in Hiberno-Latin Literature', in *Celtic Cosmology: Perspectives from Ireland and Scotland*, ed. Jacqueline Borsje *et al.* (Toronto: Pontifical Institute for Medieval Studies, 2014), pp. 93–111 (p. 102).

17 The incidents are found in a number of different versions of the *Life*; for reference I give chapters for the Oxoniensis version, *Vitae Sanctorum Hiberniae*, ed. Charles Plummer (Oxford: Oxford University Press, 1910); episodes at pp. 134–36. For a fuller account of the complexities of the voyage episodes particular to the *Life*, see Mac Mathúna, 'The Structure', pp. 326–34.

18 James Carney, for example, believed that Brendan of Birr was the original subject of Brendan's voyage tradition. See Dumville, 'Two Approaches', p. 88, n. 7.

19 See John Carey, 'Saint Brendan and the Sea Giantess', in *Scotha Cennderca cen On: A Festschrift for Séamus Mac Mathúna*, ed. Ailbhe Ó Corráin, Fionntán de Brún and Maxim Fomin (Uppsala: Acta Universitatis Upsaliensis, 2020), pp. 51–61 (pp. 57–59), where he notes the likely influence of Tirechán's *Collectanea* on the giant story in the Brendan legend, combining two stories in Tirechán concerning a *male* giant and female converts who die once baptised, but he does not discuss *Vita Sancti Machutis* in this connection.

achievement of leading his monks to the promised land, because his fame is known to lie elsewhere.

This leitmotif of a failed quest for a place of eremitic retreat can be compared to other *Vitae* from Brittany, Ireland, and Scotland, in which monks first test their vocations in the eremitical life before humbly accepting service in a more secular-adjacent community. St Samson of Dol, whom the *Vita Sancti Machutis* makes Malo's cousin, tests his own vocation first in an austere island monastery and then in a cave, before himself journeying to become a bishop in Brittany.[20] Adomnán describes the monks Cormac and Baetán, who voyage from Iona in search of 'desertum in oceano' (a desert in the ocean), but who fail to find a place to settle, instead becoming the heads of monasteries in Ireland.[21] The monk who is called to pastoral leadership thus gains dignity from his first having pursued the desert. Malo's voyage with Brendan, before his departure for Brittany, is clearly such an initiation tale.[22] We still may ask why Brendan is made Malo's companion in this Welsh connection. By this time, was Brendan simply synonymous with the ocean enterprise, to the extent that he was required to be there?[23] Even so, it is not self-evident why Brendan must be present in Wales with Malo from the latter's childhood. He could, for example, have been made by the hagiographer to simply visit Wales and bring Malo on a voyage, as Irish monks do for Samson in the *Vita Sancti Samsonis.* Or Malo could have met him on the sea itself, which is where Barre meets Brendan in Rhygyfarch's *Life* of David (see below).

The Malo *Lives,* which place Brendan, directly or implicitly, in South Wales, stand alone in the sense that there is no other direct connection of him to a site in Wales, or any other stories of him visiting Wales. There is, by contrast, a substantial cult of Brendan (locally Brandan) in northern Brittany. A medieval oratory dedicated to Brendan stood on the island of Cézambre, just to the north of Saint-

20 On Samson's monastic formation, see Jonathan M. Wooding, 'The Representation of Early British Monasticism and *Peregrinatio* in *Vita prima S. Samsonis*', in *St Samson of Dol and the Earliest History of Brittany, Cornwall and Wales,* ed. Lynette Olson (Woodbridge: Boydell Press, 2017), pp. 137–61.

21 *Vita Sancti Columbae* I.6, ed. Anderson and Anderson, pp. 222–25; I.20, pp. 249–55; III.43, pp. 440–47. Mac Mathúna ('Contributions', p. 43) notes that both Malo (anonymous version, first voyage) and Cormac visit Orkney, which might point to the Malo-hagiographer having Adomnán as a source, or perhaps to a lost source used by both.

22 Mac Mathúna, seeking a more specific context for this story in Brittany, interprets Malo's retreat from the desert as a critique of wandering insular monks in a specifically 'Benedictine' context. The narrative seems to me less pointed, however, and consistent with the insular motif. We could also note the later stories of saints such as David and Deiniol in Wales, who have both eremitic and episcopal careers.

23 It is quite likely that the *Navigatio* was itself written around this time: see Wooding, 'The Date', pp. 9–27; cf. Guglielmetti and Orlandi, *Navigatio,* pp. cii–cxix, who propose a slightly earlier date.

Malo, until it was destroyed by bombing in World War Two.[24] In Plouaret there are dedications to St Brandan at Trégrom and Lanbellec, and there is a Saint-Brandan near Quintin (Côtes d'Armor).[25] Yet there is cause to doubt the antiquity of this cult. At Saint-Brandan the form *Brandan* interchanges with *Bedan*, while at other sites St Brandan is apparently conflated with St Brévelaire – the English saint Branwaladar.[26] The Breton cult of Brendan is therefore possibly only a development later than Bili's time, perhaps secondary to his literary association with Malo. That Brendan features in literary narratives in Wales, without any cult, but has a Breton cult, may thus be a circumstantial difference. One wonders if the situation might have been different if there had been a substantial cult of Branwaladar in Wales, or some other saint whose name resembled Brendan's.

Two further British saints are claimed to have been educated by Brendan, implicitly in Wales, as the records of both seem to derive their detail from the *Vita Sancti Machutis*. One of these is St Gurval, the bishop of Alet in succession to Malo. A late text, 'Lessons for the Feast of St Gurval', claims that he was born in Britain, where he served as a monk 'sub Brandano, magni nominis viro' (under St Brandan, a man of great name).[27] The 'Lessons' do not specify Wales as the setting, only *Britannia*, but, as Gurval's story is closely tied to Malo's, Llancarfan would seem to be implied.[28] The other saint taught by Brendan is St Mechyll of Llanfechell in Anglesey, of whom it is said in a late medieval praise poem: 'Wrth ffynnu, dy ddysgu'n dda, / Bu'r un Duw a Sain Brenda' (As you flourished, the one God and St Brendan taught you well).[29] Again, here Malo is obviously tied up with the story, with *Mechyll* conflated with Malo via the Latin form of his name *Machutus*.[30] Barry

24 Nathalie Molines and Philippe Guignon, *Les églises des îles de Bretagne* (Vannes: Institut culturel de Bretagne-Skol-Uhel ar vro, 1997), pp. 56–57.

25 Bernard Tanguy, *Dictionnaire des noms de communes, trèves, et paroisses des Côtes d'Armor: origine et signification* (Douarnenez: ArMen-Le Chasse-Marée, 1992), pp. 123–24.

26 Tanguy, *Dictionnaire*, pp. 268–69.

27 *Acta Sanctorum*, 1 Junius (Antwerp and Brussels: Société des Bollandistes), pp. 727–28: 728; Gilbert H. Doble, *The Saints of Cornwall: I. Saints of the Land's End District* (Oxford: Holywell, 1960), pp. 61–78.

28 The cult at Saint-Malo is apparently conflated with, or is a doublet of, that of a Breton-Cornish saint Gudwal or Goal, whose own cult appears to have originally been unconnected to Alet: see Oliver Padel, 'Gudwal [St Gudwal, Gurval, Goal, Gouezgal] (*supp. fl.* 7th cent.)', *Oxford Dictionary of National Biography* (Oxford: Oxford University Press, 2004) <www.oxforddnb.com> [last accessed 11th November 2023].

29 Barry J. Lewis, ed. and trans., *Medieval Welsh Poems to Saints and Shrines* (Dublin: Dublin Institute for Advanced Studies, 2015), p. 70, ll. 15–16, trans. p. 341 and notes 132–39. Though Brendan is clearly the likely candidate here, we should note the claims of a separate saint 'Brenda' in Wales, see Peter Bartrum, *Welsh Classical Dictionary* (Aberystwyth: National Library of Wales, 1993), s.v. 'Brenda ap Helig'.

30 Barry J. Lewis, 'St Mechyll of Anglesey, St Maughold of Man and St Malo of Brittany', *Studia Celtica Fennica* 11 (2014): 24–38 (27–30).

Lewis has noted that some deeds referred to in the poem are taken from episodes in the *Life* of St Malo; the poem refers to an 'ystoria', which may have been a *Life* of Mechyll based on the *Vita Sancti Machutis*, or a copy of the *Vita Sancti Machutis* itself.[31]

Brendan is nowhere mentioned in the documentary record from Llancarfan (though other Irish saints are), so it could be easy to see his presence at Llancarfan as simply a projection by a Breton hagiographer.[32] The nature of his presence in the *Vita* does suggest something more, however, and the specific choice of Llancarfan may be significant; Llanilltud Fawr arguably was the more favoured location in Breton hagiography for the education of local saints.[33] Had the *Life* of St Brendan come to Saint-Malo from Llancarfan and was there an established tradition of Brendan at Llancarfan, such that it was most expedient to base him there while involving him in Malo's formation as a monk?[34]

References in Cambro-Latin Hagiography: London, British Library MS Vespasian A.xiv

A further Cambro-Latin reference to Brendan is found in the collection of saints' Lives (*Vitae Sanctorum Wallensium*), in the manuscript London, British Library, MS Cotton Vespasian A.xiv.[35] The collection includes a fragment titled *Vita Sancti*

31 Lewis, *Poems*, pp. 133–38: 137; Lewis, 'St Mechyll', p. 28.

32 For some recent perspectives on the Llancarfan sources and their potential as evidence, see Patrick Sims-Williams, *The Book of Llandaf as a Historical Source* (Woodbridge: Boydell Press, 2019), esp. pp. 25–29, 91–92; Ben Guy, *Medieval Welsh Genealogy* (Woodbridge: Boydell Press, 2020), pp. 79–100; Ó Riain, 'Hagiography', pp. 44–46.

33 See Karen Jankulak, 'Cross-Channel Intercourse in the Earliest Breton *Vitae*', in *Multi-Disciplinary Approaches to Medieval Brittany, 450–1200: Connections and Disconnections*, ed. Caroline Brett, Fiona Edmonds, and Paul Russell (Turnhout: Brepols, 2023), pp. 207–38.

34 Caroline Brett, *'You Read it Here First': Early Traditions of Welsh Saints in Brittany*, Kathleen Hughes Memorial Lectures 19 (Cambridge: Department of Anglo-Saxon, Norse and Celtic, 2022), p. 18; Caroline Brett, Fiona Edmonds, and Paul Russell, *Brittany and the Atlantic Archipelago, 450–1200: Contact, Myth and History* (Cambridge: Cambridge University Press, 2021), pp. 241–43. We should note here the close connection of Brendan with St Finnbarr/Finnian, who is culted at Llancarfan. Finnbarr, as Barinthus < Barr(f)ind, is Brendan's precursor to the promised land in the *Navigatio*. See Kathleen Hughes, 'The Historical Value of the Lives of St Finnian of Clonard', *English Historical Review* 69 (1954): 353–72 (364–67); Jonathan M. Wooding, 'Island Monasticism in Wales: Towards an Historical Archaeology', *Studia Celtica* 54 (2020): 1–28 (14); Bartrum, *Welsh Classical Dictionary*, s.v. 'Barrwg, Berwyn'.

35 The text was edited by W. J. Rees in *Lives of the Cambro-British Saints of the Fifth and Immediate Succeeding Centuries, from Ancient Welsh Latin Mss* (Llandovery: W. Rees, 1853), pp. 575–79 (pp. 251–54). It was not re-edited by A. W. Wade-Evans in his new edition of most of the Vespasian Lives. The manuscript should be consulted directly at fols 104v–105v, as Rees's transcript is unreliable in its treatment of names.

Brendani, as the final text in the collection, which is otherwise concerned with saints who have a more obvious connection to Wales. The fragment provides a copy of the standard text of the *Navigatio* from the opening of the tale up to Brendan's choice of 14 companions to accompany him to the promised land. At this point it includes an interpolation into the normative text of the *Navigatio,* between the phrases 'sua electis binis fratribus septem ...' and '... conclusit se in uno oratorio'. This interpolation names Malo (Macutus) as one of Brendan's companions. It commends reading through his venerable life ('perlegens eius venerabilem vitam'), which I take to mean a written Life of Malo.[36] The fragment breaks off shortly after the interpolation.

The Vespasian text belongs to a family of manuscripts of the *Navigatio* in which the association between Malo and Brendan is made.[37] The motivation for the interpolation may be similar to that which inspired copyists to insert the text of the *Navigatio* into the *Life* of St Brendan, namely a desire to reconcile later traditions with motifs in the earlier one. The distribution of the manuscripts of this family across Brittany, England, and Normandy – regions evincing cults of Malo in the Norman period – gives a further context for this development. Joshua Byron Smith, in a recent detailed study of this question, is inclined to see the Brendan text in Vespasian as acquired through an Anglo-Norman connection, rather than from a house within Wales.[38] The Vespasian collection also presents a calendar of saints, which lists St Brendan at 17th May; Silas Harris saw this as secondary to his inclusion in the collection, where the *incipit* of the Brendan text gives the same, abnormal, date for Brendan's feast.[39] How much any of this is evidence for devotion to Brendan in Wales is thus uncertain. Harris argued that St Cadoc and the saints associated with him were a particular focus of the Vespasian collection, among which associations he included the Llancarfan links of Brendan.[40] Smith, in his

---

Rees's form 'Barurchus', for example, could lead one to think the name of Brendan's precursor has been Cambricised, but it is simply a misreading of the manuscript's *Barinthus.*

36 Rees, ed., *Lives,* p. 578.

37 For detailed treatment, see Joshua Byron Smith, 'The Legend of St Brendan in Cotton Vespasian A. xiv', in *Seintiau Cymru, Sancti Cambrenses: Astudiaethau ar Seintiau Cymru / Studies in the Saints of Wales,* ed. David N. Parsons and Paul Russell (Aberystwyth: Centre for Advanced Welsh and Celtic Studies, 2022), pp. 31–42 (esp. 35–39); also Jean-Michel Picard, 'Early Contacts between Ireland and Normandy: the Cult of Irish Saints in Normandy before the Conquest', in *Ogma: Essays in Celtic Studies in Honour of Próinséas Ní Chatháin,* ed. Jean-Michel Picard and Michael Richter (Dublin: Four Courts Press, 2002), pp. 85–93 (pp. 90–91). Orlandi and Guglielmetti, *Navigatio,* pp. clxxiv–v. I would like thank Dr Smith for kindly sending me a copy of his article in advance of publication.

38 Smith, The Legend', pp. 41–42.

39 Silas M. Harris, 'The Kalendar of the *Vitae Sanctorum Wallensium* (Vespasian A.xiv)', *Journal of the Historical Society of the Church in Wales* 3 (1953): 3–53 (30, 49).

40 Harris, 'The Kalendar', p. 23. See also, Kathleen Hughes, 'British Museum MS.

recent reassessment, observes that Brendan's appeal to a monastic audience might also explain his inclusion in this collection of Welsh saints.[41] This theme is at least consistent with Brendan's more general role as a mentor in monastic formation in the Saint-Malo–Llancarfan tradition.

References in Cambro-Latin Hagiography: Rhygyfarch

The *Vita Sancti David* by Rhygyfarch ap Sulien (d. 1099), written at Llanbadarn Fawr (Ceredigion) around 1180–90, provides a further reference to Brendan from a Welsh context. Llanbadarn Fawr in this period produced other hagiographical texts with Irish affinities, such as a *Life* of St Máedóc and a martyrology including Irish saints.[42] In the *Vita Sancti David* an episode concerning Brendan falls within a sequence exclusively concerning Irish saints, which follows closely on chapters describing the foundation of David's principal monastery (ch. 20) and the enumeration of his Rule of life (chs 21–32). As in the Vespasian collection, Brendan again stands out here for being less obviously connected to Wales than the other saints who are included. The saints who feature in Rhygyfarch's Irish sequence are: Máedóc of Ferns (chs 35–37 and 42), Scothíne of Tiscoffin (ch. 38), Barre (Finnbarr) of Cork (ch. 39), Brendan of Clonfert (ch. 40), and Modomnóc of Tibberaghny (chs 41, 43). References earlier in the *Vita Sancti David* to saints Patrick and Ailbe, as Pádraig Ó Riain observes, serve to link David to the foundational bishops over the north and south of Ireland respectively. The inclusion of these two is arguably mainly political, but chapters 35–43 seem concerned to place Irish saints into parables of monastic formation and leadership.

We encounter Brendan when St Barre desires to leave his monastery in Cork and visit the holy places in Rome. While returning home he lingers in St David's company, until he begins to fear that, in his absence, his brethren will quarrel and fall out. Unable to find a ship sailing to Ireland, he asks to borrow David's horse:

> Fidens patris benedictione ac sustentaculo equi utitur pro naui. Equus enim tumentes fluctuum cumulos ceu planum perarabat campum. Cum autem in mare longius graderetur, apparuit ubi sanctus Brendanus super marinum cetum miram ducebat uitam. Sanctus autem Brendanus, hominem in mare uidens equitantem, stupefactus, ait, 'Mirabilis Deus in sanctis suis'.

> (Trusting in the father's blessing, he used the horse instead of a ship as support. The horse ploughed its way through the swelling crests of the waves as if through a level field. When he had travelled further out to sea, he came to where Saint

Cotton Vespasian A. XIV ("Vitae sanctorum Wallensium"): Its Purpose and Provenance', in *Studies in the Early British Church*, ed. Nora K. Chadwick (Cambridge: Cambridge University Press, 1958), pp. 183–200 (pp. 191–92).

41 Smith, 'The Legend', p. 42.

42 See David Howlett, 'Rhygyfarch ap Sulien and Ieuan ap Sulien', in *The Cambridge History of the Book in Britain Vol. 1 400–1100*, ed. Richard Gameson (Cambridge: Cambridge University Press, 2012), pp. 701–06 (pp. 701, 703–04).

> Brendan was leading a wonderful life on the back of a whale. Seeing a man riding a horse on the sea, Saint Brendan was astonished and said, 'God is wonderful in his saints'.)[43]

In contrast to the other saints, Brendan is thus not presented as a disciple of David. He is only met upon the sea between Ireland and Wales. When Barre tells of David, Brendan says only that he will come and see him.[44] Brendan's appearance here, it must be said, seems pointedly liminal. All the other saints in Rhygyfarch's sequence of Irish-associated saints seem to have local cults in Menevia, or at least South Wales.[45] Is Rhygyfarch studiously separating Brendan from Wales precisely because he did not have a cult presence there? The evidence is not sufficient to make this argument with much confidence, as one could note here that two of the other saints are only attested in Wales each by a single source, but it remains a possibility.

The whale episode, in contrast to the *Life* and the *Navigatio*, here appears without its essentially brief duration and paschal context. Rhygyfarch simply states that Brendan is living on the whale. The inert quality of Rhygyfarch's motif may reflect its use as a parallelism for Barre being on the horse, though it may also reflect use of some other source. I concur with Smith that there is nothing in this episode to indicate specific use by Rhygyfarch either of the *Life* or *Navigatio* of St Brendan.[46] The motif of protagonists meeting on the sea, one in a vessel in the sea, the other travelling as if on land, is found in a short text attached to the martyology *Félire Óengusso*, which has Barre meet St Scothíne (another saint mentioned in Rhygyfarch's sequence), with Barre in the boat and Scothíne walking on a plain of blossoms.[47] The motif is arguably paralleled in the eighth-century Irish tale *Immram Brain maic Febuil*, where the protagonists are Bran, in a boat in the ocean, and the sea-god Manannán, who is driving a chariot across a flowering plain.[48] James Carney suggested that *Immram Brain* was a bowdlerisation of

43 Rhygyfarch, *Vita Sancti David*, ed. and trans. Richard Sharpe and John Reuben Davies, in *St David of Wales: Cult, Church and Nation*, ed. J. Wyn Evans and Jonathan M. Wooding (Woodbridge: Boydell Press, 2007), chs 39–40. A *Life* of Barre contains a version of the crossing, but omits the encounter with Brendan: Plummer, *Vitae*, I.69n.

44 Rhygyfarch, *Vita Sancti David*, chs 39–40.

45 Máedóc (Aidan) of Ferns is the patron of Llawhaden (Pembrokeshire); Modomnóc is commemorated on a monument at Llanllŷr (Ceredigion). We have reference to a past dedication to St Scothíne at *Elfel* – most likely Elwell in Radnorshire. These are in the territory of the medieval diocese of Menevia (St Davids). Barre, if understood to be the same saint as Barruch/Barrwg, has a cult in Glamorgan at Barry Island.

46 Smith, 'The Legend', p. 33.

47 Whitley Stokes, ed. and trans., *Félire Óengusso: The Martyrology of Oengus the Culdee* (London: Harrison, 1905), pp. 40–41. This same entry also has a further episode concerning Brendan that is not found in any other source.

48 Máire Herbert, 'The Legend of St Scothíne: Perspectives from Early Christian Ireland', *Studia Hibernica* 31 (2000–01): 27–35 (31–32). *Immram Brain*, ch. 33, in Séamus Mac Mathúna, ed. and trans., *Immram Brain: Bran's Journey to the Land*

a lost Brendan narrative;[49] perhaps this putative lost text, or an epitome of it, is the source of Rhygyfarch's motif – if so, this would be, along with the *Vita Sancti Machutis*, another example of where a small glimpse of Brendan in a Welsh context may reveal something significant that is particular to the early transmission of his voyage legend.[50]

Claimed Cults of St Brendan in Powys and the Marches

In the *Life* of Brendan, as we have already noted, Brendan makes visits to Britain where he founds two monasteries. *Britannia* (*tir Bretan* in the Irish version) could indicate anywhere from Gaelic Scotland down to Brittany.[51] The names given for the sites offer possibilities, rather than certainties, as to their locations.

The first monastery is on an island called *Ailech/Auerech* (*Ailec* in the Irish version), which may be Eileach an Naoimh in the Inner Hebrides.[52] The site of the second monastery, which has been claimed for Wales, is described in the Salmanticensis Altera version as in: 'terra Ethica, in loco nomine Bledua' (the land of *Ethica*, in a place named *Bledua*).[53] The Oxoniensis version gives alternative forms: 'nomine Bledach, in regione cui nomen Heth' (named *Bledach*, in the region of *Heth*), and in a second copy of this version, the variants *Beldach* and *Hech* for the same names.[54] The Irish *Life* reads: 'ainm Bleit i ccrich Letha' (named *Bleit*, in the district of *Letha*).[55] The variations may represent errors in transmission, different attempts to make sense of unfamiliar names, or more deliberate attempts to associate the foundation with a locale of the scribes' preference.[56] Such philological convergence or conflation is a perennial trend in the formation of cults of saints.

Bledua or *Bledach* is identified in some sources as the village of Bleddfa in Powys.[57] I can find no earlier reference to this claim than a presidential address to

of Women (Tübingen: Niemeyer, 1980); Clark H. Slover, 'Early Literary Channels between Britain and Ireland', *University of Texas Studies in English* 7 (1927): 5–111 (14–15, 108–09).

49 James Carney, 'Review of Selmer, *Navigatio*', *Medium Ævum* 32 (1963): 37–44 (44).

50 On whether the matyrologies are a possible source, see Ó Riain, 'Hagiography', p. 42; Ó Riain, 'The Irish Element', pp. 293–94; Slover, 'Early Literary Channels between Britain and Ireland', esp. pp. 108–09.

51 Adomnan, *Vita Sancti Columbae* III.17, ed. Anderson and Anderson, p. 500; for his use of *Britannia* see the Second Preface (ed. Anderson and Anderson, p. 186) where he describes Columba travelling 'de Scotia ad Brittaniam' in his *peregrinatio* in the journey that would take him to settle in Scotland.

52 Wooding, 'The Medieval and Early Modern Cult', p. 195.

53 Salmanticenis Altera, ch. 15. Heist, *Vitae*, p. 330.

54 Oxoniensis *Life* of St Brendan, chs 86–87. Plummer, *Vitae*, I.143.

55 *Betha Brénnain*, ch. 57 (178). Charles Plummer, ed., *Bethada Náem nÉrenn: Lives of Irish Saints* (Oxford: Oxford University Press, 1922), I.85.

56 W. J. Watson, *The History of the Celtic Place-Names of Scotland* (Edinburgh: Blackwood, 1926), p. 81; Plummer, *Vitae*, I.xxxvii.

57 E.g. Terry Breverton, *Wales's 1000 Best Heritage Sites* (Stroud: Amberley, 2010), s.v. 'Bleddfa – Church of St Mary Magdalene'; David Barnes, *The Companion Guide to*

the Cambrian Archaeological Society in 1951 by Edward Williamson (1892–1953), Bishop of Swansea and Brecon.[58] Williamson equated *Bledua* and *Bledach* in the Rawlinson *Life* of St Brendan with Welsh *Bleddfa* and its earlier form *Bleddfach* (assuming consonantal rather than vocalic 'u' in *Bledua*).[59] A further element was added to this claim by the local historian W. H. Howse, who noted that *Heth* is a variant form for *Hech*, a name used in Domesday for Nash, near Presteigne.[60] Francis Rodd, however, saw no grounds to associate the name with Bleddfa, which is 7.5 miles (12 kms) from Nash.[61] *Hech*, as we have noted, is the alternative form given for *Heth* in the second manuscript of the Rawlinson Life,[62] but that copyist also made *Bledach* into *Beldach*.[63]

Williamson further proposed in support of his theory that the Brendan fragment in Vespasian A. xiv (see above) was copied out of a version of the *Life* of St Brendan into which a version of the *Navigatio* had been conflated; upon this premise he speculated that the lost text might thus have included the *Bledua* passage from the *Life*.[64] As we have already noted, the text history of the Vespasian Brendan story shows it to be (the interpolation aside) a conventional *Navigatio* text. In the 1960s, reports of investigations into the mound upon which the church in Bleddfa stands (thought to be prehistoric, but found to be medieval), cited Williamson's claim *inter alia*, whence it seems to have passed into the archaeological surveys and parish histories.[65]

The tradition of *Bledua/Bledach* as Bleddfa thus appears to be of no great antiquity. It is worth observing that the Victorian editor of the Vespasian text, the Rev.

Wales (Woodbridge: Boydell Press, 2005), p. 76; R. J. Silvester, and C. H. R. Martin, *Clwyd-Powys Archaeological Trust Historic Settlements Survey: Radnorshire*, Clyde-Powys Archaeological Trust Report No. 1088 (Welshpool: Clyde-Powys Archaeological Trust, 2011), s.v. 'Bleddfa'.

58 Edward Williamson, 'Vespasian A XIV', *Archaeologia Cambrensis* 101 (1951): 91–105 (103).

59 1316 *Blethvagh*, in Public Record Office, *Calendar of Patent Rolls Edward II AD 1313–17* (London: Her Majesty's Stationery Office, 1898), p. 610 (10 Edward II, part 2); 1693 *Bleddfach*, in Edward Yardley, *Menevia Sacra* (London: Cambrian Archæological Association, 1927), p. 355 (subscription book of Bishop Watson). Further examples are listed in the Melville Richards archive, National Library of Wales; also see Richard Morgan, *A Study of Radnorshire Place-Names* (Llanrwst: Gwasg Carreg Gwalch, 1998), p. 33, who sees the loss of *-ch* here as due to English influence.

60 W. H. Howse, 'Radnor Miscellany', *Radnorshire Society Transactions* 23 (1953): 69–70.

61 Lord Rennell (Francis Rodd), 'A Note on "Hech" in the Domesday Book', *Radnorshire Society Transactions* 34 (1964): 63–64.

62 Plummer, *Vitae*, I.143n.

63 C/t confusion is common in copying medieval script, so *Hech/Heth* would seem likely to be a scribal error.

64 Williamson, 'Vespasian A XIV', p. 103.

65 Laurence Butler, 'The Excavation of a Mound at Bleddfa Church', *Radnorshire Society Transactions* 32 (1962): 25–41 (38); F. Noble, 'Further Excavations at Bleddfa Church, and associated Problems of the History of the Lordship of Bleddfa', *Radnorshire Society Transactions* 33 (1963): 57–63 (59).

William Jenkins Rees (1772–1855), lived in the parish of Cascob, a mere 2.5 miles (4 km) from Bleddfa. His silence on this topic is notable. The Bleddfa tradition of Brendan is thus likely to be a modern example of the medieval phenomenon of linking a local placename to a superficially similar name in a text, with repetition escalating it more or less into a local cult – an interesting case-study of the phenomenon if nothing else.

Of interest also is a medieval cult in the borders, 19 miles (30 km) to the east of Bleddfa (and 9 miles (15 km) east of the modern Welsh border). Ludlow Priory in 1199 claimed to have found nothing less than the resting place of Brendan's own parents, in a tumulus east of the church, conveniently with their names on a document sealed first in wax, then lead: saints *Fercher* and *Corona*, father and mother of Brendan, as well as *Cochel*, a brother of Corona.[66] The claim is patently false and one suspects was inspired by the supposed discovery, eight years previously, of the grave of Arthur and Guinevere at Glastonbury, which also had an inscription conveniently bearing the names of the incumbents. There are some vague similarities of the Ludlow names with the names of Brendan's parents in Irish sources, where they are Findlug and Cara.[67] *Corona* might possibly be a variant on 'Cara', who is only named in the extant *Vita* and not in the *Navigatio*. What precisely Brendan's appeal would have been in Ludlow is unclear. Gilbert Márkus, in an unpublished presentation (which I cite here with his kind permission) noted the presence at Ludlow, early in the second millennium, of ancestors of the Stewarts of Bute.[68] These descended from the stewards of Dol in Brittany, close to a centre of Brendan's cult at Saint-Malo, and they set up a cult of Brendan in Bute in an attempt to displace that of St Columba. As Márkus observes, it is surely significant that in the Ludlow inscription Corona is made an aunt to Columba.[69]

Aside from these controversial claims, it is satisfying to learn that Brendan did eventually achieve one definite church dedication in Wales, albeit only for a brief period in the middle of the twentieth century. In the village of Kerry (Ceri), a few miles outside Newtown in Powys, a Catholic chapel of ease was consecrated, ded-

66 John Leland, *De Rebus Brittanicis Collectanea*, ed. Thomas Hearne, *John Leland, De Rebus Brittanicis Collectanea*, 6 vols (London: Benjamin White, 1774), III.407. Brief discussion in Robert Bartlett, 'Cults of Irish, Scottish and Welsh Saints in Twelfth-century England', in *Britain and Ireland 900–1300: Insular Responses to Medieval European Change*, ed. Brendan Smith (Cambridge: Cambridge University Press, 1999), pp. 67–86 (p. 77).

67 *Finloga* (Salmanticensis 1), Finlug and Cara (Salmanticensis 2), Findluagh (Dublin), Finnlug (Recension 1, Irish Life).

68 Gilbert Márkus, 'Saints and the Names of Places: Wales and Scotland', National Library of Wales Seminar, 9th June 2012.

69 Paul A. Fox, 'The Archbishops of Dol and the Origins of the Stewarts', *Journal of the Stewart Society* 23 (2010): 249–69; J. Horace Round, *Studies in Peerage and Family History* (London: Longman, 1901), pp. 114–46. A brief look of the currency of *Fercher* as a name might also suggest a Scottish source, though this requires a more comprehensive investigation.

icated to 'St Michael and St Brendan'. The chapel was housed in a building of 1856, the Reading Room, which still stands at the southern entrance of the village.[70] It is unclear when the chapel was deconsecrated, but certainly it was gone by the 1980s. St Michael is the dedication of the pre-Reformation (now Anglican) parish, but why Brendan was paired with him in this chapel is not made explicit. Brendan is a common patron of migrants and exiles, but we should also consider it very likely that he was chosen because the name of the diocese of Kerry (Cíarrai), in its English form, is homonymous with that of Kerry in Powys. If this proves to be the case, it would be another example of how philological convergence or conflation plays a role in disseminating the cult of saints, over the widest possible period of time.

Conclusion

The absence of an obvious cult of Brendan in Wales might mainly reflect geography. The historical co-ordinates of Brendan, including his earliest ones, anchor his career firmly in the west of Ireland. His cult also has a strongly western Irish focus, in contrast to most of the other saints alongside whom he appears in Welsh sources.[71] It is clear, however, that he was consistently venerated as a monastic teacher and mentor, even before the proliferation of his voyage legend through the *Navigatio*. The appearances of Brendan in Welsh contexts are brief, but nonetheless significant for their detail. His appearance in the *Vita Sancti Machutis* offers a rare and striking glimpse into Llancarfan's role in the pre-Norman transmission of texts, as well into the legend of Brendan in its earliest form. Rhygyfarch's brief parable of Brendan may also offer us glimpses of the legend in its early state. His situation of Brendan, as a monk living in the sea, is, however, also symbolic of the ambiguously local or international quality of Brendan's veneration in Wales.[72]

70 Cadw, *Buildings of Special Architectural or Historical Interest: Ceri/Kerry, Powys* (Cardiff: Cadw, 1996), p. 7; its use as a Catholic chapel is not mentioned in the description of the Reading Room in Noel Jerman, *Kerry, the Church and the Village: A Guide* (Kerry: N. Jerman, 1976), pp. 34–35. Different reports link it to the internment of Italian prisoners of war locally, but other reports date its use to after the building of a new village hall in 1957. For their help in my attempts to trace more detail of this rather ephemeral foundation, I would like to thank the Kerry Local History Society, in particular Carolyn White, as well as the staff of the Newtown Public Library and of the Wrexham Diocese Archives.

71 For example, St Brigit, the most extensively culted Irish saint in Wales.

72 For assistance in the research for this chapter, aside from those already thanked already above, I would like especially to thank Karen Jankulak for reading a draft to its great benefit, and Victoria Flood for her patience as editor. All errors remain my own responsibility.

7

The *Lorica of Laidcenn* and Early English Glossaries

Claudio Cataldi

Loricae across the Borders of the British Isles

This homage to Professor Helen Fulton's outstanding career and scholarly achievements finds its inspiration in her research on the connections between Celtic and English literatures. In this essay I aim to demonstrate how the dissemination of a Hiberno-Latin *lorica* across the British Isles influenced early English lexicography. For this purpose, it is firstly worth summarising the main features of a *lorica*. Deriving its name from the Latin word for 'breastplate', a *lorica* is a prayer, aimed at personal protection, which is characterised by a number of recurring elements:

1. an invocation to the Trinity
2. a call to a list of heavenly hierarchies (saints, angelic orders, martyrs etc.)
3. a prolix enumeration of body parts in need of protection and/or potential dangers from which the performer wishes to be shielded.

Sometimes the request for protection is further contextualised by means of a list of circumstances or postures.[1] Enumerations have an apotropaic purpose and represent a key element of these protection prayers. On the other hand, mere listing is not exclusive to *loricae*: it is rather the request for protection and its combination with either the invocation to the Trinity or the call to the heavenly troops – or both – that is particular to these texts, and therefore distinctive.[2] Otherwise, enumer-

1 See the pivotal study, in three parts, by Louis Gougaud, 'Étude sur les loricae celtiques et sur les prières qui s'en rapprochent', *Bulletin d'ancienne littérature et d'archéologie chrétienne* 1 (1911): 265–81; Louis Gougaud, 'Étude sur les loricae celtiques et sur les prières qui s'en rapprochent', *Bulletin d'ancienne littérature et d'archéologie chrétienne* 2 (1912): 33–41, 101–27. On the recurring features of the *loricae* see Gearóid S. Mac Eoin, 'Invocation of the Forces of Nature in the Loricae', *Studia Hibernica* 2 (1962): 212–17.

2 Pierre-Yves Lambert, 'Celtic Loricae and ancient Magical Charms', in *Magical Practice in the Latin West: Papers from the International Conference held at the Univer-*

ations are likewise found in other protection prayers or formulaic texts such as excommunications and exorcisms.[3] Finally, there are also texts that make explicit reference to breastplates but do not feature the recurring elements outlined above.[4]

Loricae originate from early medieval Ireland. They are recorded in both prose and poetry, in Old Irish and in Latin. Early Irish *loricae* include the *Lorica of St Patrick*,[5] the prayer ascribed to Columcille,[6] and the hymn beginning *Dia lem fri cech snīom*.[7] Hiberno-Latin *loricae* are the prose *Lorica of St Brendan*[8] and the verse *Lorica of Laidcenn*, which is the subject of the present essay. This genre of text soon reached Britain, where it was developed both in Latin and in the vernacular.[9] *Lorica*-like texts are recorded in medieval Wales, where they were presumably carried by Irish intermediaries. The Latin *Leiden Lorica* – which, in spite of its debatable status as a *lorica*, shares part of its vocabulary with the *Lorica of Laidcenn* – has probable Welsh connections and is preserved in a Welsh manuscript.[10] The Welsh word *llurig*, a direct borrowing from Latin *lorica*,[11] was employed in a number of texts, but only a handful of them show the features that are typical of this genre of prayers.[12] Louis Gougaud makes particular mention of two Welsh *loricae*:[13] the so-called *Lorica of Alexander* found in the *Llyfr Taliesin* (Book of Taliesin),[14] and the poem *Kyntaw geir* from the *Llyfr du Caerfyrddin* (Black Book of Carmarthen).[15]

---

sity of Zaragoza, 30 Sept.–1st Oct. 2005, ed. Richard L. Gordon and Francisco Marco Simón (Leiden: Brill, 2009), pp. 629–48 (pp. 630–33).

3 On which see Jennifer Reid, 'The Lorica of Laidcenn: The Biblical Connections', *Journal of Medieval Latin* 12 (2002): 141–53.

4 Lambert, 'Celtic Loricae', pp. 630–31.

5 Edition in Whitley Stokes and John Strachan, eds, *Thesaurus Palaeohibernicus: A Collection of Old-Irish Glosses, Scholia, Prose, and Verse: Vol. 2* (Cambridge: Cambridge University Press, 1903), pp. 354–58.

6 Edition in Kuno Meyer, 'Mitteilungen aus irischen Handschriften', *Zeitschrift für Celtische Philologie* 6 (1908): 257–72 (258); an English translation is in Lambert, 'Celtic Loricae', pp. 646–47.

7 Edition in Andrew O'Kelleher, 'A Hymn of Invocation', *Ériu* 4 (1910): 235–40.

8 Edition in Patrick F. Moran, ed., *Acta Sancti Brendani* (Dublin: Bernard Kelly, 1872), pp. 27–44.

9 The dissemination of the *loricae* stretches beyond the British Isles. For example, see Gearóid S. Mac Eoin, 'Some Icelandic Loricae', *Studia Hibernica* 3 (1963): 143–54.

10 Leiden, Bibliotheek der Rijksuniversiteit, MS Voss. Q.2. See further Michael Herren, ed., *The Hisperica Famina II. Related Poems* (Toronto: Pontifical Institute of Mediaeval Studies, 1987), pp. 2, 47.

11 On multilingualism in medieval Wales, see Helen Fulton, 'Negotiating Welshness: Multilingualism in Wales before and after 1066', in *Conceptualizing Multilingualism in England, c. 800–c. 1250*, ed. Elizabeth M. Tyler (Turnhout: Brepols, 2012), pp. 145–70 (esp. p. 165).

12 Lambert, 'Celtic Loricae', p. 645.

13 Gougaud, 'Étude sur les loricae celtiques', p. 273.

14 On this poem cf. Oliver Davies, *Celtic Christianity in Early Medieval Wales* (Cardiff: University of Wales Press, 1996), pp. 81–82.

15 On the *Black Book of Carmarthen* and the *Book of Taliesin* in the context of early

In *Kyntaw geir*, a worshipper invokes protection for their pilgrimage.[16] The same theme is developed in the Old English *Journey Charm*, a metrical incantation where a traveller seeks protection from a series of dangers,[17] with a listing pattern that, in turn, can be fruitfully compared to that found in the Irish hymn *Dia lem fri cech snīom*.[18] Apart from the *Journey Charm*, several Old English incantations feature passages, often in Latin, which clearly resemble a *lorica*.[19] The influence of this genre of text on early English literature has been investigated by scholars, who have put forward arguments for an influx of poetic invocations to the Trinity,[20] as well as for corporeal descriptions in 'Soul and Body' literature.[21] Above all, the circulation of *loricae* in medieval England is witnessed by the tradition of the *Lorica of Laidcenn*, which is rooted in earlier centuries of English literacy.

The Lorica of Laidcenn

A Latin *carmen* comprised of 24 stanzas of hendecasyllables, the *Lorica of Laidcenn* is a specimen of the distinctive Hiberno-Latin language found in works such as *Hisperica Famina*,[22] and the *Altus Prosator* hymn.[23] In the *Lorica* a request of divine

---

Welsh literature see Helen Fulton, 'Britons and Saxons: The Earliest Writing in Welsh', in *The Cambridge History of Welsh Literature*, ed. Geraint Evans and Helen Fulton (Cambridge: Cambridge University Press, 2019), pp. 26–51.

16 See Davies, *Celtic Christianity*, pp. 42–45.

17 See, especially, Marion Amies, 'The *Journey Charm*: A Lorica for Life's Journey', *Neophilologus* 67 (1983): 448–62.

18 'In t-Athair in Mac in Naemh-spirat án | in Tréidhe dom dhīon ar nēlaibh na plágh. | Ar díen-bhás ar bed gar bradaibh na mbercc / rom-ain Íosa ard ar in ngalar ndercc' (The Father, the Son, the shining Holy Spirit, the Trinity to shield me against the clouds of plagues. Against swift death, against shock, against the ravages of the plunderers, against the red disease, may high Jesus protect me). O'Kelleher, ed. and trans., 'A Hymn of Invocation', pp. 236–37.

19 See especially Godfrid Storms, *Anglo-Saxon Magic* (The Hague: Martinus Nijhoff, 1948), pp. 222–33, 236–44, 285; Reid, 'The Lorica of Laidcenn', p. 149.

20 Thomas D. Hill, 'Invocation of the Trinity and the Tradition of the Lorica in Old English Poetry', *Speculum* 56 (1981): 259–67.

21 Glenn Davis, 'Corporeal Anxiety in *Soul and Body II*', *Philological Quarterly* 87 (2008): 33–50. On the 'Soul and Body' literature in medieval England see Claudio Cataldi, 'A Literary History of the "Soul and Body" Theme in Medieval England', Unpublished PhD dissertation (University of Bristol, 2018); on the Irish and Welsh tradition, see Helen Fulton, 'Body and Soul: From Doctrine to Debate in Medieval Welsh and Irish Literature', in *Sanctity as Literature in Late Medieval Britain*, ed. Eva Von Contzen and Anke Bernau (Manchester: Manchester University Press, 2015), pp. 96–115.

22 Editions in Francis J. H. Jenkinson, ed., *The Hisperica Famina* (Cambridge: Cambridge University Press, 1908); Michael Herren, ed., *The Hisperica Famina I. The A-Text* (Toronto: Pontifical Institute of Mediaeval Studies, 1974).

23 Edition in John Carey, ed., *King of Mysteries: Early Irish Religious Writings* (Dublin: Four Courts Press, 2000), pp. 29–50. On Hiberno-Latin, see Anthony Harvey, 'The Non-Classical Vocabulary of Celtic-Latin Literature: An Overview', in *Spoken and*

protection against the attacks of the forces of evil is developed in minute detail. The supplicant invokes the Holy Trinity, the angelic orders, the hosts of heaven, and enumerates all body parts from head to toe. The poem was formerly attributed to St Gildas (the author of *De excidio et conquestu Britanniae*) and, as such, was known as the *Lorica of Gildas.* Subsequent scholarship challenged this attribution, and the poem is now ascribed to the Irish monk Laidcenn mac Buith Bannaig, the author of the *Egloga moralium Gregorii in Iob*, who, according to the *Annals of Ulster*, died in 661.[24]

Studies by Michael Herren and Patrick Sims-Williams have investigated the sources of the *Lorica of Laidcenn*, focusing on its rich anatomical vocabulary.[25] Collectively, the text lists more than 120 names of body parts, including rare words, the interpretations of which are still open to debate, plus several other learned words not related to anatomy. Book XI of Isidore's *Etymologiae* has been shown to have made an essential contribution to the vocabulary of the *Lorica*. In fact, the *Etymologiae* can be considered a *terminus post quem* for the composition of the poem.[26] Other closely-related anatomical catalogues are found in the glossaries of the *Hermeneumata pseudo-Dositheana*, part of late antique didactic material used to teach Latin to Greeks and Greek to Latin speakers.[27] Herren has noted that the *Hermeneumata* account for most of the bodily vocabulary found in the carmen.[28] However, unlike the *Etymologiae*, there are no known copies of the *Hermeneumata* preserved in early Medieval Ireland. A number of words are also shared between the *Lorica of Laidcenn* and *Hisperica Famina*;[29] the *Lorica*, in turn, served as a lexical source for the Hisperic poem *Rubisca*, which was also known in medieval England.[30]

The structure of the *Lorica* has been compared to exorcisms, such as the one found in the *Antiphonary of Bangor*: this formula, which also dates from seventh-century Ireland, features a head-to-toe list of parts of the body.[31] Other

Written Language: Relations between Latin and the Vernacular Languages in the Earlier Middle Ages, ed. Mary Garrison, Arpad P. Orbán, and Marco Mostert (Turnhout: Brepols, 2013), pp. 87–100.

24 Michael Herren, 'The Authorship, Date of Composition and Provenance of the So-Called Lorica Gildae', *Ériu* 24 (1973): 35–51. Edition in Herren, ed., *Hisperica Famina II*. The *Annals of Ulster* can be accessed online at *CELT: The Corpus of Electronic Texts*, available at <https://celt.ucc.ie//published/T100001A/index.html> [last accessed 10th November 2022].

25 Herren, 'Authorship, Date of Composition and Provenance', 39–51; Patrick Sims-Williams, 'Thought, Word and Deed: An Irish Triad', *Ériu* 29 (1978): 78–111.

26 Herren, 'Authorship, Date of Composition and Provenance', pp. 39–51.

27 See, for example, the chapter on body parts in the *Hermeneumata Monacensia*, in George Goetz, ed., *Hermeneumata Pseudodositheana* (Leipzig: Teubner, 1892), pp. 174–77.

28 Herren, *Hisperica Famina II*, pp. 39–41.

29 See especially Herren, *Hisperica Famina II*, p. 17.

30 Michael Herren, 'Some Conjectures on the Origins and Tradition of the Hisperic Poem *Rubisca*', *Ériu* 25 (1974): 70–87.

31 Sims-Williams, 'Thought, Word and Deed', pp. 91–93. Edition in Frederick E. Warren, ed., *The Antiphonary of Bangor. An Early Irish Manuscript in the Ambrosian*

formulaic texts, such as excommunications and prayers to the Cross, also include anatomical catalogues *a capite ad calcem*.[32]

The *Lorica of Laidcenn* is recorded in English manuscripts as early as the ninth-century *Book of Cerne* (Cambridge University Library, MS Ll.1.10) and *Book of Nunnaminster* (London, British Library, MS Harley 2965). However, a copy of the text was presumably carried into England more than a century earlier. Sustainable evidence for this date comes from Aldhelm, *De virginitate*: 'loricam fidei inextricabilem cum tuta pelta protecti' (240.11), which seem to quote from *Lorica* 30.[33] Further evidence comes from the Épinal-Erfurt Glossary, which includes a few entries apparently derived from the *Lorica*. The glossarial tradition also includes continuous interlinear glossing in Old Irish, as shown by Dublin, Royal Irish Academy, MS 23 P 16 (*Leabhar Breac*),[34] as well as Old English interlinear glossing, which is found in two of the manuscripts of the English tradition (the *Book of Cerne* and the *Lacnunga*).[35] These glosses presumably go back to a shared tradition of glosses in Latin, which were subsequently translated into the vernacular.[36] In other words, an early stage of glossing to the text was carried out in Latin, with these Latin explanations later turned into Old Irish on the one hand and Old English on the other. Apart from Épinal-Erfurt, words from the *Lorica* entered several Latin–Old English glossaries, with some entries still in need of adequate discussion.

A transcript of the *Lorica of Laidcenn* and its Old English interlinear glosses is provided below from one of its chief witnesses, the *Book of Cerne*, fols 43r–44v.[37]

Library at Milan, Part 2 (London: Harrison and Sons, 1895), pp. 28–29. Sims-Williams even argues that both the *Lorica of Laidcenn* and the exorcism formula in the *Antiphonary of Bangor* stem from a shared tradition of glosses to Book XI of Isidore's *Etymologiae*. See also Marina Smyth, 'Isidorian Texts in Seventh-Century Ireland', in Andrew Fear and Jamie Wood, eds, *Isidore of Seville and his Reception in the Early Middle Ages* (Amsterdam: Amsterdam University Press, 2016), pp. 111–30 (pp. 121–22).

32 On which see Reid, 'The Lorica of Laidcenn', pp. 141–53.

33 Jenkinson, *Hisperica Famina*, p. xxii.

34 The *Leabhar Breac* is the one manuscript representative of an independent Irish textual tradition and also preserves the only version where we find the attribution of the poem to Gildas. Before Herren's critical edition, the glosses were discussed by Whitley Stokes, ed., *Irish Glosses. A Mediaeval Tract on Latin Declension* (Dublin: Irish Archaeological and Celtic Society, 1860), pp. 133–51.

35 Overall, the *Lorica of Laidcenn* is preserved in seven manuscripts dating from the ninth to the sixteenth centuries; see Herren, *Hisperica Famina II*, pp. 3–14.

36 Herren, *Hisperica Famina II*, p. 5.

37 Available digitally at *Cambridge Digital Library* <https://cudl.lib.cam.ac.uk/view/MS-LL-00001-00010/139> [last accessed 11th November 2023]. An earlier edition is in A. B. Kuypers, ed., *The Prayer Book of Aedeluald the Bishop, Commonly Called the Book of Cerne* (Cambridge: Cambridge University Press, 1902), pp. 85–88. Jenkinsom, *Hisperica Famina*, pp. 51–54 prints the Latin text only.

Abbreviations are shown by italics; interlinear additions are put between vertical bars; erasures are put between square brackets. A translation follows the transcript.[38]

***Lorica of Laidcenn*, Latin text**		**Old English interlinear glosses**
Hanc[39] luricam Loding cantauit ter in omne die		
Suffragare trinitati unitas		gemiltsa sio þrynes sio annes
unitatis miserere trinitas		þære annesse gemiltsa
Suffragare quaesso mihi posito		ic bidde me gesecum
maris magni uelut in periculo	4	sæs micles swa swa on frecennesse
Ut non secum trahat me mortalitas		þætte no mid hi*m* getio me wol
huius anni neque mundi uanitas		þyses geares ne middangeardes idelnes
Et hoc idem peto a sublimib*us*		7 ðæt ilce ic bidde fro*m* þa*m* hyhstan
caelestis militiae uiritutib*us*	8	þa*m* hiofoncundan compwerodes mægnum
Ne me linquant lacerandum hostib*us*		þylæs me forlæton to slitenne fiondum
sed defendant iam armis fortib*us*		ac gescylden soþlice wæpnu*m* strangu*m*
Et illi me p*re*cedant in acie		ðæt hio me foregangan on feþan
caelestis exercitus militiae	12	þæs hiofenlican werodes wig þreatas
Cheruphin et seraphin cum milib*us*		wisdomes gefylnes 7 godes lufan onbærnn*es*
Et Mihahel Gabrihel similib*us*		strengeo godes gelicu*m*
Opto thronos uiuentes archangelos		ic wysce þry*m* setles ða lifigendan heh englas
principatus et potestates angelos	16	ealdordomas 7 duguðmihta englas
Ut me denso defendentes agmine		þ*æt* me þy ðiccan gescyldende werode
inimicos ualeam prosternere		fionda ic mæge gefyllan
Tum deinde ceteros agonithetas		syþþan þonan oðere cempan
patriarchas quattuor quater prophetas	20	heahfæderas 7 þa feower siðan fiower
Apostolos nauis Chr*ist*i p*ro*retas		scipes stioran
et martyres omnes peto anthletas d*ei*		ic bidde cempan
Ut me p*er* illos salus sepiat		þ*æt* me þurh hio ym|b|sylle
atq*ue* omne malum a me pereat	24	7 eal yfel fro*m* me gewite

38 On the translation of rare Latin words of the *Lorica of Laidcenn*, see Herren, *Hisperica Famina II*, pp. 76–89, 113–37.

39 Fol. 43r.

Chr*istus*[40] mecum pactum firmum feriat[41]	were trume fæstnie
timor tremor tetras turbas terreat	7 þa sweartan werod abrege
D*eus* inpenetrabili tutela	god mid þy unþurhsciotendlicre gescyldnesse
undiq*ue* me defende potentia	æghwanan gescyld me mid mihte
Mei gibrae pernas omnes libera	mines lich*oman* leower ealne gefria
tuta pelta protegente singula	ðine plæg sceldæ *ge*scyldendum anra *ge*hwylc
Ut n*on* tetrae demones in latera	þ*æt* þa sweartan dioflu on minre sidan
mea librent ut solent iacula	cueccen swa swa *ge*wuniað scytas
Gygram cephalem cum iaris et conas	hnoll heafudponn*an* mid loccu*m* 7 ða egan
patha*m* liganam sennas atq*ue* michinas	on|d|wlitan| tungan toeð 7 ða næs ðyrel
Cladam crassum madianum talias	swioran[42] breost sidan lendana
bathma exugiam atq*ue* binas idumas	ðeeoh midirnan 7 twa honda
Meo ergo cum capillis uertici	minu*m* soþlice
galea salutis esto capiti	
Fronti oculis et cerebro triformi	h|n|eofulan egan 7 brægene þa*m* þryfealdan
rostro labiae faciei timpori	nebbe weolure onsyne ðunnwongan[43]
Mento barbae sup*er*ciliis aurib*us*	cinne bearde oferbruu*m* earum
genis buccis internasso narib*us*	heagospinnu*m* smerum næsgristlan nosu
Pupillis rotis palpebris tautonib*us*	sion eghringu*m* bræwan |ofer|bruu*m*
gingis anile maxillis et faucib*us*	toðreomu*m* oroðe ceacum 7 goman
Dentib*us* lingue ori uuae guttori	hrectungan hræcean
gurgilioni et sublinguae ceruice	ðrotbollan tungeðru*m* swioran
Capitali ceutro cartilagini	heafudponnan swiran gristlan
collo clemens ad esto tutamine	gescyldnesse
Deinde esto lorica[44] tutissima	þonan wes ðu byrne sio gehealdfæste
erga membra erga mea uiscera	ymb lioma mine innoðas

40 Fol. 43v.

41 MS *fereat* altered to *feriat*. On this scribal alteration and those that follow see Willard J. Rusch, 'Philology and the Dynamics of Manuscript Glossing', in Gerard F. Carr, Wayne Harbert, and Lihua Zhang, eds, *Interdigitations: Essays for Irmengard Rauch* (New York: Peter Lang, 1998), pp. 219–29.

42 MS *swiran* altered to *swioran* by a later scribe.

43 MS *ðunnwengan* changed to *ðunnwongan* by a later scribe.

44 MS *lurica* altered to *lorica* by a later scribe.

Ut retrudas a me inuisibiles	þætte þu ascufe fro*m* me ða ungesewenlican
sudes clauos quos figunt odibiles	slegeas næglas ða fæstniað þa hatiendan
Tege ergo de*us* forti lurica[45]	gescyld strongre
humeros cum scapulis et[46] brachia	eaxla mid gescyldrum 7 earma
Tege ulnas cum cubi|ti|s et manib*us*	ða elna mid fæðmu*m*
pugnas palmas digitos cum unguib*us*	fyste hondbryda fingras mid þa*m* næglu*m*
Tege spinam et costas cum artub*us*	ðone hrycg 7 ða rib mid þa*m* lioðu*m*
terga dorsumq*ue* et neruos cum ossib*us*	bæc hrycg 7 sina mid ða*m* banu*m*
Tege cutem sanguinem cum renib*us*	ða hyd lundleogu*m*
cata crinas nates cum femorib*us*	huppbaan ersendu mid þa*m* ðeohgelætu*m*
Tege cambas su[r]ras femoralia	homme speoruliran genitalia
cum genuclis po|p|lites et genua	mid þa*m* cniewu*m* þa hwiorfban 7 þa cniowa
Tege talos cum tibis et calcib*us*	helan sconcu*m* helu*m*
crura pedes plantarum cum ba[s]ib*us*	sconcan fet illa mid þa*m* stæpu*m*
Tege ramos concrescentes decies	telgam emnweaxende
cum mentagris ungues binos quinquies	mid tanum næglas twiga fife
Tege iugulam pectusculum	ðearmgewind briostban
mamillas stomachum et umbilicum	briost magan þone nafelan
Tege uentrem lumbos genitalia	þa wambe 7 þa gecyndlica lima
et album et cordis uitalia	7 hrif 7 þære heortan þa liflican
Tege trifidum iecor et ilia	þa þryfealdan lifre 7 rysle
marsem reniculos fithrem cum obligia	bursan lundleogan snedelðearm nettan
Tege toleam toracem cum pulmone	readan feoluferð mid lungenne
uenas fibras fel cum bucliamine	ædran smælðearmas geallan mid þy heorthoman
Tege iunginam cum medul|l|is	þa sceare mid þa*m* meargu*m*
splenem tortuosis cum intestinis	milte gebegdu*m* isernum
Tege uesi|c|cam adipem et pantes	ða blædran gelynd 7 ealle
conpaginum innumeros ordines	þara gefoga ða unarimedan endebyrdnes
Tege pilos atq*ue* membra reliqua	hær 7 þa oðre lima forlæten
quorum forte praeterii nomina	ðara wen is ic beferde
Tege totum me cum quinq*ue* sensib*us*	ongytu*m*
et cum decim fabrefactis forib*us*	smicre geworhtu*m* duru*m*

45 A later scribe tried to change *lurica* to *lorica*.

46 Fol. 44r.

Ut[47] a plantis usq*ue* ad uerticem	þ*æ*tte fro*m* þa*m* ilum oð þæs heafdes heanesse
nullo membro foris intus egrotem	nænegu*m* limo ic geuntrumige
Ne de meo possit uitam trudere	ascufan
pestis febris langor dolor corpore	wolnes fefor ald
Donec iam dante d*eo* seneam	ær þan soðlice
et peccata mea bonis deleam	
Ut de carne iens imis caream	utfarende ic mæge gefliogan
et ad alta euolare ualeam	to ð*am* hean gefliogan ic mæge
Et miserto d*eo* ad aetheria	7 gode miltsiendu*m* to ð*am* roderlican
laetus uehor regni refrigeria	bliðe ic sio wegen rices celnessa
amen	sy swa

(O unity in Trinity, assist me; o Trinity in unity, have pity on me. I ask you to assist me, being in danger as in a wide sea, so that neither the mortality of this year nor the vanity of the world may take me away with them; and I ask the same to the high virtues of the heavenly army (8), so that they do not leave me torn apart by enemies, but defend me now with strong weapons; and may they precede me in battle-array, the host of the heavenly troops: Cherubim with Seraphim and thousands; Gabriel and Michael and the like; I beseech Thrones and the living Archangels, Principalities, Powers and Angels (16), so that I may have the strength to strike down the enemies with this dense defensive army. Then I ask all the other champions of faith, patriarchs, the four-times-four prophets, apostles – helmsmen of Christ's vessel – and all the martyrs, athletes, to enclose me within health by their intercession and that all evils disappear from me (24). May Christ strike a firm covenant with me; may fright and fear affright the foul multitudes. O God, defend me everywhere through your unyielding protection and power. With your light-shield that protects every single member, deliver all the limbs of me, a mortal, so that the dark demons do not throw their darts into my side, as they are used to (32); deliver my skull, head with hair and cones of the eyes, opening of the mouth, tongue, teeth and nostrils, neck, breast, flank, loins, hollow in the joints, wrinkles of fat, and pair of hands. Together with the hair on the top, be a helmet of well-being to my head, forehead, eyes, and triform brain; to my snout, lip, face, temple (40); to my chin, beard, eyebrows, ears, cheek-bones and cheeks, septum, nostrils; to my pupils, irises, eyelids and the like; to my gums, breath, jaw-bone and jaws; to my teeth, tongue, mouth, uvula, throat, gullet, epiglottis, cervix. Be a merciful means of protection to the centre of head, gristle, neck (48). Then be a most secure breastplate for my limbs and for my innards, in order to push back from me the invisible nails of the stakes driven by the hateful ones. O God, then protect my shoulders, along with shoulder-blades and arms, by means of your strong breast-

47 Fol. 44v.

plate; protect my elbows, along with cups of the hand and hands, fists, palms, fingers with their nails (56); protect my spine and ribs with joints, bottom, back, sinews with their bones; protect my skin, blood with kidneys, hipbones, nates with thighs; protect my legs, calves, femurs, hams with knees and knee-joints; protect my ankles with shin-bones and heels, shanks, feet with their soles (64); protect my ten branches that grow together, along with toe-tips and twice-five nails; protect my breast, collar bone, small breast, nipples, stomach and navel; protect my belly, loins, genitals, abdomen and the vital parts of the heart; protect the three-cleft liver and groin, pouch, little kidneys, intestine with its fold (72); protect my tonsil, chest with lung, veins, entrails, gall-bladder with bile; protect my flesh, loins with marrow, spleen and the winding intestines; protect my bladder, fat, and all the innumerable sorts of connections; protect my hair and all the remaining members whose names I may have passed by (80); protect all of me with the five senses and with the ten forged orifices, so that, from the soles of my feet to the top of my head, may I not be ill in any member of my body; nor may plague, fever, weakness, pain drive life away from my body, until I grow old, God willing, and I erase my sins by means of good deeds (88), so that, when I leave my flesh, I may avoid the depths and be able to fly to the heights and, by the mercy of God, I may be borne, joyful, to the ethereal relief of His kingdom. Amen.)

Rusch has recently discussed the Old English glosses to the *Lorica* in the *Book of Cerne*, noting that they are in two hands. The first one is a Mercian hand that interpreted several rare anatomical terms, as well as – rather obscurely – some common words. The second hand, somewhat later, wrote in West Saxon dialect and aimed at a continuous interlinear glossing by completing and correcting the earlier glosses. This later hand is also responsible for the changes in the Latin text.[48]

Methodology

In the pages that follow, a group of glossarial entries supposedly influenced by the *Lorica* will be compared to the text and the glosses transcribed above from the *Book of Cerne*. These glossarial entries have been identified adopting these criteria:

'*Lorica* words' are those entries that are likely to derive directly from the tradition of vernacular glossing to the Latin *carmen*. These are rare Latin terms, mostly related to the anatomical vocabulary, which carry vernacular *interpretamenta* that parallel the interlinear glosses in the *Book of Cerne* quoted above, as well as in the *Lacnunga*. In most cases, the glossarial entries are in the nominative case rather than in the oblique forms found in the poem.

48 Rusch, 'Philology and the Dynamics of Manuscript Glossing'. The essay also offers a discussion of the *Lacnunga* glosses. For an edition of the *Lorica* text in the *Lacnunga* and further analysis of its interlinear glosses see Edward Pettit, ed., *Anglo-Saxon Remedies, Charms, and Prayers from British Library MS Harley 585*, 2 vols (Lewiston, NY: Edwin Mellen Press, 2001), I, pp. 41–57; II, pp. 82–93.

Another class of words is comprised of entries that are found in the *Lorica* but may have reached the Latin–Old English glossaries only indirectly – for example, through glosses to Aldhelm or to Isidore's *Etymologiae* (which is, in turn, a source of the *Lorica*) or by means of other Hiberno-Latin works such as the *Hisperica Famina* or the *Rubisca*.

A last class of words is comprised of clusters of entries that, taken individually, do not represent rare or uncommon words, but that may collectively indicate a batch derived from the *Lorica*.

The Épinal-Erfurt and Corpus Glossaries

The Épinal-Erfurt Glossary is a key witness to the date of the earliest archetype of the *Lorica of Laidcenn* with Old English glosses, which is supposed to be latter half of the seventh century, 'probably [...] the last quarter'.[49] Épinal-Erfurt is, in fact, the earliest representative of Latin–Old English glossaries that include words supposedly derived from the *Lorica*; given its influence on subsequent Latin–Old English glossaries, it is also of key importance for the present discussion. The relevant batch of glosses in Épinal-Erfurt is a small one and, according to Herren, includes the five entries that follow: 456 'Gurgulio: throtbolla / ðrotbolla';[50] 702 'Oligia: nectae / nettae'; 970 'Slens / Splenis : milti'; 1027 'Torax : felofearth / felufrech' and 1077 'Uessica : bledrae'.[51] Of these glosses, *splenis* 'spleen' and *uessica* 'bladder' cannot be ultimately traced back to the *Lorica*, being widely recorded in anatomical lists and carrying glosses that do not point towards a specific tradition.[52] Herren ascribes *uessica* to the influence of the *Lorica* on the basis of its peculiar spelling with double *-s*, which is found in some versions of the *carmen* (but not in the *Book of Cerne*).[53] *Gurgulio* (windpipe) is also in the *Etymologiae* XI.i.58 and in Aldhelm: therefore, it cannot be considered to be unique to the *Lorica*.[54] On the other hand, a likely *Lorica* entry is Épinal-Erfurt 1027 'Torax :

49 Herren, *Hisperica Famina II*, p. 12.

50 Regardless of the edition they are quoted from, all glosses cited in this study will be edited as follows: *lemmata* are capitalised; *interpretamenta* begin with a small letter; *lemmata* and *interpretamenta* are separated by a colon.

51 All glosses from Épinal-Erfurt are quoted from J. D. Pheifer, ed., *Old English Glosses in the Épinal-Erfurt Glossary* (Oxford: Oxford University Press, 1974). Glosses from the Corpus Glossary are quoted from Wallace M. Lindsay, ed., *The Corpus Glossary* (Cambridge: Cambridge University Press, 1921).

52 Recorded in Isidore, *Etymologiae* XI.i.127 and XI.i. 137, respectively.

53 Cf. Herren, *Hisperica Famina II*, p. 137.

54 The word is recorded in several glossaries discussed in this essay: Second Cleopatra Glossary 197 'Gurgilio : þrotbolla'; Brussels Glossary 133 'Gurgulium : ðrotbolla'; Antwerp–London Class Glossary 1815 'Gurgulio : þrotbolla'. All glosses from the Cleopatra and the Brussels Glossaries are quoted from Philip Guthrie Rusche, 'The Cleopatra Glossaries: An Edition with Commentary on the Glosses and their Sources', Unpublished PhD dissertation (Yale University, 1996). Glosses from the Antwerp–London class glossary are quoted from David W. Porter, ed.,

felofearth / felufrech'. Apart from the *Lorica* 73, the lemma is also recorded in the *Etymologiae* XI.i.73; additionally, the Épinal-Erfurt interpretamentum is clearly related to the tradition of the interlinear glosses represented by *feoluferð* (*Book of Cerne*). The Old English word is of uncertain origin. It is mainly recorded in glossaries, where it explains *centipellio,* which indicates the second (or third) stomach of ruminating animals.[55]

One of the most distinctive '*Lorica* words' is *oligia*. The lemma supposedly derives from Greek *ὠλίγγη*, 'wrinkles beside the eyes, crow's feet'.[56] In the *Lorica* 72 the Latinised forms *oligia* and *obligia* (both recorded in manuscripts) presumably indicates a wrinkle of skin ('oligia');[57] the interlinear gloss *nettan* interprets the lemma as the caul.[58] The entry is also in the Corpus Glossary O147 'Oligia . nettae'. It is worth reminding ourselves that the Corpus Glossary represents a sort of 'third text' of Épinal-Erfurt; as such, it is likely that the gloss for *o(b)ligia* goes back to their common archetype. The same applies to Corpus G180 'Gurgulio : ðrotbolla', S472 'Splenis : milte' and U95 'Vesica : bledre' – provided that these lemmata are directly drawn from the *Lorica*, which, as stated above, I remain sceptical about. Two further entries shared by Épinal-Erfurt and Corpus parallel the *Lorica*: Corpus A374 'Agonitheta : princeps illius artis' and T34 'Tautones : palpebrae'.[59] The word *agonitheta* 'champion' is also in Aldhelm's *De virginitate*, which may be the source behind Corpus and Épinal-Erfurt. As regards the all-Latin entry 'Tautones : palpebrae', *tauto* is another typical '*Lorica* word', which presumably goes back – as Herren notes – to a misinterpretation of Greek *τὸ αὐτό*, 'the same, the like', which likely followed an entry indicating eyelids in some unknown Latin–Greek glossary.[60] Along with *agonitheta*, the presence of a Latin *interpretamentum* in fact points

The Antwerp–London Glossaries. The Latin and Latin–Old English Vocabularies from Antwerp, Museum Plantin-Moretus 16.2 – London, British Library Add. 32246. Volume 1: Texts and Indexes (Toronto: Pontifical Institute of Mediaeval Studies, 2011).

55 S. v. 'centipellio', in *Dictionary of Medieval Latin from British Sources (DMLBS)* <https://logeion.uchicago.edu/> [last accessed 10th November 2022]; s.v. 'felaferþ' in *Dictionary of Old English* (University of Toronto, 2018) <www.doe.utoronto.ca/pages/index.html> [last accessed 10th November 2022]; Pheifer, *Old English Glosses in the Épinal-Erfurt Glossary*, p. 129.

56 S. v. 'ὠλίγγη' (definition 3), in *Liddell, Scott, Jones Ancient Greek Lexicon* <https://logeion.uchicago.edu/> [last accessed 10th November 2022].

57 S. v. 'oligia', in *DMLBS* <https://logeion.uchicago.edu/> [last accessed 10th November 2022].

58 Cf. Pheifer, *Old English Glosses in the Épinal-Erfurt Glossary*, p. 106; Herren, *Hisperica Famina II*, pp. 134–35.

59 Cf. Épinal-Erfurt 'Ago[...]theta : princeps illius artis' and 'Tautone palpebrae', quoted from George Goetz, ed., *Placidus Liber glossarum. Glossaria reliqua* (Leipzig: Teubner, 1894), pp. 338.16, 398.31. The entry 'Tautones palpebre' is in the monolingual alphabetical glossary *Affatim*, quoted from George Goetz, ed., *Glossae codicum Vaticani 3321 Sangallensis 912 Leidensis 67F* (Leipzig: Teubner, 1889), 572.30. Cf. Herren, *Hisperica Famina II*, p. 126.

60 See Herren, *Hisperica Famina II*, p. 126; s.v. 'tauto', in *DMLBS* <https://logeion.

towards a tradition that differs from that of the *Book of Cerne* and the *Lacnunga*; the word *tauto* is also found in the *Rubisca*, v. 45, which may well be the ultimate source of these glossarial entries.[61]

Corpus, in turn, preserves three further likely *Lorica* entries not found in Épinal-Erfurt: C250 'Catagrinas : bleremina meest', E543 'Exugia : gescincio', and G96 'Gibra : mare'. Meritt is probably right in interpreting *bleremina* as arising from a misinterpretation of *catacrinas* (supposedly 'hip-bone') with **cata crinis*, 'without hair', which would have yielded the gloss *blere* 'bald'.[62] Similarly problematic is the vernacular entry *gescincio*,[63] while the form *exugia* for Latin *axungia* 'fat' is typical of the *Lorica*: Aldhelm has *axungia*[64] and Corpus A961 the doublet 'Axungia : rysel', also found in Épinal-Erfurt 2. *Gibra*, a Hisperism for 'body', is also attested to by the *Hisperica Famina* and is not therefore exclusive to the *Lorica*.[65]

Taken collectively, the entries in Épinal-Erfurt and Corpus constitute the core on which most *Lorica* glosses in subsequent glossaries are built, as is shown in particular by the First Cleopatra Glossary.

The First Cleopatra Glossary

London, British Library, MS Cotton Cleopatra A.iii preserves three glossaries collectively known as Cleopatra Glossaries. Cleopatra I is a rather long alphabetical Latin–Old English glossary stretching from the letter A to P and compiled from a variety of sources, especially from Isidore's *Etymologiae*, Aldhelm's *De virginitate*, as well as Corpus and Épinal-Erfurt. Additionally, two further sources of Cleopatra I are, in fact, variant versions of the two other glossaries preserved in the same manuscript.[66] Cleopatra II is a class glossary; Cleopatra III features *glossae collectae*

uchicago.edu/> [last accessed 10th November 2022].

61 Nevertheless, Antwerp–London 1780 'Tauto : hringban þæs eagan' (on which see below) and Brussels Glossary 96 'Tautones : bruwa' indicate that the tradition represented by the vernacular glosses to the *Lorica* also entered other Latin–Old English glossaries.

62 See Herbert Dean Meritt, *Some of the Hardest Glosses in Old English* (Stanford, CA: Stanford University Press, 1968), pp. 51–52. According to Meritt's interpretation, *mina* refers to *caelatura*, an entry that follows *catagrinas* in Corpus; *mina* would have been wrongly attached to *blere*.

63 Meritt, *Some of the Hardest Glosses in Old English*, p. 39.

64 s.v. 'axungia', in *DMLBS* <https://logeion.uchicago.edu/> [last accessed 10th November 2022].

65 Herren, *Hisperica Famina II*, p. 117.

66 On the sources of the Cleopatra glossaries see especially Rusche, 'The Cleopatra Glossaries'; Patrizia Lendinara, 'The Glossaries in London, BL, Cotton Cleopatra A.iii', in *Mittelalterliche volkssprachige Glossen. Internationale Fachkonferenz des Zentrums für Mittelalterstudien der Otto-Friedrich-Universität Bamberg, 2. bis 4. August 1999*, ed. Rolf Bergmann, Elvira Glaser, and Claudine Moulin-Fankhänel (Universitätsverlag Winter: Heidelberg, 2001), pp. 189–215; David W. Porter, 'The Antwerp–London Glossaries and the First English School Text', in *Rethinking and*

from *De virginitate*. As noted above, Aldhelm presumably knew the *Lorica*, along with other Hiberno-Latin poems,[67] and several Hisperisms entered his language. In three cases, entries apparently drawn from Aldhelm carry glosses analogous to those in the *Book of Cerne* and in the *Lacnunga*. Cleopatra I A66 'Agonizans : campiende' parallels *Lorica* 19 *agonithetas*, which is glossed by the interlinear explanation *cempan*. As stated above, *agonithetas* is also recorded in Corpus and Épinal-Erfurt. Cleopatra I A240 'A triplici cerebre : from þæm ðriefealdan brægene' is drawn from Cleopatra III 467 'Cerebre : þriefealdan brægene', which in turn glosses Aldhelm's prose *De virginitate* xxxii *triplicis summitate cerebri* (272.6–7). This entry is evidently related to the *cerebro triformi* 'threefold brain' of *Lorica* 39 but it might have reached Cleopatra only indirectly, through Aldhelm. Similarly, F342 'Fibras: þearmas' parallels the *Lorica*, but the Latin headword *fibra* 'bowels' is also in Aldhelm's *Aenigmata*, LVI, and in the *Carmina ecclesiastica*, V.7.[68]

The same process – that of '*Lorica* words' entering Cleopatra I via another source – involves the entries that are most likely drawn from Épinal-Erfurt and Corpus: Cleopatra I C713 'Catacrinis : hupban'; E89 'Exugia : gihsinga ł micgern'; O68 'Oligia : nette'. The entry C713 is of particular interest because, in Cleopatra I, it is part of an alphabetical sequence on body parts: C703 'Capitale : heafodpanne'; C704 'Cacumen capitalis : heannes þære heafodpannan'; C705 'Cerebrum : seam þære heafodpannan'; C706 'Ceruellum : brægen'; C707 'Coma : feax. sceacga'; C708 'Cesaries : þæs wonges locfæx'; C709 'Cartilago : se reoma þæs braegenes'; C710 'Chautrum : al se þrotbolla'; C711 'Cuba : elnboga'; C712 'Cubitus : se earm betweonan elnbogan 7 handwyrste'; and C713 'Catacrinis : hupban'. Taken individually, *cerebrum* and *cartilago* should not be considered here. However, this cluster includes words that are related to anatomy and that strongly indicate derivation from Hisperic poems, if not from the *Lorica* itself, which features the words *capitali* (v. 47), *cerebro* (v. 39), *cartilagini* (v. 47), *cubitis* (v. 55), and *cata crinas* (v. 60). Furthermore, *chautrum* is presumably a corruption of *centrum*, *Lorica* 47 *centro* (also recorded as *ceutro*, as in the *Book of Cerne*); the word is related to *capitali* in *capitali centro*, with the latter word that was subsequently often interpreted as a separate entry by glossators.[69] Glosses C711 and C712 are also remarkable. Manuscripts of the *Lorica* attest both *cubis* and *cubitis*, with the latter being later in the tradition than *cuba*, which is presumably the archetypal reading; this is proven by the reading of the

Recontextualizing Glosses. New Perspectives in the Study of Late Anglo-Saxon Glossography, ed. Patrizia Lendinara, Loredana Lazzari, and Claudia Di Sciacca (Porto: Fédération Internationale des Instituts d'Études Médiévales, 2011), pp. 153–77.

67 A gloss to the passage from *De virginitate* quoted above entered Cleopatra I; P 'Pelta : plegscylde' is referred to *tuta pelta protecti*; see Meritt, *Some of the Hardest Glosses in Old English*, p. 92.

68 s.v. 'fibra', in *DMLBS*<https://logeion.uchicago.edu/> [last accessed 10th November 2022]; Rusche, 'The Cleopatra Glossaries', p. 295.

69 Herren, *Hisperica Famina II*, p. 128.

Book of Cerne, which features *cub|it|is* with *it* as an interlinear addition.[70] It seems that the compiler of Cleopatra I recorded both variants and employed two discrete *interpretamenta* to explain them. It is significant that these entries are followed by C714 'Centumpellis : feleferd': as discussed above, the vernacular gloss came to be associated with *thorax* in the tradition of interlinear glosses to the *Lorica* and in Épinal-Erfurt (as well as in Cleopatra II 697 'Torax : feolufor').[71] The presence of anatomical batches built upon the *Lorica* has been posited by Herren as regards the Harley Glossary (on which see below).[72] Cleopatra I provides sustainable evidence of the existence of such batches.[73]

The Antwerp–London Class Glossary

That entries from the *Lorica* are found in the Antwerp–London class glossary is not surprising, given that it features by far the most extended chapter on body parts of all Latin–Old English class glossaries. Yet, to my knowledge, the contribution of the *Lorica* to the Antwerp–London class glossary has never been properly investigated. A collection of bilingual lexicographic material, Antwerp–London features a rich glossary arranged by subject, the bulk of which includes entries derived from Isidore. This core has been presumably expanded by means of several other sources, which have yet to be fully unravelled. The *Lorica* is doubtlessly one of these sources. Glosses from the poem recorded in Antwerp–London can be divided into two groups: 1. Entries that parallel both a word from the *Lorica* and its corresponding Old English gloss; 2. Entries that combine a word from the *Lorica* with material derived from a different source.

To the first group belong Antwerp–London entries 1780 'Tauto : hringban þæs eagan'; 1817 'Chautrum : eal þrotbolla'; 1824 'Rostrum : Foreweard feng þære lippena togædere'; 1828 'Cuba : elboga'; 1937 'Obligia : nytte'; 1944 'Mentagra . tan'; 1993 'Exugium : micgern'; 2000 'Bucleamen : heorthama'. To the *lemmata* already commented on above, it must be added that *bucleamen* can be safely ascribed to the Hisperic poem (v. 74), where it presumably indicates the eruption of the bile; the Latin word has been – rather obscurely – interpreted as the midriff by the vernacu-

70 Herren, *Hisperica Famina II*, p. 130, underlines the parallel occurrences of *cubis* and *cubitis* in the *Hisperica Famina*, pp. 103, 282.

71 Further entries that may be associated with the *Lorica of Laidcenn* are I352 'Internasus: nosgristle' and B143 'Bassis : stepe'; the latter is, however, also recorded in the *Hisperica Famina*. See Rusche, 'The Cleopatra Glossaries', p. 118.

72 Michael Herren, 'Hiberno-Latin Lexical Sources of Harley 3376, a Latin–Old English Glossary', in *Words, Texts and Manuscripts. Studies in Anglo-Saxon Culture Presented to Helmut Gneuss on the Occasion of his Sixty-Fifth Birthday*, ed. Michael Korhammer, with the assistance of Karl Reichl and Hans Sauer (Cambridge: D. S. Brewer, 1992), pp. 371–79 (pp. 375–76).

73 The possibility that at least part of this sequence is comprised of *Lorica* glosses would shed a new light on Porter's discussion of the C-entries in Cleopatra I; see Porter, 'The Antwerp–London Glossaries and the First English School Text', p. 172.

lar glossators.[74] The relationship between *rostrum* (muzzle) and 'a forward clasp of the lips together' (that is the literal meaning of the gloss) can be explained by the reading of the *Book of Cerne*, which has *rostro labiae* (instead of the juxtaposition of *rostro* and *labio* as two different body parts, as found in other manuscripts), with *labiae* interpreted as a genitive referred to *rostro*.

The second group of entries includes 1789 'Oculus et cona : eage'; 1798 'Internasus . ł interfinium : nosegristle'; 1941 'Fibre . lifrelæppan . ł þearmas'; 1988 'Tolia ł Porunula : reada'; 1992 'Torax ł centumpellis : feloferð'. The combined evidence of the gloss in the *Book of Cerne* 33 and of the additional *interpretamenta oculus* in Antwerp–London leaves little doubt that the entry *cona* in Antwerp–London ultimately derives from the *Lorica*.[75] The same process – that of the combination of different *lemmata* – underlies the entry 1794, where *internasus* (also in Cleopatra I I352 and Cleopatra II 121) is paired with *interfinum*, and entry 1992, where *feloferð* explains both *torax* (as in the tradition of the *Lorica*) and *centumpellis* (as in Cleopatra I). Similarly, the misinterpretation of *tolia* 'tonsils' by *reada* 'intestines'[76] is witnessed to by the *Book of Cerne* and marks this gloss as a sure *Lorica* word. The compiler of Antwerp–London added the obscure lemma *porunula* – perhaps a corruption of Latin *furunculus* 'furuncle' influenced by *porus* 'pore'? Elsewhere, the same combinatory approach involves the *interpretamentum*: the entry 1941 associates the meaning of *fibrae* as 'lobes of the liver', as is found in Épinal-Erfurt 405 'Fibrae librlaeppan', with that of *Lorica* 74. Overall, the *Lorica* batch in Antwerp–London shows a further development in our textual tradition: that is, the adaptation and combination of the earlier tradition of glosses with other material from different sources.

The Harley Glossary

The Harley Glossary is the last and perhaps most elaborate fruit of the tradition of Latin–Old English alphabetical glossaries. Its main witness (London, British Library, MS Harley 3376) stretches from the letter 'A' to 'F'; two further scattered folios preserve entries in 'I'. The Harley Glossary is a mammoth work built from a variety of sources – including earlier bilingual glossaries – some of which must still be adequately unravelled.[77] Among these, Herren has identified and thoroughly discussed a batch of Hiberno-Latin entries, which also include several 'nearly certain'

74 Herren, *Hisperica Famina II*, pp. 135–36.

75 On Hiberno-Latin *conas* see Herren, *Hisperica Famina II*, p. 119.

76 Herren, *Hisperica Famina II*, p. 135.

77 On the sources of the Harley Glossary see especially Jessica Cooke, 'Worcester Books and Scholars, and the Making of the Harley Glossary (British Library MS. Harley 3376)', *Anglia* 115 (1997): 441–68.

'*Lorica* words': *catacrinas, ceutrum, conas, crasum, cuba*,[78] plus *fither*,[79] to which I would now add *bucleamen, exugia* and *internasum*. As in the case of Antwerp–London, one can identify entries that directly parallel the *Lorica* – such as B405 'Bucleamen : heorthama'; C502 Catacrinas : hypban; C866 'Ceutrum : þrotbolla'; C1985 'Conas : oculos'; C2013 'Crasum : dorsum'; F387 'Fither : snædelþearm' – and entries that combine elements from the *Lorica* with other material: B104 'Bathma .i. femora : Þeoh'; C2168 'Cuba .i. ulna : elnboga . uel hondwyrst'; E765 'Exugia i. minctura : micgerne uel spolia'; I169 'Internasum : betuw nasum . uel nasu gristle . uel medietas naris'.[80] To the glosses already discussed in the sections on earlier glossaries, it must be added that the lemma *bathma* supposedly indicates a bone joint:[81] its interpretation *þeoh* 'thigh' is found in both the *Book of Cerne* and the Harley Glossary and points towards a shared tradition. Finally, the gloss *minctura* in entry E765 arises – as Meritt suggests – from confusion between *micgernu* 'fat' and *micge* 'urine'.[82]

It is remarkable that, as shown by Herren, the Harley Glossary also includes an entry that can be traced back to the *Leiden Lorica*: E83 'effaria', which bears no gloss and was presumably drawn from *Leiden Lorica* 15 *effare* 'liver'.[83] Additionally, I would argue that C58 'Calcina : calciamenta' seems related to *Leiden Lorica* 22 *calcina*, which is a *hapax* presumably meant to indicate the heels.[84] In Harley, the glossator has rationalised the lemma by interpreting it as a shoe (*calciamenta*).[85] These occurrences suggest that, from Wales, the *Leiden Lorica* may also have had some circulation in England.

Conclusion: The Old English Period and Beyond

The discussion above shows that a group of words from the *Lorica* – rare words mostly related to body parts – attracted the interest of early medieval English glossators, who included them among several of the major bilingual glossarial compilations of the Old English period.[86] This textual tradition can be roughly

78 Michael Herren, 'Hiberno-Latin Lexical Sources of Harley 3376', pp. 375–76. *Conas* and *crasum* had already been identified by Jenkinson, *Hisperica Famina*, p. xv.

79 Herren, *Hisperica Famina II*, p. 135.

80 Glosses from the Harley Glossary are quoted from Robert T. Oliphant, ed., *The Harley Latin–Old English Glossary, edited from British Museum MS Harley 3376* (The Hague/Paris: Mouton, 1966). The gloss *internasum* is quoted from Luisa Mucciante and Edoardo Scarpanti, eds, *La sezione del glossario Harley 3376 contenuta nei fogli di Oxford e Lawrence* (Alessandria: Edizioni dell'Orso, 2012).

81 Herren, *Hisperica Famina II*, p. 124, who also notes that the lemma is attested in the *Hisperica Famina*.

82 Meritt, *Some of the Hardest Glosses in Old English*, p. 39.

83 Herren, *Hisperica Famina II*, p. 140.

84 Herren, *Hisperica Famina II*, p. 141.

85 S.v. 'calceamentum', in *DMLBS* <https://logeion.uchicago.edu/> [last accessed 10th November 2022].

86 A notable exception is Ælfric's *Glossary*, from which *Lorica* entries are absent. The one possible exception is the gloss 'Catacris : hupeb', added in the version in

summarised as follows. At an early stage, the glosses to the *Lorica* were the object of individual glossarial entries. These entries show a textual relationship with the interlinear glosses to the *Lorica* as they are found in the *Book of Cerne* (as well as in the *Lacnunga*). At a later phase, the *Lorica* glosses were reworked by glossators who combined them with other material. This stage of development is represented by the Antwerp–London class glossary and by the Harley Glossary.

The lexicographic interest in the *Lorica* waned after the end of the Old English period. Isidore's *Etymologiae*, Book XI, kept on being employed as the standard repository of words related to body parts, and new works such as Walter of Bibbesworth's *Tretiz* started to exert a deep influence on anatomical catalogues. However, a notable exception is recorded in a thirteenth-century class glossary in Oxford, Bodleian Library, MS Bodley 730. This glossary (the fourth of the glossarial collection found in the manuscript) includes a catalogue of body parts, based on Ælfric's *Glossary*, that has been enriched by means of batches of glosses derived from Isidore's *Etymologiae* and the *Lorica*. This latter addition seems to go back to the early tradition of glosses represented by the *Book of Cerne* and the *Lacnunga* and does not feature combinations with other material as in Antwerp–London and in the Harley Glossary.[87] As antiquarian as interest in this material might have been, the Fourth Bodley Glossary witnesses to the continuing use of *Lorica* glosses in lists of body parts, a use that endured for over five centuries of English literacy.

Later collections of anatomical words, such as that found in the fifteenth-century *Mayer Nominale*, are virtually free from *Lorica* entries.[88] The same applies to the two so-called 'Metrical Vocabularies' of the fifteenth-century manuscript London, British Library, MS Harley 1002, both of which include sections related to body parts.[89] Remarkably, the parallel tradition of the Old Irish glosses to the *Lorica* was still vital in that period: the only surviving manuscript of the poem with interlinear Old Irish glosses, the *Leabhar Breac*, dates back to the fifteenth century, although the language of the glosses points towards a tradition at least four centuries earlier.[90] The poem kept on being copied until the sixteenth century in continental Europe, with a transmission of codices ultimately descending from the English manuscript tradition.[91]

Oxford, St John's College, MS 154.

87 I have discussed this glossary and the *Lorica* entries in Claudio Cataldi, '*Nomina membrorum* in Oxford, Bodleian Library, MS Bodley 730', *Journal of English and Germanic Philology* 118 (2019): 468–84.

88 See Thomas Wright and Richard P. Wülcker, eds, *Anglo-Saxon and Old English Vocabularies* (London: Trübner & Co, 1884), pp. 673–80.

89 Printed in Wright and Wülcker, *Anglo-Saxon and Old English Vocabularies*, pp. 622–32.

90 Herren, *Hisperica Famina II*, p. 5.

91 Herren, *Hisperica Famina II*, pp. 3–14.

8

A Romance of England and Wales: 'Logres' in *Sir Gawain and the Green Knight*

Victoria Flood

This essay is inspired by Helen Fulton's pathbreaking research into the relationship between Welsh and English literature – an area of work that formed the basis of my own training with her while I was a doctoral student at the universities of Swansea and York.[1] It also builds on a longstanding critical awareness that there are aspects of English romance that we cannot understand without an appreciation of the place of Wales within, and Welsh influences on, medieval English literary production. This is an awareness that, as Helen has noted, has taken many different forms over the past century and a half, from nineteenth-century English imaginings of 'romantic Wales', to more recent scholarship on the linguistic and cultural dimensions of literary contact between the two nations, a project that must necessarily strip away the 'Celtomania' of earlier scholarship to uncover viable hypotheses of influence.[2] Fundamental to this revised field of study is an appreciation of the connectedness, and vibrancy, of English-language literary production in Wales and the

1 For an overview of Helen Fulton's scholarship see the Introduction to this volume and select bibliography. I have in mind, in particular, in this essay Helen's research into the relationship between Welsh and English prophecy, set out in *Welsh Prophecy and English Politics in the Later Middle Ages* (Aberystwyth: Centre for Advanced Welsh and Celtic Studies, 2008); and her recent publication on the representation of Wales in English and French romance, 'Romantic Wales: Imagining Wales in Medieval Insular Romance', in *Cultural Translations in Medieval Romance,* ed. Victoria Flood and Megan G. Leitch (Cambridge: D. S. Brewer, 2022), pp. 21–44.

2 In addition to Fulton, 'Romantic Wales', see Helen Fulton, 'Matthew Arnold and the Canon of Medieval Welsh Literature', *Review of English Studies* NS 63 (2011): 204–24; Patrick Sims-Williams, 'The Visionary Celt: The Construction of an Ethnic Preconception', *Cambrian Medieval Celtic Studies* 11 (1986): 71–96; Aisling Byrne, *Otherworlds: Fantasy and History in Medieval Literature* (Oxford: Oxford University Press, 2016), pp. 7–10.

March.[3] This context has been applied in recent years to the late fourteenth-century alliterative poem *Sir Gawain and the Green Knight*. It has been a growing suspicion of scholars of the poem that a Welsh or Marcher context for *Sir Gawain and the Green Knight* ought to be considered. This is a particularly germane possibility in light of the uncertainty now cast on the long-accepted Cheshire–Staffordshire border identification of the poem in the *Linguistic Atlas of Late Middle English*, which previously resulted in a critical tendency to situate the poem largely beyond Welsh influence.[4] Simon Meecham-Jones has recently suggested that we might, instead, contextualise the poem within the 'Welsh penumbra': Wales and the Marcher lordships.[5]

This essay does not set out to present the poem indisputably as the work of an author within a Welsh or Marcher context, although I do not discount this possibility. Rather, it explores the discursive affinities of Gawain's journey across England and Wales, in lines 691–701, to a geographical and historical understanding derived from Welsh sources with an active role in contemporary historiographical conceptualisations of the insular past, present, and future in both England and Wales. I suggest that the passage can be situated in relation to one of the most significant medieval authors who was associated with a Welsh or Marcher context, although his influence stretched far beyond this: Geoffrey of Monmouth.[6] In the generations after Geoffrey's legendary history of the British past, *Historia regum Britanniae* (c. 1138), English and Welsh writers (among others) drew on Geoffrey's version of the British past and future, and made use of his engagements with Welsh place and personal names.[7] I propose that

3 For an account of surviving Middle English manuscripts in the National Library of Wales, including significant Middle English material produced in Wales and the March, see William Marx, *The Index of Middle English Prose. Handlist 14: Manuscripts in the National Library of Wales (Llyfrgell Genedlaethol Cymru), Aberystwyth* (Cambridge: D. S. Brewer, 1999). Helen Fulton's work on literary connections in the Welsh March has most recently been pursued in the context of the 'Mapping the March of Wales Project' <https://mappingwelshmarches.ac.uk/about/> [last accessed 7th February 2022]. For a discussion of multilingualism in Marcher manuscripts, see Helen Fulton, 'The Red Book and the White: Gentry Libraries in Medieval Wales', in *Crossing borders in the Insular Middle Ages*, ed. Aisling Byrne and Victoria Flood (Turnhout: Brepols, 2019), pp. 23–45.

4 Ad Putter and Myra Stokes, 'The "Linguistic Atlas" and the Dialect of the "Gawain" Poems', *Journal of English and Germanic Philology* 106.4 (2007): 468–91.

5 Simon Meecham-Jones, 'Code-switching and Contact Influence in Middle English Manuscripts from the Welsh Penumbra – Should we re-interpret the evidence from *Sir Gawain and the Green Knight*?', in *Multilingual Practices in Language History: English and Beyond*, ed. Päivi Pahta, Janne Skaffari, and Laura Wright (Berlin: De Gruyter, 2018), pp. 97–119.

6 For the most recent overview of Geoffrey's work see Joshua Byron Smith and Georgia Henley, ed., *A Companion to Geoffrey of Monmouth* (Leiden: Brill, 2021).

7 For important assessments of the role of Latin historians with Welsh and Marcher connections in transmitting the Matter of Britain in England and France, see Siân Echard, *Arthurian Narrative in the Latin Tradition* (Cambridge: Cambridge University Press, 2001); Joshua Byron Smith, *Walter Map and the Matter of Britain*

Sir Gawain and the Green Knight shares its sense of insular geography and history with English and Welsh Galfridiana, as well as independent Welsh formulations, as components of a live cross-border political discourse that emerged with especial visibility in Wales and the March. I approach these affinities as a single chapter in this very particular cross-border history, alert to the political conditions, and ambiguities, of late-medieval cultural contact and literary reuse.[8]

Sir Gawain and the Green Knight and Wales

In a departure from the Celtic source-hunting of previous generations, scholars have begun again to explore the possibility of Welsh influences on the romance, although the precise date and nature of any putative linguistic debt remains uncertain.[9] Others have argued for the *Gawain*-poet's use of Welsh poetic features, although again these are by no means widely accepted.[10] Yet there is one word in the poem that intersects with a Welsh context, and it appears at precisely the moment where the poet negotiates English, Welsh, and British space: in Gawain's journey from Camelot to Hautdesert. We here encounter the word 'Logres', a French form of the Welsh 'Lloegyr' (England):[11]

Now rides this renk thurgh the ryalme of Logres –
Ser Gawan on Godes halve, thagh him no game thoghte:
Oft ledeless alone he lenges on nightes,

(Philadelphia, PA: University of Pennsylvania Press, 2017); Patrick Sims-Williams, 'Did Itinerant Breton "Conteurs" Transmit the *Matière de Bretagne*?', *Romania* 116 (1998): 72–111.

8 There are, of course, other very productive avenues for the multilingual and postcolonial contextualisation of the romance, not least its possible affinities to Arabic traditions and English imaginings of the eastern origins of the Trojan diaspora. Su Fang Ng and Kenneth Hodges, 'Saint George, Islam, and Regional Audiences in *Sir Gawain and the Green Knight*', *Studies in the Age of Chaucer* 32 (2010): 257–94.

9 Meecham-Jones, 'Code-Switching and Contact Influence in Middle English Manuscripts from the Welsh Penumbra', pp. 111–16.

10 Ordelle G. Hill, *Looking Westward: Poetry, Landscape, and Politics in Sir Gawain and the Green Knight* (Newark, NJ: University of Delaware Press, 2009), 22–24. Hill notes some affinities in versification, a relationship between *gair cyrch* of the Welsh *englyn* and the bob and wheel of *Sir Gawain and the Green Knight,* although the most immediate influence on the poet in this respect would appear to be drawn from Latin song or other English poems to utilise the schema. Hill also notes thematic correspondences, including interests in nature and hunting in common with Welsh poetry, although these remain inconclusive. Hill's thesis rests primarily on the identification of the Marcher lord, Henry Grosmont (d. 1361), as the patron of the romance. However, Grosmont does not appear to have had any particular interest in Wales or his Welsh lands and spent most of his time in the context of the French and English courts.

11 This is noted by J. R. R. Tolkien as a Welsh loan word, although he does not comment on its likely French mediation. J. R. R. Tolkien and E. V. Gordon, eds, *Sir Gawain and the Green Knight* (Oxford: Oxford University Press, 1967), p. 98.

There he fonde not him before the fare that he liked;
Had he no fere bot his fole by frithes and downes,
Ne no gome bot God by gate with to carpe,
Til that he neghed ful negh into the north Wales.
And the isles of Anglesay on lyft half he holdes,
And fares over the fordes by the forlondes,
Over at the Holy Hed, til he had eft bonke,
Into the wyldrenesse of Wyrale ...

(Now this knight rides through the kingdom of Logres, on a mission from God, he thought it was no game: often without attendants he spent the nights, where he found no fare that he liked; he had no companion but his horse by woods and downs, and no one but God with whom to speak on the way, until he neared North Wales. He kept the Isles of Anglesey on his left, and went over the crossings to the headlands over at the Holy Head until he was on the opposite bank, in the wilderness of the Wirral.)[12] (ll. 691–701)

Scholarly discussion concerning the route taken by Gawain, and its wider cultural significance, has largely turned on where we might locate the *Gawain*-poet's Camelot, from which the hero sets out, and so whether we might understand 'Logres' as a reference to England or to Britain. For many scholars engaged with the cultural relationship between the two countries, the relationship the poem traces between England and Wales has hinged on the identification of Gawain's journey as from England *into* Wales, and the interactions that follow this in the poem have been approached as a mirror to Anglo-Welsh encounters of the later Middle Ages.[13] While some tantalising theoretical possibilities have been explored in postcolonial readings of this type – not least Patricia Clare Ingham's recognition of colonised Wales and the March as a site of supernaturalised slippage between English and Welsh identities, the 'magic by which the stranger becomes familiar' – these arguments are marked by an interest in the Welshness of Bertilak and Hautdesert as distinct from the Englishness of Gawain.[14] Rather than looking for a reflection of cross-cultural personal relationships within the text, I suggest that we might instead explore the poem's postcolonial context through the political geographies of its English and Welsh source traditions and analogues. These present a space of analysis that allows us to appreciate the hybridity and multiplicity of cross-border cul-

12 Quotations from the poem are taken from Ad Putter and Myra Stokes, eds, *The Works of the Gawain Poet* (London: Penguin, 2014). Modern English translations are my own.

13 Patricia Clare Ingham, *Sovereign Fantasies: Arthurian Romance and the Making of Britain* (Philadelphia, PA: University of Pennsylvania Press, 2001), pp. 107–36; Rhonda Knight, 'All Dressed Up with Someplace to Go: Regional Identity in *Sir Gawain and the Green Knight*', *Studies in the Age of Chaucer* 25 (2003): 259–82; Lynn Arner, 'The Ends of Enchantment: Colonialism and *Sir Gawain and the Green Knight*', *Texas Studies in Literature and Language* 48.2 (2006): 79–101.

14 Ingham, *Sovereign Fantasies*, p. 108.

tural formations between medieval England and Wales, alert to the ways in which Galfridiana disrupt modern categorisations of national literatures. In my approach, I draw on Helen Fulton's recent modification to the postcolonial study of English and Welsh cultural interactions. Helen warns against the assumption of:

> a monologic process by which Wales is dismissed as a nowhere place far from courtly civilisation, whose only function is to provide the setting for an Arthurian origin myth that can be appropriated for England. We can recover some agency and a voice for Wales by recognising that the process of romanticising Wales through literary texts was dialogic rather than monologic – that is, the Welsh and the Normans talked to each other through written (and oral) stories.[15]

This is a welcome reminder of the active role of Welsh cultural constructions and source content (both mediated and direct) in English literary traditions and perspectives, a recognition that avoids simplistic cultural identifications and is alert to the possibility of cross-linguistic and cross-cultural influence.

The most plausible reading to me (as suggested in the critical notes of Putter and Stokes' edition) locates Gawain's starting point in South Wales, potentially Caerleon, the location of Arthur's court in Geoffrey's *Historia.*[16] Gawain's movement across 'Logres' would therefore refer to a journey from South to North Wales, then across the Dee estuary, and from there to Cheshire and the Wirral.[17] This was a familiar itinerary. We find it in Gerald of Wales's route from Caerleon to North Wales in the *Itinerarium Cambriae* (c. 1191), along the settlements of the Welsh coast.[18] In more closely contemporary terms, a similar journey was undertaken by Richard II upon his ill-fated return from Ireland to Chester in 1399.[19] As Joshua Byron Smith has noted, we might understand Gawain's sense of geography as navigated via the English towns of North Wales in the century following Edward I's conquest (1282–83), sites of companionship and succour.[20] Yet for all these familiar and contemporary spatial markers, the relative emptiness of Gawain's Welsh journey is distinctly 'romantic'. As Helen Fulton notes, 'this is a deliberately romantic view of north Wales as an empty and challenging wilderness, but it would

15 Fulton, 'Romantic Wales', p. 24.

16 Putter and Stokes, *Works of the Gawain-Poet*, p. 658.

17 For discussion of possible sites of crossing potentially intended by the *Gawain*-poet see Ralph V. Elliott, 'Landscape and Geography', in *A Companion to the Gawain-Poet*, ed. Derek Brewer and Jonathan Gibson (Cambridge: D. S. Brewer, 1997), pp. 105–18 (p. 115). Elliott suggests Aldford, south of Chester, or a crossing close to Holywell, where St Winifrede lost her head.

18 Putter and Stokes, *Works of the Gawain-Poet*, p. 658; Fulton, 'Romantic Wales', p. 41.

19 Michael J. Bennett, *Community, Class and Careerism: Cheshire and Lancashire Society in the Age of Sir Gawain and the Green Knight* (Cambridge: Cambridge University Press, 1983), pp. 233–35; Michael J. Bennett, 'The Historical Background', in *A Companion to the Gawain-Poet*, pp. 71–90 (pp. 83–90).

20 Joshua Byron Smith, '"Til þat he neȝed ful neghe into þe Norþe Walez": Gawain's Postcolonial Turn', *Chaucer Review* 51.3 (2016): 295–309.

also clearly signify an imaginary description to anyone who knew the area', occluding the townships along the North Wales coast.[21] The social and cultural reality of this journey finds an articulation near-contemporary with the *Gawain*-poet in John Trevisa's (d. 1402) Middle English translation of the Cheshire monk Ranulf Higden's (d. 1364) description of Wales in his *Polychronicon*. Higden notes that Welsh rusticity is remedied by life in, and in proximity to, the English towns, which foster a cultivation both agricultural and intellectual. To quote Trevisa's translation:

> Oft gyled was this brood,
> And ȝerned batail al for wood,
> For Merlyns prophecie,
> And ofte for sortelegie.
> Best in maneres of Bretouns,
> For companye of Saxouns,
> Beeþ i-torned to beter riȝt;
> þat is knowe as clere as liȝt.
> Thei tilieþ gardyns, feeld, and downes,
> And draweþ hem to gode townes[22]

> (This brood were often deceived and yearned madly for battle, on account of Merlin's prophecies, and often for prognostication. The Britons' manners are best in the company of the English, where they are bettered; that is as clear as day. They tend gardens, fields, and downs and draw themselves to good [English] towns.)

This allusion might be understood as a recognition of sites of conquest as sites of plantation, a familiar feature of medieval English attitudes towards Wales and Ireland, regarding the pre-conquest agrarian contexts of these nations (primarily livestock farming) as unadvanced, elevated by the practices of the incoming English.[23] This growing cultivation is juxtaposed with a prophetic interest understood to be synonymous with Welsh pastness, defined in relation to a set of recognisable historiographical signifiers including, first and foremost, Merlinian prophecy, understood as a type of violent nostalgia. The warlike Welsh (the 'Bretouns') are driven by their belief in the words of Merlin. This allusion is presumably both to the prophecies of Welsh restitution in Book VII of Geoffrey's *Historia*, the *Prophetiae Merlini* (by which English authors knew a modified version of the Welsh prophetic tradition), and in-

21 Fulton, 'Romantic Wales', p. 41.

22 Charles Babington, ed. *Polychronicon Ranulphi Higden, Monachi Cestrensis; together with English translations of John Trevisa and of an Unknown Writer of the Fifteenth Century*, 8 vols (London: Longman, 1865-86), I, p. 411.

23 For discussion of the expansion of cereal cultivation in 'newly colonised parts of Europe', in both the west and the east of the continent, perceived by medieval writers as 'bringing productive labour and arable technology to an idle people and an uncultivated land', see Robert Bartlett, *The Making of Europe: Conquest, Colonisation and Cultural Change 950–1350* (London: Penguin, 1993), pp. 152–56. With thanks to Ad Putter for suggesting to me the association of Welsh cultivation with the medieval plantation.

dependent Welsh prophecies apparently in oral circulation, such as those noted in Higden and Trevisa's source texts, Gerald of Wales's *Itinerarium* and *Descriptio*. It is a compulsion associated with a broader set of prognostic practices classed as 'sortelegie' (presumably, the reading of prodigious events, weather conditions, animal behaviours etc. rather than prophetic formulae), superstitions of which the Welsh are cured through their engagements with the English towns.

The association of the Welsh, and Welsh and Marcher landscapes, with prophecy and prodigy is a familiar feature of English historical and geographical writing from as early as the twelfth century.[24] Gerald, for example, writes of the Dee, and its apparently elusive fords, as the subject of a local legend:

> Item, ut asserunt accolae, aqua ista singulis mensibus vada permutat; et utri finium, Angliae scilicet an Kambriae, alveo relicto magis incubuerit, gentem illam eo in anno succumbere, et alteram prevalere, certissimum prognosticum habent.
>
> (Also, those who live beside it assert that its streams change every month; and by whichever country, England or Wales, the channel passes more, that people will succumb, or prevail, they prognosticate most certainly.)[25]

Yet this is not necessarily, as we find in Higden and Trevisa, an account of baseless Welsh superstition. The prognostications appear to be regarded by Gerald as accurate ('certissimum'), and the communities with which Gerald is concerned may be just as easily English as Welsh, if not indeed both, situated on either side of the Dee. Although he is most consistently engaged with Welsh prophecy, Gerald's record of prophetic and prognostic practices is not confined to the Welsh but rather is regional. For example, in his *Itinerarium* Gerald notes the use of goat bones to divine the future by Flemish settlers in Pembrokeshire, apparently an imported practice.[26] As, in the final instance, Higden and Trevisa imply of the Welsh inhabitants of the English towns in Wales, cross-cultural influences can complicate cultural distinctions. Gerald's account of the prophecies of the Dee might be read as an English perception not simply of Welsh behaviours but also an English appreciation of the

24 This appears to be distinct from the association of Wales with magic, in particular weather magic, which is a distinctively late English act of 'romanticism' (to use Helen Fulton's term, see above n. 1). A good example of this is the various English chronicle treatments of the demonic magic of Owain Glyn Dŵr (a likely distortion of the associations of the Welsh *mab darogan*). Cf. 'John Hardyng's Chronicle', trans. Michael Livingston, in *Owain Glyn Dŵr: A Casebook*, ed. Michael Livingston and John K. Bollard (Liverpool: Liverpool University Press, 2013), pp. 206–11, 391 (p. 208). For discussion of English misinterpretations of Owain see Helen Fulton, 'Owain Glyn Dŵr and the Uses of Prophecy', *Studia Celtica* 39 (2005): 105–21.

25 Giraldus Cambrensis, *Opera*, 8 vols, ed. J. S. Brewer, James F. Dimock, and George F. Warner (London: Longman, Green, Longman, & Roberts, 1868), VI, p. 139. My translation.

26 *Opera*, VI, p. 87.

border between England and Wales as a site of prodigy and prophecy. This is the world through which Gawain travels.

'Logres' and the *Brut* Tradition

In our understanding of this type of localised supernaturalism, nomenclature matters – and the *Gawain*-poet invokes an explicitly legendary placename for his region of wonders: 'Logres', a term apparently appropriate to writing about movement between Wales and England. In this specific usage, the poet is clearly indebted to French Arthurian romance. 'Logres', used to encompass all Britain, is a space of marvels in the *Prose Lancelot*, a text that other details of the poem suggest was known to the *Gawain*-poet (we might note, for example, his reference to 'Morgue the Goddes' in line 2452, an allusion shared with the *Prose Lancelot*, although it appears in the Arthurian writings of Gerald also).[27] This fits with the chronological context that Putter has proposed for *Sir Gawain and the Green Knight*, located in the years of peace between Arthur's conquest of Britain and Mordred's usurpation, the time of the adventures of Wace's *Brut* (c. 1155) from which French Arthurian romance takes its inspiration.[28] In its French context 'Logres' is not obviously anchored in a clear or distinct geographical understanding, and it might simply refer to a space of antique marvels. As Putter observes, when compared with the journeying knights of French Arthurian romance, Gawain's experience (however 'easily mappable' it might appear to be) remains 'symbolic [...] geographical precision does not transform the nature of the wild forest. For Gawain the lands remain "contrayez straunge" (l. 713)'.[29] The genre conventions of French Arthuriana are clearly in place. Yet, it remains that the *Gawain*-poet does not use 'Logres' only in the sense of his French source. It is not a space of pure literary invention, marked only by monsters and the hero's isolation (although we do see these); it is also defined by familiar places and itineraries, however these are romanced.

I suggest that there are certain historiographical conventions through which this contemporary perception of place, and its self-conscious archaisms, were filtered, including nomenclature derived from Geoffrey's *Historia*. In relation to this, we might note Geoffrey's use of 'Loegria' for England, the source of the

27 For discussion of this source relationship, see Michael W. Twomey, 'Morgain le Fée in *Sir Gawain and the Green Knight*: From Troy to Camelot', in *Text and Intertext in Medieval Arthurian Literature*, ed. N. J. Lacy (London: Routledge, 1996), pp. 91–116 (pp. 96–98). For notice of the phrase as common to Gerald of Wales's account of Arthur's journey to Avalon and the *Prose Lancelot*, see Tolkien, *Sir Gawain and the Green Knight*, p. 129.

28 Ad Putter, 'Finding Time for Romance: Medieval Arthurian Literary History', *Medium Ævum* 63.1 (1994): 1–16 (6).

29 Ad Putter, *Sir Gawain and the Green Knight and French Arthurian Romance* (Oxford: Oxford University Press, 1997), p. 14.

French 'Logres' (Arthurian Britain). While 'Loegria' and 'Logres' represent two distinct discursive contexts (romance on one hand, history on the other) and have two distinct referents (England and Britain), the literary codes of romance and history meet in *Sir Gawain and the Green Knight*, as do the cultural resonances of 'Loegria' and 'Logres'. The *Gawain*-poet's Galfridian interests are stated clearly in the poem's opening, which is generally understood to be generically aligned with those romances (including the *Alliterative Morte* and the *Destruction of Troy*) that John Finlayson has termed 'chronicle' romances.[30] More specifically, the *Gawain*-poet invokes the first books of Geoffrey's *Historia*. The poem begins with the fall of Troy and the journey of the eponymous Brutus to Britain, which becomes a space of marvels not only in the sense of the *merveille* of French Arthurian romance (supernatural antagonists, magic, great feats of daring) but of cross-generational political upheaval:

> And when this Bretayn was bigged by this burn riche,
> Bolde bredden thereinne baret that lofden,
> In mony turned tyme tene that wroghten.
> Mo ferlyes on this folde haf fallen here ofte
> Then in any other that I wot syn that ilk tyme.

> (And when Britain was founded by this noble man [Brutus], many bold men were born therein who loved battle, who made trouble as the years went round. More marvels in this land have befallen more often than in any other that I know, since that same time.) (ll. 20–24)

With this framing context in mind, 'Logres' might be positioned in relation to Geoffrey of Monmouth's 'Loegria'. In Book II of the *Historia*, 'Loegria' is identified as the central part of the island, east of the River Severn, which takes its name from Brutus's eldest son, Locrinus. Locrinus is a high king under whom his brothers, Kamber (who rules the territory to the west of the Severn, and from whose name Geoffrey derives Cambria, Wales) and Albanactus (who rules the northern part of the island, from whose name comes Albion, Scotland), govern their territories. Brutus's sons face multiple challenges upon his death, from the Huns, and, finally, Corineus, the eponymous founder of Cornwall, and his daughter Guendoloena. Guendolena is the spurned wife of Locrinus, and after his death she murders his lovechild, Habren (the Welsh name for the River Severn), and scatters her ashes in the river between England and Wales, from which event the Welsh take the river's name.[31] Geoffrey writes that this naming secures Habren's immortality, but we

30 John Finlayson, 'The Expectations of Romance in *Sir Gawain and the Green Knight*', *Genre* 12 (1979): 1–24 (4–5). For a useful account of the generic difficulties of Middle English romance, and a laudably flexible solution, see Yin Liu, 'Middle English Romance as Prototype Genre', *Chaucer Review* 40.4 (2006): 335–53; and for recent work on the generic hybridity of Middle English romance see the essays collected in Flood and Leitch, *Cultural Translation in Medieval Romance.*

31 Geoffrey of Monmouth, *History of the Kings of Britain*, ed. Michael D. Reeve and

might note also that the violent death of his daughter is associated with the very limit that marks the boundary of Locrinus's immediate rule, between Wales and England. The *Gawain*-poet's understanding of insular history would appear to be fundamentally aligned with this: a sequence of bloody narratives written onto the insular landscape.

The legend of Locrinus was live political material during the later Middle Ages. Edward I made use of the precedent of the eldest son of Brutus, alongside Arthur, in his claim to rule over Scotland in his papal letter of 1301, an ambition that followed the conquest of Wales.[32] These very conditions, however, appear to have led to the elision of 'Loegria' in the English *Brut* tradition. In the Middle English *Brut*, Brutus's first son 'Lotryn' (from the Latin 'Locrinus'), rules, as does his father, over Britain, a territory distinct from two additional territories subsequently conquered by Brutus in the west and north, Wales and Scotland, and gifted to his two younger sons, 'Camber' and 'Albanak', from whom these locations derive their Latin names:

> And whan Brut had sowte all þe lond in lengthe & brede, he fonde a land þat ioyned to Brytaigne in þe north; and þat land Brut ȝaf to Albanac his sone, and he lete calle yt Albanye after his name, þat now is called Scotland. And Brut fonde anothir Cuntre toward þe west; & þat he ȝaf to Cambre his other sone, & he lete calle yt Cambre aftyr his name, & now is called Walys. And whan Brut had regnyd xx ȝeer, as byfore is sayd, he dyde in þe Cytee of newe Troy, & þere his Sones hym entered with mychil honowr. And Lotryn, Brutes sone, was Crowned kyng with myche solempnyte of all þe land of Brytaigne.[33]

The history is engaged with the origins of Wales and Scotland but not England, which is understood, both implicitly and explicitly, as Britain. This is a familiar feature of representations of Britain in a number of world and European maps, including Gerald of Wales's early thirteenth-century map of Europe, which occludes the identification 'Anglia' and names both the island and England 'Britannia', with 'Scotia' and 'Wallia' noted on its margins (whether a statement of English *imperium* or a reassertion of British antiquity, I would hesitate to say; in Gerald's case it may well have been both!).[34] The legend of Brutus's sons was used by Welsh political figures in the later Middle Ages as well as English. In his early fifteenth-century letter to Robert III of Scotland, seeking support for his opposition to the English crown, Owain Glyn Dŵr drew on the common kinship and Saxon oppression of the children of Kamber and Albanactus, noting also their brother Locrinus as a British king

---

trans. Neil Wright (Woodbridge: Boydell Press, 2007), I. ll. 1–64.

32 R. R. Davies, *First English Empire: Power and Identities in the British Isles 1093–1343* (Oxford: Oxford University Press, 2000), pp. 41–42.

33 Friedrich W. D. Brie, *The* Brut *or the Chronicles of England* (London: K. Paul, Trench, Trübner, 1906–08), p. 12.

34 For discussion of the map see Thomas O'Loughlin, 'An Early Thirteenth-Century Map in Dublin: A Window onto the World of Giraldus Cambrensis', *International Journal for the History of Cartography* 51.1 (1999): 24–39.

in no way prefigurative of English overlordship.[35] Allusions to 'Lloegyr' appear in the wider Welsh *Brut* tradition also, which, as we might expect, preserves its identification as a distinct space: as in the *Historia*, the territory east of the River Severn which takes its name from a British high king. In the fifteenth-century London, British Library, MS Cotton Cleopatra B. v version of the *Brut* we read that after the death of Brutus:[36]

> Ac yna y rannwyt yr ynys yn deir ran rwg y tri broder. nyd amgen. nogyd y locrinus canys hynaf oed agauas ohen deuawd gwyr groec y lle pennaf. sef oed hynny lloygyr mal y dycho yteruynev o vor humyr hyt yn hafren. Ac oy henw ef ehun y dodes ar y ran lloygyr.
>
> (And then the island was divided into three parts between the three brothers. That is, to Locrine for he was oldest – he got by ancient custom of the men of Greece the chief place which was Loegria as it bears its bounds from the Humber Sea to the Severn. And from his own name he called his part Loegria.)[37]

'Lloygyr' is the chief place of the island of Britain – it is, and yet is not, recognisable as England, for it is an assertion of an older political–geographical designation that, in time, would become England. It is in this respect a double, or split, referent. The placename appears similarly in the *Brenhinedd y Saesson* (Kings of the English), the sequel to *Brut y Brenhinedd* which survives in three variant versions produced between the late-thirteenth and early-fourteenth centuries.[38] The text in Cotton Cleopatra B.v and Aberystwyth, National Library of Wales, MS 700D (the Black Book of Basingwerk) begins with an account of the decline of the Britons and the rise of the English (Saxons), following the departure of the last British king, Cadwaladr (a paraphrase of the episode with which the *Historia*, and so *Brut y Brenhinedd*, concludes). We read of a time of plague and famine in the age of Cadwaladr, after which:

> y doeth y Saesson a goresgyn Lloegyr o'r mor pwy gilid, a'y chynal a dan pymp brenhin, val y buassei gynt yn oes Hors a Hengist, pan deholassant Gortheyrn Gortheneu o deruynev Lloegyr, ac a'y rannassant yn pymp ran ryngthunt. Ac yna y symvdassant henweu y dinessyd a'r trefi a'r randiroed a'r cantrefoed a'r

35 Helen Fulton, 'Owain Glyndŵr and the Prophetic Tradition', in *Casebook*, pp. 475–88 (p. 478).

36 For an overview of the Welsh *Brut* tradition see Brynley F. Roberts, 'Geoffrey of Monmouth, *Historia Regum Britanniae* and *Brut Y Brenhinedd*', in *The Arthur of the Welsh: The Arthurian Legend in Medieval Welsh Literature*, ed. Rachel Bromwich *et al.* (Cardiff: University of Wales Press, 1995), pp. 97–116.

37 John Jay Parry, ed. and trans., *Brut y brenhinedd: Cotton Cleopatra Version* (Cambridge, MA: Medieval Academy of America, 1937), fol. 11v, trans. p. 23.

38 For an overview of the variant versions, and their manuscripts, see David N. Dumville, ed. *Brenhinoedd y Saeson, 'The Kings of the English', AD 682–954: Texts P, R, S in Parallel* (Aberdeen: Department of History, University of Aberdeen, 2005), pp. vii–x.

> sswidev a'r ardaloed herwyd ev yeith wynt ehvn: London y galwassant Caer Llud; Evirwic nev Jorck y galwassant Caer Effrauc; ac val hynny holl dinessyd Lloegyr a symdvdassant ev henweu, o'r rei yd aruerwyt yr hynny hyt hediw onadunt.
>
> (the Saxons came and conquered *Lloegyr* from one sea to the other, and held it under five kings, as it had been formerly in the time of Hors and Hengist, when they expelled Gwrtheyrn Gwrthenau from the bounds of England, and they divided it into five parts between them. And then they changed the names of the cities and the townships and the *rhandiroedd* and the cantrefs and the *swyddau* and the *ardaloedd* according to their own language: they called Caer Ludd, London; they called Caerefrawg, Evirwic or York; and thus all the cities of England changed their names, which have been used from that day to this.)[39]

This recounts the fragmentation, and subsequent renaming, of British space associated with the coming of the English – a wider change to the understanding and management of space itself enacted on the linguistic level of the forgotten *cantrefi*. The passage draws a legendary scene of loss generations prior to the departure of Cadwaladr: the vilified British king Vortigen's ill-fated alliance with the first Saxon invaders, Horsa and Hengist, who appear in Welsh history, prophecy, and Geoffrey of Monmouth's *Historia* (and *Brut y Brenhinedd* after it), under whom the land was foolishly divided into British and Saxon holdings. The precise geographical referent intended in *Brenhinedd y Saesson* is clearly as in *Brut y Brenhinedd*: the passage is followed by an account of the division of 'Lloegyr' into component kingdoms, from the Severn to 'the Pictish sea'. This might be read in relation to a tradition in common with English insular geographies, reading the Severn and the Firth of the Forth as seas, seemingly a perception of British space shared across linguistic and cultural boundaries.[40] However, this material is also indicative of an interest in the dimensions of British rule conceptualised in more fully pan-insular terms (or rather, near pan-insular, as the imagined extent of British rule at its historical zenith generally does not extend beyond southern Scotland). In the ninth-century *Historia Brittonum*, one of Geoffrey's source texts with a likely correspondence to Welsh vernacular prophetic traditions, we find a very similar geographical imagining.[41] In the prophetic warning issued to Vortigern on the eve of the first Saxon invasion, we

39 Thomas Jones, ed. and trans., *Brenhinedd y Saesson, or The Kings of the Saxons: BM Cotton MS. Cleopatra B v and The Black Book of Basingwerk NLW MS. 7006* (Cardiff: University of Wales Press, 1971), pp. 2–3.

40 We find this in Higden's *Polychronicon,* and in at least one of its accompanying maps, London, British Library, MS Royal 14. C. ix, fols 1v–2r. For a discussion of the prevalence of this interpretation of the rivers see Alan MacColl, 'The Meaning of "Britain" in Medieval and Early Modern England', *Journal of British Studies* 45 (2006): 248–69.

41 For discussion of the possible early Welsh vernacular contexts of the *Omen* see Patrick Sims-Williams, 'Some Functions of Origin Stories in Medieval Wales', in *History and Heroic Tale: A Symposium*, ed. T. Nyberg *et al.* (Odense: Odense University Press, 1985), pp. 91–131 (p. 106).

read of the prodigious warring between two 'vermes' (serpents or worms), representative of the red dragon of the Britons and the white dragon of the Saxons, 'quae occupavit gentes et regiones plurimas in Brittannia, et paene *a mari usque ad mare* tenebunt' (who have seized many peoples and countries in Britain, and will reach almost *from sea to sea*; my italics).[42] If recognisable as a prophetic-legendary formula, the allusion in *Brenhinedd y Saesson* to rule from sea to sea, won and lost, recalls Welsh loss and the possibility of Welsh reconquest, similarly conceived on a (near) pan-insular scale. Indeed, read in the context of *Brut y Brenhinedd*, which precedes *Brenhinedd y Saesson* in both manuscripts, the establishment of the five kingdoms would seem to be an unhappy parallel to the division of Britain between the sons of Brutus. In the Welsh *Brut* tradition 'Lloegyr' refers to the space of English (*Saesson*) rule, but thereby it is necessarily also an allusion to the contraction of British sovereignty, and hostile English incursions upon British space. It is a spatialisation of the age of the English, but it also speaks to what was once British (Welsh). To think of 'Lloegyr' in these contexts is to think in terms of the palimpsest of insular space, encompassing British foundation, Saxon occupation, and more contemporary histories of conquest.

While I am not implying that the *Gawain*-poet was in receipt of a Welsh *Brut* or was necessarily familiar with Welsh prophecy and history beyond Geoffrey's *Historia*, his word choice reads intriguingly in relation to a Welsh context. Both *Brenhinedd y Saesson* and *Sir Gawain and the Green Knight* appear to have been written with a similar Galfridian awareness of a relationship between historical insular geographies and contemporary colonised space, and 'Logres' might as easily speak to memories of British high kingship as to the age of the Saxons. Whether the Welsh context was an active influence or not, use of the placename is certainly indebted to the conflations of English and British space that mark English Galfridiana, and its French reception (a recognised influence on the *Gawain*-poet). After all, the conflation of the two locations (Britain and England) in the *Prose Lancelot*, regardless of its status as an imaginary or non-referential place, is not one that we can understand without recognition of the international reception of Geoffrey's *Historia*, and its relationship to a broader, trans-historical, substitution of referents through which England and Britain came to be coterminous. Insular nomenclature speaks to the history of conquest beyond the territories conquered.

Prophetic Geography

Literary–political tropes derived from the Brutus/Locrinus legend appear in Galfridian historiographic works, including political prophecy, with a particular interest in the relationship between Britain and England, and the border between England and Wales. Like Galfridian historiography, of which it is effectively an extension,

42 John Morris, ed. and trans., *Nennius: British History and the Welsh Annals* (London: Phillimore, 1980), § 42.

English political prophecy, derived from Geoffrey's *Prophetiae,* has its origins in Welsh prophetic models, specifically, of the restoration of British (that is, Welsh) insular rule.[43] This is the type of superstition that we have seen Higden and Trevisa associated with the uncultivated credulity of the Welsh, a long historical rejection of Welsh prophecy by the English that goes back to the twelfth century.[44] Yet even as Welsh prophecy was met with scepticism, in its English Galfridian manifestations it was received as visions of the destinies of English kings, reimagined as British high kings. These texts participated in a wider discourse in which, I suggest, we find a very similar conflation of England with Britain to that in *Sir Gawain and the Green Knight,* similarly deployed in the writing of legendary-geographical itineraries. Political prophecies provide a closely (if not indeed precisely) contemporary model through which we might continue to approach the assumptions that underscore the British geography of Gawain's journey. I do not mean, however, to imply that Gawain's journey is prophetic, although it might be regarded as prefigurative in that its legendary scene points to contemporary conceptualisations of the balance of insular power.

One of the clearest examples of this type of prophecy is the fourteenth-century *Romance and Prophecies of Thomas of Erceldoune,* which forecasts the insular conquests of a hero in the vein of Arthur, called the bastard (the origins of which name remain uncertain). The earliest historical referent of the prophecy appears to have been Richard II, and the prophecy most plausibly belongs to a period of English celebration of the king following his military successes in Scotland in 1385. As in *Sir Gawain and the Green Knight,* the prologue to the romance found in the Lincoln Thornton manuscript positions insular history as an account of bloody marvels 'þe maste meruelle ffor owttyne naye, / That euer was herde by-fore or syene' (ll. 5–6),

43 In addition to Fulton, *Welsh Prophecy and English Politics,* for discussion of the relationship between English and Welsh prophecy see Victoria Flood, *Prophecy, Politics, and Place in Medieval England: From Geoffrey of Monmouth to Thomas of Erceldoune* (Cambridge: D. S. Brewer, 2016), esp. chs 1 and 4. For discussion of the English tradition see further, Lesley A. Coote, *Prophecy and Public Affairs in Later Medieval England* (York: York Medieval Press, 2000), and for the Welsh, Aled Llion Jones, *Darogan: Prophecy, Lament and Absent Heroes in Medieval Welsh Literature* (Cardiff: University of Wales Press, 2013).

44 We find this most notably in English rejections of prophecies of Arthur's return, although, as I have written elsewhere, the precise dimensions of any such belief (if any) in an early Welsh context remain uncertain. See further, Victoria Flood, 'Arthur's Return from Avalon: Geoffrey of Monmouth and the Development of the Legend', *Arthuriana* 25.2 (2015): 87–110. This begins with *Willelmi Malmesbiriensis Monachi Gesta Regum Anglorum atque Historia Novella,* ed. Thomas Duffus Hardy (London: Sumptibus Societatis, 1840), I, p. 51; and finds famous articulations in William of Newburgh, *The History of English Affairs: Book 1,* ed. and trans. P. G. Walsh and M. J. Kennedy (Oxford: Aries and Philips, 1988), pp. 30–31; and across the writings of Gerald of Wales, whose relationship to Welsh prophecy was notably fraught, for a comprehensive discussion of which see Ad Putter, 'Gerald of Wales and the Prophet Merlin', *Anglo-Norman Studies* 31 (2008): 90–103.

an account 'Of doghety dedis þat hase bene done / Of felle feghtyngs & batells sere' (ll. 9–10), although ultimately victorious for those allied with the prophesied hero, the bastard. There are variant versions of the bastard's victory in each surviving witness of the prophecy, and it was a highly adaptable formula (he is sometimes born in the south, beyond England, or emerges from a forest or the west), but I here give the version we find in one of its earliest witnesses, Cambridge, Cambridge University Library, MS Ff. 5. 48 (c. 1475; the material is excised from the very earliest witness of *Thomas of Erceldoune*, the Lincoln Thornton manuscript):

> A bastarde shal cum fro a forest,
> Not in ynglond borne shall he be;
> And he shalle wyne þe gre for þe best,
> Alle men leder of bretan shal he be.
> And with pride to ynglond ride,
> Est and west as [...] layde (ll. 609–14)[45]

The potential ambiguity of this itinerary lies in the uncertain use of 'bretan' and 'ynglond', potentially even as near-synonyms, and indeed both in this period (like 'Logres') might refer to a perception of pan-insular rule. The British hero will ride into England, laying claim to both the eastern and western limits of the island, yet quite what this signifies is uncertain, and is entirely a matter of the perspective of the community within which the prophecy, and its ambiguous geography, is read. He may be a Briton restoring the ancient name of the island; or he may be an English king in exile who returns to conquer the island's constituent nations. Indeed, precisely the point of the imagining is that he might be both, and, from an English perspective, after Geoffrey – however counterintuitive this might feel – what is British might also be English. This Anglo-Welsh indeterminacy is compounded still further by the sequence's recollection of Geoffrey's Brutus, ancestor to the Welsh and predecessor of the English. The bastard's trajectory recalls the insular rule established by Brutus and divested to his sons. Although with the distinctly late medieval addition of a parliament, like Brutus, the bastard declares the island Britain and establishes new laws and customs:

45 James A. H. Murray, ed., *The Romance and Prophecies of Thomas of Erceldoune* (London: Trübner, 1875). The earliest manuscripts of the prophecy can be dated no earlier than 1440, although the internal historical allusions of the text suggest a date of composition in the late fourteenth century. *Thomas of Erceldoune* appears to have seen fairly rapid dissemination across England, although its origins have been located in northern England, on the basis of residual northern English dialect features. One possible Gaelic loan (*spraye* from Gaelic *spréidh*, 'plunder'), and use of the Middle Scots *bese/beys* for second and third person singular present tense of 'to be', may suggest its origin is relatively close to the Scottish border. Ingeborg Nixon, ed., *Thomas of Erceldoune, Part 2: Introduction, Commentary & Glossary* (Copenhagen: University of Copenhagen, 1983), pp. 9–18. While a more fully localised identification is desirable, this is beyond the scope of my current research.

Alle false lawes he [shalle laye doune],
Þat ar begune in þat cuntre;
Truly to wyrke, he shal be boune;
And alle leder of bretans shal he be. (ll. 617–20)[46]

Prophecies of this type very plausibly circulated in a western and Marcher context roughly contemporary with the work of the *Gawain*-poet. The precise circuits of this are difficult to reconstruct. *Erceldoune* prophecy spread relatively rapidly across England, and from the mid-fifteenth century it survives in at least three geographically diffuse English manuscripts; and a single quatrain relating to the bastard's return is preserved in a mid-fifteenth-century manuscript from Wales. In the mid-fifteenth-century Aberystwyth, National Library of Wales, MS Peniarth 50 (a multilingual English, Welsh, and Latin manuscript, probably produced at Neath Abbey, in Glamorgan), we read the account of the bastard's first victory, given as a short, stand-alone prophecy:

A bastar schall come owte of the west
In sowth England borne shall be
He schall wyne the gre for the best
And then thys lande schall Briten be[47]

I have suggested elsewhere that this brief prophecy most likely was associated with Edward IV, given the inclusion of Yorkist content in the manuscript emphasising Edward's status as an English-born king with a Welsh genealogy.[48] This fragment of the prophecy remained in Welsh circulation, and we find it in a sequence of English-language prophecies in an otherwise Welsh-language prophetic collection, in the commonplace book of seventeenth-century Caernarfonshire recusant and physician, Thomas Williems (Aberystwyth, National Library of Wales, MS Peniarth 94). The prophecy's reapplication is facilitated by the ambiguity of the insular borders traced in its political geography; and these reworkings appear to affirm the geographical distinction between Wales and England muddied by the original prophecy, envisaging a united Britain ruled by an English-born Welsh king.

We might orient *Thomas of Erceldoune* – at least in terms of its Welsh and Marcher reception – as part of a complex of late medieval imaginings, which read the border region between England and Wales as a place of politicised marvel, or rather marvellously encoded politics. This is the same tradition to which *Sir Gawain and the Green Knight* belongs, a geographically engaged work which operates in direct correspondence with Galfridian historiography and carries a prophetic resonance that speaks directly to the political present and the long legacy of the English presence in Wales. The *Thomas*-author and the *Gawain*-poet both trace marvellous itineraries that engage with extra-textual spatialisations and must be understood as

46 Cf. *Historia*, II, ll. 504–05.
47 p. 117, my transcription.
48 Flood, *Prophecy, Politics, and Place*, p. 142.

part of the long historical reception of Geoffrey of Monmouth's account of Brutus and the bloody marvels that characterise early insular history. It is through this palimpsest that Gawain travels, which, while it is in part the marvellous terrain of Arthurian romance, is also the tumultuous land once held by Brutus and his sons.

Conclusion

It is sometimes noted as a curious historical vicissitude that, while the twelfth-century Norman colonisation of Wales saw the flourishing of an interest in Welsh history and geography among readers in England (an interest facilitated by writers such as Geoffrey of Monmouth and Gerald of Wales), there is no corresponding movement following the Edwardian conquest until the accession of Henry Tudor.[49] Yet, as Helen Fulton has noted, imaginings of Wales are significant presences within Middle English romance, if only we possess the cultural codes by which to read them.[50] Among these cultural codes we must necessarily include the Galfridian, which shaped the geographical and prophetic habits of thought of chroniclers and poets in England, as they did in Wales. They also, I have suggested, facilitated literary–cultural perceptions of journeys between England and Wales as loci of prophecy and prodigy. This awareness demands a recentring of our understanding of the cultural geography of poems like *Sir Gawain and the Green Knight,* and, indeed, our own historical sense of centre and periphery. To think of Wales and the March in this period is to contemplate the whole island, navigating trans-historical and cross-linguistic meanings.

49 Simon Meecham-Jones, 'Where was Wales? The Erasure of Wales in Medieval English Culture', in *Authority and Subjugation in Writing of Medieval Wales,* ed. Ruth Kennedy and Simon Meecham-Jones (London: Palgrave Macmillan, 2008), pp. 27–55.

50 Fulton, 'Romantic Wales'.

9

Female Spirituality as Spectral Presence in the Medieval Welsh March and its Writings

Liz Herbert McAvoy

In her contribution to the 2008 *Mapping Medieval Chester* project, run by Catherine A. M Clarke, Helen Fulton argued for the medieval city of Chester as subject to different definitions by its Welsh and English occupants, with both sets of people left unaffected by any sense of a 'hard border' lying between the two territories. This, she argued, was in spite of Chester's geographical position on the English side of the River Dee – the official marker of the official Welsh–English 'divide'. As Helen also suggested, both demographics of the post-Edwardian conquest experienced the city in rather different ways, occupying the space accordingly and bearing diverse relationships to it.[1] As she made clear, Chester thus joined forces with the other English towns across Wales and the March to house systematic violence and oppression against the Welsh people, something that evidences itself richly in the Welsh poetry of the period.[2]

Elsewhere in her essay, however, Helen also points out that an area in which both Welsh and English *did* come together was that of pilgrimage to Chester's many religious sites – particularly the Collegiate Church of St John that housed a relic of the Holy Cross.[3] In a number of ways this observation, again based on evidence from the Welsh poetic corpus, chimes loudly with the findings of my own contribution to the same project, in which I focused on the large numbers of female anchorites positioned along the English–Welsh borderlands – and the lack of them within the Welsh territories themselves. The sites of this reclusion, moreover, conglomerated in centres such as Chester, Shrewsbury, and Ludlow, and were attached

1 Helen Fulton, 'The Outside Within: Medieval Chester and North Wales as a Social Space', in *Mapping the Medieval City: Space, Place and Identity in Chester c. 1200–1600*, ed. Catherine A. M. Clarke (Cardiff: University of Wales Press, 2011), pp. 149–68.

2 Fulton, 'Outside Within', p. 155.

3 Fulton, 'Outside Within', p. 157.

to their urban churches or else positioned along those strategic roadways or river bridges that connected them.[4]

This prominence of reclusive holy women in the Marcher region is attested in the locally written thirteenth-century guide for anchoresses, the widely read *Ancrene Wisse,* that was penned initially for such a group, possibly living at Wigmore, on their request sometime before or around 1230.[5] Here, the author impresses upon the holy women the need to look outward as well as inward: that is, they should be cognisant of a sense of wider community as well as of their own individual calling; they should feel united with others like them in their shared purpose to serve God, 'For euch is wiðward oþer in a manere of liflade, as þah ȝe weren an cuuvent of Lundene ant of Oxnefort, of Schreobsburi oðer of Chester' (because each of you is turned towards the other in one way of living, as if you were a single religious community of London and of Oxford, of Shrewsbury or of Chester), he reminds them.[6] For this author, at least, the intensity of female spirituality in the Marcher towns of Shrewsbury and Chester equates easily to that of centres of authoritative female spirituality in the larger urban centres of England, including London and Oxford. Thus, when Helen attests that 'Welsh pilgrims overflow into Chester as a matter of right, undermining English efforts to keep them in their place',[7] I would add that the main centre of their religious piety – the church of St John – had long been associated with anchoritic activity, as well as housing a holy relic.[8] This was

4 Liz Herbert McAvoy, '"Ȝe beoð þe ancren of Englond ... a þah ȝe weren an cuuent of ... Chester": Liminal Spaces and the Anchoritic Life in Medieval Chester', in *Mapping the Medieval City,* pp. 99–113. See also Liz Herbert McAvoy, *Medieval Anchoritisms: Gender, Space and the Solitary Life* (Cambridge: D. S. Brewer, 2011), pp. 147–77.

5 Bella Millett, ed., *Ancrene Wisse: A Corrected Edition of the Text in Cambridge, Corpus Christi College, MS 402 with Variants from Other Manuscripts,* Early English Text Society Original Series 325 (Oxford: Oxford University Press, 2005). The translation is taken from Bella Millett, trans., *Ancrene Wisse, Guide for Anchoresses: A Translation based on Cambridge, Corpus Christi MS 402* (Exeter: University of Exeter Press, 2009). Page numbers are the same in each instance. This text was rapidly rewritten by the same author within five years for a much larger group of anchoresses and was widely adapted and excerpted for a wider lay audience over the next two centuries; for which, see, for example, Catherine Innes-Parker, 'The Legacy of *Ancrene Wisse:* Translations, Adaptations, Influences and Audience with Special Attention to Women Readers', in *A Companion to Ancrene Wisse,* ed. Yoko Wada (Cambridge: D. S. Brewer, 2003), pp. 145–73.

6 *Ancrene Wisse,* pp. 96–97.

7 Fulton, 'Outside Within', p. 158.

8 Legend had it that King Harold of England was enclosed there, having escaped the Battle of Hastings in 1066. Gerald of Wales reports this in his *Itinerarium Cambriae,* for which see Giraldus Cambrensis, *Opera,* 8 vols, ed. J. S. Brewer, James F. Dimock, and George F. Warner (London: Longman, Green, Longman, & Roberts, 1868), VI, p. 140. Other independent sources also attest to a one-eyed anchorite living

also true of many of the other churches of note within the town during the period, as I have attested previously.[9]

The same can be said of Shrewsbury, which enjoyed its own level of intermingling and permeability as a border town, based largely on trade and military activity. Indeed, the long consecutive presence of female anchorites at the Chapel of Saint George near the 'Welsh Bridge' just outside the 'Welsh Gate' of the town, testifies to an important strategic presence of holy women at the margins of the town.[10] These would have been sought out by travellers for spiritual advice and prayers as they embarked upon their way, or as they entered the town, after – or having faced – what would often have been a dangerous and arduous journey.

Both Chester and Shrewsbury, of course, had long both been subject to an intense militarism during repetitive attempts at colonising Wales, first by the Normans and then by the English.[11] As I have previously argued, such violent militarism, allied to an equally intense expression of female spirituality and its practices in the same locations, was not without coincidence. As I concluded about the ubiquitous presence of female anchorites and other types of female spirituality evidenced in these locations during the twelfth to fifteenth centuries: 'they [...] inscribe a permanence and stability in the chimeric shape-shifting of the dangerous borderland soil itself, an act which announces an unmovable spiritual and physical resolve to the world beyond the anchorhold'.[12] In what follows, I wish to develop this thesis, arguing that it is exactly where the violence of male-orchestrated in-fighting and warfare takes place in these Marcher regions that female spirituality, whether home-grown or developed out of more continental influences, is turned to as solace, solution, or salvation. Time and time again, if we look more closely at the implicated families of that borderland violence, as well as at the writings emerging from or associated with that region, we find expression of a female spirituality that draws almost obsessively upon anti-militaristic discourses of nurture, growth, and flourishing, as opposed to violent, 'heroic' retribution. Such discourse, moreover, forms an insistent spectral presence that attempts to alleviate the physical and intellectual landscape of its entrenched obsession with death and oppression.

---

there during the eleventh century, whose uncorrupted body was interred in St Werburgh's Abbey and discovered in 1332. The full legend is recounted in the *Vita Haroldi, quodam Anglorum Regis,* in London, British Library, MS Harley 3776, fols 1–25.

9 McAvoy, *Medieval Anchoritisms*, pp. 166–75.

10 H. Owen and J. B. Blakeway, *History of Shrewsbury*, 2 vols (London: Harding, Lepard and Co., 1825), I, p. 315n; II, p. 475.

11 The most authoritative discussion of this remains R. R. Davies, *Conquest, Coexistence and Change: Wales 1063–1415* (Oxford: Oxford University Press, 1987).

12 McAvoy, *Medieval Anchoritisms*, p. 177.

Female Anchoritism and Marcher Dynasty

In 1310 the strategic Welsh-Bridge anchorhold at Shrewsbury is recorded as occupied by one Emma Sprenghose, who had apparently decided upon the anchoritic life as a small child. Emma was from a prestigious noble Marcher family, which had long occupied the lordship of Longnor, in the hundred of Condover, as well as the lordship of the castles of Montgomery and Oswestry.[13] As such, she stands as a paradigm for the prevalence of a personally-chosen reclusion for Marcher women from some of the leading families during this turbulent period.[14] Perhaps the most elite of such women, however, were the congenital sisters, Lorretta and Annora de Braose, daughters of the powerful Marcher lord, William de Braose (d. 1211), a man who outdid many of his peers in his acts of violence and brutality in the service of King John. Having fallen out with the latter, William's family was subject to prolonged royal cruelty in retribution for what was regarded as the nobleman's disloyalty, culminating in the king's walling-up of William's wife, Maud de St Valery, along with their son and heir (also William) in a cell at Windsor Castle, where they starved to death in 1210.[15]

The de Braose Marcher lands lay in exactly the same location as the production of *Ancrene Wisse*, where, as we have seen, there was a particularly rich proliferation of female anchoritism during the same period. Indeed, this culture of female anchoritism, allied to the region's violence and the particular experience of its excesses to which the de Braose family was particularly accustomed, may well have been the impetus behind the decision of two of the de Braose daughters, Loretta and Annora, to enter the anchoritic life as young women upon their widowhood. Loretta was Countess of Leicester, whose husband, Robert de Beaumont, fourth Earl of Leicester, had died in 1204 without issue. Annora was married to the powerful Hugh de Mortimer, who died in 1227, also without issue. Both women were therefore rendered extremely vulnerable as potential heiress-brides without offspring – but were also left without immediate access to their own finances and estates. In the light of the king's murder of her mother and older brother, Loretta had fled to France with her father and another brother, Giles, but returned to settle her affairs and entered an anchorhold in Hackington, Kent, sometime between 1219 and 1221.[16] Meanwhile, Annora, too, had been imprisoned by the king in Bristol

13 Owen and Blakeway, *History of Shrewsbury*, I, p. 315n.

14 Owen and Blakeway, *History of Shrewsbury*, I, p. 132.

15 For a detailed account of Loretta and her family history, see F. M. Powicke, *The Christian Life in the Middle Ages and Other Essays* (Oxford: Clarendon Press, 1935), pp. 147–68. For a focus on the wider family tradition of anchoritism and its relationship to the Marches and *Ancrene Wisse*, see Catherine Innes-Parker, 'Medieval Widowhood and Textual Guidance: The Corpus Revision of *Ancrene Wisse* and the de Braose Anchoresses', *Florilegium* 28 (2011): 95–124. What follows here is indebted to both Powicke and Innes-Parker.

16 Powicke, *Christian Life*, p. 262.

between 1210 and 1214, subsequently withdrawing to the anchorhold in the village of Iffley, near Oxford, in 1232.[17] As if this was not enough to exorcise the obscene violence embedded within the family history, another sister, Flandrina, became a nun, then abbess, at Godstow Abbey, Oxford, an institution with close links to her mother's family; and another sister, Margaret, would go on to found the Abbey of Acornbury, near Ludlow in her mother's memory in 1218.[18] As Catherine Innes-Parker has pointed out, in the light of the violence wrought upon the family by their father's dealings with his peers and the king, the de Braose offspring turned overtly towards their matrilineal inheritances for their 'patterns of religious participation', adding: 'In the light of William de Braose's abandonment of his family at the time of his exile, the death of his wife and eldest son, and the exile or imprisonment of his other children, the matrilinear bias of his daughters' religious patronage is understandable'.[19] Read within this wider context, it is also unsurprising that at least two extant *Ancrene Wisse* manuscripts carry with them close connections to this family's women.[20] Indeed, Innes-Parker has demonstrated that if *Ancrene Wisse* was not actually written for the de Braose sisters, it certainly was written for a group of anchoresses who were very much like them.[21]

While these experiences of the remarkable de Braose sisters may seem to present an exceptional set of circumstances, a hundred years or so later another Marcher woman of equally high status also withdrew into the local anchorhold – this time at Ledbury – upon her early widowhood: Katharine de Audeley. Katharine's father was the formidable John Giffard (d. 1299), who had received extensive Marcher lands and Welsh territories as reward for his support of the king during the Welsh rebellion of 1264–65 – including leading the force that killed and beheaded Llewelyn in the upper Wye valley in 1282.[22] Katharine's mother, Maude de Longspée, was Giffard's second wife, an exceptionally high-born young widow who was also granddaughter of the Welsh leader Llywelyn ab Iorwerth (d. 1240) and great-granddaughter of King John. In 1271, Maude wrote to the king, accusing Giffard of having abducted her from her home and having imposed marriage (for which, read rape) upon her against her will. The matter was settled when Giffard paid the sum of 300 marks for marrying her without permission from the king, by which time Maude, already pregnant and infirm, was unable to represent herself

17 Powicke, *Christian Life*, p. 265.
18 Innes-Parker, 'Medieval Widowhood', p. 98.
19 Innes-Parker, 'Medieval Widowhood', p. 101.
20 Innes-Parker, 'Medieval Widowhood', p. 97.
21 Innes-Parker, 'Medieval Widowhood', p. 98.
22 Davies, *Conquest*, p. 353. For an account of this episode, see Theophilus Jones, *A History of the County of Brecknock* (London: W and G. North, 1805), p. 137. I have traced in some detail the history of Katharine's progress through two marriages and widowhood into the anchorhold in Liz Herbert McAvoy, 'Uncovering the "Saintly Anchoress": Myths of Medieval Anchoritism and the Reclusion of Katharine de Audeley', *Women's History Review* 22.5 (2013): 801–19.

at court.[23] Katharine was the first of three daughters born to Maude under these circumstances, and the latter died soon afterwards in 1283.

Katharine, as a highly desirable heiress, therefore seemed destined for a similar trajectory. Having married a powerful nephew of her mother's, Nicholas de Audeley, in 1288, she bore three children before her husband died a decade later in 1299. Thus, like Annora and Loretta before her, Katharine was overnight rendered another highly desirable young widow vulnerable to strategic capture in the Marcher region. Unusually, however, Katharine seems to have been allowed to withdraw quietly into domesticity soon after her husband's death, where the records suggest she was waiting for her children to come of age before she took advantage of such room for manoeuvre.[24] Tragedy struck in 1307, however, when she lost her elder son at the age of 19; and, in the same year, her 17-year-old daughter, Ela, was also widowed, two events that initiated frenetic activity on Katharine's part to set her affairs in order and secure Ela's future, as she disposed of her goods to her children and other family members before entering the anchorhold at Ledbury in or around 1213. Thereafter, she surfaces in the records a number of times, primarily petitioning to maintain the subsistence allowance accorded to her from her remaining lands, until her death sometime after 1325.[25] That she became known as a deeply respected holy woman in the region is attested by her entering the realm of legend in the intervening period between her enclosure and the early twentieth century, when poets, musicians, playwrights, and novelists took up her story with some measure of creative licence.[26]

Female Spirituality and the Literature of the March

The particular importance of female spirituality as an underpinning mechanism within the Marcher regions is also testified to in its literary contexts. For example, the anonymous fourteenth-century Anglo-Norman romance, *Fouke le Fitz Waryn*, based on a now lost earlier thirteenth-century verse rendition, recalls the dramatic experiences of the twelfth-century Fitz Waryn dynasty, including how the wealthy widow and heiress, Mathilda de Caus, was sold into a transactional second marriage against her will to the Marcher lord, Fouke le Fitzwaryn.[27] A mixture of verifiable historical

23 *Calendar of the Close Rolls* 1268–72, p. 294; *Calendar of the Patent Rolls* 1266–72, p. 520. For an account of Maude's life, see Gwenyth Richards, *Welsh Noblewomen in the Thirteenth Century* (Lampeter: Edwin Mellen Press), pp. 99–124.

24 *Calendar of the Close Rolls* 1308–13, pp. 199–200.

25 For a summary of these incursions of the world upon Katharine's anchoritism, including episodes of violence leading to murder on her lands, see again McAvoy, 'Uncovering the "Saintly Anchoress"', pp. 811–13.

26 See again McAvoy, 'Uncovering the "Saintly Anchoress"'.

27 The surviving tale is written in Anglo-Norman prose and is extant in one later manuscript only: London, British Library, MS Royal 12.C.XII, dating from about 1330. The original thirteenth-century poem is lost to us. For an account of this history, see Thomas Ohlgren, 'General Introduction', in *Medieval Outlaws: Ten Tales in Modern*

detail and romance mythology celebrating an eventful family history, the text tells of how Fouke became a renowned 'outlaw' after joining the baronial rebellion against King John and how he received a pardon and restoration of his lands.[28] His return to power at his Marcher seat of Whittington Castle is testified to by this marriage to Mathilda as a high-status woman, which was enacted in or before 1207.[29]

In the romance tale, however, Mathilda is married to Fouke when he is still an outlaw and she quickly produces three children, although her three birthing experiences are surrounded by an ignominy and abjection fully suggestive of the excesses to which King John would go to punish the wives and families of those men deemed to have betrayed him. Beneath the drama of the romance conventions, therefore, lie the very real dangers inherent to any family who fell the wrong side of the king in these highly volatile environments. Pregnant with a daughter soon after her marriage, the text recounts how Mathilda was forced to flee to Canterbury to escape the malign attentions of the king, ultimately giving birth to her daughter in a Canterbury church.[30] Such a delivery within danger, exile, and alien circumstances, of course, is subtly allied in the text with the childbirth experience of the Virgin within the discomfort of a lowly stable. Indeed, this biblical correlation is further underlined when, having been rescued from Canterbury by her husband and pregnant again, she is forced to seek shelter in the church of St Mary in Shrewsbury for her second parturition:

> E le roy la fist espier, e ele s'en ala de yleoqe privément a Saloburs, e ileqe fust espié, e ele fust si grosse qe ele de yleqe ne poeit traviler, e s'enfuy a la eglise Nostre Dame, a Saloburs, e ileqe fust delyvre de une file, qe fust baptize Johane, qe pus fust mariee a sire Henri de Penebrugge.[31]

> (The king had her spied upon and she went secretly from there to Shrewsbury. She was spied upon there too and was so heavily pregnant that she could not travel. She fled to the church of Our Lady in Shrewsbury where she was delivered of a daughter, who was baptised Joan and later married to Sir Henry de Pembridge.)[32]

English, ed. Thomas H. Olhgren (Stroud: Sutton, 1998), p. xix. For an edition of the Anglo-Norman text, see *Fouke Le Fitz Waryn*, ed. E. J. Hathaway, Anglo-Norman Text Society (Oxford: Blackwell, 1975). For a modern English translation, see Thomas E. Kelly, trans., 'Fouke Fitz Waryn', in *Medieval Outlaws*, ed. Olhgren, pp. 106–67.

28 Janet Meisel, *Barons of the Welsh Frontier: The Corbet, Pantulf, and Fitz Warin Families 1066–1272* (Lincoln, NE: University of Nebraska Press, 1980), pp. 38–39.

29 *Calendar of the Close Rolls* October 1, 1207. For an account of what we know about the historical Fouke, see Meisel, *Barons*, pp. 38–39.

30 'E ele fuy a moster, e ileqe fust delyvre de une fyle, e l'archevesqe la baptiza Hauwyse, qe pus fust dame de Wemme' (she fled to the church, where she was delivered of a daughter. The archbishop baptized her Hawyse and she later became the Lady of Wem). Hathaway, *Fouke le Fitz Waryn*, p. 38, ll. 35–37; Burgess, *Two Medieval Outlaws*, p. 163.

31 Hathaway, *Fouke le Fitz Waryn*, p. 39.

32 Burgess, *Two Medieval Outlaws*, p. 164.

This Shrewsbury church of St Mary had a long history of female anchoritism and still bears evidence of a cell on the north side of the church (now the vestry) and another in the parvise above the porch to the main entrance on the south.[33] It may well have been that the succour and safety Mathilda received was proffered by one or other of the anchoresses who lived in this church during the period.

In a similar vein, but this time without even the basic home comforts of church or anchorite cell, according to this text, Mathilda's third and last child was again born in exile – in the open air of a Welsh mountainside: 'nee sur un[e] montaigne de Gales, e fust baptizee Johan en une russele qe vyent de la Fontaigne dé Puceles' (born on a mountain in Wales and baptised John, in a stream which comes from the Fountain of Maidens).[34] This allusion, while likely caught up in tales of the *tylwydd teg* of Welsh folklore,[35] and clearly linked to the sacred feminine, also has biblical underpinnings connected to the birth of John the Baptist, his wilderness baptism of Christ and wider prophetic mission. Again, then, Mathilda is also being cast as a biblical figure, this time as Mary's cousin Elizabeth, who produces a special son in anticipation of Christ. As Helen Fulton, drawing on Michel de Certeau, has pointed out about these borderlands and their belief systems: 'the constructed outside inevitably leaves traces of itself on the inside, thus revealing the partial and mythical nature of the boundary itself'. If Wales was considered 'outside' of England and the Marches 'through a hegemonic discourse of borders and exclusion', medieval Wales nevertheless left its traces upon borderlands writings, 'inscribing itself as a type of "presence-in-absence"'.[36] While childbirth on a Welsh mountain, then, may seem like a type of biblical abjection to reflect badly on the 'satanic' acts of the king in this tale, nevertheless, the folkloric 'presence-in-absence' of the Welsh mountainside dissolves the boundaries of borders and nations, as much it does those of class, status, and faith.

A similar incursion of Welsh legend – in this case, sixth-century hagiographic legend – is to be found in another borderlands text, written by a canon at Lilleshall Abbey, Shropshire, in the late fourteenth century. The *Festial*, constituting a collection of sermons embedded with widespread *exempla* and reworked hagiography, was penned by John Mirk for the purposes of educating parish priests and providing them with material to assist in their pastoral care of parishioners.[37] It appears to have been immensely popular, gaining what its editor refers to as 'a prominence unique amongst vernacular sermon collections before the Reformation'.[38] In Mirk's

33 R. W. Eyton, *Antiquities of Shropshire*, 12 vols (London: John Russell Smith, 1854–60), VI, pp. 89–90.

34 Hathaway, *Fouke le Fitz Waryn*, p. 39; Burgess, *Two Medieval Outlaws*, p. 164.

35 The *tylwydd teg* is the term for mythical fairy-like creatures in Welsh folklore.

36 Fulton, 'Outside Within', p. 151.

37 John Mirk, *Festial*, ed. Susan Powell, 2 vols, Early English Text Society Original Series 334 and 335 (Oxford: Oxford University Press, 2009 and 2011). Hereafter *Festial*. Translations are my own.

38 *Festial*, I, p. xix.

own words, as a man of 'febul letture', he was driven to write the *Festial* to help others in the same position to 'teche hore pareschonus' (teach their parishioners) of the church's chief festivals, to increase the knowledge, understanding and faith, not only of the priests but the laity more generally.[39] He claims as his main source the ever-popular *Legenda aurea* (Golden Legend) of Jacobus de Voragine (d. 1298), but 'wyth more adding to' (with additions), meaning that he inserts some of his own material gleaned from elsewhere to embellish the entire work, which he proceeds to name himself: 'I wolle and pray that it be called a *Festial*' (I wish and pray that it be called a *Festial*).[40]

One of the most significant of these additions is an English rendition of the Welsh life of St Gwenfrewy (in English, Winefride), from which, as Powell also suggests, Mirk may have been 'working from memory'.[41] As Jane Cartwright has pointed out, Gwenfrewy was one of the most renowned of Welsh saints, beheaded at Sychnant because of her refusal to accept the sexual advances of the local prince Caradog, but resurrected by the intervention of her brother, Beuno, when he reunites her head to her body. At that moment, the *Life* explains, a holy well appears on the spot of her attempted murder, a site known forever after as Holywell, and sacred to this virgin saint.[42] The fact that Mirk saw fit to include this Welsh virgin-martyr hagiography in his *Festial*, specifically 'not ordeynid to be haly-day bot þeras men han devocion' (not ordained as a holy day but wherever men may show devotion), testifies not only to its local importance in the Marches, but also to the fact that he deems it important enough to have far wider significance ('þeras men han devocion').[43] Indeed, Winefride's inclusion in the thirteenth-century *South English Legendary*, in circulation until at least the fifteenth century, the *Gilte Legende* (1438), and Caxton's 1483 printed edition of the *Golden Legend* would attest to her more widespread popularity as a 'home-grown' virgin saint. In fact, as Richard Turner has comprehensively established, royal interest in a growing cult of Saint Winefride had begun during the reign of Richard II, whose patronage of the holy site of Holywell may have been connected to his establishment of the principality of Cheshire in 1398. In this sense, the saint provided a strong regional equivalent to the cult of the Virgin, which was coming to ascendance at this time. As Turner also argues, the king's beheading of

39 *Festial*, I, p. 3.

40 *Festial*, I, p. 3.

41 *Festial*, I, p. xxiv.

42 Jane Cartwright, *Feminine Sanctity and Spirituality in Medieval Wales* (Cardiff: University of Wales Press, 2008). For an account of the manuscript and other history of Gwenfrewy's *Life*, see p. 72.

43 *Festial*, I, p. 162. The sermon on Saint 'Wenefreda', like the others, is headed by a Latin *incipit* ('De sancta Wenefreda sermo'), for which see *Festial*, ed. Powell, I, pp. 162–67. Cartwright points out that the Welsh version of Gwenfrewy's *buchedd* (saint's life) preserved in Aberystwyth, National Library of Wales, MS Llanstephan 34 closely resembles a Latin *vita* written by a Prior Robert of Shrewsbury. *Feminine Sanctity*, p. 72.

Richard Fitzalan, earl of Arundel, and his later haunting by this episode 'for the rest of his life', may well have found its resonance within the hagiography and served, in part, to ease the sense of guilt by providing a source of devotional penance. In January 1398, the king brought parliament to Shrewsbury Abbey (the site of Winefride's relics and a rare iconographic depiction of her, still extant), later making grants and a pilgrimage to the saint's well at Holywell.[44] As such, he was 'making a public demonstration of his power in the region, tempered by deference to its local saint and her relics'.[45] Here, I would add to Turner's assessment to claim that, once more, we witness a turning towards an intensely realised female spirituality to mitigate the effects of male violence and warfare by bringing to bear upon it not only notions of purity but also elements of a determined non-militaristic devotion that offered a stable hot-line to redemption – a route that the war-mongering royals and noblemen could only dream about and which, at best, they could only access by proxy. As Turner surmises: 'For a man haunted by the spectre of Arundel, whose head and body he feared had miraculously re-joined, Winefride would have been a highly appropriate saint to pray to and from whom to seek forgiveness'.[46]

But royal devotion to Saint Winefride did not stop with Richard: it was also a feature of the pious performances of kings Henry IV and Henry V – but for somewhat different reasons. Indeed, on the eve of the Battle of Shrewsbury, fought by Henry IV and his 15-year-old son (later Henry V) on 20th July 1403 against the forces of Owain Glyndŵr, royal prayers in the Abbey were directed towards Winefride; and, when the young Henry was seriously wounded during the battle, four days later both prayers and an offering of 20 shillings were offered at Winefride's shrine at Holywell.[47] Indeed, Henry IV's foundation of a chapel at the site is also attested to in a later account of the life of Saint Winefride by the East Anglian writer, Osbern Bokenham (d. c. 1464), who includes a brief account of this in his own hagiographic retelling:

> King henry the fourte for the tendyr love
> Wich he had to this virgin pure
> Dede maken a chapel over the welle above
> Myhty and strong for to endure
> On thre partys closing yt in sure

44 Richard Turner's work on the cult of St Winefride and its royal associations examines the material evidence within Shrewsbury Abbey, including a stone carving of St Winefride and St Beuno, her brother, alongside John the Baptist, adding to the association between the local saints and the biblical martyr I have suggested above in the context of the romance of *Fouke le Fitzwaryn*.

45 Richard Turner, 'Sir Gawain and the Cults of the Assumption of the Blessed Virgin Mary and St Winefride in Late Medieval England and Wales', Unpublished PhD dissertation (Swansea University, 2018). For the chapter focusing specifically on Saint Winefride, see pp. 153–93 (p. 192).

46 Turner, 'Sir Gawain', p. 182.

47 Turner, 'Sir Gawain', p. 182.

And that no man presumy should to com ther ny
A gret grate ys sette on the fourte party.

(King Henry the fourth, for the tender love
Which he had to this pure virgin,
Did make a chapel over and above the well,
Mighty and strong to endure
On three sides, safely closing it in,
And, so that no man should come near there presumptuously,
A large grating is set on the fourth site.)[48]

Similarly, in March 1465, Edward IV issued letters patent specifying his own financial support for a chaplain at the chantry established at Holywell by Richard II,[49] verified by another poem dedicated to Gwenfrewi, this time in Welsh by the poet, Tudur Aled (d. c. 1525). Here, Aled writes of Edward's own pilgrimage to Holywell during his reign, when he apparently wreathed moss from Winefride's well into his royal crown: 'Edwart daeth i dir at hon, / a'r gweryd ar i goron' (Edward came to the land of this woman [Winefride], and [placed] the moss on his crown).[50]

Here, we have a mossy image that is highly reminiscent of the type of 'green poetics' common to some of the widely popular writings of earlier continental holy women in England – Mechthild of Hackeborn (d. 1398), in particular, whom I discuss further below – but also summons up resonances with the mysterious and enigmatic, green-decked knight in the late fourteenth- or early fifteenth-century borderlands poem, *Sir Gawain and the Green Knight.* Indeed, Turner has gone some way to setting out a convincing case for the cult of Saint Winefride as major driver of the poem and the author, whoever it was, as a clear devotee.[51]

The Works of the *Gawain*-Poet: *Sir Gawain and the Green Knight* and *Pearl*

Sir Gawain and the Green Knight is one of four poems collected together in a single manuscript witness, written in the borderlands by an anonymous poet, possibly a priest from the local gentry, at the turn of the fifteenth century.[52] Written in alliterative verse (as are all the poems extant from this particular poet), it famously hinges on a supernatural beheading episode, during which the enigmatic, seemingly gigantic, Green Knight incites the more naïve Sir Gawain to behead him with his own green axe during the former's intrusion into the Camelot celebration of

48 James Ryan Gregory, ed. and trans., 'A Welsh Saint in England: Translation, Orality and National Identity in the Cult of St. Gwenfrewy 1138–1512', Unpublished PhD dissertation (University of Georgia, 2012), p. 418, ll. 540–46.

49 Chester Recognizance Roll 4–5, Edward IV, M.8.

50 Tudur Aled, *Gwaith Tudur Aled*, ed. T. Gwynn Jones (Cardiff: University of Wales Press, 1926), p. 526, ll. 97–98.

51 Turner, 'Sir Gawain', p. 153.

52 London, British Library, MS Cotton Nero A.x.

Christmastide. Having duly obliged, the court is horrified to witness the Green Knight's reconjoining of his head to his body before laying down another challenge to Gawain – to meet him at the 'Green Chapel' in a year's time to enact a reciprocal beheading, but this time of Gawain by his supernatural opponent.[53] The resonances here with the equally supernatural 'survived' beheadings of both Winefride and Arundel are hardly subtle. Gawain's later travels that take him to what is almost certainly St Winefride's well, 'Holy Hede' in North Wales (l. 700), not only reinforce this resonance, but also serve to place the poem geographically, politically, and spiritually in this turbulent region.[54]

The strong underpinnings of the St Winefride cult outlined above, however, are not the only elements of female spirituality anchoring the poem to a socio-religious culture that, as we have seen, was in many ways dependent upon female spirituality to provide an element of stability – what Sarah McNamer has identified, moreover, as predicated on a performance of compassion that was gendered as decidedly 'feminine' in England during the later Middle Ages.[55] For McNamer, the rise of affective devotional practices, including those of cults devoted to the Virgin and other female saints, had a 'gendered logic' to them, ultimately rendering female spirituality an exciting new conduit for lay access to God, whatever the sex or gender of the devotee.[56] Indeed, it is just such a 'gendered logic' that characterised the anchoritic and other retreats from male violence made by women of the Marcher regions, discussed above. Time and time again, the spirituality of women appears to have served as a palliative mechanism within male, pugilistic contexts – and this is something that emerges particularly strongly in the literature of this enigmatic and unpredictable region, as also demonstrated above. However, in the case of the two works of the *Gawain*-poet I wish to discuss here (*Sir Gawain* and *Pearl*), not only do these texts manifest strong affinities with such female-coded

53 All quotations from *Sir Gawain and the Green Knight*, as well as from *Pearl*, are taken from Malcolm Andrew and Ronald Waldron, eds, *The Poems of the Pearl Manuscript: Pearl, Cleanness, Patience and the Green Knight* (Exeter: University of Exeter Press, 2007). The translations are my own. For Andrew and Waldron's overview of debates regarding common authorship, see their introduction, p. 26. See also Sarah Stanbury's introduction to *Seeing the* Gawain*-Poet: Description and the Act of Perception* (Philadelphia: University of Pennsylvania Press, 1991), pp. 1–11; Ad Putter, *An Introduction to the Gawain-Poet* (London: Routledge, 1996).

54 Again, see Turner, 'Sir Gawain'; but see also Joshua Byron Smith, '"Til þat he neȝed ful negh into þe Norþe Walez": Gawain's Postcolonial Turn', *The Chaucer Review* 51.3 (2016): 295–309. Here Smith reassesses how the poem's apparent romantic mystification of Wales as 'exotic other' has been subject to misreading. Instead, he argues that Gawain's Welsh journey points towards a more nuanced perspective, in which the English Welsh territories of North Wales are deemed to be safe havens for the knight in an otherwise hostile environment.

55 Sarah McNamer, *Affective Meditation and the Invention of Medieval Compassion* (Philadelphia, PA: University of Pennsylvania Press, 2010), p. 21.

56 McNamer, *Affective Meditation*, p. 7.

spirituality, but, as I shall suggest, they resonate closely with many of the 'green' hermeneutics deployed within the writings of earlier continental holy women. In turn, this points towards another form of turning outwards from this region: that is, towards female-authored writings that had been making their mark in wider continental contexts for over a century and more.

The *Gawain*-poet's familiarity with the writings of the thirteenth-century German visionary, Mechthild of Hackeborn (d. 1298), is a tantalising possibility suggested not only by the new availability of Mechthild's writing in a range of vernaculars throughout Europe during the late fourteenth and early fifteenth centuries, but also by the many internal allusions and resonances of her *Liber Specialis Gratiae* (Book of Special Grace), that everywhere haunt *Sir Gawain* and *Pearl*.[57] Mechthild's *Liber* was written down by some of her sister nuns at the Helfta nunnery at the end of the thirteenth century, and documents her extraordinary visions, direct conversations and union with Christ.[58] Translated into English at some point in the early fifteenth century, the text is shot through with an enigmatic hermeneutics of gardens, flowers, and the greening of the natural world, and soon became a staple text, known, for example, to Dante, Boccaccio, Birgitta of Sweden, the nuns of Syon Abbey, and Margery Kempe, among others.[59] When read alongside *Sir Gawain*, the spectral presence of this visionary work is sometimes startling and unexpected. For example, Mechthild regularly depicts her visionary – and frequently feminised – Christ in terms of a foliage-decked or arboreal 'green' man who, like the Green Knight in the poem, becomes indistinguishable from this foliage, its greenness, and its hermeneutic anti-worldly, anti-masculinist associations.[60] Indeed, on one occasion, Christ appears to Mechthild on the altar in the guise of 'a fayr tree of

57 See Liz Herbert McAvoy, *The Enclosed Garden and the Medieval Religious Imaginary* (Cambridge: D. S. Brewer, 2021), pp. 195–260, for my case in the context of *Pearl*.

58 The Latin *Liber* has been edited alongside the writing of one of its likely scribes, Gertrude of Helfta, in Dom Louis Paquelin, ed., *Revelationes Gertrudiannae ac Mechtildiannae*, 2 vols (Paris: Oudin, 1875–77). It was translated into English early in the fifteenth century as *The Boke of Gostely Grace*, although only two later manuscript versions are extant. For the purposes of this present essay – and because of the text's relevance to the Middle English texts under scrutiny here – I will be quoting from the version in Oxford, Bodleian Library, MS 220. For a new edition of this text see: Anne Mouron and Naoë Kukita Yoshikawa, ed., with the assistance of Mark Atherton, *The Boke of Gostely Grace, Edited from Oxford, MS Bodley 220 with Introduction and Commentary* (Liverpool: Liverpool University Press, 2022). All quotations are taken from this edition. The translations are my own.

59 On this, see Liz Herbert McAvoy, 'Textual Phantoms and Spectral Presences: The Coming to Rest of Mechthild of Hackeborn's Writing in the Late Middle Ages', in *Women's Literary Cultures in the Global Middle Ages: Speaking Internationally*, ed. Liz Herbert McAvoy, Vicki Kay Price, Kathryn Loveridge, and Sue Niebrzydowski (Cambridge: D. S. Brewer, 2023).

60 For a nuanced discussion of the queerness of the tale and its male protagonists, see Carolyn Dinshaw, 'A Kiss is Just a Kiss: Heterosexuality and Its Consolations in *Sir Gawain and the Green Knight*', *Diacritics* 24.2–3 (1994): 205–26.

hyeth and bredyth' (a beautiful tree, high and broad), before morphing into the officiating priest 'cloþed ande arayed with þe leves of þe same tree' (clothed and decked out with the leaves of the same tree).[61] Meanwhile, for the *Gawain*-poet, the Green Knight is 'al grayþed in grene þis gome and his wedes' (bedecked in green, this man and his garments), so that 'alle his vesture uerayly watz clene verdure' (his entire clothing was truly bright greenness) (l. 151 and l. 161). Elsewhere in her text, Mechthild twice presents this green Christ as a 'gyaunt' (giant), who is 'þe waye of oure redempcion and heylth' (the way of our redemption and health): the first in the context of a vision of the heavenly Jerusalem; the second in relation to a vision of the Virgin, for whom Christ was 'as a gyaunte' (as a giant) in her womb, 'joyng and gladyng' (being joyful and happy).[62]

This latter allusion is incorporated into one of the Virgin's speeches to Mechthild regarding the need for humankind to celebrate her Seven Joys, the first of which is her joy at the Incarnation. Similarly, we find that Gawain is also devoted to the 'fyue joez' (five joys) of the Virgin, invested in one of the points of the pentangle painted on the exterior of his shield; indeed, the inner side of his shield bears an image of the Virgin herself. Elsewhere in Mechthild's writing, a shield-bearing Christ in his guise as Christ-the-Knight also appears, but, unlike most such depictions, he, too, is a green knight, decked out with foliage 'in lykenes of grene braunches' (like green branches), and carrying a shield painted with deeply female-coded imagery – the rose and the lily – signifying both Mary and the 'innocence' and 'pacyence' (patience) of his own humanity.[63] In the light of such poetic resonances between the two texts, Gawain's shield provides an ambivalent and slippery signifier in the poem. While a symbol of knightly – and divine – masculinity, drawing on popular representations of Christ-the-Knight, nevertheless, its female-coded imagery dominating the inside of the shield reminds the reader not only of the feminine underpinnings of attempts to ameliorate the violence invested in knightly masculinity, but also the feminine underpinnings of the chivalric code itself.

Indeed, this dilemma of codes is exactly one that will test Gawain to the core in his escapades in Haut Desert with Bertilak (the Green Knight in another guise) and his lady, who famously seduces Gawain, not with her body (although nearly that) but with the supernatural green girdle that will ultimately save his life. Again, Turner has dealt with the episode of the Lady's green girdle in great depth, arguing convincingly for its being a secular reworking of the apocryphal tale of the Virgin's dropping her own life-enabling girdle to Thomas the Apostle from Heaven during the Assumption.[64] Given what I am also arguing here, that such episodes are likely deeply indebted to continental women's visionary accounts, it comes as no surprise that Mechthild's gender-fluid writing should also feature girdles as well as shields.

61 Mechthild, *Boke*, I.xxxi.
62 Mechthild, *Boke*, I.lxxvii, I.lxxxi.
63 Mechthild, *Boke*, I.xxxiii.
64 Turner, 'Sir Gawain', esp. ch. 4.

In *Sir Gawain*, the lady's girdle given to the knight in his moment of weakness, of course, substitutes for the sexual act he ultimately – although barely – eschews. It is a magical talisman that will protect his life, if worn next to his own flesh; but it is also a symbol of that flesh: a female-coded umbilical signifier that reminds him of his own vulnerability and human mortality. Such an umbilicus conjoined the Virgin and Christ, too, something that is not lost on Mechthild in her own use of this image set. For example, early in her text, she describes how the Virgin appears to her on the right side of Christ and, as Mechthild watches, draws a golden girdle from her side, bedecked with cymbals that the angels and saints come forward to touch in turn.[65] A few chapters later, however, the Virgin's girdle appears around Christ's waist. Here his garment is specifically 'gerte above ande tuckyd up with a gyrdyll made of sylke to here siȝt curyouslye wrouȝte with three diverse colours, with rede, grene, and white' (girded around and tucked up with a girdle made of silk, to her sight curiously woven with three different colours). These colours, woven into 'þis gyrdyll of humanyte' (this girdle of humanity) are green, red, and white, signifying Christ's innocence, his passion, and his humanity. Moreover, it is also a symbol, he tells Mechthild, of the joy and happiness he brings as a strong 'geaunte' as he makes his way on the 'harde and grevouse' (hard and burdensome) route towards the redemption of humankind.[66] In typical fashion, in the space of a few chapters, Mechthild is able to combine, and collapse into one another, traditions of divine femininity and divine masculinity, male-coded violence and female-coded flourishing, masculine and feminine modes of salvation and all the discourses pertaining to them, in much the same way as would the *Gawain*-poet a century or so after the production of her book.

Similarly spectral resonances are to be found between the work of Mechthild and the poem, *Pearl*, which documents a dreamer's vision of his recently deceased two-year-old daughter, who appears to him in the heavenly paradise in her guise as a transcendent bride of Christ. The poem subsequently documents how this now-reconfigured female 'child' becomes the spiritual guide of her parent, attempting with care and patience to lead him out of his abject grief on a female-directed journey towards the realisation of divine grace and love. So, too, from the onset of her text, Mechthild generates an equally powerful young-child hermeneutic that she shapes carefully into another important articulation of female-coded flourishing. Like *Pearl*, the *Boke* uses an infant frame-narrative to trace the origins of the nuptial spirituality of their female protagonists, embedding it in the drama of an untimely death – or, in Mechthild's case, a brush with death in the first few hours after birth close enough to effect a very hasty baptism. In both cases, this death, or near-death, is justified in terms of God's desire to forge a paradigm for Christianity out of the goodness of the child: for Mechthild, as a 'halowyd ... temple' (holy temple) for Christ's 'habitacion anon as she come fro her moderes wombe' (habitation as soon

65 Mechthild, *Boke*, I.ii.
66 Mechthild, *Boke*, I.vii.

as she exited her mother's womb); in *Pearl*, as a bride of Christ who is destined to become united with Christ as 'holy Hysse' (entirely His) (l. 418). Similarly, both texts foreground a deep parental reluctance to release a daughter to God, in what is configured as a type of parental shortcoming: in Mechthild's case, her parents' attempts at thwarting her determination as a seven-year-old to become an oblate at Helfta; in *Pearl*, the dreamer's worldly grief clouding his belief in the possibility of his daughter's heavenly elevation.[67]

The use of the child hermeneutic is not limited to this single comparison, however. In Book V of Mechthild's text – a section devoted to her redemptive gifts – she recounts one of her own visionary encounters with the soul of a dead child – also a two-year-old girl – whose mother had pledged to devote her to God as an oblate.[68] This child, however, had died before this could be achieved. Like the maiden in *Pearl*, moreover, the girl appears to Mechthild as an adult woman, announcing her own mature transcendence by means of rose-hued clothing and a mantle of gold embroidered with snow-white lilies. In this manifestation, she clearly anticipates the pearl-maiden, whose garments are similarly 'Blysnande whyte' (gleaming white) (l. 163) and 'glysnande golde' (glistening gold) (l. 165). In both cases, too, the visionary or dreamer is transformed into a non-comprehending child-like figure, with the actual child taking on the role of all-seeing and all-knowing divine adult. Just as Mechthild demands of this holy maiden, 'Howe and for what cause cam all þis joy and blisse to þe?' (How and for what reason were you bestowed all this joy and bliss?), the dreamer demands of the pearl-maiden, 'may þis be trwe?' (may this be true?) (l. 420). In Mechthild's text, too, it is similarly the child's father who disbelieves any possibility of his daughter's transcendence; indeed, we are told that the girl was taken by God prematurely because 'here fader wolde have nullyd her moderis vowe and wold have kepte her still in þe world' (her father would have annulled her mother's vow [of oblation] and would have kept her living in the world).[69] Both texts, therefore, present paternal intransigence as running counter to God's plan for the spiritual flourishing of their daughters, thus necessitating a radical divine intervention.

But the resonances go on. In *Pearl* the maiden's powerful and protracted response to her father's incredulity does not manifest frustration but instead causes her to launch into a lengthy reworking of the biblical Parable of the Vineyard, as recounted in Matthew 20:1–16. Here, the vineyard's owner, although having paid his early workers a penny to toil in the vineyard all day, pays the same amount to those who come to the vineyard to work late in the day – to the great annoyance of those who had arrived early. Such transcendence, the pearl-maiden (herself a

67 Mechthild, *Boke*, I.i.

68 Mechthild, *Boke*, V.vi. Barbara Newman also notes this resonance, pointing out that the episode 'anticipates *Pearl*' in *Mechthild of Hackeborn: The Book of Special Grace* (Mahwah: Paulist Press, 2017), p. 268, n.13.

69 Mechthild, *Boke*, V.vi.

'late-comer') intimates, is her reward just as if she had toiled in Christ's vineyard – Holy Church – during a long lifetime. Indeed, this lively retelling and its lengthy exegesis take up nearly 20 stanzas at the epicentre of the poem before segueing into a retelling of Luke 18: 15–17, in which Christ rebukes his disciples for attempting to send away those children who had been brought to him by their mothers for blessing or healing ('Suffer children to come to me, and forbid them not: for of such is the kingdom of God'). Thus, in *Pearl* the hermeneutics of the child and those of the vineyard collapse into one another, with these parabular juxtapositions serving as an entangled metanarrative and allowing the pearl-maiden to ventriloquise the master narrative in seemingly orthodox fashion. Simultaneously, however, she realigns its components to create an altogether new dialogue that prioritises the sanctity of her own experience as child, transcendent woman, and gardener in the vineyard-of-the-Lord.

Similar strategies are at work in Mechthild's writing, where the sacred vineyard also makes a number of important appearances – and in similar contexts – sometimes comprising a multivalent image for Christ himself or, sometimes, his sacred heart. On one occasion, Mechthild is encouraged by Christ to draw grapes with her mouth from grafted vines emerging from Christ's heart.[70] On another, Christ invites Mechthild into the vineyard of his heart, entered via his wounded side.[71] In yet another significant vision, received in the monastic church during the singing of the *Vinea facta est* (A vineyard is planted), Mechthild sees her own heart transformed into the vineyard of God in which grapes productive of four different types of wine to feed the faithful are growing.[72] Thus, in Mechthild's text we see another realigned vineyard of biblical parable, within which she traces her own paradigmatic labour in the vineyard, again in terms of contemporaneous identities: as infant and holy woman, as gardener and transcendent *sponsa Christi*. As she explains in her exegesis of the reworked parable, the wine flowing from it signifies, 'our lorde delyted hym and moch was plesyd in such a man or woman whiche lyvyth worshipfully and commendably all hys lyfe to God from childhod' (our lord takes great delight and pleasure when such a man or woman who lives commendably with worship all their life, devoted to God from childhood).[73] By means of her own flourishing vineyard-heart, in which the child morphs into transcendent soul, Mechthild also provides a reconfigured, female-coded version of the parable of the Lord's vineyard and its potential to reflect the truths of human salvation.

In a final flourish, both texts align with a culminating vision figuring the transcendent maiden – Mechthild and the pearl-maiden respectively – who join the company of 'þe holy virgynes which folowe þe holy lombe' (the holy virgins who

70 Mechthild, *Boke*, II.xviii.
71 Mechthild, *Boke*, II.ii.
72 Mechthild, *Boke*, I.li.
73 Mechthild, *Boke*, I.li.

follow the holy lamb).[74] Moreover, both texts carefully remind the reader of the child-origins of its sanctified protagonist: Mechthild's holiness stems historically from the piety she displayed from 'þe seveneth yer age' (the age of seven), while the pearl-maiden remains to the dreamer 'my lyttel quene' (my little queen) (l. 1147) in spite of her magnitude and elevation.

A number of commentators have aligned these types of hermeneutics with those prevalent in the works of Dante and Boccaccio, claiming the author's familiarity with the writing of these male precursors.[75] I am not doubting such familiarity here, but it is worth noting that both Dante and Boccaccio were certainly acquainted with Mechthild's work and drew on it in their own.[76] In turn, this renders the directions of influence multifaceted and circular. Whether the *Gawain*-poet had read or discussed Mechthild's work will, perhaps, never be known for certain, but there is absolutely no doubt that some of the hermeneutic sets that were so important to this Saxon woman visionary also feature large in the writing of the late fourteenth-century anonymous borderlands poet. And if, as many critics have suggested, this poet was deeply embedded and embroiled in the warring factions and families of the Marcher regions, then his turning towards the spiritual comfort of a female-coded – or, indeed, feminine – way of seeing the divine project for humankind, may well have offered a similar comfort to the poet's early readership. Far from celebrating a pugilistic enterprise and environment, like many of the actors presented in this present essay, he was proffering an alternate vision based on a female, rather than male, version of Christian spirituality and its poetics of greening and salvation.

Conclusion

In her early essay on the Harley Lyrics – another set of borderlands writings not under scrutiny here – Helen Fulton ultimately dispelled arguments for a strong set of Welsh borrowings in the lexis deployed within these poems.[77] For Helen, the poems engage more with a 'looking outwards' from the English vernacular to draw on both French and wider Latinate traditions, rather than Welsh. The latter developed a love-lyric tradition occurring later than the type recorded in the Harley manuscript, rather than earlier, pointing towards another example of a literary 'inward-outward' dynamic extending over centuries.[78] Such a combination of simultaneously looking outwards and inwards, therefore, appears to have been a strong

74 Mechthild, *Boke*, V.xxii.

75 See, in particular, Putter, *Introduction*, pp. 5–6.

76 This was first posited by Edmund Garratt Gardner, *Dante and the Mystics* (London: J. M. Dent and Sons, Ltd., 1913), pp. 283–97. More recently Barbara Newman has made out an even more convincing case in 'The Seven Storey Mountain: Mechthild of Hackeborn and Dante's Matelda', *Dante Studies* 136 (2018): 62–92.

77 Helen Fulton, 'The Theory of Celtic Influence on the Harley Lyrics', *Modern Philology* 82.3 (1985): 239–54.

78 Fulton, 'Celtic Influence', p. 254.

component of borderlands writings that rendered the resultant mix eclectic, often scintillating, sometimes spectral, and, ultimately, a form of inherent protest against centuries of a patriarchal and dynastic warmongering that took its toll in ways that were often dire on local families and royalty alike. Led both by material women withdrawing into anchoritic enclosure and by literary women as authors and protagonists, the region's literature also often reflected such protest, turning outward and inward to offer glimpses of other ways of living, of being, and of approaching the spiritual world.

10

Adam Usk's Epitaph(s): Shaping Identity in a Medieval Borderland

Catherine A. M. Clarke

In the Monmouthshire market town of Usk, inside the Priory Church of St Mary, a small and easily missable brass plaque is fixed to the chancel side of the magnificent fifteenth-century painted rood screen. In many ways, this very specific, precise location in the Welsh Marches is a place I arrived at as a result of collaboration with Helen Fulton. Formatively for me, our work together on the 'Mapping Medieval Chester' project led me to further research on the England–Wales border region: the 'City Witness' project on medieval Swansea and, more recently, the St Thomas Way, which reimagines the late thirteenth-century pilgrimage of William Cragh, medieval Swansea's 'hanged man', as a modern-day heritage route from Swansea to Hereford.[1] The St Thomas Way includes the Priory Church of St Mary, Usk, as one of its locations, inviting visitors to pause at the rood screen and notice that small brass plaque. Engraved with Welsh, in cramped fifteenth-century Gothic script, it commemorates the life of Adam Usk (c. 1350–1430): born in Usk and later priest, lawyer, academic, and most widely known today for his *Chronicle*, a continuation of the *Polychronicon* of Ranulph Higden, covering the years 1377–1421.[2] With a strong

1 For these projects, see *Mapping Medieval Chester* (2008) <www.medievalchester.ac.uk> [last accessed 1st December 2022]; Catherine A. M. Clarke, ed., *Mapping the Medieval City: Place, Space and Identity in Chester, c. 1200–1600* (Cardiff: University of Wales Press, 2011); *City Witness* (2014) <www.medievalswansea.ac.uk> [last accessed 1st December 2022]; *Journal of Medieval History* 41 (2015), Special issue *Power, Identity and Miracles on a Medieval Frontier*; *The St Thomas Way: Swansea–Hereford* <www.thomasway.ac.uk> [last accessed 1st December 2022]; Catherine A. M. Clarke, ed., *The St Thomas Way and the Medieval March of Wales: Exploring Place, Heritage, Pilgrimage* (Amsterdam: Amsterdam University Press, 2020).

2 For the textual history of the Chronicle and its manuscript, see Chris Given-Wilson, 'The Dating and Structure of the Chronicle of Adam Usk', *Welsh History Review* 17 (1995): 520–33. For a short overview of the life and career of Adam Usk, see Chris Given-Wilson, 'Usk, Adam (c. 1350–1430), chronicler', in *Oxford Dictionary of National Biography* (Oxford: Oxford University Press, 2004) <www.oxforddnb.

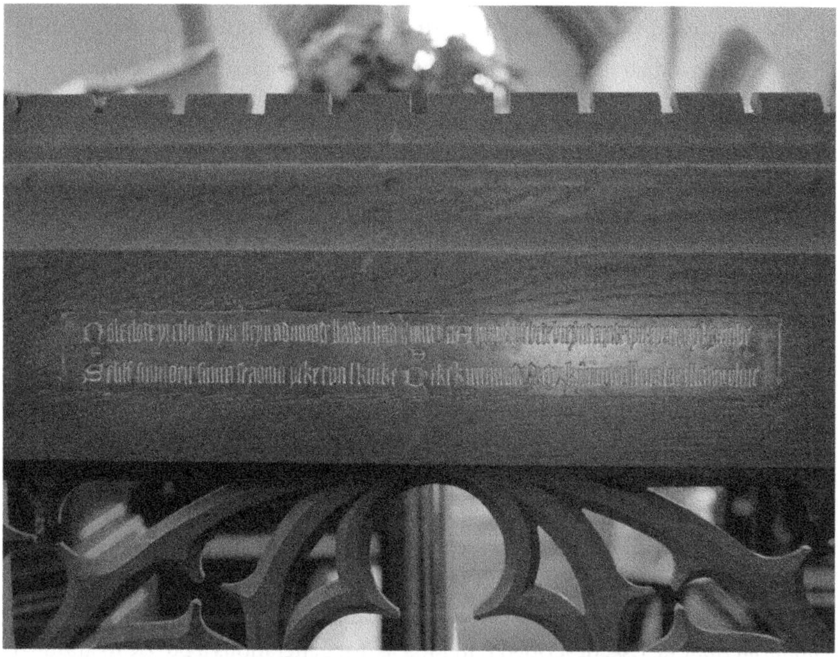

Plate 1 The Adam Usk Epitaph Brass, Priory Church of St Mary, Usk. Photograph: Catherine Clarke, 2023.

autobiographical emphasis, Adam's *Chronicle* details, often in partial or evasive ways, his own participation and shifting allegiances in turbulent early fifteenth-century events, including Richard II's deposition, court politics of Henry IV, and the rebellion of Owain Glyn Dŵr. My discussion of the epitaph of Adam Usk in this essay was developed in part through a paper Helen invited me to give at a 2016 workshop on 'Borders and Borderlands in Medieval and Early Modern Europe' at the University of Bristol, and I am conscious of how my analysis of this intriguing and difficult textual artefact draws on so much I have explored with, and learned from, her: the rich multilingual cultures of medieval Britain, the complexity of border, hybrid, and Marcher identities, and the production of self and place through varied modes and genres of late-medieval writing, both in Latin and the vernaculars.[3]

The epitaph of Adam Usk, inscribed on the brass plaque in St Mary's Priory Church, was transcribed by John Morris-Jones and transliterated and translated as follows:

---

com> [last accessed 1st December 2022]; or the fuller discussion in Given-Wilson, ed., *The Chronicle of Adam Usk 1377–1421* (Oxford: Oxford University Press, 1997), pp. xiv–xxxviii.

3 I also gave an earlier version of some of this paper at a 'Region and Nation' workshop at the University of Oxford, September 2012, at the invitation of David Clark and Kate McClune. I am grateful for all the feedback and advice I have received on this essay, especially from Adam Chapman, Geraint Evans, and Barry Lewis.

Nôl clod i veddrod iar vein	After fame, to the tomb, from on the bench,
advocad llawnhad llundein	The most skilled advocate of London,
A barnwr byd breint arab –	And judge of the world by gracious privilege,
ty nev a vo [i] ti, ha vab!	May the heavenly abode be thine, good sire.
Selyf swnnwyr, synna, sy,	Lo! a Solomon of wisdom,
Adam Wsk, yna yn kwsky,	Adam Usk, is sleeping here,
Dec kwmmwd doctor kymmen –	Wise doctor of ten commotes,
llyna le yn llawn o lên!	Behold a place full of learning![4]

While the inscription presents many linguistic and stylistic eccentricities and difficult features – acknowledged and discussed in detail by Morris-Jones, and the source of many strange outcomes in earlier attempts at translation, which I will examine later in this essay – later scholars have, as Chris Given-Wilson notes, 'had no hesitation in accepting' this text and translation,[5] and it remains the authoritative version, though with some unresolved uncertainties and ambiguities. Yet the text has never received serious attention as a literary source – rather, only as a philological conundrum to be solved. Edward Maunde Thompson, the first editor of the *Chronicon Adae de Usk*, described it in 1904 as 'for generations a puzzle to antiquaries and philologists'.[6] The tangled Welsh of the St Mary's epitaph, which remained stubbornly unreadable for centuries, and which still resists definitive interpretation, embodies Adam's complex, ambivalent relationship with his Welshness: both his proximity to and distance from his roots as a Marcher boy, and his often precarious place on Britain's cultural and political borders.[7] As a text, the epitaph continues to evade easy readings or 'solutions', recalling the similarly intractable, slippery nature of Adam's *Chronicle*, characterised by influential, important recent readers such as Andrew Galloway and Steven Justice as a 'riddle or a puzzle' (Galloway) or in terms of 'puzzles' and unyielding 'secrets' (Justice).[8] Yet Adam Usk's epitaph – a rich, complex, elusive but rewarding text – has been strangely neglected in scholarship

4 J. Morris-Jones, 'Adam Usk's Epitaph', *Y Cymmrodor* 31 (1921): 112–34; transcription and transliteration p. 124 (also p. 135, with image of the plaque); Latin translation p. 125, and English translation assembled from the Notes, pp. 125–34.

5 Given-Wilson, *Chronicle*, p. xxxvii.

6 Edward Maunde Thompson, ed., *Chronicon Adae de Usk* (London: Henry Frowde, 1904), p. xxxi.

7 For a detailed discussion of poetry and cultural identities in the region in the period, see Dylan Foster Evans, '"Talm o Wentoedd": The Welsh Language and its Literature in Gwent, c. 1070–1530', in *The Gwent County History, Vol. 2*, ed. R. A. Griffiths, T. Hopkins, and R. Howell (Cardiff: University of Wales Press on behalf of the Gwent County History Association, 2008), pp. 280–308.

8 Andrew Galloway, 'Private Selves and the Intellectual Marketplace in Late Fourteenth-Century England: The Case of the Two Usks', *New Literary History* 28 (1997): 291–318 (314); Steven Justice, *Adam Usk's Secret* (Philadelphia: University of Pennsylvania Press, 2015).

on Adam, even as readers such as Galloway and Justice have focused on questions of self-presentation or the challenges of interpretation in the *Chronicle*. The epitaph as text has been completely disconnected from recent literary scholarship on Adam, with no mention of it at all from Galloway or Justice (who comments in an introductory note on translations and orthography that 'I know no Welsh'),[9] as have many of the traces of Adam's linguistic identity and networks of cultural production as a Welsh speaker. This essay seeks to address this serious omission and gap in current scholarship on Adam Usk and the complex textual assemblages around his life.

This essay will offer a new study of Adam Usk's epitaph, moving out from the brass plaque in St Mary's, Usk, to traces of what I suggest could be understood as 'epitaphic' writing in the *Chronicle* and other texts associated with Adam. Through close textual analysis, I will reflect on questions around the authorship, purpose, and intended audience(s) of these epitaphic texts, and the work they do in performing identity, negotiating hybridity, and asserting a place at and across varied kinds of borders. My reading will draw on the valuable insights advanced by Galloway, Justice, and the most recent editor of Adam's *Chronicle*, Given-Wilson, as well as wider work on identity and performativity by scholars such as Susan Crane, who sites such performances of selfhood 'at the intersection of agency and prescription, innovation and memory, self and social group'; and David Gary Shaw, whose analysis of the medieval 'social self' urges attention to the value of small 'biographical moments'.[10] In what ways do Adam Usk's epitaphic texts assemble a repertoire of different social selves? And how can they help nuance our understanding of borderland identities, multilingualism, and self-fashioning in medieval Britain? I also want to pay attention to the reception and translation history of the St Mary's epitaph in the post-medieval period. What can early attempts at translation of the epitaph – problematic and erroneous, but also imaginative and lively – tell us about memory, scholarship and the desire for origins in the formation of Welsh and Marcher history and identity in the eighteenth and nineteenth centuries? Finally, taking a cue from Justice's work on Adam, what is there to say about the St Mary's epitaph as an uninterpretable text, a resistant cultural artefact, which fails to co-operate in straightforward ways with the conventional practices of textual criticism, and which evades a definitive, stable reading? How do we engage with Adam Usk's brass epitaph as unreadable, flawed, and faulty, and what value might a text like that hold? How might a close analysis of Adam's epitaph open up wider questions about how we treat not only textual puzzles, but also textual accidents, mistakes, and the unmeant?[11]

The two lines of the epitaph text inscribed in St Mary's Church comprise four couplets in the Welsh *cywydd* metre. This form of Welsh *cynghanedd*, as Morris-

9 Justice, *Adam Usk's Secret*, p. 10.

10 Susan Crane, *Performance of Self: Ritual, Clothing, and Identity during the Hundred Years War* (Philadelphia, PA: University of Pennsylvania Press, 2002), p. 3; David Gary Shaw, *Necessary Conjunctions: The Social Self in Medieval England* (Basingstoke: Palgrave Macmillan, 2005), pp. 5, 196.

11 I pick up the term 'unmeant' from Steven Justice; see discussion below.

Jones summarises, 'consists of two lines of seven syllables each; one line must end in an accented, the other in an unaccented, syllable; and these two end-syllables must rhyme'.[12] In line 5, Usk's name itself – though not discerned by the text's first translators – is folded aurally into the patterns of the *cynghanedd* with 'Adam Wsk, yna yn kwsky' ('Adam Usk is sleeping here').[13] The lines display a confident command of the rhetorical features of the epitaph form, playing with ideas of 'here', place, transaction, and exchange, as well as direct address to the reader and the invitation to decode the riddle of the verse. The poem centres on the conventional *hic* of the epitaph: the 'here-ness' or 'locative declaration' identified by Scott Newstok as the 'core statement' of all epitaphic writing.[14] While the 'here' located by the text is most obviously the site of Adam's burial (the 'yna' or 'here' of line 5), the poem also plays with other sites and places, figured in a pattern of negotiation and transaction that engages with another key element of epitaphic form: what Anne Carson describes as the 'central shaping metaphor' of 'exchange'.[15] The inscription initiates the conventional epitaphic exchange between text and reader in its appeal for attention, memory, and (implicitly) prayer in return for a moral exemplar and edification. Yet Adam's epitaph also skilfully combines the metaphorical systems of the 'here' and exchange, playing with the idea of *lle* (place) throughout. The first line begins a series of transactions, as Adam exchanges 'fame' for the 'tomb'; 'the bench' and 'London' for 'the heavenly abode'. Multiple, overlaid geographies of power and authority operate in the poem, from the allusion to London as a site of secular prestige (l. 2) to the invocation of an Old Testament world with the reference to Solomon (l. 5), the heavenly realm (l. 4), and, in the penultimate line, the very Welsh landscape of the 'ten commotes' – the ten administrative divisions of land in Wales. The poem's final line, pointing to a 'place full of learning', imagines not just the tomb, but Adam's body itself as a site and container, echoing a well-known line from an elegy by Dafydd ap Gwilym on Gruffudd Gryg: 'Llyna gist yn llawn o gerdd!' (Behold, a casket full of song!).[16] Even as the epitaph locates

12 Morris-Jones, 'Adam Usk's Epitaph', p. 119.

13 David Callander looks at 'kwsky' in Adam Usk's epitaph in his recent discussion of *cusky* (to sleep) in Middle English, pointing to linguistic borrowing from Welsh, especially in texts associated with the Marches or border region. See David Callander, 'Cywydd epitaff Adam Wsg a "Cusky" Saesneg Canol', *Llên Cymru* 43 (2020): 96–100.

14 Scott L. Newstok, *Quoting Death in Early Modern England: The Poetics of Epitaphs Beyond the Tomb* (Basingstoke: Palgrave Macmillan, 2009), pp. 1, 34.

15 Anne Carson, *Economy of the Unlost (Reading Simonides of Keos with Paul Celan)* (Princeton, NJ: Princeton University Press, 1999), p. 74. For further discussion of medieval epitaphic traditions, see Günter Bernt, *Das lateinische Epigramm im Ubergang von der Spätantike zum frühen Mittelalter* (Munich: Arbeo-Gesellschaft, 1968); André Vauchez *et al.*, eds, *Encyclopaedia of the Middle Ages*, 2 vols (Cambridge: James Clarke and Company, 2000), I, p. 492, and the overview of epitaph conventions in Catherine A. M. Clarke, *Writing Power in Anglo-Saxon England: Texts, Hierarchies, Economies* (Cambridge: D. S. Brewer, 2012), pp. 44–79.

16 See Morris-Jones, 'Adam Usk's Epitaph', pp. 132–33; Dafydd ap Gwilym, 'Marwnad

Adam in his final resting place in the Priory Church of St Mary, it plays with the concept of his many dwelling places, past, present, and future, and self-consciously troubles any straightforward notion of belonging. As the verses present Adam's multifaceted, diverse claims to fame, status, and spiritual stature, they also inscribe his divided, fractured identity. The tomb itself, in the epitaph, functions as a kind of border space, its tensions, hybridities, and multiplicities internalised within Adam's own body.

While the epitaph, then, plays confidently with elements of form and convention, its Welsh is tangled, difficult, and full of errors. These are discussed in detail by John Morris-Jones in his analysis of the text, and range from flaws in the use of *cynghanedd* – arising either from lack of skill or discipline, Morris-Jones suggests – to serious problems with orthography and apparent misunderstanding of the text being engraved.[17] As I will discuss later in this essay, the problems and errors in the epitaph inscription presented enormous obstacles for early readers, resulting in numerous (themselves revealing, telling) mistranslations. Morris-Jones is reasonably confident in his translation: as an authority on Welsh philology and orthography, his version can be treated as reliable, but stands on the basis of numerous corrections and adjustments from transcription to transliteration.[18]

In his analysis, Morris-Jones distinguishes between the three separate roles of 'scribe, or writer of the copy', 'engraver', and the text's 'author'.[19] He observes that the scribe who produced the text for the engraver was 'unacquainted with the standard spelling of Welsh words'.[20] Where certain Welsh sounds are correctly represented by their standard symbols in Welsh, notably *ll* and *aw*, Morris-Jones argues that this suggests that the scribe may have been 'a member of one of the learned professions, probably a lawyer', familiar with these forms from place-names (*Ll* in all the Welsh place-names beginning with *Llan-*, and *aw* in the common place-name

Gruffudd Gryg', in *Cerddi Dafydd ap Gwilym*, ed. Dafydd Johnston *et al.* (Cardiff: University of Wales Press, 2010), p. 100, l. 50.

17 Morris-Jones's detailed account of the text and its problems is extensive, and the substance of the entire article is cited above as the source for the transliterated epitaph text and translation. There is not space to reproduce its analysis here, and my aim in this essay is to move from Morris-Jones's textual reconstruction to a critical reading: instead, I would refer readers directly to the Morris-Jones's article for a full discussion of all these features.

18 In preparing this essay, I consulted Professor Barry Lewis of the School of Celtic Studies, Dublin Institute of Advanced Studies, and Geraint Evans, Swansea University, for advice on the epitaph text and Morris-Jones's translation: both pointed to Morris-Jones's authority as a philologist and translator, and I am grateful for their generous help and advice. For an account of Morris-Jones's standing and legacy as a Welsh historical linguist, see Patrick Sims-Williams, 'John Morris-Jones and his *Welsh Grammar*', *Transactions of the Honourable Society of Cymmrodorion* 22 (2016): 134–53.

19 Morris-Jones, 'Adam Usk's Epitaph', pp. 119–21.

20 Morris-Jones, 'Adam Usk's Epitaph', p. 119.

element *mawr* or 'large / great').[21] Beyond these, the 'peculiarities of the orthography' presented a huge impediment for readers of the text in the post-medieval period – and, potentially, even soon after Adam's death and burial. Morris-Jones further concludes that the 'engraver clearly did not understand a word of Welsh', suggesting that the engraver was English, possibly from Bristol or London.[22]

Morris-Jones's consideration of the possible authorship of the epitaph is especially intriguing. He is dismissive of the possibility that 'the author and the scribe may … have been the same person', declaring 'I do not think this is likely', and rejecting Edward Maunde Thompson's suggestion that the author may have been Adam himself, on the grounds that 'if [the author] had taken enough interest in Welsh poetry to compose these verses, he could not help being familiar with it in its written form, and could scarcely be such a stranger to Welsh orthography'.[23] Yet Morris-Jones goes on to build a compelling case that Adam may have been, at the least, the scribe who wrote down the text for the engraver. He observes that:

> [T]he orthography is just what one would expect from a person like himself, who was thoroughly conversant with English and French, and probably possessed only a colloquial knowledge of Welsh. But the case is really much stronger than that: when Adam's own spelling of Welsh names is examined it is found to tally in almost every particular with the spelling of our scribe [...] it is therefore very probable that he wrote out the lines himself.[24]

Morris-Jones refers readers to a meticulous comparison of the orthography of Adam's *Chronicle* (in instances of Welsh names), and the epitaph, printed on pages 125–27 of the article. While cautioning that 'it is perhaps idle to speculate', he goes on (in the main text) to offer the following hypothesis:

> [I]t is not inconsistent with what we know of Adam to suppose that the verses were inspired by him; they may have been composed by a friend of his with a local reputation as a poet; they were probably put in writing by himself, and perhaps handed to a copyist to engross for the engraver.[25]

Our understanding of medieval cultures of multilingualism, literacies, and modes of authorship has advanced significantly since Morris-Jones wrote this analysis in 1921. Yet his imagined scenario already attends to the complex processes of medieval literary production: in his formulation, the enmeshed and interwoven roles of patron as 'inspiration' and poet as 'composer'. Reading the textual evidence assembled by Morris-Jones today, we might interpret it more boldly, or with different nuance. The evidence that leads to his awkward insistence on Adam as source of 'inspiration' for the poem, and possibly scribe – but emphatically not author – could instead be read in terms of collaborative modes of authorship and fluidity of agency shared between

21 Morris-Jones, 'Adam Usk's Epitaph', p. 120.
22 Morris-Jones, 'Adam Usk's Epitaph', p. 120.
23 Morris-Jones, 'Adam Usk's Epitaph', p. 120.
24 Morris-Jones, 'Adam Usk's Epitaph', pp. 120–21.
25 Morris-Jones, 'Adam Usk's Epitaph', p. 121.

patron and poet, allowing Adam a more central, active role in the production of his own epitaph. Further, we might review Morris-Jones's assertion that an author capable of composing the epitaph *cywydd* 'could not help being familiar with it in its written form, and could scarcely be such a stranger to Welsh orthography'. Instead, we might imagine a multilingual world in which Adam Usk engaged with multiple languages in varying formats and contexts, and in which cultural literacy would have accommodated encounters with languages and literary traditions through oral and aural, as well as written, experience.[26] While Adam may have read and written in Latin and English, is it so unlikely that his engagement with Welsh could have been primarily oral and aural? *Cywydd* emerged as the most popular metre among the 'bards of the gentry' in the fourteenth century and later, 'used for all kinds of genres ranging from formal praise-poetry and religious poetry to popular and comic types of verse'.[27] Is it not possible that Adam was familiar with this common *cynghanedd* form through oral performance and transmission, even as his orthography slips into the written conventions of Latin, Anglo-Norman, and English? My primary aim in this essay is not to identify the authorship of the epitaph of Adam Usk in St Mary's, Usk. However, it seems to me that Morris-Jones resists what might be considered the most obvious conclusions from his own evidence, while more recent developments in our understanding of medieval authorship, multilingualism, and literacy lend still greater weight to the argument that Adam may well, at the very least, have played an active and central role in the production of his own epitaph. His lifelong interest in textual self-representation, his detailed preparations for his death in his will, and his other attempts at what I describe as 'epitaphic' writing – all of which I will consider later in this essay – strengthen the case further.

In Adam's will (20th January 1430, 'Datum apud Usk'), he asks for his body to be buried 'in ecclesia parochiali de Vsk, coram ymagine beate Marie uirginis' (in the parish church of Usk, before the image of the blessed Virgin Mary).[28] Given-Wilson refers to this as the 'statue of the Virgin',[29] but the choice of language here may allude to a more specifically Welsh tradition: the 'living image' statues, usually of Christ or the Virgin Mary, which were found in churches across Wales in the Middle Ages. As Helen Fulton comments, '[i]t is assumed that they were wooden statues with some mechanical parts which enabled them to move', with references in texts including Welsh poetry (for example, 'y ddelw fyw' in Maredudd ap Rhys, *I'r Groes o Gaer*).[30] In this detail, it may be that Adam expresses, and identifies with,

26 Ground-breaking texts in this field have included, of course, Michael Clanchy, *From Memory to Written Record* (Oxford: Wiley Blackwell, 2012), and more recent work on multilingualism in medieval Britain, such as that collected in Jocelyn Wogan-Browne *et al.*, eds, *Language and Culture in Medieval Britain: The French of England, c. 1100–c. 1500* (York: York Medieval Press, 2009).

27 Helen Fulton, 'Metres of Medieval Welsh Poetry', in *Mapping Medieval Chester* <www.medievalchester.ac.uk> [last accessed 1st December 2022].

28 Given-Wilson, *Chronicle*, pp. 272, 273.

29 Given-Wilson, *Chronicle*, p. xxxvii.

30 See Maredudd ap Rhys, 'I'r Groes o Gaer', ed. Helen Fulton in *Mapping Medieval*

a particularly Welsh kind of devotional sensibility and reverence. Given-Wilson notes that Adam's will 'reveals a man of some wealth, and strong local attachment'.[31] The will includes several bequests to Usk and those associated with it:

> lego ecclesie parochiale predicte [Usk] unum librum appellatum 'Racionale Diuinorum'. Item, lego domino Iohanni, uicario de Vsk, tres solidos quattor denarius. Item, lego cuilibet moniali prioratus de Vsk uiginti denarius.
>
> (I bequeath a book called the *Racionale Diuinorum* to the aforesaid parish church. Also, I bequeath three shillings and fourpence to John, vicar of Usk. Also, I bequeath twenty pence to each nun of the priory of Usk.)

There is also a gift to another local man: 'Thome Went de Castell Cwm uiginti solidos' (twenty shillings to Thomas Went of Castle Combe).[32]

The gifts outlined in Adam's will are also reflected in a passage of his *Chronicle*, amid entries covering the years 1400 and 1401 (but likely written significantly later). At this point, following musings on the corruption of the priesthood and the certainty of mortality, Adam outlines his intentions for bequests and commemoration at his death:

> *Ornamenta ecclesie de Vsk.* Ideo benedicatur Deus, in mei originis, scilicet de Vsk, ecclesia, iam mori adiscens, memorial meum in competentibus missali, gradali, tropario, sequencia, antiphonario, nouiter et cum nouis addicionibus et notis compositis, ac plena uestimentorum secta cum tribus capis ornanter compositorum, meis signis, scilicet nudi fodentis in campo nigro, oracionum suffragiis ibidem me comendando, relinquo; ulterius, si Deus dederit, ecclesiam eandem reparacione honestiori ad beate Virginis gloriam, in cuius natiuitatis honore est dedicata, perornare proponens; hoc ad mei laudem non reputando, quia presentis fatuitatis mee scripturam in uita mea uideri detestor.
>
> (*The ornaments of the church of Usk.* Blessed be God, therefore – for, anticipating my death, I have already left to the church of Usk, my birthplace, my own memorial in the form of a proper missal, gradual, tropary, sequentiary, and antiphonal, newly copied out, and with new additions and notation, and a full suit of vestments together with three copes ornately embroidered with my badges, namely a naked man digging on a black background, commending myself thereby to the intercession of those who pray there. Furthermore, should God spare me, I intend to embellish this same church with even finer ornaments, to the glory of the blessed Virgin in honour of whose nativity it is dedicated; but I do not say this in order to win praise for myself, for I should hate this account of my present follies to be seen during my lifetime.)[33]

Chester <www.medievalchester.ac.uk> [last accessed 1st December 2022], n. 5 l. 29. See also Glanmor Williams, *The Welsh Church from Conquest to Reformation* (Cardiff: University of Wales Press, 1962), pp. 481, 491.

31 Given-Wilson, *Chronicle*, p. xxxvii.

32 Given-Wilson, *Chronicle*, pp. 172, 173.

33 Given-Wilson, *Chronicle*, pp. 118, 119.

This passage underlines the extensive attention paid by Adam to preparations for his own death and commemoration, and his acute awareness of his burial and memorial as an opportunity for self-fashioning and self-presentation for posterity. The text here also reflects the characteristic ambivalence and tensions in Adam's writing, as well as questions about the *Chronicle's* intended audience and purpose. While Adam imagines in detail the future honour and status to be accorded to him by his carefully planned burial and memorial, he simultaneously shrinks from the notion of an audience during his lifetime. (His *Chronicle*, described as 'unum librum uocatum "Policronica"' – a book called the *Polychronicon* – was gifted to his kinsman Edward ab Adam in his will.)[34] Adam's gifts to Usk are designed to consolidate his prestige as a successful local-born man and to exhibit his piety and devotion, yet the prose self-checks these ambitions with the note that 'hoc mei laudem non reputando' (I do not say this in order to win praise for myself). Strikingly, it is only in death, and in his posthumous commemoration, that Adam seems ready for an audience, when, as the text here hints, his motives will no longer be under question, and he will no longer be present to be discomfited by public scrutiny. These lines in the *Chronicle* further reinforce the likelihood that Adam – so focused on the details of his commemoration – was directly involved in the composition of his own epitaph at Usk. They also suggest a strangely deferred – hesitant, doubting – project of self-presentation, delaying commitment to a definitive, stable public identity or posture – such as that solidified in the epitaph – until after death. I shall return later in this essay to Adam's reference here to his 'badges', and his personal sign of the digging man (an allusion to the biblical Adam): another intriguing moment of self-fashioning that operates alongside his long-term (auto-)epitaphic projects.

Beyond the instructions in Adam's will, the original location of his epitaph plaque cannot be known with complete certainty. Thomas Wakeman, writing in 1847, comments that the plaque had been fixed to the rood screen 'time out of mind', at a section 'inclosing a spare [read square] space, the use and intention of which are not very obvious'.[35] Morris-Jones suggests this could have been the site of the statue (or 'living image') of the Virgin: a Lady chapel, quite possibly enclosed and decorated through Adam's own gift, as detailed in his *Chronicle*.[36] The plaque was moved to a new position on the rood screen during church alterations in 1844. While it is not possible to be certain it was the plaque's original location, its present place on the chancel side of the Usk rood screen (as it would similarly have been previously, if sited in a small Lady chapel) seems a curiously appropriate place for Adam's epitaph. Rood screens, of course, have a longstanding association with preaching and speaking in the later Middle Ages: pulpits developed as an attachment to them, and earlier preachers may even have climbed the screens themselves to speak. The siting of Adam's epitaph is a place of public proclama-

34 Given-Wilson, *Chronicle*, pp. 172, 173.

35 'Inscription in Usk Church, Monmouthshire', *Archaeologia Cambrensis* 2.5 (January 1847): 34–41 (35).

36 Morris-Jones, 'Adam Usk's Epitaph', p. 123.

tion and instruction to the parish, as well as a gesture towards his own identity as a man of words: lawyer, chronicler, and poet. Within a Marcher landscape, the rood screen also enacts liminality in microcosm: between chancel and nave, between clergy and laity, and between the linguistic worlds of clerical Latin and vernacular Welsh, as well as Anglo-Norman and English. The position of the epitaph – both in its probable fifteenth-century location as well as its site today – also troubles, once again, notions of self-presentation, commemoration, and audience. Facing towards the chancel and high altar, and away from most of the lay community within the church, the epitaph is ambivalent about its intended audience: while it addresses the reader in typical epitaphic style, it is turned towards God. The site suggests, once again, a squeamishness or equivocation with regard to self-presentation and self-memorialisation, and continuing self-doubt around motive, or the perception and judgement of motive by others (the danger of inviting 'ad mei laudem' to which Adam alludes in the *Chronicle*). In its position, the epitaph is strangely both public and secret, simultaneously a confident statement of status and identity, and a gesture of humility, doubt, and erasure. It makes a grand statement but is tiny. It is also, of course, deeply ironic – as well as suggestive and significant – that the tangled Welsh of Adam's epitaph proved unreadable by local people – and, indeed, by scholars of Welsh literature – for so many centuries. I will return to that notion of the epitaph as an unreadable text, through discussion of its translation and reception history, later in this essay.

The brass plaque in St Mary's Church, as is already becoming apparent, is not the only potential epitaph for Adam Usk that survives today. The manuscript of the *Chronicle*, which became separated sometime between 1600 and 1836, is now comprised in two separate manuscripts: London, British Library, MS Additional 10104 (termed by Given-Wilson 'MS A') and a manuscript in the possession of the Duke of Rutland at Belvoir Castle, discovered in 1904 (Given-Wilson's 'MS B').[37] The first epitaphic text we will consider appears on fol. 177r of the full *Chronicle* manuscript; now the flyleaf of MS A. There are traces of more than one hand on this folio (Given-Wilson counts 11 different hands over the full extent of the *Chronicle*), including Hand Five – the one that Given-Wilson considers most likely to be that of Adam himself.[38] The notes in (possibly) Adam's hand concern earlier medieval royal marriages and succession (Given-Wilson comments that 'they demonstrate an interest in succession questions which is revealed elsewhere in the chronicle').[39] Following these notes, in a different hand, are several lines of Latin verse, described by Given-Wilson as 'a series of attempts at an epitaph for Usk'.[40] The first editor of the *Chronicle*, Edward Maunde Thompson, dismissed them as 'vile literary productions'.[41] Yet, questions of stylistic value or merit aside, they present another

37 See Given-Wilson, *Chronicle*, pp. xxxviii–xxxix.

38 See the full discussion in Given-Wilson, 'The Dating and Structure', esp. pp. 529–31.

39 Given-Wilson, *Chronicle*, p. xliii.

40 Given-Wilson, *Chronicle*, p. xliii.

41 Maunde Thompson, *Chronicon Adae*, p. x.

intriguing moment in Adam's self-fashioning through (auto-)epitaphic writing. I suggest that we might consider these lines as epitaph 'trial pieces', exploring and experimenting with varied, multivocal ways of shaping and commemorating Adam's identity and achievements.

The trial epitaph lines are translated by Given-Wilson as follows (while Given-Wilson presents the lines as a single verse text, I have separated them to better indicate that they are a series of different epitaph attempts rather than a coherent piece):

O dolor immensus! satis ars uel gloria sensus, Non rediment census, quin casus sit tibi pensus. Sortitum nostri prothoplausti nomen, ab inde Vsk dictum, sub se continet iste lapis.	(O grief unmeasured! Skill, or the virtue of insight, or wealth, will not compensate [for it], so that your case has not been weighed. This stone encloses beneath itself one given the name of our common progenitor [Adam], thereafter named Usk.)
Iustinie, tuas leges docuit, uice fungens Doctoris, necnon ius, Graciane, tuum.	(Justinian, he taught your laws, fulfilling the role of doctor; and your law too, Gratian.)
Qui docui mores mundi uitare fauores, Inter doctores sacros sortitus honores, Vermibus hic ponor, et sic ostendere conor Quod, sicut hic ponor, sic ponitur omnis honor.	(I, who instructed [human] character to shun the favours of the world, having attained ecclesiastical rank among the teachers, am here laid for worms, and thus try to show that, just as I am laid here, so too is all honour.)
Legit hic Oxonie doctor ciuilia iura; Hic iacet in requie, uiuat sine fine futura.	(This man read civil law as a doctor at Oxford; here he lies in peace, may he live henceforward in peace without end.)[42]

While the lines are not in Hand Five, that which Given-Wilson thinks is most likely to be Adam's own, he notes that 'it is not impossible that Usk composed them himself'. He observes '[t]he emphasis, once again, on his legal attainments – clearly regarded by Usk as the chief memorial to his fame'.[43] Once again, as with the epitaph in St Mary's, Usk, we must imagine a medieval process of textual production in which patron / author (Adam) and scribe worked closely together. Again, these verses show confident familiarity with the epitaph form and conventions – this time in Latin rather than nuanced by the poetic idioms of Welsh. They foreground,

42 Given-Wilson, *Chronicle*, pp. xliii–xliv.

43 Given-Wilson, *Chronicle*, p. xliv.

in alignment with the choice of language, Adam's achievements as an inheritor of classical learning and an Oxford scholar. They also play with the biblical resonances of his name, 'Adam': a recurrent motif across his wider work.

The first group of lines ('O dolor ... iste lapis') play knowingly with epitaph conventions. As well as pointing to the 'here' of the burial site ('iste lapis', this stone), the text engages with the imagery of reckoning, calculation, and transaction traditionally prominent in epitaphic writing, joining it with a conceit based on Adam's career as a lawyer. While the performative opening exclamation ('O dolor immensus') counts grief as unmeasured, the text goes on to play with the paradox that salvation – heavenly judgement – relies on careful reckoning and weighing, mirroring at the level of divine authority Adam's practice as an earthly lawyer. Although the verb *reddo* more typically appears in Latin epitaphs to express the expected 'return' from the reader – prayer and memory in exchange for edification – here it articulates the impossibility of redressing such loss with (Adam's) earthly achievements of skill, insight, and wealth: '[n]on rediment census' (they will not compensate [for it]). The assertion that Adam's 'case has not been weighed' obviously alludes to conventional medieval imagery of the scales of judgement (both earthly and divine), suggesting that there is still time for intercession to aid Adam's soul before the Day of Judgement, and making the text's only, implicit, invitation to prayer. The play on Adam's name – that of our 'common progenitor' – presents him as an everyman (as with his badge of the digging man; see discussion below) and deserving of prayers as a kind of mirror for the reader, translating the individual life into a more general *memento mori*. The second epitaph trial piece, of just two lines ('Justiniae ... tuum'), centres Adam's scholarship, presenting him as a follower of Justinian and Gratian. The third ('Qui docui ... honor') follows familiar *memento mori* or *contemptus mundi* conventions, though there is something slightly telling about Adam's refusal to fully inhabit the role of the proud brought low in death. Instead, despite having attained high rank, he reminds us that he also 'docui mores mundi vitari favores' (instructed [human] character to shun the favours of the world) and, even as he is laid as food for worms, he insists that this is a didactic act of his own intention ('ostendere conor') – a final claim to agency. The dense internal and end-rhymes in these stanzas, together with the wordplay on *ponor*, are typical of the highly-artificed conceits of Latin epitaphs. Finally, the last epitaph ('Legit hic ... futura') presents an exchange of past for present: Adam's former legal career for an eternity in peace; Oxford (and the world of human learning and authority it represents) for the tomb. 'Hic' shifts in meaning from the first to the second line of the couplet: from a reference to Adam, who read law ('Legit hic ...') to a reference to the 'here' of the grave, with the core epitaphic phrase 'Hic jacet' (Here lies ...).

It is significant that these lines are a collection of epitaph trial pieces, not a single coherent text (as the combined presentation by Given-Wilson could suggest, even though he does describe them as a 'series of attempts').[44] They present an intriguing

44 Given-Wilson, *Chronicle*, p. xliii.

and unusual insight into what appears to be a process of drafting or composition: a series of experiments and varying approaches. Indeed, we might read these lines as a list of failures: literary misfires, false starts, rejected versions. Yet, they also represent a testing out of differing voices, diverse selves, and varied authorising topoi. Both Justice and Galloway have discussed Adam's meticulous processes of 'self-making' in the *Chronicle*: the effort taken to 'portray [himself] in terms consistent with [his] social and professional ideals'; 'to fashion and elaborate, fantastic, indeed, nearly allegorical social identities'.[45] The epitaph trial pieces on folio 177 of the *Chronicle* present a repertoire of different tropes and social selves that can be variously selected and performed, each foregrounding different aspects of Adam's identity and accomplishments. Yet it is striking that they cannot cohere: the epitaph trial pieces remain disconnected, disjointed failures. They suggest a fractious, uncontainable plurality, which can be expressed as an assemblage of vivid, dynamic parts, but not as a whole – even in Latin texts that do not begin to encompass or make manifest Adam's Welshness. Traces of that jostling, intractable hybridity remain, as we have seen, in the epitaph finally chosen for the inscription at St Mary's, Usk.

In addition to these epitaph trial pieces, the *Chronicle* includes several other fragmentary texts, outside the main *Chronicle* continuation itself, which explore the name Adam and experiment with self-presentation through various idioms. I discuss these here, together with the more obviously epitaphic sources in the *Chronicle* and St Mary's, Usk, as they also reflect some of the same stylistic impulses and preoccupations of epitaphic writing: the focus on a central figure or name, the play between an individual life and 'everyman' tropes, and the deliberate use of dense conceits or riddling, demanding active decoding and 'solution' from the reader. Unlike epitaphs proper, such as the trial pieces in the *Chronicle* or the plaque in St Mary's Church, they lack the focus on the 'here' of burial and are not tied explicitly to death. But they are further instances of engagement in that wider project of self-fashioning and the crafting of a lasting, 'nearly allegorical' and didactic image of the self. Together with their notably provisional and liminal quality, jotted in the space between Higden and the *Chronicle* continuation, this leads me to consider them, similarly, as 'trial pieces' in Adam's iterative project of self-presentation and quasi-epitaphic self-commemoration. First, two meditations on the name 'Adam' occur, together with some other short notes, between the end of the Higden *Polychronicon* and the beginning of Adam's continuation (fols 154v–155r). The first of these texts, which, according to Given-Wilson, 'allude in tortuous and ungrammatical fashion to events concerning Usk',[46] is as follows:

> Ade quamuis, propter sui uirtutes omni carentis miseria, finaliter principiis obstet inuidia, tamen praecipua in eo reperitur gracia, ut patet Genesi .i.; qui, expulsus paradiso per inuidiam diaboli, fuit restitutus celo per sangiunem Dei filii. Et quamuis per inuidiam cuiusdam militis fuit priuatus beneficio, ecce quam solempnis

45 Galloway, 'Private Selves', p. 292.
46 Given-Wilson, *Chronicle*, p. xl.

> fuit eius restitucio, exacta de testimonio ex parte Ade. Et, quamuis uenatorum inuidia eorum ducis concilio expellebatur et consorcio, ecce quam gloriosa eciam eius reparacio, exacta de iurribus: ueniens Adam iuxta naturam Aprilis, in quo fuit creatus primo uarias et asperas aurarum et turbinum subeuntis procellas, tamen finaliter Maii ac tocius estatis flores causantis et dilicias.
>
> (Albeit that jealousy of Adam, who was devoid of all misery on account of the virtues of his person, intervenes decisively between him and his origins [i.e. God], nevertheless special grace is found in him, as appears in Genesis I; for, having been expelled from paradise through the envy of the devil, he was restored to heaven through the blood of the son of God. And, albeit that he was deprived of his benefice by the jealousy of a certain knight, hearken to how splendid was his restoration, as was required by the evidence on behalf of Adam. Also, albeit that, through the jealousy of the hunters, he was expelled from the company and council of their leader, hearken to how glorious too was his reparation, as was required by the laws: Adam thereby conforming to the character of April, in which he was created, and which submits to the manifold and perilous blasts of wind and storms, but eventually to that of May, which brings forth the flowers and other delights of all the summer.)[47]

Explicitly a reflection on Adam, the biblical first man, the text's coded (auto)biographical allusions are foregrounded by its juxtaposition with the second text on the name 'Adam' immediately following. Given-Wilson suggests that this first meditation on 'Adam' may well establish an analogy between the biblical Adam's expulsion and exile, and Adam's own loss of the benefice of Llandygwydd (St David's diocese), at the protest of Walter Aumeney (also known as Walter Jakes), who claimed to be the existing legal incumbent. This episode led to a protracted dispute, advancing as far as papal appeal and counter-appeal, and also formed the background to the indictment of Adam, Edward Usk, and others as thieves, following an incident involving Aumeney / Jakes in Westminster in November 1400. Although Adam and Edward Usk were pardoned, and Adam was restored to his benefice, Given-Wilson suggests that this messy, extended business may still have been ongoing and unresolved when this note was written into the *Chronicle* manuscript, likely in the spring of 1401.[48] This meditation on 'Adam', then, may function as a kind of prophecy or personal mobilisation of biblical typology, with the journey of the scriptural Adam – as the type of everyman, exiled at the Fall but restored to his place in paradise through Christ's blood – promising the ultimate success of Adam Usk's own legal case. The mention of the jealousy of a certain knight ('per inuidiam cuiusdam militis') rather strains the allegorical appropriation of the Genesis narrative (a stretch as an allusion to the serpent / devil), and uses the term

47 Given-Wilson, *Chronicle*, p. xl.
48 Given-Wilson, *Chronicle*, pp. xxi--xxii, xli.

miles somewhat freely, but probably references Aumeney specifically. The passage reflects many of Adam's continual preoccupations – disappointment, a sense of injustice and persecution – covertly folding them into this sententious, apparently universalising meditation on his name.

The second meditation on 'Adam' also plays with naming and prophecy, this time moving from the conventions of scriptural exegesis and typology to Welsh prophetic traditions and writing:

> Ecce, omnis miserie reiciendo uangam, quam gloriosus uirtutibus efficitur Adam! Vsk: de isto cognomina canit uates Merlinus, 'Fluuius Vsk per septem menses feruebit, cuius calore pisses morientur et serpentes grauabunt' – serpentes in bona parte sumendo, ut intelligo, iuxta illud euangelii, 'Estote prudentes sicut serpentes'. Sed de quo ista canit Merlinus? Credo quod (de) comite Marchie, domino loci et graciosi regis Edwardi pronepote, et domini Lionelly ducis Clarencie, eius filii, nepote; quem regem Edwardum dictus uates uocat aprum bellicosum, qui suos dentes infra tutamina Francie accuere deberet; quod, ut contstat, fecit partes deuincendo (et) depredando, necnon eorum regem in campestri bello captiuando, regemque Boemie eodem dencium accumine perimendo.
>
> (Hearken! – abandoning the spade of all misery, how glorious, with his manly qualities, becomes Adam! Usk: the prophet Merlin says of this name, 'The River Usk shall be boiling hot for seven months; the fish shall die of its heat, and serpents shall proliferate' – thereby showing approval of serpents, as I take to be correct, according to what the gospel says, 'Be ye wise as serpents'. But of whom does Merlin say these things? I believe it to be the earl of March, the lord of that place, and the great-grandson of the noble King Edward and grandson of Lord Lionel, duke of Clarence, his son; the aforesaid prophet describes this King Edward as the warlike boar who should sharpen his tusks in the strongholds of France; for, as is well known, he succeeded not only in conquering and laying waste those parts, but also in capturing their king on the battlefield and, through that same sharpness of his tusks, slaying the king of Bohemia.)[49]

The key to Adam himself is more explicit here, with the playful juxtaposition of 'Adam' and 'Usk' writing his personal name into the text. It opens with another reference to the biblical Adam, the 'spade of all misery' alluding to traditional depictions of Adam digging or delving, perhaps, once again, connecting this implicitly to Adam Usk's sense of his own personal trials, efforts, and misfortunes. Yet the biblical precedent promises, again, future glory and triumph. From the name 'Adam', the reflection moves to 'Usk', drawing on prophecies of Merlin as gathered and circulated in texts including Geoffrey of Monmouth's twelfth-century *Prophetiae Merlini* or *Libellus Merlini*. The prophetic allusion to Usk takes Adam into present-day politics, with his interpretation of the passage as an allusion to the house of March.

49 Given-Wilson, *Chronicle*, p. xli.

In addition to these two textual meditations on the name 'Adam', we have already noted Adam's reference to his 'badges' in the list of his gifts to the church of Usk (see discussion above). In this list, Adam describes his bearings as 'a naked man digging on a black background': another representation of Adam, the first man, delving, which maintains that playful allegorical or analogous connection between Adam Usk and his biblical forbear – a figure synonymous with labour, suffering, effort, and exile, but also ultimate redemption and triumph. The *Chronicle* manuscript (Additional 10104) also includes a 'crude representation of this image' at the bottom of fol. 9r, which Given-Wilson describes as 'presumably drawn by Usk'.[50] Again, this strengthens a picture of Adam's own interest and active agency in these processes of self-representation and self-identification, as well as the consistency of this 'Adam' motif and analogy across text and image. These are not epitaphs, but an integral part of that wider autobiographical and auto-epitaphic project traceable across the sources I explore here, from the *Chronicle* to the St Mary's plaque: the ongoing, iterative endeavour of producing short, discrete, outward-facing representations of the self in textual and visual forms, which play with allegory, analogy between the individual and the 'everyman' type, didactic messages, and dense, riddling, ludic linguistic conceits. The conceit of Adam Usk as Adamic everyman serves, deftly, to deflect or transcend questions of national or ethnic identity: by drawing this analogy with the first man, Adam's difficult Welshness is elided; his identity is ciphered as common and shared, rather than as other or potentially treacherous. In the context of Adam's slippery associations with Wales, and the revolt of Owain Glyn Dŵr in particular (including longstanding suspicion regarding his support for the rebellion and the formal declaration of him as a rebel in 1407),[51] this appears calculated and politic. And yet the prominence of prophecy and prophetic traditions in these epitaphic pieces (as well as throughout the *Chronicle*) marks out a particularly Welsh literary and political sensibility.

Adam's epitaphic texts experiment with varying presentations of the self, from the Latinate lawyer and cleric, inheritor of the classics, to the biblical type of the everyman, to the firmly Welsh figure of prophetic writing and – most prominently of all – the 'skilled advocate of London' (commemorated in Welsh) in the epitaph at St Mary's, Usk. These multimodal texts carry traces of loss, alienation, and exclusion: career disappointments, divided or contested allegiances, the delicate negotiation of Welsh origins and a life that swings from political and religious centres to peripheries. Yet these texts also present the 'social and professional ideals' identified by Galloway: Usk's idealised versions of himself, his desires, ambitions, and fantasies for his memorialisation.[52] Returning now to Adam Usk's epitaph in St Mary's Priory Church, I want to examine some of the post-medieval reception and translation history of this difficult text, exploring how early scholars brought to it

50 Given-Wilson, *Chronicle*, p. 118, n. 4.

51 See, again, the full discussion of Adam's life and career in Given-Wilson, *Chronicle*, pp. xiv–xxxviii and, especially, pp. xxxix–-xxxiii, 'Outlawry and Excommunication, 1406–11'.

52 Galloway, 'Private Selves'.

their own ideals, and made it signify in new ways to shape Welsh and borderland identities. Morris-Jones and Maunde Thompson are dismissive of these early translation attempts; however, their imaginative misreadings reveal intriguing desires for origins and narratives of early Welsh history.[53]

The first surviving post-medieval translation of Adam Usk's epitaph is found in a substantial article by the Rev. William Harris on the 'Julia Strata' or Via Julia and other Roman remains in south Wales and the Welsh Marches, published in the journal *Archaeologia* of the Society of Antiquaries of London, volume 2, 1773. Writing on Usk, Harris notes that 'No man living has ever heard of any relict of the Romans being discovered there, or in the neighbourhood, unless it be the uncommon epitaph upon the brass plate now chained to the wall within the church'.[54] Harris's presentation of the text draws on an earlier translation (no longer extant) 'by the celebrated Dr Wotton':[55] it is discussed in detail in Morris-Jones's article on the epitaph, with a detailed analysis of its errors and misreadings. Harris, following Wotton, reads the epitaph as the commemoration of a learned professor of astronomy, who was leader of a huge school of philosophers, at Caerleon, in the time before the coming of the Saxons to Britain. He remarks on the tangled Welsh – often a result of misreading ascenders and ligatures in the engraved Gothic script – and suggests that 'the British language, at the making of this inscription, seems to have been greatly corrupted by the provincial Roman'. He adds that this 'broken language' thus reflects the intermixing of British and Roman cultures and languages before the arrival of the Saxons.[56] There are several key misreadings that produce the interpretation advanced by Wotton and accepted by Harris. First, the opening line of the epitaph is mistranscribed and read as 'Nole clodde ur Ethrod Caerlleon …', rendered in Latin as 'Noli effodere Professorem (Scientarium) Caerlegionensem'.[57] Morris-Jones comments that '"Don't dig up the Professor" seems scarcely a necessary injunction',[58] though Harris, in 1773, anticipates this objection, and argues that 'it is frequent enough in old sepulcral [sic] monuments to use this form', pointing to formulae on ancient tombs which warn the viewer against damage or destruction of the grave.[59] Wotton and Harris interpret line 5 of the poem as a reference to a 'Selif Synwoepr', recognising the conventional Welsh form for 'Solomon' ('Selif'), but reading 'Synwoepr' as '*Synwybr*, a word compounded of *Syniaw* and *Wybyr*, i.e. *Coelos contmplari* [sic]' – a contemplator of the stars or astronomer. The name 'Adam Usk' is entirely missed: instead, the placename 'Usk' is interpreted as part of the reference to the location of the professor's school.[60]

53 Morris-Jones, 'Adam Usk's Epitaph'; Maunde Thompson, *Chronicon Adae.*

54 William Harris, 'Observations on the *Julia Strata*, and on the *Roman* Stations, Forts, and Camps, in the Counties of *Monmouth, Brecknock, Caermarthen*, and *Glamorgan*', *Archaeologia* 2 (1773): 1–24 (19).

55 Harris, 'Observations', p. 19.

56 Harris, 'Observations', p. 20.

57 Harris, 'Observations', p. 19.

58 Morris-Jones, 'Adam Usk's Epitaph', p. 113.

59 Harris, 'Observations', p. 20.

60 The full translation by Dr Wotton, as reproduced by Harris, is: 'Noli effodere Professorem Caerlegionensem, Advocatum dignissimum Londinensem, et Judicem

This reading of the epitaph draws on apparent supporting historical evidence in Camden's *Britannia,* which includes in its account of Caerleon (on Usk) the note that 'a little before the comming in of the English Saxons, there was a Schoole heere of 200 Philosophers, who being skilfull in Astronomie and all other arts, diligently observed the course and motion of the starres, as wrote Alexander Elsebiensis, a rare Author and hard to be found'.[61] Camden has this information via a Thomas James of Oxford, evidently working as a kind of research assistant, who takes it from Alexander of Ashby (Alexander Essebiensis), 'a twelfth-century prior, poet and religious writer'.[62] Filling the gap from the twelfth century back to pre-Saxon Britain, Harris, in his analysis of the epitaph, suggests that 'Elsebiensis' 'no doubt had it from some British records now lost'. He understands the epitaph as part of a proud tradition of early medieval British history writing or oral tradition, arguing that 'it is not unlikely that this *Selif Synwybr* was long after remembered by our British poets, who generally kept memoirs of these things'.[63] Thus, medieval myth-making meets early modern chorography and antiquarianism: the story of the school of philosophers and the reading of the plaque are mutually affirming, but both mistaken. Yet they produce, in Harris and Wotton's reading of the Usk epitaph, an awe-inspiring vision of culture and learning in Wales in the centuries after the Roman withdrawal and before the coming of the Saxons. The 'professor' commemorated is the 'most noble lawyer of London', but also a judge at Roman sites – and, for 'Fanum Julii' or the Temple / Shrine of Julius, Wotton suggests substituting 'Avaloniae': the Temple of Avalon. Romano-British and Arthurian resonances mingle in this mythologised vision of a pre-Saxon Britain. The misread final line, transcribed as 'Leua loer i lawn O leue', is rendered in Latin 'Lunam lucidam in plenilunio lucentem': Harris argues that this supports the entire proposition of the professor and school of astronomy, since there could be 'no elogy [sic] more poetical, or more proper for a professor of astronomy, than the comparing him to one of the great luminaries, which had been the subject of his contemplation'.[64]

The reading of the epitaph advanced by Wotton, and reproduced by Harris, was accepted by Theophilus Evans and appears in his *Drych y Prif Oesoedd* (Mirror of the Early Centuries, 1716, revised 1740): a foundational work of early medieval Welsh history. Later, in 1801, in his *An Historical Tour in Monmouthshire,* William

Sacri Privilegii (vel Cancellarium) apud Fanum Aaronis, et Fanum Julii (potius forsan Avaloniae) Solomonen Astrologum, Summum vel Praepositum Civitatis Usk, tenentis circiter decem Commotes, Lunam lucidam in plenilunio lucentem.' See Harris, 'Observations', p. 19.

61 William Camden, *Britain: Or, a Chorographicall Description of the Most Flourishing Kingdomes, England, Scotland, and Ireland, and the Ilands Adioyning, Out of the Depth of Antiquitie* (London, 1610), p. 693.

62 Angus Vine, *In Defiance of Time: Antiquarian Writing in Early Modern England* (Oxford: Oxford University Press, 2010), p. 91.

63 Harris, 'Observations', p. 20.

64 Harris, 'Observations', pp. 19–20.

Coxe treats this critical tradition with more scepticism, noting that Evans 'never saw the inscription', and proposes some revisions to the existing interpretation.[65] On the suggestion that the epitaph text represents some kind of hybrid form of Latin and Welsh, he argues that 'the best judges of the Welsh language, are decidedly of opinion, that the interpretation is wholly Welsh, and written in the dialect of Gwent used in the middle ages'.[66] Further, he asserts that 'there is not the smallest reference to Caerleon' and throws into doubt the existence of the 'college of two hundred philosophers' and the text's reliability as 'proof of the long residence of the Romans in these parts'.[67] Coxe claims the text more firmly as Welsh, but the seductive vision of the Marches as an unparalleled centre of classical learning in the first millennium recedes. The next most notable publication on the epitaph appears in 1847 in *Archaeologia Cambrensis*, in an article that, intriguingly, brings together three different authors (two of them anonymous) to offer varying interpretations of the text – a fascinating acknowledgment of its difficulty and the diversity of possible readings.[68] Thomas Wakeman reads lines 5 and 6 as 'Lo! Adam is a Solomon in intellect and resides at Usk', but proposes the thirteenth-century Adam ab Iorwerth ap Cradoc as the subject, and argues that 'his resting place' must be 'place of abode' rather than burial.[69] The two further, anonymous, correspondents offer alternative readings, with the third rendering the epitaph (clearly influenced by Wotton's translation) in English thus:

> In praise of the Teacher, Lord of Lleyn,
> The accomplished advocate of London,
> And justice of the peace, who was a privilege about a place:
> May the residence of Heaven, the abode of rights, be his portion.
> A Solomon he was, of astounding wisdom,
> And under Usk is now his sleeping bed:
> He effected reconciliations, was an eloquent Doctor,
> Brighter than the moon, and full of light.[70]

The school of philosophers has disappeared, but the (unknown) subject remains a teacher or professor (from the reading 'ur Ethrod'), but, in his depiction as advocate, wise scholar and doctor, a character somewhat closer to that of Adam Usk. Why, then, might these mistranslations be worth our attention? They offer readings of a text that never existed, but through this they reveal changing assumptions and narratives about medieval Welsh history, as well as a desire for origins, an

65 William Coxe, *An Historical Tour in Monmouthshire* (London: Printed for T. Cadell and W. Davies, 1801), p. 132.
66 Coxe, *Historical Tour*, p. 132.
67 Coxe, *Historical Tour*, p. 132.
68 'Inscription in Usk Church', p. 38.
69 'Inscription in Usk Church', p. 38.
70 'Inscription in Usk Church', p. 41.

idealised image of early medieval Welsh culture as the heir of classical learning and civilisation, and the place of myth-making in early modern Welsh historiography. Intriguingly, even in the earliest surviving (mis)translations, the epitaph remains a relic of cultural hybridity, redolent of borderland identity, multilingualism, and colonialism, even as its intended subject – Adam Usk and his life – are erased.

Even with Morris-Jones's translation of the Welsh, widely accepted by scholars today, Adam Usk's epitaph remains a challenging text that raises difficulties of interpretation, but also generates questions and insights that cut straight to the heart of recent scholarship on Adam, and extend and nuance our understanding of this historical figure, his work and context, in new ways. Adam Usk's epitaph – and, indeed, his Welshness more broadly – seem to have become disconnected from the body of scholarship on his writing. Could a more multilingual approach, and one that attends to the multimodal, manuscript, and material texts surrounding Adam – including the plaque in Usk Church – help to answer some of the questions framed, for example, by Steven Justice in his landmark study of Adam's *Chronicle*, *Adam Usk's Secret*? Justice comments that Adam's orthography in the *Chronicle* is 'consistent and interestingly eccentric', but explores this no further; while Morris-Jones argues that Usk's Welsh spelling (evidenced in the epitaph) was affected by English and French conventions, Given-Wilson thinks more flexibly about how Adam's multilingualism – both written and oral or aural – may have affected his orthography in Latin.[71] Justice observes patterns of rhythm in the *Chronicle* that constitute failures of well-disciplined Latin, yet comments that '[t]hese failures are choices, not lapses, and throughout the book we can see him choosing emphatically rhythmical or emphatically arhythmical cadences for dramatic purpose'.[72] Justice does not pursue this, but is there scope to explore the unusual mannerisms and aural patternings of Adam's Latin as potentially influenced by the idioms of vernacular Welsh *cynghanedd*? All commentators on the *Chronicle* observe its prominent interest and engagement in prophetic writing, and the Welsh traditions informing this.[73] Adam's epitaph in Usk Church centres his identity and self-presentation on his Welshness and invites us to do the same in a reappraisal of the *Chronicle* as a textual production. That the epitaph has dropped out of recent critical analyses of Adam Usk, even as those studies attend closely and productively to processes of self-fashioning and the production of self-image in the *Chronicle*, is a serious loss and one that needs restoring.

Finally, how do we acknowledge and recuperate error and accident in our reading of Adam Usk's epitaph(s)? The plaque in St Mary's Priory Church, described by Morris-Jones as so 'hopelessly misread and misunderstood'[74] for centuries, remains,

71 Justice, *Adam Usk's Secret*, p. 10; Morris-Jones, 'Adam Usk's Epitaph', pp. 126–27; Given-Wilson, *Chronicle*, pp. lxxxvi–lxxxvii.

72 Justice, *Adam Usk's Secret*, p. 118.

73 See for example Given-Wilson, *Chronicle*, pp. lxvii–lxxi.

74 Morris-Jones, 'Adam Usk's Epitaph', p. 113.

even in its current scholarly edition, an uncertain text. In the epitaph's fifteenth-century textual mistakes and problems we have been able to read, productively, traces of cultural hybridity, multilingualism, ambivalence, and the fraught complexities of collaborative textual production. Earlier translations of the epitaph, while often serious misapprehensions, further reveal the defining irony of the text's obstinate unreadability – its failure as a legible memorial – as well as important ideas and ideals of late antique and early medieval Welshness that inform its later reception. In his study of Adam's *Chronicle*, Justice explores the limits of 'New Criticism' and close reading, imagining what may lie beyond the tools of critical analysis and the assumption that every text is an 'interpretable artefact'.[75] His discussion raises important questions about whether there are, indeed, uninterpretable artefacts, as well as what kinds of technique can be used to recover authorial intention and authenticity from a complex textual performance. He explores the value of accidents – moments where the text goes awry or slips out of control – and the use of 'misfires to find the unmeant traces of history in an intentional performance'.[76] In the pages of the *Chronicle*, we have examined the 'misfires' of Adam's epitaph trial pieces: abortive, fragmentary texts on his name and identity that betray the divisions and ambivalences undermining his lifelong project of self-presentation. But what about the epitaph in Usk Church? What can we learn from paying attention to a text so utterly riven with errors and uncertainty? From the mistakes of the fifteenth-century scribe to the engraver, to early modern (mis)translations and critical interpretations, this is an artefact in which the accidental and the unmeant has continually dominated over intentionality. Indeed, its very textual porousness and precarity means that, as we have seen, the values, cultural (il)literacies, and desires of many participants have written themselves, across centuries, peculiarly powerfully over any original intention or design. Justice attends to the secrets and puzzles of the *Chronicle*, but Adam's Usk epitaph emerges as the most enduring puzzle he has left us: ultimately, perhaps, a text that can never be fully or definitively interpretable, as the multiauthored experiment in the 1847 volume of *Archaeologia Cambrensis*, with its collection of anonymised counter-readings, tacitly acknowledges. Perhaps only such inconclusive plurality and multivocality, the jostling voices and interpretations over the centuries, the contingent readings and vested interests, come close to capturing the rich and fractious hybridity presented by that small brass plaque in Usk Church. Adam Usk's epitaphs have been dismissed on the grounds of literary merit, textual faultiness, or (most egregiously) linguistic inaccessibility to present-day non-Welsh-speaking scholars. The plaque in Usk Church has been treated as a mere philological challenge or curiosity. Yet this unique collection of sources sheds new light on the fashioning of identity, self-representation, and textual production in a multilingual medieval borderland.

75 Justice, *Adam Usk's Secret*, pp. 136–37.
76 Justice, *Adam Usk's Secret*, p. 139.

11

Borders in Translation: English Resistance to Borderless Empire in Jean d'Arras's *Mélusine*

Jan Shaw

Helen Fulton's important work on Wales, which concerns much of this volume, is contextualised within a broader interest in the richness of the border literatures of medieval Britain. At the time of writing, Helen is leading the Borders and Borderlands project at the University of Bristol, a collaborative research network that asks how topography and built environments contribute to our understanding of medieval borders and border identities. This chapter considers the deployment of borders in one late medieval romance and its English translation, thereby representing the Borderlands project in this celebratory volume.

Medieval borders cannot be understood within the conceptual framework that explains the borders of modern nation states. Unlike the modern state, where sovereignty stretches from one legally defined border to another, operating more or less equally across the territory, Benedict Anderson argues that 'dynastic' realms are defined by centres, leaving borders 'porous and indistinct'.[1] Saskia Sassen observes that the conception of territorial boundaries remained underdeveloped in Europe until the late Middle Ages, noting that political authority was based on the allegiance of peoples through whom authority over territory was acquired, rather than on direct territorial control.[2] For Sassen, medieval Europe was little more than a collection of 'scattered de facto mini-sovereignties' that existed within 'a vast system of often loose overlapping jurisdictions', including loyalties both local (to lords) and far-flung (to popes and kings).[3] From this perspective, rather than mutually recognised sovereign states with borders delimited by agreement, European kingdoms in the late Middle Ages retained vestiges of empire in the complexities

1 Benedict Anderson, *Imagined Communities: Reflections on the Origin and Spread of Nationalism* (London: Verso, 2006), p. 19.

2 Saskia Sassen, *Territory, Authority, Rights: From Medieval to Global Assemblages* (Princeton, NJ: Princeton University Press, 2006), pp. 33–35.

3 Sassen, *Territory, Authority, Rights*, p. 33.

of local and centralised authority, and in the self-imposed border limitations that Paul La Pradelle referred to as 'the voluntary halting place'.[4] Indeed, Randy Schiff proposes that empire is the 'more apt model' for considering late-medieval polities, particularly in cases where militarised zones without stable borders signal ongoing expansionary tensions.[5]

From a legal perspective, however, La Pradelle identifies the evolution of precise border delimitation by mutual agreement from the Middle Ages in Europe.[6] The evidence in medieval romance suggests that there was an acute awareness of different border types and of the strategic opportunities they presented. The romance of *Mélusine* is one such example.[7] The romance was written at the behest of the powerful Jean, Duc de Berry, to intervene in a looming political crisis that was threatening to take from him his favourite fortress of Lusignan.[8] At the time of

4 Paul La Pradelle, translated and cited in S. Whittemore Boggs, *International Boundaries: A Study of Boundary Functions and Problems* (New York: Columbia University Press, 1940), p. 7.

5 Randy P. Schiff, *Revivalist Fantasy: Alliterative Verse and Nationalist Literary History* (Columbus, OH: Ohio State University Press, 2011), p. 100.

6 Benjamin Perrier, 'The "Frontier" According to Paul de La Pradelle', *Borders in Globalization Review* 2.1 (2020): 130–34.

7 I cite two critical editions: for the English text, A. K. Donald, ed., *Melusine. Compiled by Jean D'Arras Englisht about 1500* (London: Kegan Paul, Trench, Trübner and Company, 1895); for the French text, Matthew W. Morris, ed. and trans., *A Bilingual Edition of Jean d'Arras's Mélusine or L'Historie de Lusignan* (Lewiston: Edwin Mellon Press, 2007). The translations, while informed by Morris, are sometimes modified. Any errors, therefore, are my own. Important studies of the French *Roman de Mélusine* include Louis Stouff, *Essai sur 'Mélusine,' roman du XIV siècle par Jean d'Arras* (Paris: Editions Picard, 1930); Jacques Le Goff and Emmanuel Le Roy Ladurie, 'Mélusine maternelle et défricheuse', *Annales* 26 (1971): 587–622; Laurence Harf-Lancner, *Les fées au Moyen Âge: Morgane et Mélusine; La naissance des fées* (Paris: Champion, 1984); Françoise Clier-Colombani, *La fée Mélusine au Moyen Âge: Images, mythes et symboles* (Paris: Le Léopard d'or, 1991); Jean-Jacques Vincensini, *Pensée mythique et narrations médiévales* (Paris: Champion, 1996). For a comprehensive discussion of modern reinterpretations of the Mélusine myth see Misty Urban, Deva Kemmis, and Melissa Ridley Elmes, eds, *Melusine's Footprint: Tracing the Legacy of a Medieval Myth* (Leiden: Brill, 2017). For the only monograph-length discussion of the English *Melusine* to date, see Jan Shaw, *Space, Gender and Memory in Middle English Romance: Architectures of Wonder in Melusine* (New York: Palgrave Macmillan, 2016).

8 Studies that explore historical and political contexts and implications of the romance include Laurence Harf-Lancner, 'Littérature et Politique: Jean de Berry, Leon de Lusignan et le Roman de Mélusine', in Danielle Buschinger, ed., *Histoire et littérature au Centre d'études médiévales de l'Université de Picardie, Amiens, 20–24 mars 1985* (Göppingen: Kümerle, 1991), pp. 161–71; Donald Maddox and Sara Sturm-Maddox, eds, *Mélusine of Lusignan: Founding Fiction in Late Medieval France* (Athens, GA: University of Georgia Press, 1996); Marie-Thérèse de Medeiros, 'L'idée de croisade dans la *Mélusine* de Jean d'Arras', *Cahiers de recherches médiévales et humanistes: Journal of medieval and humanistic studies* 1 (1996): 147–55; Catherine

writing, between 1387 and 1393, Lusignan, in western Poitou, was part of the contested borderland of the Hundred Years War between the crowns of England and France.[9] To lend popular legitimacy to the continuation of the Duc's tenure as lord of Lusignan, Jean d'Arras drew on the local legend of the fairy Mélusine to craft a romance of origin that reached back to legendary time and folded vast swathes of what is now western France into an empire with Lusignan as its imperial core. Mélusine's sons further increase the family's holdings, reaching as far east as Bohemia and Cilician Armenia. Given the then political context, it is, perhaps, not surprising that examples of border delimitation and demarcation, usually associated with more modern conceptions, are found in this text alongside imperial organisations of power.[10] Precise border agreements are also found that extend beyond the purely geographical into the geo-political space of religion. The most significant border that this text negotiates to transcend, however, is that of time.

The political impact that the romance may have had on the Duc de Berry's immediate problem is unclear, but its wide circulation evidences popular success. After its initial appearance in prose, the romance was reworked in verse, and both forms were translated and circulated throughout Europe, including a unique translation of Jean d'Arras's prose version into English in about 1500.[11] The political location of this translation, both on the opposite side of the Hundred Years War and the tussle over Lusignan, lends it a singular authority to illuminate further the political implications of Jean d'Arras's efforts. For his or her most significant revision, however, the translator singled out as the main target the strategy to extend the Lusignan empire throughout human time. This chapter argues, then, that the romance of *Mélusine* uses different conceptions of borders, imperial and modern, geo-political and temporal, selectively and strategically to establish an empire that extends across the known world and throughout human time. In the second half of this chapter, the analysis homes in on Geoffroy's visit to Jerusalem, in which the temporal limits

Gaullier-Bougassas, *La tentation de l'Orient dans le roman médiéval: Sur l'imaginaire médiéval de l'autre* (Paris: Champion, 2003); Catherine Léglu, 'Nourishing Lineage in the Earliest French Versions of the "Roman de Mélusine"', *Medium Ævum* 74.1 (2005): 71–85; E. Jane Burns, 'Magical Politics from Poitou to Armenia: Mélusine, Jean de Berry, and the Eastern Mediterranean', *Journal of Medieval and Early Modern Studies* 43.2 (2013): 275–301. For a consideration of the political patronage of Couldrette's poetic version of the romance from 1400, see Tania M. Colwell, 'Patronage of the Poetic Mélusine romance: Guillaume l'Archevêque's Confrontation with Dynastic Crisis', *Journal of Medieval History* 37 (2011): 215–29.

9 Harf-Lancner, 'Littérature et Politique', p. 169.

10 For border terminology, see Perrier, 'The "Frontier"'; A. Henry McMahon, 'International Boundaries', *Journal of the Royal Society of Arts* 84.4330 (1935): 2–16; Bradley Parker, 'Toward an Understanding of Borderland Processes', *American Antiquity* 71.1 (2006): 77–100.

11 For a comprehensive study of the medieval afterlife of the romance throughout Europe, see Lydia Zeldenrust, *The Mélusine Romance in Medieval Europe: Translation, Circulation, and Material Contexts* (Cambridge: D. S. Brewer, 2020).

of the empire are dissolved. The English translation, however, deletes Geoffroy's visit completely, leaving only the pilgrimage of two other brothers. In this way, the English text removes the temporal complexity of the origins and future reach of the Lusignan empire, effectively resisting Jean's ambitious claims. The English translation, therefore, reintroduces the limit of time, bringing the Lusignan/French empire neatly to an end in the recent past, never to rise again.

Borders

In the romance, the establishment and growth of the Lusignan holdings and their familial and political relationships suggest an imperial organisation of power. As Bradley Parker observes, imperial structures employ a number of potential relationships between core and periphery, from direct administrative control, to control by delegates imported from the centre, to retaining local control but implementing varying degrees of intervention, taxation, military assistance and control of foreign policy.[12] These relationships, by focussing on satellite administrative hubs and the people who rule them, tend to leave physical borders undefined, as becomes evident in the romance. Various modes of control are inscribed in the romance as the Lusignan sphere of influence grows, and personal relationships are key to both local and distant authority. Lusignan, the core of empire, is established on land free of vassalage, but is enmeshed with family connections as it is granted to Mélusine's husband, Raimondin, by his cousin, the Earl of Poitiers, for services rendered to his recently deceased father (as discussed further below). From Lusignan, Mélusine and Raimondin increase their personal holdings into western Poitou, expanding into previously uninhabited lands.[13] The lack of habitation suggests that Mélusine and Raimondin are opening up new territories, obviating the need to define borders. La Pradelle's definitions of *limitation* and *delimitation* are helpful here. *Limitation* is the self-imposed territorial limit within imperial structures: 'The *Limes imperii* is not the result of an agreement, even an imposed agreement, but a mere voluntary halting place'.[14] *Delimitation*, on the other hand, is a territorial limit mutually agreed between two sovereignties: 'the modern frontier [is] a delimitation of equal jurisdictions', 'the modern boundary presuppose[es] equal jurisdictions'.[15] The demesne of Mélusine, therefore, as it expands into new territories without habitation, with no negotiation with another sovereignty, has the imperial quality of the self-imposed limitations of La Pradelle's 'voluntary halting place'.[16] Mélusine marks these new acquisitions through the building of a series of castles, towns, and towers, which she and Raimondin visit in a peripatetic style, travelling from one

12 Parker, 'Borderland Processes', pp. 83–84.

13 'Pays n'est habitez et peupliz'. Morris, *Jean d'Arras's Mélusine*, p. 208. 'Countre is nat enhabyted with people'. Donald, *Melusine*, p. 100, l. 27.

14 La Pradelle, translated and cited in Boggs, *International Boundaries*, p. 7.

15 La Pradelle, translated and cited in Boggs, *International Boundaries*, p. 7.

16 La Pradelle, translated and cited in Boggs, *International Boundaries*, p. 7.

location to another, fostering community through the judicial management of their estates and entertaining the surrounding noble families.[17] These locations, therefore, function as satellite administrative hubs from which direct supervisory control is maintained over the district.

While this built infrastructure represents the limits of Mélusine and Raimondin's direct control, their influence extends further. Raimondin travels to Brittany to recover his patrimony, successfully defending his claim through trial by combat. He then replicates his Poitevin cousin's generosity, distributing his rich inheritance freehold to his Breton cousins, thereby securing their lifelong allegiance and the favour of the king: 'the king of Bretons & hys baronye made grete honour to Raymondyn in so moche that I can nat reherce it'.[18] Supported by a comfortable buffer of patrilineal connections to the north and east, Mélusine and Raimondin's influence quickly extends south through a mixture of vassalage, family connections, and diplomatic ties. Indeed, by the time Mélusine has given birth to her fourth son, the romance tells us that Raimondin had acquired so many lands in Poitou, Brittany, Guyenne, and Gascony, that 'no prynce was about hym / but he doubted to dysplaise hym'.[19] The resultant collection of allied and tributary states is under varying levels of control, from influence to direct rule, but there is no invasive colonisation of previously occupied lands. Control and influence radiate outwards from Lusignan, effected through a network of nodal points of power, connecting with the rulers of the surrounding communities, rather than identifying and defending delimited borders.

As noted by Anderson, the flexibility presented through imperial structures enables networks of power to span vast distances, as indeed is evident in the Lusignan case.[20] In a loose adaptation of historical events, the second generation expands the imperial project to reach the eastern fringes of Christendom.[21] Four Lusignan sons embark on chivalric quests in the pursuit of honour, fighting righteous battles and winning the hands of vulnerable heiresses. They acquire Cyprus,

17 Morris, *Jean d'Arras's Mélusine*, p. 142; Donald, *Melusine*, p. 63, ll. 7–10. Also, 'the feste was made grete / and many noble men, ladyes, and damoyselles were there ... and bygan the Abbey there, and moche good she died to poure folk' (Donald, *Melusine*, p. 103, ll. 7–15).

18 Donald, *Melusine*, p. 90, ll. 17–19.

19 Donald, *Melusine*, p. 104, ll. 6–7; Morris, *Jean d'Arras's Mélusine*, p. 214. The English text adds that these acquisitions occur 'through the polycye & good gouernaunce of Melusyne' (Donald, *Melusine*, p. 104, ll. 3–4).

20 Anderson, *Imagined Communities*, p. 19.

21 The romance incorporates but embellishes upon the historical reach of the Lusignan crusader kings in the eastern Mediterranean, collapsing time in these episodes to suit the narrative imperative. See Emmanuéle Baumgartner, 'Fiction and History: The Cypriot Episode in Jean d'Arras's *Mélusine*', in Maddox and Sturm-Maddox, eds, *Mélusine of Lusignan*, pp. 185–211. See also Daisy Delogu, 'Jean d'Arras makes History: Political Legitimacy and the *Roman de Mélusine*', *Dalhousie French Studies* 80 (2007): 15–28.

Cilician Armenia, Luxembourg, and Bohemia through these means. In their travels they also secure the fealty of Alsace and the friendship and support of Rhodes. A fifth brother, Geoffroy, who is the heir of Lusignan, spends a considerable amount of narrative time flitting across Europe, from one satellite centre to another, assisting his brothers and father in fighting off assaults and enforcing tribute payments. Geoffroy's travels serve to scope out the expanse of empire. Jean d'Arras has him travelling as far as Ireland when he hears of 'un people qui pas ne vouloit obeir enc e quílz devoient a son pere' ('peple that wold not obey to hys fader').[22] The English translator, however, pushes this conflict back across the English Channel to Guerande in Brittany, containing the western limit of empire in the second generation to that which had been established by Raimondin in the first.[23] Geoffroy's exploits supporting his brothers in the Holy Land mark the eastern limit. While this extent is repeatedly reinforced in the narrative, the borders themselves remain undefined. Rather than territorial control, central authority reaches to the extremities through a complex web of the loyalty and obligation of 'ryght true & loyal peuple'.[24] It would seem, therefore, that the romance is clearly setting up the House of Lusignan's tentacular reach across a huge expanse as an empire, founded upon a network of human connection, with borders remaining porous and indistinct.

This is not to say that legally agreed borders, those inscribed in documentation, demarked on the landscape and so on, were not understood. Indeed, these forms of borders are strategically invoked in the narrative. There are two borders described in the text that are reflected in legal agreements drawn up between mutually recognised sovereign entities. One defines the land around Lusignan, setting the core of empire apart, and the other is the impervious divide between Muslim and Christian, forming the religious limit of empire.

Lusignan is built upon land secured by a hard border. As noted above, it is legitimately gained, granted freehold to Raimondin by his cousin, the Count of Poitiers, for services rendered to the count's recently deceased father. The land is delimited by legal agreement, secured in 'the best and moost surest wyse that could be deuysed', with documents 'Seelled of the grette Seal of the Erle, by thassent and relacion of alle the Barons of the land / whiche also dide putte theire seeles thereto'.[25] It is then marked out on the landscape by a thong made from a single hart's skin, and its extent is appropriately (and accurately) recorded by the count's agents. This is the only landholding in the narrative that is defined in this way, secured in legal contract and drawn on the surface of the land, echoing both La Pradelle's *delimitation* (of border lines legally agreed between two neighbouring sovereignties, rather than the limit self-imposed from within) and McMahon's *demarcation* (of a border line

22 Morris, *Jean d'Arras's Mélusine*, p. 462; Donald, *Melusine*, p. 246, ll. 16–17.

23 Donald, *Melusine*, p. 89.

24 Donald, *Melusine*, p. 246, l. 28.

25 Donald, *Melusine*, p. 42, ll. 2–6.

on the ground).[26] These formal legitimising processes mark the land upon which Lusignan is built as quantitatively and qualitatively different from any other lands in the romance. Such processes not only distinguish it unreservedly from the holdings of Raimondin's family, but the physical separation on all sides also reinforces the potential political independence of Lusignan. In this deft manoeuvre, therefore, under Mélusine's instruction, Raimondin secures an independent nucleus for the emergent empire. Consequently, the real-world geo-political vulnerability of the historical castle of Lusignan, which was the primary driver for the writing of the romance, has been transformed in the romance to a core of empire, heavily protected by every means possible.

The border between Christian and Muslim is also sharp and clear, even though the dividing line between Christendom and the Muslim world is left unspecified in geographical terms. The limits of Christendom are instead delineated in the recognition of irreconcilable difference between Muslim and Christian, as Urien reflects: 'Pay foy, c'est grant dommage que ce Turc ne croit en Dieu, car il est moult preux' ('By my feyth, it is grete pyte & dommage that yonder Turcke byleueth not on god, For he is moche preu & valyaunt of his hand').[27] The recognition of this difference leads to unexpected narrative outcomes. Unlike the unrestrained expansion into foreign territory that the imperial structure enables through its lack of acknowledgement of other sovereign entities, the Muslim world is recognised as a separate sovereign polity. This is evidenced by the treaty that the Lusignans and the 'Saracens' eventually negotiate.[28] In a similar way to the written agreement of the land grant at Lusignan, the treaty is inscribed in letters patent affixed with appropriate seals.[29] Such an agreement can only be made between legally sovereign entities. With this insurmountable distinction firmly established, the terms of the treaty can allow for a long and fruitful collaboration, without any risk of their fundamental differences being dissolved.

It is evident, therefore, that border types were well understood and that the choice of which border type to use in a given situation was strategic. Lusignan, the core of empire, is secured behind delimited borders, agreed and recorded in legal documentation, and demarked on the surface of the land. From here, imperial structures enable unfettered expansion. Indeed, in the very early stages, there is almost an obligation on Mélusine and Raimondin to populate and exploit the landscape of western Poitou, as suggested by the 'grant dommage' of leaving the lands uninhabited.[30] As they expand farther afield, Lusignan influence and rule invariably bring order and peace to the land. While in Brittany, Raimondin resolves disputes and

26 Perrier, 'The "Frontier"', pp. 131–32.

27 Morris, *Jean d'Arras's Mélusine*, p. 282; Donald, *Melusine*, p. 145, ll. 14–17.

28 In both Jean d'Arras's text and its English translation, the terms 'Saracen' and 'Sarrasin', respectively, are used throughout.

29 Donald, *Melusine*, p. 292, l. 7.

30 Morris, *Jean d'Arras's Mélusine*, p. 208. Donald, *Melusine*, p. 100, l. 26.

brings warring barons together in friendship.[31] Four of Mélusine and Raimondin's sons bring lasting peace to distant lands, through fighting rightful quarrels and implementing their mother's sage advice on good governance. Even tribute taking by the Lusignans leads to peace making. Tipped off by lagging tribute payments, Geoffroy delivers the country around the fortress of Sion from the rule of traitors, releasing prisoners and installing a 'vaillant homme et preudhoms' ('ryght valyaunt & wyse') knight, 'de gouverner la loyaument et tenir justice' ('to gouerne lawfully his subgets, & to keep good justice').[32] The border with the Muslims, focusing on religious difference, signals the limits of Christendom. From this point on, the Lusignans expand no farther eastward. Instead, in the third generation and beyond, the empire folds back into Europe. Lusignan strength and influence is extended and consolidated through marriage and acquisition, spreading across all southern France, south into Catalonia and Aragon, north into the Low Countries, Denmark, and Scandinavia, and even into England through marriage with the Pembrokes, who did indeed marry into the House of Lusignan in the early thirteenth century.[33] Given that Lusignan rule and/or influence leads only to peace and good governance, their expansion across and within Europe is legitimised. Indeed, in creating a pan-European empire, the Lusignans create a pan-European peace.

This apparently secure construct, however, is not flawless. The somewhat overdetermined protection of Lusignan, particularly in legal terms, inevitably draws attention to its historical vulnerability. While it is the core of empire, a trace of its borderland character, therefore, remains. The border with the Muslim world similarly retains a strategic ambiguity. As noted, this border is based on religious difference and does not define a geographical boundary. Indeed, the terms of the treaty tend toward the dissolution of such a boundary, as they include not only an agreement to share military intelligence 'assoone as they might know it', but also to 'socoure and gyue ... comfort' to each other against aggressors.[34] In this way, the treaty allows for the movement of Lusignan forces into Muslim territories, specifically for the purpose of Lusignan peace-keeping, thereby enabling the spread of Lusignan influence even beyond the borders of Christendom. In leaving this particular border ambiguous, the treaty opens up possibilities for an approach to Jerusalem, which is located in this geo-political borderland, and which was viscerally important to Christians at the time of writing. Further, the treaty extends into the future for 100 years and a day – effectively forever – making Jerusalem available to the Lusignan peace-keeping project moving forward.[35] At this moment in the narrative, when the treaty is made and the limits of Christendom recognised,

31 Morris, *Jean d'Arras's Mélusine*, p. 206; Donald, *Melusine*, p. 100, ll. 12–17.

32 Morris, *Jean d'Arras's Mélusine*, p. 482; Donald, *Melusine*, p. 256, ll. 12–18.

33 Morris, *Jean d'Arras's Mélusine*, p. 682; Donald, *Melusine*, p. 356, l. 1.

34 Donald, *Melusine*, p. 292, ll. 15–16.

35 The French text states 'cent ans et ung jour' (Morris, *Jean d'Arras's Mélusine*, p. 554), while the English translates this to one hundred and one years: 'C & one yere' (Donald, *Melusine*, p. 292).

Jerusalem sits just beyond Lusignan grasp, but the future stretches out, full of possibility. Then, at the signing of the agreement, the sultan invites Geoffroy to accompany him to Jerusalem.

Jerusalem

If Lusignan is simultaneously at the core and on the periphery of empire, Jerusalem is similarly situated. In the medieval Christian imaginary, Jerusalem existed on the one hand in a geopolitical borderland just beyond the reach of a desiring Christendom, and on the other hand as a monumental location central to Christian ideology. The Jerusalem sequence thereby implicitly aligns Lusignan with Jerusalem, while also drawing the Lusignan empire into the temporal complexity of Jerusalem. Anthony Bale, Mary Carruthers, and others have noted that the medieval Christian imaginary associated a different kind of time with Jerusalem, removing expectations of linearity, instead focussing on engagements that promoted symbolic readings.[36] The romance appears to tap into similar ideas, interrupting the linear flow of time. Including Geoffroy, the son who will inherit Lusignan, in this episode implicitly locates the foundation of Lusignan within the polytemporality there described, effectively extending the narrative as a whole, and the House of Lusignan's influence, beyond conventional conceptions of linear time. Rather than reading this as a temporal collapse, as a flattening of time, it is more in keeping with its temporal complexity to read it as offering a simultaneity of temporal multiplicity, as bringing multiple narrative trajectories together into one place in time.[37]

To expand on the implications of such a meeting, I turn to Doreen Massey, a contemporary theorist of space, place, and time, who proposes that space is a four-dimensional product of interrelations, a 'simultaneity of stories-so-far'.[38] The 'so-far' encapsulates both the past, which has been, and the future, yet to be determined, both of which will necessarily be changed by the interactions that occur in that coming together. In this view, space has potentially disruptive characteristics, because it brings together narrative trajectories in a 'happenstance arrangement-in-relation-to-each-other, of previous unconnected narratives/ temporalities'.[39] This leads to the uniqueness of place (place being the specific term and space the general term). Place is defined by the particular collections of stories that come together there, stories whose relations are influenced by the wider power-geometries that pertain in that place. For Massey, then, 'what is special about place is precisely that throwntogetherness, the unavoidable challenge of negotiating a here-and-now ...

36 Anthony Bale, *Feeling Persecuted: Christians, Jews and Images of Violence in the Middle Ages* (London: Reaktion Books, 2010); Mary Carruthers, *The Craft of Thought: Meditation, Rhetoric and the Making of Images* (Cambridge: Cambridge University Press, 1998).

37 Gaullier-Bougassas, *La tentation de l'Orient*, p. 320.

38 Doreen Massey, *For Space* (London: Sage, 2005), p. 24.

39 Massey, *For Space*, p. 39.

this is the event of place'.[40] To read the Jerusalem episode through this lens vaults the scope of Lusignan power into another temporal order. The narrative has not only extended the Lusignan empire to the limits of Christendom, it has also served to break down conventional conceptions of linear time, spreading its imperial reach across multiple spatial and temporal projections, without perceivable limit in either space or time.

Prior to this moment in the text, Jean d'Arras locates the main narrative implicitly in two main timeframes. One temporal thread draws from the time of production of the romance or just prior, as indicated by the implicit political references that pervade the text. For example, the lands Raimondin draws together in an empire-like structure, taking in the western third of modern-day France, map onto those ceded to England in the Treaty of Brétigny in 1360, while the acquisitions of Cyprus and Cilician Armenia in the second generation are a reworking of historical events during the crusades.[41] Similarly, Mélusine's patriline maps onto the Auld Alliance between France and Scotland, and Raimondin's onto the ruling Breton clans involved in the Wars of the Breton Succession.[42] This thread, therefore, implicitly invokes contemporaneous time by echoing those very particular political instabilities that caused Jean de Berry to commission the production of this text. This is not a consistent temporal location, but it contrasts with the other temporality, which is a far distant past, a legendary past, prior to the building of the many castles and towns that had already existed in western Poitou for centuries at the time of writing. The French text identifies this as the earliest of times, as these lands are identified by Raimondin, in his journey home from Brittany, as both rich and uninhabited. The tendency in the English translation, however, is to undercut such temporal distinctions. While Raimondin's reflection is translated, the English narrator adds: 'many a fayre manoyr and places were on the ryueres there that soone might be redressed as hym semed whiche had be ouerthawen in tyme of warre'.[43] The country might not be populated at this moment, but it has been in the past. Manors lie in ruins, overthrown by war, which necessarily points to a time later than a distant originary moment, and could even be a contemporaneous reference to the decimation of lands across western France during the Hundred Years War.[44] In this way, the English text chips away at Jean d'Arras's project to draw legitimacy from legendary

40 Massey, *For Space*, p. 140.

41 For the treaty of Brétigny, see Anne Curry, *The Hundred Years War* (Basingstoke: Palgrave Macmillan, 2003); Michael Prestwich, *A Short History of the Hundred Years War* (London and New York: I. B. Tauris, 2018). For the crusades, see Christopher Tyerman, *England and the Crusades: 1095–1588* (Chicago: University of Chicago Press, 1988).

42 For the Wars of the Breton Succession, see Erika Graham-Goering, *Princely Power in Late Medieval France: Jeanne de Penthiévre and the War for Brittany* (Cambridge: Cambridge University Press, 2020).

43 Donald, *Melusine*, p. 100, ll. 27–30.

44 Donald, *Melusine*, p. 100, ll. 25–29.

origins in the long distant past. The French text, however, is explicit in identifying at least two timeframes, and Geoffroy's visit to Jerusalem shakes up time even further by interrupting its linearity.

The episode that describes Geoffroy's visit to Jerusalem introduces temporal conundrums that cannot be easily resolved. As discussed below, the romance temporally places Geoffroy's visit to Jerusalem after the destruction of Jerusalem by Titus in 70 CE, but before its rebuilding, which began in the second century CE. Notably, however, the Holy Sepulchre stands, which is dated from the fourth century CE.[45] Given the impossibility of locating such a moment in historical terms, it has been proposed that the purpose of these references is to take the establishment of the House of Lusignan back to some unidentified, even mythical, time prior to the crusades.[46] Within the layering of multiple temporalities in this description of Jerusalem, however, deeper meaning unfolds.

Jerusalem has a long and complex history that has been read through multiple interpretative perspectives. For Christian pilgrims in the Middle Ages, whether they were armed crusaders, unarmed travellers, or virtual pilgrims who stayed at home, Jerusalem was much more than a destination at the end of a literal or figurative road. Bale proposes that it was 'an inherently translatable idea, a set of images rather than a place'.[47] Indeed, Carruthers explains that pilgrimage itself was 'a map of remembering', and that, having arrived, pilgrims were not looking for 'an authentic, validated historical object'. Rather, what was 'authentic and *real*' to them was 'the *memory-work*, the thinking' to which Jerusalem's holy sites 'gave clues'.[48] Importantly, for the Christian pilgrim, the multitude of events, of histories, that accrued in this place, became organised around the narrative found in the Bible: 'The pilgrims thus came not to see something new, but to recollect things well known to them already'.[49] As Bale concludes: '"Calvary" did not refer to a place as such but rather a scene with a standard narrative and a specific cast of characters'.[50] When viewed in this light, Geoffroy's visit to Jerusalem with the Sultan of Damascus becomes understandable. The scene is set: the ruined city on the one hand and the Holy Sepulchre ready for Christian worship on the other. The cast of characters is complete: Jesus, the Jews, Titus, and Vespasian. Geoffroy and the sultan bring in the Lusignan link and Urian, Guyon, and others arrive soon after to

45 Colin Morris, *The Sepulchre of Christ and the Medieval West: From the Beginning to 1600* (Oxford: Oxford University Press, 2005), pp. 31–38.

46 Baumgartner notes that chronicles, which gave more historically accurate descriptions of events, were circulating widely in the late Middle Ages. Baumgartner, 'Fiction and History', in Maddox and Sturm-Maddox, eds, *Founding Fiction*, pp. 185–200. See further, Gaullier-Bougassas, *La tentation de l'Orient*, p. 341.

47 Bale, *Feeling Persecuted*, p. 122.

48 Carruthers, *The Craft of Thought*, p. 42.

49 Carruthers, *The Craft of Thought*, p. 43.

50 Bale, *Feeling Persecuted*, 122.

complete the pilgrimage picture.[51] The narrative itself is complete: the death and resurrection of Christ, the 30 pieces of silver, the destruction of the Jews, pilgrims worshipping at the Holy Sepulchre, and the implicit rebuilding yet to come.

This narrative explicitly draws on what is now known as the Vengeance of Our Lord tradition.[52] Popular in the late Middle Ages and circulating in a number of narratives, this tradition appropriates the historical slaughter of the Jews and the sacking of their city by the Romans in 70 CE and transforms it into a Christian vengeance story through the spectacular conversion of the aggressors Vespasian and his son Titus.[53] Roger Nicholson observes that such narratives were seen to 'do God's work', as the fall of Jerusalem is a necessary part of Christian history.[54] The references in the Jerusalem episode of the romance are unmistakable:

> Et le mena le soudant en Jherusalem, qui pour lors n'estoit pas reparee ne refremee de la destruction que Vaspasien et Thitus, son filz, y orent faicte, quant ilz vindrent vengier la mort Jhesucrist apréz son crucifiement. Et donna Vaspasien, emperiere de Romme, xxx. Juifs pour un denier, en remebrance qu'ilz orent achaté le precieuz corps Jhesucrist xxx. deniers.[55]
>
> (The sultan brought him to Jerusalem, which, at that time, had not yet been repaired and rebuilt since the destruction that Vespasian and his son Titus had made there when they came to avenge the death of Jesus Christ after His crucifixion. Vespasian, the Roman Emperor, had given thirty Jews for one piece of silver in remembrance of the fact that they had bought the precious body of Jesus Christ for thirty pieces of silver.)

The romance clearly and unequivocally attributes vengeance motives to Titus and Vespasian's sacking of the city, citing the crucifixion and death of Jesus Christ as the impetus for their actions. Importantly, it is not the Lusignans who enact the Vengeance narrative. They do not explicitly take Jerusalem: they do not attack it, put in under siege, or inflict any destruction upon it. Instead, they arrive after the requisite cleansing has taken place. Nicholson also argues that the Vengeance of Our Lord tradition, in addition to explaining the necessity for destruction, points to future rebuilding. He proposes that, through their modernised chivalric settings,

51 The romance appropriates a history of English glory, when Richard I of England made a treaty with Saladin to allow Christian pilgrim access to Jerusalem to worship at the Holy Sepulchre. See Gaullier-Bougassas, *La tentation de l'Orient*, pp. 341–44.

52 See further, Michael Livingston, 'Introduction', in *Siege of Jerusalem* (Kalamazoo, MI: Medieval Institute Publications, 2004).

53 Livingston, 'Introduction'. Such narratives include *Siege of Jerusalem* and *Titus and Vespasian*. For a comprehensive discussion of Jerusalem in Middle English narrative, see Suzanne M. Yeager, *Jerusalem in Medieval Narrative* (Cambridge: Cambridge University Press, 2008).

54 Roger Nicholson, 'Haunted Itineraries: Reading the *Siege of Jerusalem*', *Exemplaria* 14:2 (2002): 447–84 (461).

55 Morris, *Jean d'Arras's Mélusine*, p. 554.

these works 'anticipate [...] the city's more distant futures', and the future history of Christ's church is projected rather than stated in these works: 'the Temple is razed and the Church raised in its place'.[56] Notably, however, the Lusignan sons do not attempt to build/rebuild the Holy Sepulchre. Given their dubious maternal heritage, in Mélusine's half-fairy nature, that might be going a little far even for Jean d'Arras's reworking of history. When Geoffroy arrives in Jerusalem with the sultan, the Holy Sepulchre stands. Nevertheless, as Nicholson anticipates, the moment in which Geoffroy arrives has within it the potential for building/rebuilding, as Jerusalem 'n'estoit pas reparee ne refremee'.

For Robert Rouse, the Vengeance tradition goes further, extending beyond the destruction of the Temple and the building of the Church to the reinscription of civic space.[57] Rouse argues that the focus of the Vengeance narratives is religious erasure through geographical effacement and urban cleansing. Spiritual rebuilding is then realised through urban architectural reconstruction and the building of a Christian community 'in the rubble of the past'.[58] The building of civic structures, of city landscapes and infrastructure, is, therefore, implicated in the spiritual rebuilding and consolidation of the city: the old Jerusalem is cleared to make way for the new. Historically, this process of erasure and rebuilding has occurred several times in Jerusalem. The romance points to the time between the destruction in 70 CE and its next rebuilding in the second century, but the city and walls were repeatedly rebuilt and torn down in an *ad hoc* fashion, reconfigured to different plans under different rulers and different kinds of religious observance, throughout the Middle Ages (and before and since). Rouse also makes clear, however, that the past is not as easily eradicated as this turbulent history might suggest. In his discussion about medieval London's walls, he proposes that the stone and masonry of the walls themselves make visible the past. They contain 'legible material' that exists as 'manifold traces' of the past, never quite extinguished. The new walls are not only built *in* the rubble of the past, but literally *of* the rubble of the past. The walls 'represent the accretion of London pasts made visible in the London present'.[59] Rouse notes that the temporal complexity of such infrastructure was understandable within the medieval imaginary, which interpreted the world as 'a polychronic palimpsest', and that different temporalities could co-exist or 'jostle against' one another within both religious and secular contexts without contradiction.[60] The past, therefore, remains; but, at the same time, literally latent within it, is the potential for the narrative futures of further building projects. If this is so for London, it can only be more

56 Nicholson, 'Haunted Itineraries', pp. 461, 457.

57 Robert Allen Rouse, 'Emplaced Reading, or Towards a Spatial Hermeneutic for Medieval Romance', in *Medieval Romance and Material Culture*, ed. Nicholas Perkins (Cambridge: D. S. Brewer, 2015), pp. 41–57.

58 Rouse, 'Emplaced Reading', p. 53.

59 Rouse, 'Emplaced Reading', p. 44.

60 Rouse, 'Emplaced Reading', p. 45.

so for Jerusalem, with its more ancient stone infrastructure and its longer and more multilayered histories.

It might be tempting, then, to conclude that the Jerusalem episode locates the origins of the House of Lusignan in an historical palimpsest. For Massey, however, the metaphor of the palimpsest does not accurately describe the relations between narrative trajectories. Massey observes that the idea of the palimpsest reinforces a layering that reflects historical coherence, as the under layers of the palimpsest, those layers covered over, are always things from 'before'.[61] In such a structure, temporal coherence remains. Instead, the Jerusalem episode could better be described in Massey's terms as a radical contemporaneity, in which multiple, temporally diverse narratives are organised as a simultaneity. Geoffroy stands in a Jerusalem with multiple historical trajectories flowing through it. He is at a cross-section, a nexus, a nodal point in space that cannot be reduced to a single moment in time. Further, Massey's thinking not only brings multiple narrative trajectories together into contact with each other, each with its own past, present, and future, it also proposes that these interactions are consequential, that every narrative trajectory leaves such a meeting forever changed. This means that, as the multiple strands come together in Jerusalem and interact with each other, bringing together an array of different moments in time in full contemporaneous coexistence, temporal linearity is not the only thing that is disturbed. In this view, the narrative flows that come together in Jerusalem leak into one another, and then project forward in multiple and temporally variable futures. One of these possible futures (at some indeterminate time) is the rebuilding of Jerusalem, and Geoffroy is a descendant of a builder par excellence, Mélusine herself.

The Jerusalem episode is not the first in the romance to explore the alternative temporal flows and how they intersect with building projects. The building of Lusignan itself suggests multiple narrative threads, and the entirety of Mélusine's building programme across Poitou, in both texts, reveals temporal complications. Mélusine's building activities occur in the early years of her marriage, interwoven with, and framed by, a birthing narrative, the timing of which is precisely reported. The castle of Lusignan is built while she is pregnant with her first son, and a more expansive building programme throughout Poitou and Guyenne is completed in two phases after the births of her second and third sons. Over a period of four years, explicitly interwoven with the birthing sequence, she builds castles, towns, and towers at 12 named locations, and the list trails off with a gesture to innumerable others: 'et moult d'autres villes et forteresses'.[62] Unlike Lusignan, the building of the latter structures is not described, and the three years of extraordinary productivity is compressed into two short pages of narrative. As I have discussed elsewhere, while the temporality of Mélusine's birthing narrative is normalised as

61 Massey, *For Space*, p. 110.

62 Morris, *Jean d'Arras's Mélusine*, p. 214.

demonstrably human through the careful counting of months and years, the impossibility of the building narrative, in terms of human time, introduces a complexity that can only be resolved through different conceptions of time.[63] I argue that the apparent effortlessness of establishment of the Lusignan dynasty, in both human reproduction and massive capital works, is characterised by an 'excess' that is literally marked on the bodies of Mélusine's children in the disfigurement that each one bears (in Geoffroy's case, an abnormally large tooth). This excess spills over into the impossible temporal constraints of the building projects, at which point the narrative fractures, allowing time to expand into temporal multiplicity, where parallel and varying regimes of time simultaneously co-exist. In this expandable time, 'Mélusine builds, moves, and builds again'.[64]

This example highlights the close interconnection between building structures and building communities, the family in this case. While the second generation moves away from building structures, they instead build an empire through fighting the righteous fight, through protecting Christendom and marrying vulnerable heiresses, through building a network of relationships. When Geoffroy arrives at Jerusalem, therefore, his family has already demonstrated its capacity to construct a built environment and to foster communities. His mother has built castles, towers, and towns, and given birth to a family; and his father and brothers have extended Mélusine's demesne into an empire through their martial, political, and diplomatic expertise. When Geoffroy arrives at Jerusalem, the city has been cleansed and the Holy Sepulchre stands, but the civic infrastructure remains to be built. This is a moment of potential, of looking forward to the rebuilding of the city, at some future unspecified time, indeed at multiple future times. If we take the building capacity of the Lusignans seriously, both of infrastructure and of community, of a pan-European empire across multiple temporal trajectories with the monumental Lusignan at its core, if we interpret that empire as securing the community of Christendom into unlimited, complex, and multiple futures, then it seems to me that the Jerusalem episode has within it, in one of its narrative trajectories, the potential for Geoffroy to build the New Jerusalem.

The English translator makes an interesting intervention into the Jerusalem episode, suggesting that a keen interpretative eye has assessed its political implications. The translator cuts the episode, removing all the references to Geoffroy visiting with the sultan, to Vespasian and Titus, the ruinous state of the city, the 30 pieces of silver, and so on. Nevertheless, the flow of narrative works seamlessly, making small adjustments to allow for this deletion, indicating that the extraction of the episode was deliberate.

> And the sawdan made moche of Geffray, and proffred hym grete yeftes, but he wold nought receyue / but that he moche thanked hym of his curtoysye.

63 Shaw, *Space, Gender and Memory*, pp. 110–23.

64 Shaw, *Space, Gender and Memory*, p. 118.

> Thystorye sayth that Vryan & Guyon entered in to the see, & vowed themself to Jherusalem. Wherfore they toke leue of geffray theire broþer, and hym moche thanked of hys noble ayde & socours / and syn they departed fro the porte of Japhe, and rowed toward Jherusalem. And Geffray toke hys way by the see toward Rochelle.[65]

All that is left of the episode, in the English translation, is Urian and Guyon heading towards Jerusalem. Geoffroy leaves for Lusignan immediately after the treaty between the Lusignans and the Muslims is concluded. In this way, the English translation deletes a whole series of simultaneous polychronic narrative flows. It removes the connection between Jerusalem and the building of Lusignan in a polytemporal context, the link with Lusignan building expertise, and the latent potential of Geoffroy as builder of the New Jerusalem. It also erodes the specific link between Lusignan and the early Christian, pre-Crusade past. The English translation, therefore, reintroduces temporal limit to the otherwise limitless Lusignan empire. It effectively contains the narrative of the Lusignan empire into a single linear timeframe in the recent past, closing off the potential for future trajectories, snuffing out any hint of enduring pan-European, or even trans-continental, Lusignan rule.

Conclusion

The romance of *Mélusine* suggests that medieval people well understood the strategic implications of borders of different types. The English translation reflects a similar understanding. It repeats the recording of agreements between sovereign entities in letters patent and the demarcation of the border around Lusignan on the surface of the land. It tracks imperial expansion and the organisation of power in the Lusignan world that is maintained through a network of personal relationships. It replays the bringing of peace and order in the wake of this expansion, acknowledging chivalric honour in religious difference in a treaty between Christendom and the Muslim world. The English translation allows this empire to stand relatively unchanged. The exception is the border of time. Jean d'Arras, in the Jerusalem episode, introduces a temporal complexity and potential futurity that erases the limit of time. The English translation, by deleting this episode, removes this temporal destabilisation and thereby reintroduces time as a limit. In this way, the English translation reinstates a border around the otherwise borderless Lusignan empire. In so doing, it nullifies the audacious claims, both political and spiritual, that are implicit in the Jerusalem episode. These were, evidently, more far-reaching than the English translator was prepared to entertain in a world where England had only recently lost all its possessions in France save Calais. Both versions of the romance, therefore, demonstrate that different border types were used strategically to achieve varying political outcomes.

Reintroducing the limit of time to close off the past also reflects the passing of time between 1393, when Jean d'Arras's romance first appeared, and the time of the

65 Donald, *Melusine*, p. 292, ll. 23–33.

English translation, around 1500. For Jean d'Arras, the Lusignan empire brings peace to a Europe wracked by the Hundred Years War and divided by the Papal Schism. Such a peace echoes the desire of many of his contemporaries who were calling for an end to the Hundred Years War. Indeed, Philippe de Mézières was arguing at that time that the Hundred Years War led to the loss of the Holy Land and only when this war came to an end could Jerusalem be regained.[66] Jean d'Arras writes the narrative of European peace that Philippe promotes as an answer to the Hundred Years War. Jean inscribes upon Christendom, and even beyond, a peace wrought by the Lusignans, and only then does Geoffroy approach Jerusalem with the potential for its rebuilding in sight. In narrative terms, Geoffroy's visit to Jerusalem sacralises the Lusignan imperial project, opening the potential for the reclamation of and rebuilding of Jerusalem by the Lusignans, and rewriting domination as unity and peace. This project necessarily begins with the establishment of the fortress of Lusignan, protected by multiple legal and physical borderlines. In political terms, Geoffroy's visit to Jerusalem marks the end of the Hundred Years War, and the beginning of this most desirable end is to settle once and for all the dispute over Lusignan, thereby securing his favourite fortress in the Duc de Berry's hands. By removing Geoffroy's visit to Jerusalem, the English translation closes off the potential of a political history whose time has already passed. By 1500, the Hundred Years War was over, the Schism was healed, and the regaining of Jerusalem was no longer the goal that it once was. While the English translator seems content with replaying the romance of empire, removing the Jerusalem episode writes out the prospect of the Lusignans as the saviours of Christendom, which may well have seemed political and spiritual overreach by 1500.

It is evident, therefore, that the conceptual framework that explains the borders of modern nation states cannot be easily mapped onto medieval borders, but this does not mean that borders, limits, and negotiated boundaries were not understood by medieval people. An understanding of complex border types is clearly demonstrated in Jean D'Arras's *Mélusine* of 1393 and the English translation 100 years later. In this romance, borders extend from the concrete into abstract, spiritual, political, and polytemporal realms. They are manipulated and translated in sophisticated ways to achieve desired ends. Indeed, the strategic use of the borderless construct of empire, within a context of other carefully negotiated borderlines, highlights an understanding of the varying political implications of different forms. The limitations that negotiated borders present, particularly in the necessary acknowledgement of a neighbouring sovereign entity, are easily cast aside within the temporal context of the putative legendary past of a romance of origin, thereby naturalising the narrative use of the imperial construct. When the limits of time, however, are similarly eschewed in a polytemporal simultaneity of historical narrative trajectories, the apparent innocence of the invocation of imperial power structures is lost within the skilful narrative play that resonates with an imbrication of historical, political, and

66 Yeager, *Jerusalem*, p. 158.

religious implications. Moreover, the consequences of the deft removal of one short sequence by the English translator point to a keen awareness, both in 1393 and 1500, of the significance of different border forms.

As the evolution of the imperial model into the modern nation state in Europe continued along its long and convoluted route, the use of imperial structures waned under the pressures of the centralisation of power, the rise of bureaucracy, and the more formal demarcations of borders. In these conditions, while borders remained contested it became difficult to sustain the fiction of the 'voluntary halting place' that the imperial project required. As lines were being drawn on the maps of Europe, however, the rest of world was opening up. The focus of the imperial project shifted to this more favourable ground. The strategic use of different kinds of borders to achieve desired political ends, particularly the idea of uninhabited lands and the imperial 'voluntary halting place', continued. Indeed, it was to become one of the most effective tools of power and exploitation in the global empires of the modern age.

12

The Cely and Johnson Letters and the Languages of Calais, 1347–1558

Ad Putter

Historians have always been fascinated by the fact that England had an outpost on the continent of Europe for over two centuries, from the capture of Calais by Edward III in 1347 until its loss to France in 1558. Entire books have been written on the town during this period, but they say little, if anything at all, about the languages that could be heard and read in colonial Calais.[1] We might be tempted to conclude from this silence that the language of Calais was English when the town fell into English hands, and French before and after the English occupation, but the silence more probably simply reflects the lack of any investigation into the facts of the matter. Although questions about what languages people in the past used to communicate with one another, about how they acquired them, and how well they managed them, are basic historical questions, they are not ones that many historians ask themselves.[2]

It is fortunate, therefore, that literary historians have also become intrigued by the existence of an English colony in mainland Europe, for it is in their work

1 I have consulted Georges Daumet, *Calais sous la domination anglaise* (Arras: Répressé-Crépel, 1902); G. A. C. Sandeman, *Calais under English Rule* (Oxford: Blackwell, 1908); Fernard Lennel, *Histoire de Calais: Calais sous la domination anglaise* (Calais: Peumery, 1910); Susan Rose, *Calais: An English Town in France, 1347–1558* (Woodbridge: Boydell Press, 2008); and David Grummitt, *The Calais Garrison: War and Military Service in England, 1436–1558* (Woodbridge: Boydell Press, 2008).

2 There are, of course, exceptions, such as Michael Richter, *Sprache und Gesellschaft im Mittelalter: Untersuchungen zur Mündlichen kommunikation in England von der Mitte des elften bis zum Beginn des vierzehnten Jahrhunderts* (Stuttgart: Hiersemann, 1979), where it is pointed out (p. 1) that 'the question of how people understand each other, which language they use, how they negotiate and master difficulties in communication, touches on issues which in any form of human society are of fundamental importance. In relation to medieval society these problems have hardly been addressed' (my translation).

that we find a keener interest in the linguistic dimension of this phenomenon. The English language at this time had no currency abroad, and so an important cultural consequence of the imposition of an English plantation on the county of Artois was that it confronted continental visitors with the presence of an alien language on their own doorstep. David Wallace has drawn attention to a remarkable ballade by Eustache Deschamps, which registers the incursion of the English language into the continent in the form of a macaronic dialogue between two English guards and Eustache himself.[3] Accompanied by his fellow poet Oton de Granson, Eustache had travelled to Calais without an official permit, and was rudely turned back by two English soldiers:

> Je fu l'autrier trop mal venuz
> Quant j'alay pour veir Calays;
> J'entray dedenz comme cornuz,
> Sans congié; lors vint .II. Anglois,
> Granson devant et moy après,
> Qui mi prindrent parmi la bride:
> L'un me dist: 'dogue', l'aultre 'ride';
> Lors me devint la coulour bleue:
> 'Goday', fait l'un, l'autre 'commidre' [contraction of *com hider*].
> Lors dis: 'Ouil, je voy vo queue'.[4]

> (Things turned out very badly for me the other day when I went to see Calais. Like a fool, I went without permission. Then two Englishmen came up to Granson and then to me. They took me by the bridle. One said to me 'dog', and the other 'ride'. I turned pale. 'Good day', said one; the other 'come here'. Then I said, 'indeed I see your tail'.) (ll. 1–10; my translation)

The joke here lies in the way Deschamps repays the affront he receives in the same figurative currency. 'Dog' was the word of choice when a medieval English speaker wanted to insult a Frenchman',[5] and Deschamps retorts by fitting the term of abuse to the speaker: it is the latter who has a 'tail'. The retort rests on the common ethnic myth that the English had tails.[6] The jeer seems really to have riled the English. When,

3 David Wallace, *Premodern Places: Calais to Surinam, Chaucer to Aphra Behn* (Oxford: Blackwell, 2004), pp. 22–90 (pp. 54–56).

4 Ballade 893. Eustache Deschamps, *Oeuvres completes*, ed. Auguste Henri Edouard Queux de Saint-Hilaire and Gaston Raynaud, 11 vols (Paris: Firmin-Didot, 1878–1903), V, pp. 79–80.

5 Compare Deschamps's Ballade on the English, no. 868, '"Franche dogue", dist un Anglois', and, from a French parliamentary record, dated 7th May 1406, 'Ceulx dedens respondirent et appelerent les François chiens, dogue, et trahirent saietes [shot crossbows] et canons plusieurs' (Those inside responded and called the French hounds, dog, and fired crossbows and many canons), in *Mémoire sur le commerce maritime de Rouen*, ed. Ernest de Fréville, 2 vols (Rouen: Le Brument, 1857), II, pp. 28–283 (p. 281).

6 Peter Rickard, '*Anglois coué* and *l'Anglois qui couve*', *French Studies* 7 (1953): 48–55,

during the Whitsun Fair of 1457, Antwerp harbour officers insulted some English merchants by saying they had tails, the English community of Merchant Adventurers, who did business in Antwerp, took umbrage: in protest, they all decamped to Bruges and boycotted the Antwerp fairs, until eventually peace was restored.[7]

The interlinguistic encounters prompted by the English conquest of a town in mainland Europe have also been explored by Ardis Butterfield, who has highlighted the dramatic role of language choice in the famous story of the burghers of Calais surrendering the keys of the city to Edward III.[8] Froissart records them deliberating in French, but when they plead for mercy King Edward pointedly returns his verdict in English: 'quant il parla, il commanda en langage englois que on lor copast les teste tantos' (when he spoke, he ordered in the English language that their heads should be cut off at once).[9] Luckily for them, Edward III's Queen, Philippa of Hainaut, intervenes and pacifies her husband; incidentally, Froissart records her words to her husband as being in French.

Calais has thus emerged, for good reason, as a place of special interest in the multilingual context of Middle English language and literature. Predictably, since so much work on multilingualism in medieval England has focused on the 'Big Three' – Latin, French, and English – the vernacular languages that have dominated the discussion of Calais as a multilingual contact zone have been French and English.[10] The aim of this essay is to bring some other languages of medieval Calais into the frame, notably Dutch. In doing so I follow the lead of Helen Fulton, who has consistently championed the cause of another minority language that has been overlooked in the 'trilingual' model of multilingual medieval England, namely Welsh.

---

and for the earliest history of this myth see also James William Lloyd, 'The West Country Adventures of Saint Augustine of Canterbury', *Folklore* 131 (2020): 413–34.

7 Marie-Rose Thielemans, *Bourgogne et Angleterre: relations politiques et économiques entre les Pays-Bas Bourgoignons et l'Angeterre, 1435–1467* (Brussels: Presses Universitaires de Bruxelles, 1966), pp. 277–82; Anne Sutton, 'Caxton was a Mercer: His Social Milieu and his Friends', in *England in the Fifteenth Century: Proceedings of the 1992 Harlaxton Symposium*, ed. Nicholas Rogers (Stamford: Paul Watkins, 1994), pp. 118–48 (pp. 127–28).

8 Ardis Butterfield, *The Familiar Enemy: Chaucer, Language and Nation in the Hundred Years War* (Oxford: Oxford University Press, 2009), pp. 163–64.

9 Jean Froissart, *Chroniques. Dernière rédaction du premier livre. Édition du manuscrit de Rome Reg. lat. 869*, ed. George T. Diller (Geneva: Librairie Droz, 1972), p. 847.

10 The simplifying characterisation of medieval England as a 'trilingual' culture is a feature of much recent scholarship. See, for example, William Rothwell, 'The Trilingual England of Geoffrey Chaucer', *Studies in the Age of Chaucer* 16 (1993): 45–67.

Welsh was spoken in parts of England bordering on Wales,[11] and was also to be heard in Calais. The 'English' garrison stationed at Calais numbered many Welsh soldiers. The push-and-pull factors that encouraged many Welshmen to go out to Calais have been discussed by Helen Fulton in 'Mobility and Migration: Calais and the Welsh Imagination in the Late Middle Ages',[12] and the Welsh poem that she cites and translates in an appendix to this essay, *Cywydd i Galais a'i Milwyr* (Poem to Calais and its Soldiers) by Robert Leiaf (fl. c. 1440–90), is a memorable tribute to the Welsh of medieval Calais:

Pan Gollo Cymro, p'le cais
Oni gweler 'n y Galays?
Mi a welais y milwyr
Oedd are goll. Pand oedd dda'r gwŷr?
Selays wŷr a gollais gynt,
Sawdwyr yng Nghalais ydynt!

(When a Welshmen goes missing, where can he be found except in Calais? I've seen the soldiers who went missing – were they not fine men? – I looked for men I'd lost touch with a while ago, and they are soldiers in Calais!) (ll. 7–12)

Robert Leiaf had been to Calais himself, and so fulsome is his praise for the Welsh soldiers that you could read the poem and think that Welshmen were the only people there: 'Cymry sy'n hon' (it's Welshmen who are in that town) (l. 52). Although in fact the English dominated, Leiaf asks us not to forget the Welsh speakers of Calais.

There were Welshmen, or at least men of Welsh extraction, too, among the merchants and lords who frequented or inhabited Calais. William Cely, writing from Calais in 1487, mentions 'John Flewelen, mercer' in a couple of letters (more about the Cely letters later).[13] The name 'Flewelen' is evidently an Anglicised spelling of the Welsh Llywelyn – compare 'Fluellen' (also spelt 'Flewellen' in some early editions) in Shakespeare's *Henry V*.[14] This same 'John Flewelen' also appears in the Acts of the Mercers' Court as 'Thlewellen' and 'Lewel(l)en'.[15] His last mention in

11 See Llinos Beverley Smith, 'The Welsh and English Languages in Late-Medieval Wales', in *Multilingualism in Later Medieval Britain*, ed. David Trotter (Cambridge: D. S. Brewer, 2000), pp. 7–24; and in the same collection Michael Richter, 'Collecting Miracles along the Anglo-Welsh Border in the Early Fourteenth Century', pp. 53–62.

12 Helen Fulton, 'Mobility and Migration: Calais and the Welsh Imagination in the Late Middle Ages', in *The Hundred Years War and European Literary History*, ed. Daniel Davies and R. D. Perry (Manchester: Manchester University Press, 2024), pp. 145–67.

13 Alison Hanham, ed., *The Cely Letters, 1472–1488*, Early English Text Society Original Series 273 (Oxford: Oxford University Press, 1975), letters 238/5 and 296/6.

14 Alison Hanham, *The Celys and Their World: An English Merchant Family of the Fifteenth Century* (Cambridge: Cambridge University Press, 2002), p. 356.

15 Lætitia Lyell, ed., *Acts of Court of the Mercers' Company, 1453–1527* (Cambridge:

the Mercers' records occurs in a report of a 'sclaunderous bargayn of grete Summes of mony' that he had struck with another mercer of London, Thomas Wyndoute.[16] Wyndoute was to pay Llywelyn this great sum as soon as he had married the widow of the mercer Thomas Shelley, the problem being that Thomas was not dead yet. The money promised to Llywelyn was in effect the fee he charged for taking care of that problem.

A letter dated 28th November 1534 from Thomas Speke asks Lord Lisle, Governor of Calais, for a letter of safe conduit for 'Richard Appowell',[17] who is perhaps to be identified as Richard ap Hywel of Mostyn (d. 1540).[18] The courtier Sir John Donne (John ap Gruffydd Dwn) lived in Calais from 1468 onwards and owned a house there. A patron of the arts, he was immortalised by Hans Memling in the Donne triptych, now in the National Gallery, London, and by Simon Marmion in the Book of Hours known as the Louthe Hours (Louvain-la-Neuve, Archives de l'Université, MS A2, fol. 100v).[19] The fine Flemish manuscripts that Donne commissioned and received as gifts from Margaret of York contain no Welsh, but only Latin, French, and English.[20] However, Welsh written texts could certainly be found in Calais. The Welsh chronicler and translator Elis Gruffudd was active in Calais from the 1530s onwards, writing numerous books in his native tongue. He claims to have consulted other Welsh sources while researching his universal chronicle in Calais.[21]

Another language of medieval England and medieval Calais that has been neglected by Anglophone scholars is Dutch, and in the pages that follow I would like to remedy that neglect. The first point to make is that, before the town was conquered, Dutch was the spoken vernacular of Calais. Ardis Butterfield assumes, quite rightly, that the burghers who surrendered to Edward III spoke French to him, but, if this story reflects what actually happened, it is not unlikely that French would have been their second language and Dutch their first. For while Calais is now in France and in francophone country, the town had once belonged to the domains

Cambridge University Press, 1936), pp. 112, 124, 130.

16 Lyell, ed., *Acts*, p. 130.

17 Muriel St Clare Byrne, ed., *The Lisle Letters* (Harmondsworth: Penguin, 1985), letter 42 (pp. 100–01).

18 On the Mostyn family, see Antony Carr, 'The Mostyn Family and Estate, 1200–1642', Unpublished PhD dissertation (Bangor University, 1975).

19 George Holmes, 'Donne [Dwn], Sir John', in *Oxford Dictionary of National Biography* (*ODNB*) (Oxford: Oxford University Press, 2004) <www.oxforddnb.com> [last accessed 26th July 2023].

20 See Janet Backhouse, 'Sir John Donne's Flemish Manuscripts', in *Medieval Codicology, Iconography, Literature and Translation: Studies for Keith Val Sinclair*, ed. Peter Rolfe Monks and D. D. R. Owen (Leiden: Brill, 1994), pp. 48–57; Anne Dubois, 'The *Donne Hours*: A Codicological Puzzle', *Journal of Historians of Netherlandish Art* 6 (2014) <https://jhna.org/articles/donne-hours-codicological-puzzle/> [last accessed 26th July 2023].

21 Brynley F. Roberts, 'Gruffudd, Elis', in *ODNB* <www.oxforddnb.com> [last accessed 26th July 2023].

of the Count of Flanders. And, just as territorial borders have their histories, so do linguistic borders. In the medieval period, Calais was still on the Dutch side of the Germanic/Romance language boundary.[22] Today, this boundary runs in a roughly horizontal line from Visé (11 miles (18 km) south of Maastricht) in the east to Mouscron (10 miles (16 km) north of Lille) in the west. But local charters from the medieval period show that the present border lay further south. In the fourteenth century, it ran roughly from Wissant (Witsant = 'white sand' in Dutch) to Saint-Omer (Sint Omaars), and from there eastwards to Merville (Mergen).[23]

In the case of Calais, the evidence is complicated by the fact that, prior to the English conquest, the official town records were kept first in Latin and then, from 1300, in French.[24] However, the Germanic naming patterns and the amount of code-switching in these records reveal that Flemish was the spoken language. Below are some examples of the kind of language-mixing that pervades the Calais charters (Dutch words in italics):[25]

1. in de *kerkdic* nec in *de let* nec *int fesseid* (dated 1293)

(in the church fosse nor in the canal nor in the moat)

2. quil falirent a metre l'estake sur le *banc* ou *hauene* (dated 1301)

(that they failed to put up the chained barrier on the bank or the harbour)

In example 2, *banc* (present-day *bank*) is the Dutch word for an elevated region of the seabed, while *hauene* (present-day *haven*) is Dutch for 'harbour'. In example 1, *kerkdic* is the Middle Dutch compound *kerke + dyc*; *de let* is *de lede*; and *fesseid* is Middle Dutch *fosseit*, with *int* being a contraction of the preposition *in* and the neuter article *het*.[26] The scribes of the charters code-switched to Dutch when mentioning places in and around the town, because that is how people referred to them. Thus, even though the records of pre-conquest Calais were kept in Latin and French, they give us snippets of the spoken Dutch language. Taken together, these snippets have given Middle Dutch specialists enough data to reconstruct the phonology of the Flemish dialect that was once spoken there.[27]

22 Hugo Ryckeboer, 'Dutch/Flemish in the North of France', *Journal of Multilingual and Multicultural Development* 23 (2002): 22–35.

23 The excellent study by Godefroi Kurth, *La frontière linguistique en Belgique et dans le Nord de la France*, 2 vols (Brussels: Société belge de Librarie, 1896–98), remains the best guide to the early history of the shifting French/Flemish language border in present-day Belgium and northern France.

24 Serge Lusignan, *Essai d'histoire sociolinguistique: Le français picard au Moyen Âge* (Paris: Garner, 2012), p. 202.

25 I owe the examples to Maurits Gysseling and Peter Bougard, *L'onomastique Calaisienne a la fin du 13e siècle* (Leuven: Instituut voor Naamkunde, 1963), pp. 102, 104.

26 The Middle Dutch words are given in the spellings selected for their entries in *Het Middelnederlandsch Woordenboek* (Institute for the Dutch Language, 2007–18) <https://gtb.ivdnt.org> [last accessed 26th July 2023].

27 See Maurits Gysseling and Carlos Wijffels, 'Diets in schepenverordeningen van

Since Calais was close to French-speaking territory, bilingualism must have been common, especially among the higher echelons, who were beginning to regard French as a language of prestige. That said, Dutch was the majority language of medieval Calais and its environs. The implications of this fact are worth spelling out: during the 200 years and more when Calais was an English colony, England had a hard language border on Dutch-speaking lands.

Did Dutch have any future in Calais after it was captured? The official policy was to purge the town of all 'strangers' (as the locals were now designated), who were expelled by royal decree in 1347. In the words of Jean Froissart, Edward III hated the local inhabitants ('moult haoit les habitans de Calais') and was determined to repopulate the town with 'pure English' ('je veoil la ville repeupler de purs Engles').[28] But policy and practice are different things. Edward III himself found it necessary to make a few exceptions for locals who understood how things worked in Calais or knew the lie of the land.[29] Locals also made good spies: they could blend in without arousing suspicion and were able to report on the latest gossip and news, which in written form was often disseminated in the form of pamphlets written in the Dutch vernacular and nailed on doors of public buildings and churches.[30] Remarkably, these spies sometimes reported back in Dutch: one such report (1540), signed by one 'Willen de Vrient' and addressed to the Master Porter of Calais, was written to inform the English of the Emperor Charles V's plans for a tour around the Low Countries.[31] The porter was presumably expected to be able to read the Dutch. Other locals probably stayed unofficially to become what we would now call 'illegal workers'. In Susan Rose's words, 'there remains a suspicion [...] that many ordinary townsfolk either did remain in the town for at least the first years of the English occupation or melted into the general body of anonymous poor folk in northern France, leaving no trace in the records.'[32]

Calais uit het einde der XIIIe eeuw', *Studia Germanica Gandensia* 4 (1962): 9–30.

28 Froissart, *Chroniques. Livre I (première partie, 1325–1350) et Livre II. Rédaction de manuscript de New York Pierpont Morgan Library M. 894*, ed. Peter F. Ainsworth and George T. Diller (Paris: Livre de Poche, 2001), pp. 644, 646.

29 Sandeman, *Calais*, p. 84.

30 On late medieval Calais as a 'centre for spies' (p. 84) and on the appointment of 'French and Flemings [who] could speak the enemy's language as natives', see J. R. Alban and C. T. Allmand, 'Spies and Spying in the Fourteenth Century', in C. T. Allmand, ed., *War, Literature and Politics in the Late Middle Ages* (Liverpool: Liverpool University Press, 1976), pp. 73–101. The adventures of one Calais spy, apparently an Englishman, who went to Dunkirk in 1527 and found writing on the church door and learned that the same news had been spread all over Flanders in the same fashion, are related by Sandeman, *Calais*, p. 45.

31 The report is now available online at *State Papers Online: Early Modern Government in Britain and Europe* (Gale International, 2023) <https://www.gale.com/intl/primary-sources/state-papers-online> [last accessed 11th November 2023], and summarised in *Letters and Papers, Foreign and Domestic, of the Reign of Henry VIII, Vol. 15: 1540*, ed. J. Gairdner and R. H. Brodie (London: Her Majesty's Stationery Office, 1896), p. 84.

32 Rose, *Calais*, p. 28.

Officially, only subjects of the English king were allowed to own property in Calais and to house guests, but again it is doubtful that the law was strictly observed. In 1364, an inquiry found that a large number of 'strangers from diverse nations kept inns in the town, to the great damage and danger of the town.'[33] Calais had by this stage become the official wool staple and was full of 'diverse nations' – many of them Dutch-speaking merchants or their agents from Holland, Brabant, and Flanders – who went to Calais to buy the English wool that was turned into cloth by textile workers from the Low Countries. These visitors to Calais were evidently able to stay at inns that were being run by their own countrymen who could speak their language and help them do business in Calais, for in this period innkeepers also made themselves useful as brokers.[34] By the sixteenth century, the pipedream of turning Calais into a 'pure English' town was just a fond memory. When Lord Lisle was Governor of Calais in the 1530s, he reported that the English had begun to be outnumbered by Flemish and French 'strangers'.[35]

At this point, I would like to introduce some primary sources that can shed further light on the multilingualism of this 'English' town: the Cely letters and the Johnson letters. Both the Celys and the Johnsons were merchants of the Staple.[36] The Celys dealt mainly in wool and cloth, and their surviving correspondence covers the 1470s and 1480s. The Johnsons also dealt in wool and cloth, but they had diversified and ventured into other merchandise, notably wine, which they imported from France and from Spain. Their letters cover the 1540s and early 1550s. The family homes of both the Celys and the Johnsons were in England, but since Calais was the international hub of the staplers, both families found it indispensable to have a branch of the business across the Channel. The continental branch was typically run by junior members of the family and by agents posted to Calais.

The Cely and Johnson letters, many dispatched to and from Calais, are full of interest for anyone concerned with multilingualism, and they have rather more to say about Dutch than is generally known. Both letter collections were included in the *Corpus of Early English Correspondence*, a database recently investigated by Arja Nurmi and Päivi Pahta in their study of cross-linguistic code-switches in relation to the social ranks of the letter writers.[37] The findings of this study can only be described as discouraging to anyone who is interested in what these letters might have to say about the languages of Calais beyond the 'Big Three'. As far as code-switching is concerned, their statistics show plenty of code-switches into Latin and French, but only two examples of code-switches into other languages, one into Dutch and one into Italian, both of them occurring in the Johnson letters.

33 My translation, based on the original record as cited by Daumet, *Calais*, p. 80.

34 John Hare, 'Inns, Innkeepers and the Society of Later Medieval England', *Journal of Medieval History* 39 (2013): 478–97.

35 *Lisle Letters*, p. 61.

36 There are excellent studies of the Celys and Johnsons by Hanham, *Celys*, and Barbara Winchester, *Tudor Family Portrait* (London: Cape, 1955).

37 Arja Nurmi and Päivi Pahta, 'Social Stratification and Patterns of Code-Switching in Early English Letters', *Multilingua* 23 (2004): 417–56.

The letter that code-switches into Dutch is dated 16th August 1547 and was sent by Robert Andrew from Antwerp to John Johnson, 'merchant of the Staple [...] in Callais'. The letter reports political developments and the highly sensitive matter of religion:

> For newes yt ys brutyd [rumoured] that agrementt ys taken betwene the Emperoure's Majestie and the Duke of Saxson, the said Duke being restoryd to as hight power as ever he was of. Besyde, ther ys commandentt subscrybid with the Emperoure's owne hand, and popliched [published] in 2 or 3 of the chieff townes in Duchlonde, straytly charging them from thensforth to speke no dishonour agayne the said duke, nameyng hym in the same commandment 'de machtych ende hooghebore prynce' [the mighty and high-born prince]. Towchyng theyr religion, je ne scay rien.[38]

The emperor in question is Charles V and the 'duke of Saxson' is probably Philip I, Landgrave of Hesse, who had been captured by Charles V at the Battle of Mühlberg. As a staunch supporter of Protestant reform, Philip had set up a Lutheran alliance in opposition to the Holy Roman Empire,[39] and the rumour that Philip had been restored to his former dignity would have been music to the ears of John Johnson, who was himself an ardent Protestant.[40] Lutherans could be burned for heresy under Henry VIII, so what Andrew actually says about religion is guarded and deliberately coded in French: 'je ne scay rien'.[41] This is consistent with the use of French elsewhere in the letters. In the case of news that was too hot to handle, or that had to be kept private for personal reasons, the Johnsons and their business partners elsewhere switch to French to imply that there is more to be said, but not in spontaneous writing. Here, for example, is Otwell Johnson writing to his brother John on 15th January 1547:

> Th'Erle of Surray was indited, arraigned, and condemned to dye like a traytour, at the Guyldehall in London on Thursday last, God be mercifull unto him; and the duke his father, by his owne writing, hath submitted himself to the King his majes-

38 'The Johnson Letters, 1542–1552', ed. Barbara Winchester, 4 vols, Unpublished PhD dissertation (Birkbeck College, 1954), letter 519, III, pp. 915–16. I have corrected Winchester's word division to make sense of the Dutch. All subsequent references to the Johnson letters are from this edition.

39 T. Kolde, 'Philip of Hesse', in *The New Schaff-Herzog Encyclopedia of Religious Knowledge*, ed. Samuel Macauley Jackson, 12 vols (Grand Rapids, MI: Baker Book House, 1951) <https://www.ccel.org/ccel/schaff/encyc09/cache/encyc09.pdf> [last accessed 26th July 2023].

40 Winchester, 'Johnson Letters', I, p. 67.

41 The same caution is seen in the Lisle Letters. Here is Lord Lisle (c. 17th November 1538) trying to reassure Cromwell that the folk of Calais do not hold extremist views: 'The gentlemen also accused the people of Calais of being all Lutherans, but he replied that we were good Christian men, and do as we were wont to do, but just not in pilgrimages nor the Pope's pardons': letter 1301a, in Muriel St Clare Byrne, ed., *The Lisle Letters*, 6 vols (Chicago: Chicago University Press, 1981), V, p. 325.

tie as a consular of his treason, butt whether he shall araigne or suffer I heare not. *Du filz j'ay merveilles a vous compter de bouche* [About his son I have astounding things to tell by word of mouth] at our next meeting.[42]

The Dutch in Robert Andrew's letter, 'de machtych ende hooghebore prynce' (the mighty and highborn prince) was presumably taken from a version of the emperor's edict as disseminated in the towns of 'Duchlonde'; it described the anti-Catholic Philip of Hesse in deferential terms that chimed with the sympathies of Robert Andrew and his addressee.

According to Nurmi and Pahta, this is the only letter in the *Corpus of Early English Correspondence* that switches to Dutch. However, there is more Dutch and more Dutch code-switching to be found in this corpus. Perhaps the most interesting letter in the Cely correspondence is a love letter by a lady named Clare to George Cely, who had been sent to Calais to run the continental branch of the family business. Clare later became George's mistress. The place she was writing from is unknown – presumably she lived somewhere George travelled to on business, perhaps Bruges. The love letter has been edited by Alison Hanham, who dates it speculatively to 'before 26th May 1479'.[43] The original document (TNA SC 1/59/41) is written in a fluent and stylish hand. It was probably written for Clare by a professional scrivener. The love letter itself is in French. George Cely had some French, for on the dorse of another letter to him (undated) he wrote some rudimentary French phrases with English glosses.[44] For the present purposes, however, the most interesting thing about the letter is the endorsement, written in the same hand. It reads: 'Desen brief zij ghegeuen tot Jorge Sely' (Let this letter be given to George Cely).[45] The instruction was intended for George's *serviteur*, who is named in a postscript to the French love letter: 'Sachies que j'envoye vne ansaigne a Bietremeulx vostre serviteur, et se me recomande à lui. Je lui promis caint il estoiet pardecha' (Know that I am sending a token[46] of myself to Bartholomew, your servant, and I recommend myself to him. I told him this before while he was over here). Bartholomew was evidently a Dutch speaker. As Hanham notes, 'the Dutch address suggests that the letter was handed to one of George's servants, many of whom were Dutch'.[47] The case confirms Susan Rose's suspicion that not all the Dutch-speaking locals of Calais vanished when the area was anglicised. Colonists need servants, and Dutch speakers could make themselves useful, for example, as messengers carrying letters between Calais and Flanders.

42 Letter 465, III, p. 820.

43 Letter 54, in Hanham, *Cely Letters*, pp. 49–50.

44 Letter 49.

45 Hanham reads 'zy'.

46 The handwriting of a letter offered reassurance as to the identity of its author (see Winchester, 'Johnson Letters', I, p. 130); if the letter was written by someone else, a 'token' (for instance, a ring, or a piece of information that would have meant something only to the sender and the recipient) could be entrusted to the messenger.

47 Hanham, *Cely Letters*, p. 262.

The Celys themselves also needed Dutch. Most of their clients were Dutch speakers and George Cely was often in Antwerp or Bruges for business or entertainment. In fact, his correspondents did not always know where he might be, and some endorsements of letters written to him hedge their bets: 'To Jorge Cely at Caleys or Bregys be thys letter delyuerd'.[48] One letter in the Cely collection is entirely in Dutch.[49] It was written to George Cely at Calais by Jan Vanderheyden in Mechelen (Mechlin), in the Duchy of Brabant. The translation offered by Hanham is loose, so it is worth presenting the Dutch text with a translation that I think is more accurate:

> Ghemynde wrient, wet dat Ic U seere groete, messter Soersse, ende ic late U wetten by myn hantghescryfte hoe dat ghy wel wet dat wy te gaeder ghesproken hebben van wollen die ghy my sendden sout by Ryken, Joes Wranx factoer, ghelijc also ghy wel wet. Ende daerum scrywe ic, Jan Vanderheyden, aen U, Soersse Seely, goede wrient, ende late U wetten dat ghy my wylt senden iiij sacken myddel Cutsewout, schoen ghebont, ghelyc als Ic my toet U betrowe: te wettene, iij nwe ende j out. Item, wet, Soersse, soe sullen wy te Bergghen alle dynch wel eens sijn, wylt God. Sent my de beste, Soerse, ende scrijft my ghelieft U yet dat ic voir U doen maech. Ghescreuen te Mechelen, anno lxxvij xi in October.
>
> By Jan Vanderheyden.
>
> *Dorse*: Den erbaren Soersse Seely, coepman vanden Stappel at Caelijs, salut.
>
> (Beloved friend, know well that I greet you wholeheartedly, master George, and I let you know in my own handwriting that, as you well know, we spoke together about some wool which you were to send to me via Ryken, Joes Wranx's factor, as you well know. And for this reason, I, Jan Vanderheyden, am writing to you, George Cely, good friend, and I am letting you know to please send four sarples of medium-grade Cotswold, properly packed, just as I trust you will: to wit, three new and one old. Also George, know that we will settle everything at Bergen-op-Zoom, God willing. Send me the best, George; and write to me if there is anything I can do for you. Written at Mechlin, 9th October 1477.)

Bergen-op-Zoom, along with Antwerp, hosted the annual fairs of Brabant. At Bergen-op-Zoom the fair was held around Eastertime.[50] The two merchants agree to settle up there. I construe 'eens sijn' as idiomatic Dutch for 'come to an agreement' (literally 'be at one'). Hanham, on the other hand, construes 'sijn' as the verb 'to see'. As these and other differences of interpretation show, the Dutch is not exactly straightforward. This makes it all the more remarkable that Jan Vanderheyden could assume it would not give George any trouble. George needed reminding of

48 See letters 67 and 80.

49 Letter 14.

50 Anne Sutton and Livia Visser-Fuchs, eds, *The Book of Privileges of the Merchant Adventurers of England, 1296–1483* (Oxford: Oxford University Press for the British Academy, 2009), p. 3.

promises he had made and needed to know when and where payment would be made: all this information is given to him in Dutch.

Dutch Literature, with a capital 'L', does not feature in the Cely letters. Except for some French songs,[51] the literacy on display is pragmatic, and practical utility also lies behind the one foreign-language book (possibly in Dutch) that makes an appearance in the Cely letters. It is mentioned in a letter dated 12th March 1486/87 from William Dalton, based in Calais, to George, who was now a senior partner in the business and was back home in London: 'I [...] sent you the letter of payment wyth a prognosticacon and an almynake of the making of master John Laete, and this I sent you all bounden and seled togeder be William Drynklow'.[52] The book in question is the *Prognosticationes* by the contemporary astronomer Jan Laet from Borgloon in Limburg.[53] Every year Jan Laet (and later his son Jasper) published a set of forecasts and prophecies for the forthcoming year. The earliest surviving edition is for the year 1476 and was published in Latin by Johan van Westfalen in Leuven (Louvain) in 1475. However, Laet's readership widened considerably when Dutch- and French-language editions began to appear from the printing presses of the Low Countries.[54] We can only speculate about the language (Dutch, French, or Latin?) of the bound copy acquired for George Cely by William Dalton of Calais. If George shared the linguistic preferences of a contemporary English merchant, William Caxton, he probably preferred reading French or Dutch to reading Latin.[55]

We do not know how George Cely acquired his Dutch. Middle Dutch and Middle English were close enough to make some words guessable, but it is certainly not the case that the languages were mutually intelligible, as is sometimes

51 Discussed by Alison Hanham, 'The Musical Studies of a Fifteenth-Century Wool Merchant', *Review of English Studies* 8 (1957): 270–74.

52 Letter 228.

53 On Jan Laet, see Eustace Fulcrand Bosanquet, *English Printed Almanacks and Prognostications: A Bibliographical History to the Year 1600* (London: Chiswick Press for the Bibliographical Society, 1917), pp. 18–19; Jonathan Green, *Printing and Prophecy: Prognostication and Media Change 1450–1550* (Ann Arbor, MI: University of Michigan Press, 2011), pp. 116–17, 233.

54 Surviving copies recorded in the *Incunable Short-Title Catalogue* (British Library, 2016) are il00022125 (French: Bruges, Colard Mansion, 1476–77), il00022150 (Oudenaarde: Arend de Keysere, 1480), and il00022200 (Louvain: Johan van Westfalen, 1484/5). See <https://data.cerl.org/istc/> [last accessed 26th July 2023]. On the Dutch editions, see also Georges Colin *et al.*, *De Vijfhonderdste verjaring van de boekdrukkunst in de Nederlanden* (Brussels: Koninklijke Bibliotheek Albert I, 1973), pp. 141–42.

55 On Caxton's multilingualism, see Ad Putter, 'Caxton's Linguistic and Literary Multilingualism: English, French, and Dutch in the *History of Jason*', in *Middle English in a Multilingual Context: Current Methodologies and Approaches*, ed. Louise Sylvester and Sara Pons-Sanz (London: Palgrave Macmillan, 2023), pp. 213–36.

suggested.[56] It seems to have been customary among the English Merchant Adventurers and Staplers who traded with the Low Countries to send apprentices abroad for a year so that they could acquire Dutch.[57] The Ordinances of the Merchant Adventurers (though not written down until 1608) allude to the practice of boarding young apprentices with Flemish speakers so that they could learn the language. The ordinances stipulate that apprentices should not normally take up lodging other than in the housing of approved hosts except if they were given leave 'for learning of language' to 'boord in a straungers house for a year after his first Cominge over or shorter tyme'.[58] The Johnson letters provide glimpses of this arrangement. Ambrose Saunders, writing from Antwerp to his brother John Johnson, then in London, on 26th December 1551, recommends his son for employment: 'If ye so thawght yt good, I thincke yf my boy did continu here he wold do us good service, having good instruccyon, nothing dowbting his diligence nor treuthe. And yf ye thawght yt mete [thought it appropriate], I could bestowe hym at a Fleminge's howse'.[59] The children of the governing classes in Calais were also sent off to learn a language, though in their case Latin and French are mentioned. Both the Johnson letters and the Lisle letters mention Saint-Omer as a place where the children of both the merchant- and the governing classes of Calais could go to learn French.[60] The town had been largely Dutch-speaking in the twelfth century,

56 Martina Häcker argues that 'English and Dutch must […] have been close enough for English sellers to understand Dutch buyers and vice versa': 'French-English Linguistic and Cultural Contact in Medieval England: The Evidence of Letters', *AAA: Arbeiten aus Anglistik und Amerikanistik* 36 (2011): 133–60 (144–45). But Flemish merchants wrote to the Celys and the Johnsons in French or in Dutch, and English merchants who did not know Dutch relied on compatriots who knew the language to do business in the Low Countries. Note the testimony of Richard Able given at the court of the Hague: Algemeen Rijksarchief, Sententiën van het Hof, 1499–1500, 1499/100, ed. H. J. Smit, *Bronnen tot de geschiedenis van den handel met Engeland, Schotland en Ierland*, 2 vols (The Hague: Martinus Nijhoff, 1928), II, pp. 1, 140: 'alzoe hy alhier in den landen van mynen genadichen heere verkerende was omme zijn copmanscap te doen ende de tale ten besten niet en konde, zoe hadde hy tot diversche stonden zijn copmanscap gedaen by middele van eenige andre Engelschen, die haerwairds verkeerden ende de tale verstonden' (Because he was here in the lands of my merciful Lord to do business and because he did not know the language very well, he at various times had done his business by means of some other Englishmen who resided in these parts and knew the language). Digitised by Huygens Institute <http://resources.huygens.knaw.nl/handelengeland> [last accessed 26th July 2023].

57 Oskar de Smedt, *De Engelse Natie te Antwerpen in the 16e Eeuw*, 2 vols (Antwerp: De Sikkel, 1954), II, p. 464.

58 William E. Lingelbach, ed., *The Merchant Adventurers of England, Their Laws and Ordinances with Other Documents* (Philadelphia, PA: Longmans, 1902), p. 46.

59 Letter 870, IV, p. 1532.

60 See letter 106 of the Johnson letters (II, p. 217) and letter 72 of the Lisle Letters (p. 142).

but French had established itself as the language of public affairs by the thirteenth century and became dominant among the bourgeoisie and nobility in the later Middle Ages. The ordinary people of Saint-Omer, however, continued to speak Flemish, and so the courts of Saint-Omer had to make provision for pleading in French or Flemish – 'sera cascun receu a parler franchois au flameng tel langage qu'il sara' (Let anyone be allowed to speak French or Flemish, whichever language he might know) – and continued to do so in the early sixteenth century.[61] Because Dutch still mattered in Saint-Omer, some French speakers there made an effort to learn Dutch by immersion as lodgers in households across the Dutch-language border. Writing (9th October 1536) from Saint-Omer to Peter Beckwith, secretary to Lord Lisle in Calais, Willebrordus Montanus reported that his mother was currently staying in Bailleul (Belle in Flemish) to learn Flemish.[62]

Given the importance of Dutch in the Calais area, it is not surprising that the language features more prominently in the Johnson letters than Nurmi and Pahta's statistics indicate. John Johnson not only received letters in Dutch, but also himself wrote in Dutch to his clients in the Low Countries. Barbara Winchester, who edited the Johnson correspondence in four volumes, relegated all the Dutch letters to an appendix. Unfortunately, this appendix was never digitised, and the hard copy appears to have gone missing.[63] Only the originals survive in the National Archives.[64]

Because John Johnson knew Dutch so well, he was sometimes asked to act as an interpreter and intermediary by those who did not know the language, and several letters show his linguistic prowess. On 3rd November 1545, he wrote to Richard Wethill in London. Richard was owed money by Victor Meaw, a Flemish merchant from Bruges, and John had been present when Victor had promised to repay Richard. But Victor had now died, and Richard had evidently asked John in Calais to write to Victor's widow to get his money back. In his reply, John tactfully declines, but he does offer to translate Richard's own letter into Dutch:

> I thincke it were moche better that you devised your lettre to Victor Meawe's widow yourself and to requyer an answer thereof then for me to writ unto her, having nothing to do in the matter (save only that I am witness of the consculsion [sic] that was made between you). Ye shall not thincke therby that I will not take so moche paynes for you as to writ a lettre at youre request, but I pray you rather thincke (as the very trewthe is) that if I were in youre case I wolde do as I audvise

61 Kurth, *Frontière linguistique*, II, p. 76.

62 'Henry VIII: October 1536, 6–10', in *Letters and Papers, Foreign and Domestic, Henry VIII, Vol. 11 (July–December 1536)* (London: Her Majesty's Stationery Office, 1888), online at *British History Online* (Institute of Historical Research, 2019) <www.british-history.ac.uk> [last accessed 26th July 2023].

63 I would like to thank Jessica Kauffman of Birkbeck College Library for trying to locate this missing volume.

64 For example, Dutch letters to John Johnson, TNA SP 46/188/126, SP 46/188/114; Dutch letters written by him, SP46/5/Part1 fo1. 73; SP 46/fo303.

> you. Yf ye please not to wret youre lettre to her in Frengis (which I knowe you can do veary well), send me a draught of that ye wolde have writon in Englyshe, and I will the best I can trans[l]ate the same into Flemyshe.[65]

The letter shows not only Johnson's secure grasp of Dutch but also his sound metalinguistic understanding of what would be linguistically possible and desirable. Mr Wethill in London could not be expected to produce a letter in Dutch, but he might be able to manage one in French. The widow of a wealthy merchant from Bruges could also be expected to read a letter in French. However, if Mr Wethill wanted to write his letter in English rather than French, John would be happy to translate it. The translation would be into Flemish, for Johnson knew that that would be the preferred language of a Flemish merchant's wife.

The same year, again writing from Calais, John composed a letter to Henry Southwick in Antwerp that code-switches into Latin, French, and Dutch. Headed 'Jhesus *anno* 1545 [Latin], the 10 *jour* [French] June, at Callais', the letter proposes an efficient solution to a debt owed to John Grant by another widow, Janekis Vergowse, 'dwelling in Andwerpe on the Lynnen Clothe Market, at the Signe of the Golden Lettis [Lattice], called in Flemysche the Gulden Trayle'.[66] John Grant himself owed money to the Antwerp merchant Symond Pollard, and the proposal was for Janekis to settle John's debt to Symond, on the understanding that John would acquit her of her debt to him. To communicate this proposal to Janekis Vergowse, John enclosed a letter that Henry Southwick was to deliver to her. The reason why John Johnson thought it necessary to give her address in Dutch as well as English will now be understood: to find her house Henry would need to know its name in the local language. (The house appears to have had a sign displaying the name in Dutch.[67]) And what language did John use for the enclosed letter to Janekis? The letter, no longer accessible in Barbara Winchester's edition, survives in the National Archives (SP/46/5/Part1 fol. 73): it is written in Dutch. Janekis from Antwerp would probably have been able to cope with French, too,[68] but since Dutch would have been her first language and John had no trouble writing it, Dutch is the language he picked.

Of course, the personnel of the English branch of the Johnson business could not be expected to know Dutch as well as the agents of the Calais branch. There is a clear indication of this in a letter, dated 28th February 1552, sent to John

65 Letter 2422, II, p. 452.

66 Letter 167, II, p. 330.

67 Anna and Thomas Haukens lived in this house later in the sixteenth century. When they moved, they took the house sign with them and hung it up outside their new house (in the Warmoesstraat in Amsterdam), which thus became known as *De Gulden Tralie*. See Janny Venema, *Kiliaen van Rensselaer (1586–1643): Designing a New World* (Hilversum: Verloren, 2010), p. 40.

68 Ludovico Guicciardini in his description of Antwerp (published 1567) praised the enterprising people of Antwerp for their linguistic versatility, *scavant parler de trois ou quatres langues* ('knowing how to speak three or four languages'), cited by Winchester, I, p. 101.

Johnson, who had now moved back from Calais to the family manor in Glapthorn in Northamptonshire. The letter was from John's business partner Bartholomew Warner:

> I have gon thorough with a ship for Spaine for lxx toonne, and as I understond by a lettre from John de Mydlebrouque of Syvill which I received this daye, written in Flemishe, wherof I understond almost nothing [...] the sayd lettre youe shall receyve herwith, and thus fare youe well.[69]

Bartholomew could not make much sense of the Dutch letter, but he knew that John could, so he enclosed it. John kept the Flemish letter on file: it is now TNA SP 46/7/fo1. 18. The writer signs himself as Jehan de Millebrouque, that is, Jan van Millebroek (a placename in west Flanders), and he sent the letter from Seville (2nd January 1552).[70]

'Colonization', as Andrew Bennett and Nicholas Royle write, 'always works in two directions: to colonize is, however imperceptibly or insidiously, to be colonized'.[71] The former colony certainly seems to have altered John Johnson and, after he retired to Glapthorn, he dreamed of bringing it back to England. When Calais fell in 1558 and the English Wool Staple moved to Bruges, Johnson championed the idea of establishing the Staple in Ipswich. His plan, which unsurprisingly did not recommend itself to the authorities, was to reform Ipswich town governance on a Dutch model. The governor was to be a viscount 'which they name in the Flemysche tounge *markegrave*'; there was to be a chief mayor and 'two *burghemeesters*, in Engliche masters of the burgeyse', ten aldermen, 'a *pentioner* or recorder as we call hym',[72] a collector of taxes or '*tollenare*', and various minor officials. Dutch had really got under his skin.[73]

There is further evidence of code-switching into Dutch in Otwell Johnson's letter to his brother, dated 10th April 1548, reporting on negotiations between representatives of the staplers and the Dutch cloth merchants 'Jacob Stevinzon of Haerlem and Dirik Franszon Goile'.[74] The trade agreement between England and Flanders, known as the Magnus Intercursus, had been suspended, and attempts to renew it had stalled when it was discovered that the English and Dutch versions of it contained substantive differences.[75] The two Hollanders, both well known to

69 Letter 910, IV, p. 1606.

70 J. Langohr and H. J. van de Wijer, 'Plaatsnamen uit het Aalstersche', *Mededeelingen Uitgegeven door de Vlaamse Toponymie Vereeniging te Leuven* 15 (1939): 17–44 (32).

71 Andrew Bennett and Nicholas Royle, *An Introduction to Literature, Criticism and Theory* (London: Routledge, 2016), p. 288.

72 A 'pensioner' in the Low Countries was a municipal official who acted as legal adviser.

73 'Johnson letters', I, p. 507.

74 Letter 545, III, p. 956.

75 Winchester, 'Letters', III, p. 957.

the Johnsons,[76] had therefore travelled to London to plead with the staplers 'for thayer lawfull favour to be shewed them by all thayer factoures at Calleis'. Their case must have been favourably received, for, as Otwell continues, they 'theruppon obtained lettres somewhat to thayre contentacion, as I suppose, for they departed hense *vroelike*'. That last word is Otwell's code-switched wink to his brother John, who could be relied upon to know the Dutch equivalent for 'merrily'.

In an essay dedicated to Helen Fulton, co-editor of *Anglo-Italian Cultural Relations in the Later Middle Ages*,[77] it seems appropriate to end by mentioning one further language that makes the occasional appearance in the Cely and Johnson letters: Italian. In the Cely Letters, there is an intriguing mention of the Italian nation in Bruges. On 26th January 1480/1, Richard Cely wrote to George in Calais to find out the latest news about Rhodes, which had been attacked by the Turks: 'My Loorde [the Grand Master of the Order of St John] prays you when ye cwm to Brygys that ye will enqwer of the Whenysyans [Venetians] and Florantynys of tydynges of the Rodys'.[78] One wonders how this communication would have taken place: in Italian or in French? As has already been mentioned, Nurmi and Pahta mention one example of a code-switch into Italian in the Johnson letters. It occurs in letter 534, dated 3rd November 1547, from Otwell Johnson to Richard Johnson. Otwell seems to have conceived a plan to carry gold bullion from Flanders over to London, there to be turned into English gold coins for a favourable exchange rate: 'for I am at a pointe [agreed] with one [someone] of the Mynte to have my redy money within thre days, for howe moche soever I can bring unto hym, *a duodeze quasi percento*'. The background to the code-switch seems to be that the person at the Royal Mint with whom Otwell had come to an agreement was Italian, and had negotiated with Otwell in Italian, offering him a profit 'a duodeze quasi percento' (of around 12%). We cannot tell from this how much Italian Otwell knew, but, as the Johnson letters show, some merchants were expert. On 30th November 1544, Henry Bostock wrote to John Johnson in Calais with 'news of the Turk'. He had got hold of a copy of a letter from the Pope to the Holy Roman Emperor, 'wych I have in hast most rudely translated owt of Italyon into Englyshe'.[79] From the fact that Bostock furnished a translation we may infer that John Johnson himself could not read Italian – or, at least, not as comfortably as he managed Dutch.

I would like to conclude with some wise words from Anne Sutton and Livia Visser-Fuchs. In their introduction to the late fifteenth-century *Book of Privileges of the Merchant Adventurers*, they write: 'At no time is it advisable to underrate

76 They appear in previous correspondence, e.g. letters 389, 405, and a letter from 'Dirk Franz Goes' (in Dutch) to John Johnson is extant: TNA SP 46/188/114.

77 Michele Campopiano and Helen Fulton, eds, *Anglo-Italian Cultural Relations in the Later Middle Ages* (York: York Medieval Press, 2018).

78 Letter 114. I have modernised the yoghs.

79 Letter 87.

the language capacities of these merchants'.[80] The *Book of Privileges*, copied by an Englishman in London c. 1485, is quadrilingual, English, Latin, French, and Dutch, and makes the point for them. When scholars talk of the 'trilingualism' in medieval England, they think only of the first three languages in this list; the fourth, Dutch, however, also mattered to the mercers who commissioned the manuscript, because their trade was focused on the Dutch-speaking Low Countries.

In the case of the staplers of Calais, and other people who made their home there, we similarly need to see beyond English, French, and Latin. When in 1476 Lord Hastings, Lieutenant of Calais, needed a clerk of the kitchen, William Paston recommended a 'goodly yong man on horse and foote. He is well spokyn in Englyshe, metly well in Frenshe, and varray parfite in Flemyshe. Hys name is Rychard Stratton. Hys modyr is Mastress Grame of Caleys'.[81] Calais had been Dutch-speaking, and an underclass of local servants did menial work for the colonialists. The town was frequented by merchants from Holland, Brabant, and Flanders, and nearby Bruges and Antwerp were good places to go shopping: a working knowledge of Dutch was thus an essential requirement for a clerk of the kitchen in Calais.

For Calais-based merchants like the Celys and the Johnsons, Dutch was also necessary, and nothing could be further off the mark than Martina Häcker's opinion that: 'Since the Celys managed to run their business successfully for decades, we must conclude that they conducted their business negotiations in Flanders in English'.[82] The sixteenth-century Anglo-Italian author and teacher John Florio offers a refreshing corrective to this view. I edit below his imaginary dialogue between an Englishman and an Italian who has learned English:

> 'What thinke you of this English tongue, tel me, I pray you'?
> 'It is a language that wyl do you good in England, but, passe Dover, it is woorth nothing.'
> 'Is it not used then in other countreyes?'
> 'No, sir. With whom wyl you that they speake'?
> 'With English marchants.'
> 'English marchantes, when they are out of England, it liketh them not, and they doo not speake it.'[83]

80 Sutton and Visser-Fuchs, *Book of Privileges*, p. 37.

81 *Paston Letters and Papers of the Fifteenth Century*, ed. Norman Davis, 2 vols (Oxford: Clarendon Press, 1971–76), I, p. 600.

82 Häcker, 'French-English Linguistic and Cultural Contact', p. 144.

83 John Florio, *Florio his firste fruites which yeelde familiar speech* (London: Thomas Dawson, 1578), pp. 50–51. I have added modern punctuation, expanded abbreviations, and modernised u/v. Florio's testimony is the starting point of John Gallagher's valuable exploration of language learning in a slightly later period than the one covered here: *Learning Languages in Early Modern England* (Oxford: Oxford University Press, 2019).

As Florio indicates, trade between English merchants and ones from other nations was carried on in languages other than English, because very few foreigners could understand it. To this circumstance, we owe the fascinating insight that the Celys and Johnsons give into the use of other languages in the multilingual contact zone of 'English' Calais.

13

Shelley's Welsh Bible

Geraint Evans

This brief description of an eighteenth-century Welsh Bible, which probably belonged to Percy Bysshe Shelley, illustrates the interconnected nature of the literary histories of Wales and England, something which underpins the inclusive, outward-looking, and comparative structure of the *Cambridge History of Welsh Literature*, which was a shared endeavour with this volume's honourand. As Helen Fulton's work shows so clearly, the languages and literatures of the Island of Britain are intimately interconnected and by studying them together, as part of a larger whole, different patterns of cultural production and consumption begin to emerge. This essay about Shelley in Wales is itself part of the larger field of English Romantic writers in Wales, a field which spans the literary, political, and linguistic borders which often connect, rather than separate, the literary cultures of Wales and England.

* * *

In an early memoir of Percy Bysshe Shelley (1792–1822), Thomas Medwin, Shelley's second cousin and his childhood friend, recalls, 'as if it occurred yesterday', Shelley waking him up by knocking at his door in Garden Court in the Temple, at four o'clock in the morning, the day after his expulsion from Oxford: 'Medwin, let me in; I am expelled, (here followed a loud half-hysterical laugh) – I am expelled for Atheism'.[1]

The idea of Shelley's atheism has become one of the defining elements of his early life, if not his whole career, as it proved a fruitful starting point for the development of ideas about social equality. In his first year of study at University College, Oxford, he collaborated with his friend Thomas Jefferson Hogg on numerous satirical and anti-authoritarian pieces, culminating in an anonymous pamphlet entitled *The Necessity of Atheism*. The pamphlet consisted of a single foolscap sheet, folded in octavo to produce 16 pages, carrying the imprint 'Phillips, Printers, Worthing', and an 'Advertisement' signed 'Thro' deficiency of proof, An ATHEIST'. The text of the pamphlet covers pages seven to thirteen and concludes with the sentence,

1 Thomas Medwin, *Memoir of Percy Bysshe Shelley* (London: Whittaker, Treacher, 1833), pp. 10–11.

'Every reflecting mind must allow that there is no proof of the existence of a Deity. Q.E.D'.[2] The argument of *The Necessity of Atheism* would have been shocking enough in 1811, but Shelley provoked a crisis by sending a copy of the pamphlet to the head of every college in Oxford. Shelley and Hogg were suspected and called to account, and when both declined to deny their authorship or involvement, they were both expelled. The pamphlet was printed and circulated around the middle of February 1811, and the two young students were expelled on 25th March. While Hogg's role in the affair is not entirely clear, recent accounts have tended towards the view that Shelley was the main author while Hogg insisted on sharing Shelley's punishment.[3] The argument of *The Necessity of Atheism* was expanded and republished by Shelley as a note to Canto VII of *Queen Mab* (1813), but most copies of the original pamphlet were destroyed and only six copies are now recorded in institutional libraries, including a copy that was identified and recatalogued as recently as 2015, in the Dugald Stewart bequest at Edinburgh University library.[4]

However, despite his adoption of an atheist identity, the influence of biblical prose on Shelley's poetry was recognised at an early stage. In his *Life of Shelley*, Thomas Hogg records that Shelley 'was much addicted to reading the Septuagint', and that, when he was only 22, he claimed to have read the Bible four times.[5] In Thomas Medwin's *Life of Shelley*, a work that expands considerably on his early *Memoir*, Medwin went further, locating the 'oriental splendour' of biblical prose alongside the 'imposing grandeur' of Greek tragedy as two of the central characteristics of Shelley's writing.[6] In the same work he also recalled Shelley's own library, and his description of what 'a good library' should contain:

> Shelley's library was a very limited one. He used to say that a good library consisted not of many books, but a few chosen ones; and asking him what he considered such, he said, 'I'll give you my list [...] The Greek Plays, Plato, Lord Bacon's Works, Shakespeare, the Old Dramatists, Milton, Göthe and Schiller, Dante, Petrarch and Boccaccio, and Machiavelli and Guicciardini, – not forgetting Calderon; and last, yet first, the Bible.'[7]

2 The bibliographical description is based on Percy Vaughan, *Early Shelley Pamphlets* (London: Watts, 1905); for the text of the pamphlet see E. B. Murray, ed., *The Prose Works of Percy Bysshe Shelley* (London: Chatto & Windus, 1993).

3 See Michael O'Neill, 'Percy Bysshe Shelley', in *Oxford Dictionary of National Biography* (Oxford: Oxford University Press, 2004) <www.oxforddnb.com> [last accessed 11th November 2023].

4 Edinburgh University Special Collections, MS Df.7.97.

5 T. J. Hogg, *The Life of Percy Bysshe Shelley* (London: Routledge, 1906), p. 573.

6 Thomas Medwin, *The Life of Percy Bysshe Shelley by Thomas Medwin: A New Edition printed from a copy copiously amended and extended by the Author and left unpublished at his death*, ed. H. Buxton Forman (Oxford: Humphrey Milford, 1913), p. 419. Hereafter *Revised Life of Shelley*.

7 *Revised Life of Shelley*, p. 255.

This enlightening contradiction in Shelley's life and work, which acknowledges the cultural centrality of the Bible alongside 'the necessity of atheism', provides some useful context for a remarkable copy of a Welsh Bible, dated 1746, which survives in a private collection. The book has an eighteenth-century binding, with original brass clasps, and one of the preliminary blanks carries an ownership inscription in a nineteenth-century hand, which reads 'Percy Bysshe Shelley | 1811'.

To begin with the book itself, this is a very special edition of the Bible in Welsh. Finely printed in Cambridge and elegantly bound, this is probably the most desirable edition of the Welsh Bible to appear in the eighteenth century. The edition is described in John Ballinger's *The Bible in Wales*, which was published as a catalogue to accompany an exhibition of Welsh Bibles at Cardiff Central Library commemorating the centenary of the British and Foreign Bible Society. The exhibition contained examples of every important edition of the Bible in Welsh, and Ballinger's book contains what is still the best bibliography of Welsh-language editions of the Bible, New Testament, and Prayer Book since the sixteenth century.[8] In Ballinger's bibliography, the 1746 Bible is described as the third edition in Welsh to be published by the Society for the Promotion of Christian Knowledge (the SPCK), which had been founded in 1698. The first Welsh SPCK Bible appeared in 1717–18, and is now known as 'Beibl Moses Williams', after the Vicar of St Cynog's, the medieval church at Defynnog in the Brecon Beacons, who had edited the text for publication. The second SPCK edition of 1727 was a reprint of the 1718 edition, and the third was published in 1746. This new edition was revised and prepared for the press by Richard Morris, the eldest of the literary Morris brothers from Anglesey, who was by then working at the Navy Office in London, and after whom it is known in Welsh as 'Beibl Rhisiart Morys'. Morris also oversaw the production of a fine edition of the Welsh Prayer Book, which was also printed in Cambridge in 1770, and which the editor of the *Cambrian Bibliography* described as 'un o'r llyfrau harddaf a gyhoeddwyd yn y ganrif honno' (one of the most beautiful [Welsh] books to be published during that century).[9] It was also Richard Morris, together with his brother Lewis Morris, who founded a society for London Welsh antiquarians in 1751. Known as the Honourable Society of Cymmrodorion, the society's *Transactions* are one of the longest-running learned society journals in the world, and for many years they were edited by Professor Helen Fulton.

The Welsh Bible of 1746 is styled on the title page as *Y Bibl Cyssegr-lan, sef yr Hen Destament a'r Newydd.* It was printed by Joseph Bentham, printer to Cambridge University, and Ballinger records that 15,000 copies were printed and sold at 4 shillings 6 pence each, some bound in a single volume, but many bound in two

8 John Ballinger, *The Bible in Wales: A Study in the History of the Welsh People, with an Introductory Address and a Bibliography* (London: Henry Sotheran, 1906).

9 William Rowlands, *Cambrian Bibliography, Revised and Enlarged by D. Silvan Evans*, '1770, Item 19' (Llanidloes, John Pryse, 1869), p. 519.

volumes of equal size. The copy carrying the Shelley inscription is volume one of a two-volume set and only the first volume has survived – kept, perhaps, because of the name – but it is in the original SPCK calf binding, with clasps, as described by Ballinger.[10] This particular copy of 'Beibl Rhisiart Morys' has two marks of ownership. On the recto of the front free endpaper is the name and date: 'W.H. Rees | 1926'. Then on the verso of the same endpaper there is another name and date: 'Percy Bysshe Shelley | 1811'. So, what kind of provenance does this create? Did the book actually belong to Shelley? And does the ownership signature imply that Shelley could read Welsh?

Shelley already had links with Wales. As a boy, he had studied with a Welsh parson, the Rev. Mr Edwards, 'who recognised his pupil's talent for Latin and Greek' and encouraged an interest in languages. Peacock later records that Shelley retained a genuine affection for 'the reverend Mr Edwards of Horsham', from whom he received his first instruction.[11] Shelley was born at Field Place near Horsham in Sussex on 4th August 1792, and the Rev. Evan Edwards (d. 1839) was curate and later vicar at Warnham, a small village on the outskirts of Horsham.[12] Shelley's enthusiasm for languages and his genuine affection for his childhood tutor may well have been enough to encourage his later interest in the Welsh Bible when, in the years after his expulsion from Oxford, he visited Wales and then hoped to settle there.

In March 1811 Shelley had briefly stayed with his cousin Thomas Medwin in the Temple before moving to 15 Poland Street, east of Regent Street. While there he established a close friendship with the 16-year-old Harriet Westbrook, the daughter of a successful owner of a coffee house in Grosvenor Square, but both families were opposed to the match and in July 1811 Shelley left London to spend time at the house of his cousin, Thomas Grove, at Cwm Elan near Rhaeadr in mid Wales. Thomas Grove senior had purchased the 10,000-acre Cwm Elan estate in 1782 and, while there is no record of the transfer of ownership of the estate from Thomas Grove to his son, Tom Grove and his wife Henrietta were in residence at least by the summer of 1809 because Henrietta wrote from Wales to her sister-in-law Harriet Grove, Shelley's first sweetheart, who records in her diary entry for 25th July that she was 'happy to hear they are quite well at Cwm Elen [Elan]'.[13] Thomas Grove junior was ten years older than his cousin Percy Bysshe Shelley and there had been little contact between them before they met in the spring of 1811. When Shelley

10 See Ballinger 22; the other catalogue references are *Libri Walliae* 366, *Cambrian Bibliography* 1746 Item 1, Darlow & Moule 9599.

11 See Theresa Kelley, 'Life and Biographies' in *The Cambridge Companion to Shelley*, ed. Timothy Morton (Cambridge: Cambridge University Press, 2006), pp. 17–34.

12 See A. P. Baggs, C. R. J. Currie, C. R. Elrington, S. M. Keeling and A. M. Rowland, 'Warnham: Church', in *A History of the County of Sussex: Volume 6 Part 2, Bramber Rape (North-Western Part) Including Horsham*, ed. T. P. Hudson (London: Victoria County History, 1986), pp. 216–17.

13 'The Diary of Harriet Grove', in *Shelley and his Circle 1773–1822: Vol. II*, ed. Kenneth Neill Cameron (Cambridge, MA: Harvard University Press, 1961), p. 525.

was expelled from Oxford, Tom and Henrietta had been spending a few weeks in London, where Tom's younger brother John Grove had a house in Lincoln's Inn Fields, which he shared with the youngest of the brothers, Charles Henry Grove. After Shelley made contact with his Grove cousins they rallied round their young relative. John Grove attempted to mend the rift with Shelley's father, while Tom invited his cousin to spend July with him in the remote tranquillity of Cwm Elan.[14] Shelley accepted the invitation, although he was also hoping to use the visit as a means of continuing his connection with his future wife, Harriet Westbrook, whose family were planning to holiday in Aberystwyth, which could be reached by coach from Rhaeadr.[15]

Just as books recording 'Tours in Wales' were beginning to displace accounts of travels on the continent, so also many of the English Romantic writers were spending time in Wales or writing about its landscape and history. Wordsworth, Coleridge, and Southey all drew on visits to Wales in their writing, as did De Quincey, Hazlitt, and Shelley's friend Peacock.[16] The earliest English Romantic writer to record his impressions of the landscape around the Grove estate in particular was William Lisle Bowles, whose poem on 'Coombe Ellen' is subtitled 'written in Radnorshire, September 1798'.[17] Shelley's own poem 'Written at Cwm Ellan', which survives in manuscript in the Esdaile Notebook, was composed in the summer of 1811.[18] Reflecting, perhaps, the turmoil of recent months, the poetic voice in this poem seeks out the smothering embrace of night, as if solitude alone were not enough to banish the pain:

> More dear to me, tho' day be robed in vest of dazzling whiteness,
> Is one folding of the garment dusk that wraps thy form, O Night!

Two more poems that are the product of his first visit to Cwm Elan are 'Dark Spirit of the Desart Rude' and 'Death-spurning Rocks!', both of which explore a gothic landscape that provides a location for introspection and spiritual growth.[19] Despite his delight in the natural world around the Elan valley, Shelley told Elizabeth Hitchener that his 'only adventure' was the sudden arrival at the kitchen door below his bedroom window of a philosophical beggar. Shelley ran out and walked with him

14 See Desmond Hawkins, 'The Groves of Cwm Elan', *Radnorshire Society Transactions* 55 (1985): 47–48.

15 See Richard Holmes, *Shelley: The Pursuit* (London: Harper Collins, 2005), p. 75.

16 See Glyn Tegai Hughes, ed., *The Romantics in Wales: An Anthology* (Newtown: Gregynog, 2009).

17 The sole edition was printed by R. Cruttwell in 1798 and sold by Dilley, Cadell, and Davies in Bath.

18 See *The Esdaile Notebook*, ed. Kenneth Neill Cameron (London: Faber, 1964), pp. 73, 204; 'The Esdaile Notebook', in *Shelley and his Circle 1773–1822: Vol. IV*, ed. Kenneth Neill Cameron (Cambridge, MA: Harvard University Press, 1970), p. 962.

19 See *The Esdaile Notebook*, pp. 77, 207, 81, 211; 'The Esdaile Notebook', in *Shelley and his Circle IV*, pp. 966, 970.

for a mile or so, pestering him with questions about his life, before the exasperated traveller observed, 'I see by your dress that you are a rich man – they have injured me & mine a million times', and told Shelley that it would be an act of charity to leave him to his own company.[20]

In August 1811 Shelley left Cwm Elan and returned briefly to London. With little time to plan, he and Harriet eloped to Edinburgh, where they were joined by his friend Hogg. On the following day, 29th August, Shelley and Harriet were married. They travelled back through the Lake District, where Shelley met many of the Lake Poets and began to form friendships, later sustained by correspondence with the writer and radical thinker William Godwin and his daughter Mary. In 1812, Shelley and Harriet returned to Wales following a trip to Dublin, travelling through north Wales and staying at the Grove estate in Cwm Elan, before moving briefly to the nearby Nantgwyllt House, where Shelley considered settling permanently. Located in the parish of Llansantffraed Cwmteuddwr, Nantgwyllt was in the Claerwen valley, just a mile and a half (2.5 km) from the Groves, whose house was in the adjacent Elan valley. Shelley and his young wife, Harriet Westbrook, were entranced by the beauty of the house and the tranquillity of the surrounding countryside. On 16th April Harriet wrote to Catherine Nugent in Dublin, describing their hope of making their home at Nantgwyllt, and adding that 'the beauty of this place is not to be described'.[21] On 24th April Shelley wrote to his father, asking for security or sufficient capital to settle in this 'retired spot' with his wife: 'The farm is about 200 acres, the house a very good one. The furniture and the stock must, however, be purchased, which will cost £500'.[22] Timothy Shelley replied to the request on 5th May, through his agent William Whitton, declining to advance any money or to offer security, and by 7th June Harriet was writing again to Catherine Nugent about their 'disappointment' that 'we are not at our beloved Nantgwillt. Alas, that charming spot is, I am afraid, never destined to be ours! The possessor cannot settle with Percy, and indeed he has acted such a *villanous* part that we have been obliged to leave him, and for a few days take up our residence at Mr Grove's'.[23]

It was during this second visit to Cwm Elan, in the spring of 1812, that Shelley wrote 'The Retrospect', one of his finest early poems, and it is clear that he was still connecting the landscape of Wales with restorative escape.[24] 'The Retrospect' also contrasts his former depressive loneliness when visiting Cwm Elan the previous

20 See James Bieri, *Percy Bysshe Shelley: A Biography* (Baltimore, MD: Johns Hopkins University Press, 2008), p. 157.

21 Roger Ingpen, ed., *The Complete Works of Percy Bysshe Shelley, Volume 8: Letters 1803 to 1812* (New York: Gordian Press, 1965), p. 310.

22 Roger Ingpen, *Shelley Letters 1803 to 1812*, p. 311.

23 Roger Ingpen, *Shelley Letters 1803 to 1812*, p. 332.

24 See *The Esdaile Notebook*, pp. 155, 281; 'The Esdaile Notebook', in *Shelley and his Circle IV*, p. 1048.

year with his happiness on returning with Harriet. He recalls the consolation of 'friendless solitude', but contrasts it with the changed perception of his return visit:

> How changed since nature's summer form
> Had last the power my grief to charm,
> Since last ye soothed my spirit's sadness–
> Strange chaos of a mingled madness! (ll.132–35)

In 'On Leaving London for Wales', the poem which marks the beginning of that second visit, he writes again about the anticipation of restorative solitude, and the 'unfettered wind' of 'Mountain Liberty':

> One draught from Snowdon's ever-sacred spring
> Blots out the unholiest rede of worldly witnessing.[25]

These were turbulent times for the Shelleys, who still had no permanent home and were constantly short of money. It is therefore no surprise that they saw the Grove estate as a place of refuge, although it is clear from their letters that they found genuine delight in Cwm Elan and Nantgwyllt.

The two great collections of Shelley materials are held in the Bodleian Library in Oxford, and the Carl H. Pforzheimer collection of 'Shelley and his Circle' at the New York Public Library. So, to investigate the provenance of the Welsh Bible I visited the New York Public Library, accompanied by Helen Fulton and the Shelley Bible. With the assistance of curators from the Pforzheimer, we examined Shelley signatures, inscriptions, and manuscripts, and it was quickly established that the signature in the Welsh Bible was not in Shelley's hand. However, this might be good evidence of ownership because Shelley rarely signed his own name in books that he owned. The Pforzheimer curators have seen several examples of books carrying forged Shelley signatures, but very few that are genuine. The initial conclusion was clear: the mark of ownership was in an authentic early nineteenth-century hand, although it was not Shelley's signature, and those two things together made the attribution of ownership more likely to be authentic.

There is no comprehensive account of the books that were owned by Shelley during his lifetime. E. J. Trelawny, who was a close member of the Shelley circle in Italy in the early 1820s, made a list of books on leaves two and three of his account and commonplace book for 1820–22.[26] It is an interesting list of 63 works in 85 volumes, and some early Shelley biographers, such as Walter Edwin Peck, took this to be a list of Shelley's library in Pisa. Peck also believed the list of books to be in a 'feminine autograph', which 'is not Trelawny's and might be the hand of Jane

25 See *The Esdaile Notebook*, pp. 53, 190; 'The Esdaile Notebook', in *Shelley and his Circle IV*, p. 941.

26 See 'E. J. Trelawny, Notebook [1820–1822]', in *Shelley and his Circle 1773–1822: Vol. VIII*, ed. Donald H. Reiman and Doucet Devin Fischer (Cambridge, MA: Harvard University Press, 1986), pp. 625–28.

Williams or Claire Clairmont'.[27] But the modern edition of the notebook, in the Pforzheimer series of *Shelley and His Circle* manuscripts, is clear that this is a list of Trelawny's own books rather than Shelley's. One genuine source, which is also in the Pforzheimer collection, is the 'Marlow List', the significance of which has recently been highlighted by Bysshe Inigo Coffey.[28] Formerly owned by Thomas Love Peacock, the document consists of ten manuscript leaves of varying sizes, listing the books left with Peacock in the village of Marlow when the Shelleys went abroad in 1818. Over 300 items are recorded, in a variety of often unidentified hands, and it provides a fascinating resource for a study of the reading and book buying habits of the Shelleys in the years leading up to 1818. What it does not do, unfortunately, is help with the identification of books in which Shelley wrote his own name as a mark of ownership.

The Pforzheimer collection includes a number of books that were owned by Shelley, and although some of them carry annotations by a variety of people indicating that the book had once belonged to Shelley, very few are signed by him. The Pforzheimer has Shelley's two-volume copy of *The Poems of Ossian* (1807), signed and dated 1810 on both title pages, and Shelley's copy of Gregory's *Economy of Nature* (1804), which has Shelley's ownership inscription in the first volume: 'P.B. Shelley / ex dono / G.R. Smith / July 1810'.[29] Another example survives in the Robert H. Taylor collection at Princeton University Library. This is Shelley's schoolboy copy of Ovid's *Metamorphoses* (Amsterdam, 1729), which carries his signature on the title page. The Taylor collection also includes Shelley's two-volume copy of Milton, which he later inscribed to Mary Wollstonecraft Godwin (see below).[30] Signing his books as a mark of ownership seems to have been only an occasional early practice, and one which Shelley did not continue into his 20s. All three of the examples listed above were signed by Shelley before 1811, and the Pforzheimer has ten further books that were owned by Shelley and contain annotations in his hand, although none of them carry an autograph signature of ownership. The other major collection of manuscripts and books relating to Shelley and his circle is held at the Bodleian. The collection includes Shelley's annotated proof copy of *A Proposal for Putting Reform to the Vote* (1817),[31] together with books with a Shelley family ownership provenance, although none of these items are signed by Shelley. In fact, the largest group of books that carry Shelley's autograph are not books from his library but

27 Walter Edwin Peck, *Shelley: His Life and Work, Vol. II* (London: Benn, 1927), p. 265; an example of the booklist hand is reproduced in *Shelley and his Circle VIII*, p. 699.

28 Bysshe Inigo Coffey, *Shelley's Broken World: Fractured Materiality and Intermitted Song* (Liverpool: Liverpool University Press, 2023), p. 17.

29 New York Public Library, PBS 0250/Pforz 557R 04 and PBS 0312/Pforz 557R 03; vol. 3 of the Gregory is lacking.

30 Princeton University Special Collections, 19th-452 RHT and 19th-453 RHT; see Mary Hyde, 'Robert H. Taylor and Other Collectors', *The Princeton University Library Chronicle* 38.2/3 (1977): 97–102.

31 Oxford, Bodleian Library, MS Shelley e. 3.

books containing gift inscriptions, although even this is a list of no more than about 11 titles. They are listed here by location and date of publication:

1. [P. B. and Elizabeth Shelley], *Original Poetry by Victor and Cazire* (Worthing, 1810) inscribed to 'Thos Medwin - / a present from / one of the authors'; probably Shelley but possibly his sister and co-author Elizabeth; NYPL.

2. P. B. Shelley, *A Vindication of Natural Diet* (London, 1813) inscribed 'To John Grove Esq.r / from the author'; NYPL.

3. P. B. Shelley, *Cenci* (Italy, 1819) inscribed to 'J[ohn]. Taaffe Esqr'; NYPL.

4. P. B. Shelley, *Queen Mab* (London, 1813) inscribed to 'Mary Wollstonecraft Godwin, P.B.S.'; Sotheby's, August 1879; Brayton Ives; Huntington Library.

5. P. B. Shelley, *Adonais* (Pisa, 1821) inscribed by PBS to Sir Charles Hyde; Huntington Library.

6. John Milton, *Paradise Lost* [in two volumes] (Dublin, 1747) inscribed 'Mary. W.G. from Percy B. Shelley June 6. 1815.'; Princeton University Library.

7. P. B. Shelley, *Adonais* (Pisa, 1821) inscribed by PBS to Thomas Love Peacock; British Library.

8. Vincenzo da Filicaja, *Poesie Toscane* (Venice, 1812) inscribed to Claire Clairmont: 'To dearest Clare from her affectionate P.B.S., April 1821'; sold at Bonham's London, 23rd March 2022, lot 85; present location unknown.

9. P. B. Shelley, *Alastor* (London, 1816) inscribed 'To Mr. [Edward] Hookham / with the Author's Compts'; Christie's New York, 18th November 1988, lot 315; present location unknown.

10. P. B. Shelley, *Laon and Cythna* (London, 1818) inscribed 'From the Author'; Christie's New York, 15th December 2005, lot 525; present location unknown.

11. P. B. Shelley, *Adonais* (Pisa, 1821) inscribed 'To my dear friend Leigh Hunt / PBS'; Christie's New York, 9th October 2001, lot 106; present location unknown.

So, if we accept that the inscription in the Welsh Bible is a genuine and contemporary mark of ownership, but not in Shelley's hand, that can be read as evidence for the authenticity of the connection given how infrequently Shelley seems to have written his name in the books he owned. The fact that the signature is not even a good approximation of Shelley's autograph is also evidence that the signature is not a later fake. The likeliest explanation for the date of 1811 is that Shelley acquired the book, or was given it as a gift, during his first visit to Cwm Elan. When he left the book behind after that visit, somebody who knew him wrote his name on the endpaper of the first volume to mark the ownership and to preserve it for his expected return. This link with a Welsh Bible also suggests that Shelley's ambiguous relationship with the Church and the Bible continued through 1811 and 1812, during his visits to Wales. There is an interesting account from 1878, in which a visitor to Cwm Elan records a conversation in Welsh with an elderly woman called Elizabeth Jones, who had once delivered letters to Cwm Elan and Nantgwyllt. She recalled the poet Shelley sporting a small cap and a bare neck throughout the week, but looking very smart in a silk hat on Sundays, when he attended church with the family.[32] The family might occasionally have attended the medieval Church of Sain Ffraid (Saint Bride or Saint Bridget) at Llansanffraid Cwmdeuddwr, but regular Sunday worship would have been in the small church or chapel of ease at Nantgwyllt, which was demolished as part of the creation of the Caban Coch reservoir in the 1890s.

In 1811 and 1812 the whole valley and much of the area surrounding Rhaeadr would have been Welsh-speaking. In Ffransis Payne's *Crwydro Sir Faesyfed* (1966 and 1968), his wonderful two-volume walking-tour history of the county of Radnorshire, he notes that, until about 1830, the family of Lewis Lloyd, the owners of Nantgwyllt, would all have been fluent Welsh speakers, although some of them would also have been educated in English. Many of the other inhabitants of the valley would have spoken only Welsh, which may perhaps have made the text of the Bible in Welsh more intriguing to Shelley.[33] In her history of Nantgwyllt as a Welsh gentry-house, Ruth Bidgood relates another story about Shelley, which was recorded by Herbert Vaughan. During the weeks of his failed attempt to secure a lease on the Nantgwyllt house, Shelley left a lasting memento of himself in the house in the form of his name and a date cut into a windowpane with a diamond ring. Herbert Vaughan records that Miss Gertrude Lewis Lloyd of Nantgwyllt, who was remembered locally for running a small school, carefully removed the small pane and kept it in her room at Llwynmadog in north Breckonshire when she lived there with her friend Clara Thomas. He records that after Gertrude Lewis Lloyd's death in 1907, people looked for this memento of Shelley at Nantgwyllt but it could not be found.[34]

Occasional attendance at a church in Wales, together with Shelley's interest in languages and his admiration of the Bible as a monument of literature, are enough to account for his interest in the Welsh Bible. It is also easy to imagine that in 1811, leaving Cwm Elan but planning to return, Shelley had left certain items with his

32 Morris Thomas, 'Shelley yng Nghymru [Shelley in Wales]', *Cylchgrawn Myfyrwyr y Bala* 9.2 (1908): 75–78.

33 Ffrancis Payne, *Crwydro Sir Faesyfed* [Wandering Through Radnorshire], 2 vols (Llandybïe: Llyfrau'r Dryw, 1966 and 1968). See II for the Lloyds of Nantgwyllt.

34 See Ruth Bidgood, 'Nantgwyllt', *Radnorshire Society Transactions* 65 (1995): 33–46; Herbert Vaughan, *The South Wales Squires* (London: Methuen, 1926), pp. 178–87.

cousin, items which he perhaps reclaimed the following year when he and Harriet attempted to settle at their 'beloved Nantgwillt'. It would also make sense to leave a Welsh Bible in Wales rather than taking it back to London, so it may be that it was in August 1811, when Shelley left Wales and returned to London to pursue his relationship with Harriet Westbrook, that the name and date were written in the book to establish his ownership. The book would have been waiting for him the following year, but then, after the disastrous failure to settle at Nantgwyllt, the Welsh Bible was probably left behind once more. Events then moved quickly. Shelley never returned to Wales and the Bible perhaps remained at Cwm Elan until 1815, when the Groves sold the estate, or perhaps until what remained of the estate was dispersed later in the century. There are also other factors, of course, which help to account for Shelley leaving some possessions behind in mid Wales. One is the chaotic nature of his travels and enthusiasms during those years. A visit to Tremadoc in north Wales also resulted in boxes being left behind, some of which became the subject of disputes over unpaid debts, and the pattern is visible again in the large number of books which were left in Marlow with Thomas Love Peacock when the Shelleys left for Italy in 1818.[35] On the other hand, an important factor in leaving the Welsh Bible behind could have been Shelley's continuing fascination with Wales as a place of refuge and a possible place to settle. As late as June 1815, on a tour of the West Country with Mary Wollstonecraft Godwin, he wrote to John Williams enquiring about the possibility of renting a house in north Wales. The Grove estate near Rhaeadr was no longer available to him, but the lure of Wales was apparently still strong.[36]

Little can be deduced with certainty about the fate of the Welsh Bible after 1815. Shelley's personal life was in turmoil in the years that followed his failed attempt to settle at Nantgwyllt. In March 1814 he remarried Harriet, to ensure her legal status as his wife, but in May and June his increasingly close relationship with Mary Wollstonecraft Godwin became so intense that, on 28th July, they secretly escaped to the continent in the company of Mary's younger half-sister, Claire Clairmont, an account of which was incorporated into the anonymous travel narrative *History of a Six Weeks' Tour*, which they published in London in 1817.[37] Following his abandonment of Harriet, the Grove family had little sympathy for Shelley, and when the Cwm Elan estate was sold in 1815 there would have been no reason for the family to retain any of Shelley's belongings that were still in the house. Following Harriet's death in 1816, Shelley and Mary Wollstonecraft Godwin were married. They lived in the village of Marlow, in Buckinghamshire, close to Thomas Love Peacock, before moving to Italy in 1818, where they remained until Shelley's death in July 1822. The

35 See Donald H. Reiman and Doucet Devin Fischer, eds, *Shelley and His Circle 1773–1822: Vol. IX* (Cambridge, MA: Harvard University Press, 2002), pp. 196–209.

36 See *Shelley and His Circle IX*, pp. 215–16.

37 *History of a Six Weeks' Tour through a Part of France, Switzerland, Germany and Holland* (London: T. Hookham and C. and J. Ollier, 1817).

following year Mary Shelley returned to London, where she lived and worked as a professional writer until her death in 1851.

There is very little evidence about what exactly happened to this Welsh Bible in the years after 1815, but it seems likely that it remained in Wales, perhaps kept by somebody as a memento of Shelley's visits or as a memento of the Grove family at Cwm Elan, or perhaps given away to a local churchgoing family. It is also possible that it was simply left behind in the house at Cwm Elan until the contents were finally dispersed in the 1890s, although the likelihood is that it was already in new ownership long before long before then, as it was not then recorded as being in the possession of Gertrude Lewis Lloyd, a known Shelley enthusiast and the proud possessor of a Shelley memento from Nantgwyllt. It also seems likely that, in the years after Shelley's death, the book must have remained in Wales until, after yet another death or estate dispersal, the book was acquired by W. H. Reese, who wrote his name in the first volume in 1924, an action that perhaps indicates that it was newly acquired in that year and had not been in the Reese family prior to 1924. Then, for the next 70 years, it probably remained in one or more private collections in Wales, because, if such an intriguing inscription had ever found its way to London in the years between 1815 and 1990, it is doubtful that it would have avoided being swallowed up by the London book trade. Finally, towards the end of the century, it found its way to a bookseller who sold the orphaned single volume to its present owner.

There are so many things which have been lost from Cwm Elan and the surrounding countryside because of the creation of the reservoirs, including the houses and farms that were the heart of the local Welsh-speaking community. Also lost are the small church and nearby mill and the two mansion houses, where the young poet Shelley sought refuge in 1811 and 1812. It seems appropriate, therefore, that this fragile memorial to Shelley's life in Wales probably survived by passing from owner to owner in a Welsh-speaking community. This is especially appropriate when the memorial is written into a Bible because the survival of the Welsh language itself is linked to high levels of literacy in seventeenth- and eighteenth-centuries Wales, a literacy that was predicated on the use of *Y Bibl Cyssegr-lan* as a medium of instruction in Welsh schools of the period.[38] And whoever wrote Shelley's name and the date 1811 in this copy of 'Beibl Rhisiart Morys', it has survived as a reminder of the link between Shelley, the self-proclaimed atheist, and Shelley the linguist, whose own revolutionary writing combined the 'imposing grandeur' of Greek tragedy with the 'oriental splendour' of biblical prose.

38 See Geraint H. Jenkins, *The Welsh Language before the Industrial Revolution* (Cardiff: University of Wales Press, 1997).

Tribute: Helen Fulton and Welsh Medieval Studies

Elaine Treharne

In her consultative work as a medievalist, as an Arthurian specialist, and as a linguistic expert, in 2020 Helen Fulton invented two languages for Netflix's fantasy retelling of Arthurian legend, *Cursed*. In her explanation of how she achieved linguistic depth for the Fey and Tusk languages that she developed, Helen reminds her readers of the flexibility of medieval literature, of the importance of multilingualism, and of the acceptance of different cultures expressed through different languages. Linguistic diversity, she comments, 'brings people together rather than driving them apart'.[1] One can say of Helen's own professional life, her scholarship, collegiality, and commitment to early literary histories that she, too, 'brings people together'; this ethos has been a consistent hallmark of Helen's career.

Helen Fulton is the exemplar of the international scholar, with a worldview that is expansive and generous. She was an undergraduate at the University of Sydney, a postgraduate at the University of Oxford, a postdoctoral fellow at the University of Aberystwyth, and has held fellowships from colleges at the Universities of Oxford and Cambridge. Helen taught and administered at the University of Sydney before taking up senior academic posts at the Universities of Swansea, York, and Bristol. Her influence has been broad and profound and, wherever she has dedicated her professional efforts, both the field of Medieval Studies and the working lives of colleagues have been the better off because of her. Helen commands respect for her achievements, but also affection for her warmth and kindness; she has an entirely collaborative intellectual spirit and, through her many funded projects and awards, she has created positions for early career scholars, many of whom have gone on to permanent institutional posts.

These funded projects are inventive and multidisciplinary, engaged in research into the real world of space, place, time, and language. In the last decade, Helen's focus has been on towns, countryside, and the significance of peoples and geographies of the Atlantic, and of Welsh and English medieval borders and borderlands.

1 Helen Fulton, 'Netflix's "Cursed" and the Fey Language', 14th September 2020, <https://www.reddit.com/r/conlangs/comments/iso3xu/netflixs_cursed_and_the_fey_language/> [last accessed 27th July 2023].

This research has far-reaching implications for improving scholars' understanding of contact, connections, and colonisation in the Middle Ages. The medievalist's expertise, once applied to literature and language, is now also directly impacting understanding of localities, regions, and the present-day manifestations of the past. How, why, and where people moved; who they encountered; what marks and traces they left? – questions about these facets of human history highlight human samenesses across time, as well as allowing for the revealing of radical differences in the way we live in the present day when compared with those who came before us.

This significant work, with its important public-facing engagement, has culminated in 2023 in a major five-year project, funded by the European Research Council: 'The Medieval March of Wales, c. 1282–1550: Mapping Literary Geography in a British Border Region'. This research is, typically of Helen, deeply thoughtful, timely, and pioneering. It aims to bring to light multilingual medieval manuscripts and texts that will be instrumental in reappraising the significance of Wales to British culture more broadly, and of the Marches as a specific region of Britain meriting individual study of its later medieval history. Literary and historical texts from these borderlands have traditionally either been overlooked, misassigned, or appropriated for an English colonial history. Helen and her team's research will provide a revisionary account of the region, its culture, and its particular markers. As with so much that Helen Fulton has achieved, this collaborative research is ground-breaking for British Studies, but has wider implications for Postcolonial Studies, involving, as it does, close analysis of the make-up and traces of Marcher lords, and of those Welsh folk upon whom England subjected colonial rule. The complex situation, where some were oppressed and yet simultaneously served the ruling nobles, or where there was surface loyalty but hidden resistance through literature and a critical intellectualism, has directly fed into a contemporary legacy of Wales as both colonised and a part of a colonial British enterprise. Some of the textual evidence for this period is edited but not translated (if Welsh), and some remains unedited. As Helen proposes, until a clearer picture of the surviving body of literature emerges, the importance of the border region remains in the shadows. This capacious, consequential, and challenging work has an array of significances that will contribute to changing the shape of literary historical studies in the later medieval period, tapping into the flourishing areas of multilingual investigation and nuanced exploration of socio-political identities in the centuries following what is sometimes referred to as 'the Edwardian Conquest'. This project, with its collaborative impulse, might be thought of as one of the culminations of the exceptional career of a scholar who has created a flourishing group of researchers wherever she has been located.

In the early years of her scholarship, Helen focused on medieval poetry, and especially that of Dafydd ap Gwilym. In her first major article, 'The Love Poetry of Dafydd ap Gwilym', Helen began her publishing record by squarely insisting on the significance of the fourteenth-century Welsh poet in the broader literary context.[2] Written with a sensitive eye to an English-language audience, her lucid exposition of Dafydd's poetic brilliance read alongside his famous contemporary, Geoffrey Chaucer, helped raise the profile of pre-modern Welsh poetics and one of its finest exponents. Many more outstanding articles and a book on Dafydd ap Gwilym followed, including examinations of how Dafydd's poetry has been received and presented to modern scholarship.[3] A serious and insightful thread on the role of the editor in the mediation of texts runs through Helen's published work. In 'Editorial Method: Thomas Parry and *Gwaith Dafydd ap Gwilym*' and 'Editing Medieval Manuscripts for Modern Audiences', Helen urges scholars to think carefully about the literary works they study, interpret, and analyse.[4] Through these, and other publications, she makes an important, and persistent, set of interventions to highlight the fulcral role of critical textual studies in the transmission and reception of the literary past to present-day students of all levels. Helen's knowledge of theory and experience of praxis, and her understanding of the implications of individual editors' scholarly agenda in their presenting textual evidence that is purportedly 'original' and yet resists the scribal evidence as it is written down, is profoundly significant. With her customary expertise in comparative literatures and languages, she has shown us how to move between literary corpora with deftness. Her work has ensured that the issues of authorship, multilingualism, and the individuated nature of manuscript production that were so much a part of early British culture are foremost in scholarly apprehension of the medieval.

This desire to establish a sense of the authentic – what it is that scholars are working with, and how scholarship intervenes between author and reader, or corpus and audience –permeates several of Helen's publications throughout the last three-and-a-half decades. Frankness and clarity resonate throughout her work. Helen has helped to redefine a broader canon of literature for students and experts to take into consideration. In 'Literary History and the Medieval Canon in Wales', 'Matthew Arnold and the Canon of Medieval Welsh Literature', and 'Medieval Welsh Poetry', for example, Helen has questioned, examined, and highlighted core elements, forms, and genres of, as well as responses to, those texts considered funda-

2 Helen Fulton, 'The Love Poetry of Dafydd ap Gwilym', *AUMLA* 49 (1978): 22–37.

3 Helen Fulton, *Selections from the Dafydd ap Gwilym Apocrypha* (Llandysul: Gwasg Gomer, 1996); and, *inter alia*, 'The Poetic Construction of Authority: Dafydd ap Gwilym and the *uchelwyr*', *Parergon* 10 (1992): 15–34; 'Ceredigion: Strata Florida and Llanbadarn Fawr', in *Europe: A Literary History, 1348–1418*, ed. David Wallace, 2 vols (Oxford: Oxford University Press, 2016), I, pp. 438–54.

4 Helen Fulton, 'Editorial Method: Thomas Parry and *Gwaith Dafydd ap Gwilym*', *Proceedings of the Harvard Celtic Colloquium* 15 (1995): 12–21; 'Editing Medieval Manuscripts for Modern Audiences', in *The Cambridge Companion to Medieval British Manuscripts*, ed. Orietta Da Rold and Elaine Treharne (Cambridge: Cambridge University Press, 2020), pp. 187–213. See also, 'The Editor as Author: Re-producing the Text. A Case-study of Parry's *Gwaith Dafydd ap Gwilym*', *Bulletin of the Bibliographical Society of Australia and New Zealand* 19.2 (1995): 67–78.

mental in the long history of literary production in Wales.[5] The reach of this work is important, too: published in numerous mainstream, English-language journals and books, access to Welsh literature and its exceptional longevity and sociocultural importance has been foremost to Helen Fulton's scholarly mission. Dozens of periodical articles and chapters in books have ensured the impact of Helen's studies, which have varied in focus from fourteenth-century Welsh and English poetry to Irish epic and French romance.[6] This enviable range of expertise and language permits a broad perspective on the skilful and imaginative literary products of the Middle Ages, drawing out comparisons and differences of nuance that encourage a deeper appreciation of the work of authors, known and unknown.

This breadth of language and tradition is evident through Helen's extensive corpus of scholarly outputs. In recent years, investigations into British, Irish, and French poetry and prose have been extended to full and detailed studies of Italian cultural and literary influences on Chaucer, culminating in two notable edited books published in 2018 and 2021.[7] But it is not just cultural and linguistic diversity that has attracted Helen's attention. Throughout her remarkable career, the sociopolitical and socioeconomic infrastructure that both supports and produces literature and literate communities has been fundamental to Helen's explorations. She has produced a raft of publications that seeks to promote new knowledge of the relationships between language and class, language and education, and money and patronage. For example, in 'Literature of the Welsh Gentry: Uses of the Vernacular in Medieval Wales', Helen raises the profile of the *uchelwyr*, the Welsh gentry, who in the aftermath of conquest sought to deploy Welsh as a medium of productive resistance principally to the English, but also through the assimilation of Latin and French texts into the Welsh tradition.[8] This sensitivity to the symbiotic rela-

5 Helen Fulton, 'Literary History and the Medieval Canon in Wales', in Language and Power in the *Celtic World: Papers from the Seventh Australian Conference of Celtic Studies*, ed. Anders Ahlqvist and Pamela O'Neill (Sydney: University of Sydney Celtic Studies Foundation, 2011), pp. 37–60; 'Matthew Arnold and the Canon of Medieval Welsh Literature', *Review of English Studies* 63 (2012): 204–24; and 'Medieval Welsh Poetry', in *Oxford Bibliographies in British and Irish Literature*, ed. Andrew Hadfield (New York: Oxford University Press, 2014).

6 See, for instance, Helen Fulton, 'The Dialogic Town in the Arthurian Romances of Chrétien de Troyes', in *Epic and Romance: A Guide to Medieval European Literature*, ed. Leonard Neidorf and Yang Liu (Nanjing: Nanjing University Press, 2021), pp. 130–57; 'Gender and Jealousy in "Geraint uab Erbin" and "Le Roman de Silence"', *Arthuriana* 14.2 (2014): 43–70; and 'Magic Naturalism in the "Táin Bó Cúailnge"', in *Narrative in Celtic Tradition: Essays in Honor of Edgar M. Slotkin*, ed. Joseph F. Eska (Hamilton, NY: Colgate University Press, 2011), pp. 84–99.

7 Among these are Michele Campopiano and Helen Fulton, eds, *Anglo-Italian Cultural Relations in the Later Middle Ages* (York: York Medieval Press, 2018); and Helen Fulton, ed., *Chaucer and Italian Culture* (Cardiff: University of Wales Press, 2021).

8 Helen Fulton, 'Literature of the Welsh Gentry: Uses of the Vernacular in Medieval Wales', in *Vernacularity in England and Wales, c. 1300–1500*, ed. Elisabeth Salter,

tionships of patrons, producers, receivers, and onlookers, as well as the power of language to create identity of person, unity of purpose, and focus for nation, is critically important in redefining Welsh literary heritage. Such redefinition is key to Helen Fulton's long and distinguished scholarly track record.

In 'Literary Networks and Patrons in Late Medieval Wales', scholars can witness Helen's exceptional knowledge of how Welsh literary culture functioned politically and pragmatically in the late fourteenth and fifteenth centuries – a 'golden age of manuscript production in Wales'.[9] Examining praise poetry, and the talents and virtues of the *uchelwyr*, Helen takes us through this rich period with a compelling account of the sociohistorical significance of literary work that not only eulogised but prophesied; that not only expressed the past and present glories of Wales, but also manifested ambitions for the future nation. As always, presenting the Welsh text alongside her English translations, Helen provides access (often for the first time) to as wide an audience of present-day readers as possible. Folded into this account, too, is Helen's noteworthy expertise on place and literary expression, developed over the last decade and more of scholarship into the role of the urban in cultural production.[10]

When Daniel Hughes reviewed the *Cambridge History of Welsh Literature*, he movingly praised the book's excellence and vision: 'Most strikingly for me', he writes, 'this volume makes the history of Welsh literature present, skilfully exposing the connections between Wales's literary heritage and its contemporary condition'.[11] In his review, he highlights the work of Helen Fulton herself. For this monumental collection, which Helen conceived, nurtured, and edited with co-ed-

and Helen Wicker (Turnhout: Brepols, 2011), pp. 199–223. Also see, for example, Helen Fulton, 'The Status of the Welsh Language in Medieval Wales', in *The Land Beneath the Sea: Essays in Honour of Anders Ahlqvist's Contribution to Celtic Studies in Australia*, ed. Pamela O'Neill (Sydney: University of Sydney Celtic Studies Foundation, 2013), pp. 59–74; and 'The Red Book and the White: Gentry Libraries in Medieval Wales', in *Crossing Borders in the Insular Middle Ages*, ed. Aisling Byrne and Victoria Flood (Turnhout: Brepols, 2019), pp. 23–39.

9 Helen Fulton, 'Literary Networks and Patrons in Late Medieval Wales', in *The Cambridge History of Welsh Literature*, ed. Geraint Evans and Helen Fulton (Cambridge: Cambridge University Press, 2019), pp. 129–53 (p. 129).

10 Numerous notable major research projects and publications testify to the strength of Helen Fulton's innovative work in urban centres of textual production. Among the former are the University of Bristol project of which Helen Fulton is principal investigator, 'Making Bristol Medieval' (2020), and her co-investigation on the Arts and Humanities Research Council-funded project, 'Mapping Medieval Chester' (University of Swansea, 2006–08); and among the latter, one might note 'The Geography of Welsh Literary Production in Late Medieval Glamorgan', *Journal of Medieval History* 41.3 (2015): 325–40; Helen Fulton, ed., *Urban Culture in Wales* (Cardiff: University of Wales Press, 2012); 'The *Encomium Urbis* in Medieval Welsh Poetry', *Proceedings of the Harvard Celtic Colloquium* 26/27 (2006): 54–72.

11 Daniel Hughes, '*The Cambridge History of Welsh Literature*. Ed. by Geraint Evans and Helen Fulton', review in *Modern Language Review* 116.3 (2021): 489–91 (491).

itor Geraint Evans, Helen also wrote two chapters, and co-wrote the introduction and afterword.[12] The 35-chapter work, almost sure never to be superseded in its scope, purpose, and diverse set of approaches to a single urgent question, seeks to bridge languages (English and Welsh, and multilingual culture more broadly); to cover the full temporal range of Welsh literary production; and to insist on the addressing of knotty social, cultural, and political questions of the visibility of Wales's past, of its colonisation, resilience, legacy, and the needs of its future. Such impressive far-sightedness and optimism, generosity of scholarly spirit (which is not always reciprocated by others), and collaborative impulse as this edited volume exhibits, typify Professor Helen Fulton's work over the decades. If an academic sets out on their career with one desire – to make a difference – then our honourand has done this in abundance. In their closing words to the *Cambridge History*, the editors acknowledge the positive trajectory of contemporary Wales: 'Produced both inside and outside Wales, defining itself as inclusive rather than exclusive, Welsh literature today has the capability, in at least two languages, to mediate national preoccupations for an international audience. This is the history of Welsh literature: multilingual, many-voiced, and constantly shapeshifting.'[13] This uplifting, evidence-based, accessible, and learned synopsis of Welsh literature mirrors the lifelong career and impact of Helen Fulton herself: inclusive, multilingual, public-facing, impactful, and adaptable. It is a privilege to write about her and always a joy to read and learn from her work.

12 'Introduction', 'Britons and Saxons: The Earliest Writing in Welsh', 'Literary Networks and Patrons in Late Medieval Wales', and 'Afterword', in *Cambridge History of Welsh Literature*, pp. 1–10, 26–51, 129–53, and 715–19, respectively.

13 Evans and Fulton, *Cambridge History*, p. 718.

Bibliography of Professor Helen Fulton's Key Publications

'Cheapside in Wales: Multilingualism and Textiles in Medieval Welsh Poetry', in *Middle English in a Multilingual Context: Current Methodologies and Approaches*, ed. Louise Sylvester and Sara Pons-Sanz (London: Palgrave Macmillan, 2023), pp. 187–212

ed. with Sif Rikhardsdottir, *Charlemagne in the Norse and Celtic Worlds* (Cambridge: D. S. Brewer, 2022)

'Historiography and the Invention of British Identity: Troy as an Origin Legend in Medieval Britain and Ireland', in *Origin Legends in Early Medieval Western Europe*, ed. Lindy Brady and Pamela Wadden (Leiden: Brill 2022), pp. 338–62

'Romantic Wales: Imagining Wales in Medieval Insular Romance', in *Cultural Translations in Medieval Romance*, ed. Victoria Flood and Megan Leitch (Cambridge: D. S. Brewer, 2022) pp. 21–44

'Sir John Prise and his Books: Manuscript Culture in the March of Wales', *Welsh History Review* 31.1 (2022): 55–78

'Voice of Authority: Free Indirect Discourse in Chaucer's General Prologue', in *Medieval Literary Voices: Embodiment, Materiality and Performance*, ed. Louise D'Arcens and Sif Rikhardsdottir (Manchester: Manchester University Press 2022), pp. 37–55

Chaucer and Italian Culture (Cardiff: University of Wales Press, 2021)

'The Dialogic Town in the Arthurian Romances of Chrétien de Troyes', in *Epic and Romance: A Guide to Medieval European Literature*, ed. Leonard Neidorf and Yang Liu (Nanjing: Nanjing University Press, 2021), pp. 130–57

'Editing Medieval Manuscripts for Modern Audiences', in *The Cambridge Companion to Medieval British Manuscripts*, ed. Orietta Da Rold and Elaine Treharne (Cambridge: Cambridge University Press, 2020)

'A "Mirror of the Gentry": Vernacular Versions of the Secretum Secretorum in Medieval Wales and England', in *Prodesse et Delectare: Case Studies on Didactic Literature in the European Middle Ages*, ed. Norbert Kössinger and Claudia Wittig (Berlin: De Gruyter, 2019), pp. 57–82

ed. with Geraint Evans, *The Cambridge History of Welsh Literature* (Cambridge: Cambridge University Press, 2019)

'The Red Book and the White: Gentry Libraries in Medieval Wales', in *Crossing Borders in the Insular Middle Ages*, ed. Aisling Byrne and Victoria Flood (Turnhout: Brepols, 2019), pp. 23–39

ed. with Michele Campopiano, *Anglo-Italian Cultural Relations in the Later Middle Ages* (York: York Medieval Press, 2018)

'Caerleon and Cultural Memory in the Modern Literature of Wales', in *Germano-Celtica: A Festschrift for Brian Taylor*, ed. Anders Ahlqvist and Pamela O'Neill (Sydney: Sydney University Press, 2017), pp. 101–19

'Historiography: Fictionality vs Factionality', in *Handbook of Arthurian Romance: King Arthur's Court in Medieval European Literature*, ed. Leah Tether and Johnny McFadyen (Berlin: De Gruyter, 2017), pp. 151–66

'Ceredigion: Strata Florida and Llanbadarn Fawr', in *Europe: A Literary History, 1348–1418*, 2 vols, ed. David Wallace (Oxford: Oxford University Press, 2016), I, pp. 438–54

'Poetry and Nationalism in the Reign of Edward I: Wales and Ireland', *The Plantagenet Empire, 1259-1453: Proceedings of the 2014 Harlaxton Symposium*, ed. Peter Crooks, David Green, and W. Mark Ormrod (Donnington: Shaun Tyas, 2016), pp. 169–86

'Body and Soul: From Doctrine to Debate in Medieval Welsh and Irish Literature from Doctrine to Debate in Medieval Welsh and Irish Literature', in *Sanctity as Literature in Late Medieval Britain*, ed. Eva von Contzen and Anke Bernau (Manchester: Manchester University Press, 2015), pp. 96–115

'The Geography of Welsh Literary Production in Late Medieval Glamorgan', *Journal of Medieval History* 41.3 (2015): 325–40

'Translating Europe in Medieval Wales', in *Writing Europe, 500–1450: Texts and Contexts*, ed. Aidan Conti, Orietta Da Rold, and Philip A. Shaw (Cambridge: D. S. Brewer, 2015), pp. 159–74

'Gender and Jealousy in Gereint uab Erbin and Le Roman de Silence', *Arthuriana* 14.2 (2014): 1–28

'History and Historia: Uses of the Troy Story in Medieval Ireland and Wales', in *Classical Literature and Learning in Medieval Irish Narrative*, ed. Ralph O'Connor (Cambridge: D. S. Brewer, 2014), pp. 40–57

'A Medieval Welsh Version of the Troy Story: Editing *Ystorya Dared*', in *Probable Truth: Editing Medieval Texts from Britain in the Twenty-First Century*, ed. Vincent Gillespie and Anne Hudson (Turnhout: Brepols, 2013), pp. 214–25

'Guto'r Glyn and the Wars of the Roses', in *Gwalch Cywyddau Gwŷr: Essays on Guto'r Glyn and Fifteenth-Century Wales*, ed. Dylan Foster Evans, Barry J. Lewis, and Ann Parry Owen (Aberystwyth: University of Wales Centre for Advanced Welsh and Celtic Studies, 2013), pp. 53–68

'Magic and the Supernatural in Early Welsh Arthurian Narrative: *Culhwch ac Olwen* and *Breuddwyd Rhonabwy*', *Arthurian Literature* 30 (2013): 1–26

'Owain Glyndŵr and the Prophetic Tradition', in *Owain Glyndŵr: A Casebook*, eds Michael Livingston and John K. Bollard (Liverpool: Liverpool University Press, 2013), pp. 475–88

'The Status of the Welsh Language in Medieval Wales', in Pamela O'Neill, ed., *The Land Beneath the Sea: Essays in Honour of Anders Ahlqvist's Contribution to Celtic*

Studies in Australia (Sydney: University of Sydney Celtic Studies Foundation, 2013), pp. 59–74

ed. *Urban Culture in Medieval Wales* (Cardiff: University of Wales Press, 2012)

'Matthew Arnold and the Canon of Medieval Welsh Literature', *Review of English Studies* 63.259 (2012): 204–24

'Negotiating Welshness: Multilingualism in Wales Before and After 1066', in *Conceptualizing Multilingualism in England, c. 800–c. 1250*, ed. Elizabeth M. Tyler (Turnhout: Brepols 2012), pp. 145–70

'Literary History and the Medieval Canon in Wales', in *Language and Power in the Celtic World: Papers from the Seventh Australian Conference of Celtic Studies*, ed. Anders Ahlqvist and Pamela O'Neill (Sydney: University of Sydney Celtic Studies Foundation, 2011), pp. 37–60

'Literature of the Welsh Gentry: Uses of the Vernacular in Medieval Wales', in *Vernacularity in England and Wales, c. 1300–1550*, ed. Elisabeth Salter and Helen Wicker (Brepols: Turnhout, 2011), pp. 199–223

'Magic Naturalism in the *Táin Bó Cúailnge*', in *Narrative in Celtic Tradition: Essays in Honor of Edgar M. Slotkin*, ed. Joseph F. Eska, CSANA Yearbook 8–9 (Hamilton, NY: Colgate University Press, 2011), pp. 84–99.

'The Outside Within: Medieval Chester and North Wales as a Social Space', in *Mapping the Medieval City: Space, Place and Identity in Chester c. 1200–1600*, ed. Catherine A. M. Clarke (Cardiff: University of Wales Press, 2011), pp. 149–68

'Troy Story: The Medieval Welsh *Ystorya Dared* and the *Brut* Tradition of British History', *Medieval Chronicle* 7 (2011): 137–50

ed. *Companion to Arthurian Literature* (Oxford: Wiley-Blackwell, 2009)

'Class and Nation: Defining the English in Late-Medieval Welsh Poetry', in *Authority and Subjugation in Writing of Medieval Wales*, ed. Ruth Kennedy and Simon Meecham-Jones (New York: Palgrave Macmillan, 2008), pp. 191–212

Welsh Prophecy and English Politics in the Late Middle Ages (Aberystwyth: University of Wales Centre for Advanced Welsh and Celtic Studies, 2008)

'Autobiography and the Discourse of Urban Subjectivity: The Paston Letters', in *Early Modern Autobiography: Theories, Genres, Practices*, ed. Ronald Bedford, Lloyd Davis, and Philippa Kelly (Ann Arbor: University of Michigan Press, 2006), pp. 191–216

ed. with Ruth Evans and David Matthews, *Stephen Knight and Medieval Cultural Studies* (Cardiff: University of Wales Press, 2006)

'The Encomium Urbis in Medieval Welsh Poetry', *Proceedings of the Harvard Celtic Colloquium* 26/27 (2006): 54–72

'The Performance of Social Class: Domestic Violence in the Griselda Story', *AUMLA* 106 (2006): 25–42

'Arthurian Prophecy and the Deposition of Richard II', *Arthurian Literature* 22 (2005): 64–83

ed. *Medieval Celtic Literature and Society* (Dublin: Four Courts Press, 2005) ed. with A. Dunn, Rosemary Huisman, and J. Murphet, *Narrative and Media* (Cambridge: Cambridge University Press, 2005)

'Owain Glyn Dŵr and the Uses of Prophecy', *Studia Celtica* 39 (2005): 105–21

'The *Mabinogi* and the Education of Princes in Medieval Wales', in *Medieval Celtic Literature and Society* (Dublin: Four Courts Press, 2005), pp. 230–47

'George Borrow and the Oldest Animals in "Wild Wales"', *Transactions of the Honourable Society of Cymmrodorion* 11 (2004): 23–40

'Awdurdod ac Awduriaeth: Golygu'r Cywyddwyr [Authority and Authorship: Editing the Cywyddwyr]', in *Cyfoeth y Testun: Ysgrifau ar Lenyddiaeth Gymraeg yr Oesoedd Canol,* ed. Iestyn Daniel, Marged Haycock, Dafydd Johnston, and Jenny Rowland (Cardiff: University of Wales Press, 2003), pp. 50–76

'Medieval Studies in Australia', *AUMLA* 100 (2003): 1–12

'Mercantile Ideology in Chaucer's Shipman's Tale', *The Chaucer Review* 36.4 (2002): 311–28

'Orality and Literacy in Early Welsh Literature', *Chwileniwm: Technoleg a Llenyddiaeth,* ed. Angharad Price (Cardiff: University of Wales Press, 2002), pp. 17–35

'Individual and Society in *Owein/Yvain* and *Gereint/Erec*', in *The Individual in Celtic Literatures,* ed. Joseph Falaky Nagy (Dublin: Four Courts Press, 2001), pp. 15–50

'Tenth-Century Wales and *Armes Prydein*', *Transactions of the Honourable Society of Cymmrodorion* 7 (2001): 5–18

'Cultural Meanings in the *Mabinogi*', in *Origins and Revivals: Proceedings of the First Australian Conference of Celtic Studies,* ed. Geraint Evans, Bernard K. Martin, and Jonathan Wooding (Sydney: University of Sydney Celtic Studies Foundation, 2000), pp. 437–53

'Cyd-destun Gwleidyddol *Breudwyt Ronabwy* [The Political Context of *The Dream of Rhonabwy*]', *Llên Cymru* 22 (1999): 42–56

'Editorial Method: Thomas Parry and Gwaith Dafydd ap Gwilym', *Proceedings of the Harvard Celtic Colloquium* 15 (1998): 14–21

'Trading Places: Representations of Urban Culture in Medieval Welsh Poetry', *Studia Celtica* 31 (1997): 219–30

'Punctuation as a Semiotic Code: The Case of the Medieval Welsh *cywydd*', *Parergon* 13.2 (1996): 2–17

ed. *Selections from the Dafydd ap Gwilym Apocrypha* (Llandysul: Gwasg Gomer, 1996)

'The Editor as Author: Re-producing the Text. A Case-study of Parry's *Gwaith Dafydd ap Gwilym*', *Bulletin of the Bibliographical Society of Australia and New Zealand* 19.2 (1995): 67–78

'A Woman's Place: Guinevere in the Welsh and French Romances', *Quondam et Futurus: Journal of Arthurian Interpretations* 3 (1993): 1–25

'The Poetic Construction of Authority: Dafydd ap Gwilym and the *uchelwyr*', *Parergon* 10.1 (1992): 15–34

'Medieval Welsh Poems to Nuns', *Cambridge Medieval Celtic Studies* 21 (1991): 87–112

'Dafydd ap Gwilym and Intertextuality', *Leeds Studies in English* 20 (1989): 65–86

Dafydd ap Gwilym and the European Context (Cardiff: University of Wales Press, 1989)

'The Theory of Celtic Influence in the Harley Lyrics', *Modern Philology* 82.3 (1985): 239–54

'The Role of the Poet in the Love Poetry of Dafydd ap Gwilym', *Transactions of the Honourable Society of Cymmrodorion* 1979: 129–36

'The Love Poetry of Dafydd ap Gwilym', *AUMLA* 49 (1978): 22–37

Index

Tabula Gratulatoria

Marianne Ailes
Mary Bateman
Fred Biggs
Lindy Brady
Janet Burton and William Marx
Ardis Butterfield
Aisling Byrne
David Callander
Claudio Cataldi
Catherine A. M. Clarke
Luciana Cordo Russo
Peter Crooks
Rhiannon Daniels
Orietta Da Rold
Daniel Davies
Sioned Davies
Peter Dent
Emily Dolmans
Siân Echard
Robert R. Edwards
Joseph F. Eska
Geraint Evans
Ruth Evans
George Ferzoco
Victoria Flood
Deborah R. Furchtgott
Rachael Harkes
Marged Haycock
Liz Herbert McAvoy
Bleddyn Owen Huws
Suzanne Jamieson
Andrew James Johnston
Aled Llion Jones
Tristan Kay
John Kennedy
Stephen Knight
Matt Lampitt
Barry Lewis
Andrew Lynch
Rebecca Maloy
David Matthews
Catherine McKenna
Daniel F. Melia
Carolyn Muessig
Ronald G. Musto
Joseph Falaky Nagy
Máire Ní Mhaonaigh
Caroline Palmer
Alessandra Petrina
Benjamin Pohl
Erich Poppe
Stuart Prior
Ad Putter
Raluca Radulescu
Melissa Ridley Elmes
Philip Schwyzer
Jan Shaw
Victoria Shirley
Madeleine Smith
Jonathan Stavsky
Leah Tether
Richard Trachsler
Elaine Treharne
Elizabeth Tyler
David Wallace
Lawrence Warner
Ian Wei
Beth Williamson
Jonathan M. Wooding

University of BRISTOL

Bristol Studies in Medieval Cultures

ISSN 1757–2150

Series Editors
George Ferzoco (emeritus)
Ronald Musto
Benjamin Pohl

Editorial Advisory Board
Marianne Ailes
Rhiannon Daniels
Peter Dent
Helen Fulton
Tristan Kay
Stuart Prior
Ad Putter
Leah Tether
Ian Wei
Beth Williamson
Peter Crooks (Trinity College Dublin)
Rebecca Maloy (Colorado Boulder)
Carolyn Muessig (Calgary)
Alheydis Plassmann (Bonn)
Richard Trachsler (Zurich)
David Wallace (Pennsylvania)

Established in 2009, the Bristol Studies in Medieval Cultures series draws on a long and well-established tradition of multidisciplinary medieval research at the University of Bristol and its world-leading Centre for Medieval Studies. It is served by an international editorial advisory board of globally recognised experts and features titles from across the field of Medieval Studies. The series welcomes submissions addressing a broad range of disciplines, including literature, art, history, religion, and thought. We particularly encourage proposals that engage with medieval cultures from a comparative perspective. Our aim is to publish the best in current research and to help readers appreciate the Middle Ages in cross-cultural and global contexts.

Queries about the series, or proposals for monographs, editions, or collections of essays, should be sent in the first instance to the Series Editor.

email: rg.musto@bristol.ac.uk / benjamin.pohl@bristol.ac.uk

Bristol Studies in Medieval Cultures

PREVIOUSLY PUBLISHED

The Madonna of Humility: Development, Dissemination and Reception, c.1340–1400
Beth Williamson

The Medieval Art, Architecture and History of Bristol Cathedral: An Enigma Explored
Edited by Jon Cannon and Beth Williamson

Chaucer and the Cultures of Love and Marriage
Cathy Hume

Translators and their Prologues in Medieval England
Elizabeth Dearnley

Cross and Culture in Anglo-Norman England: Theology, Imagery, Devotion
John Munns

CHARLEMAGNE: A EUROPEAN ICON

Charlemagne and his Legend in Early Spanish Literature and Historiography
Edited by Matthew Bailey and Ryan D. Giles

The Charlemagne Legend in Medieval Latin Texts
Edited by William J. Purkis and Matthew Gabriele

The Legend of Charlemagne in Medieval England: The Matter of France in Middle English and Anglo-Norman Literature
Phillipa Hardman and Marianne Ailes

Charlemagne in Medieval German and Dutch Literature
Albrecht Classen

Charlemagne in the Norse and Celtic Worlds
Edited by Helen Fulton and Sif Rikhardsdottir

Charlemagne in Italy
Edited by Jane E. Everson